A Moment As A Police Officer

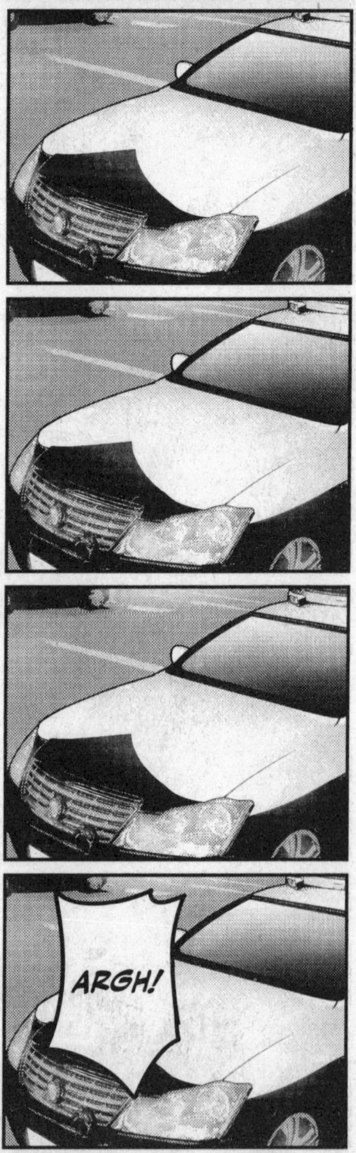
ARGH!

Waiting and Waiting...

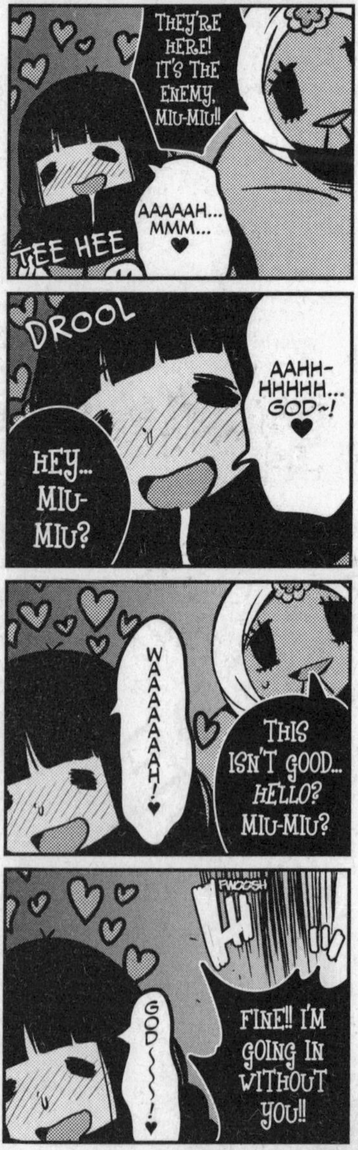
THEY'RE HERE! IT'S THE ENEMY, MIU-MIU!!
AAAAAH... MMM... ♥
TEE HEE
AAHH-HHHHH... GOD~! ♥
DROOL
HEY... MIU-MIU?
THIS ISN'T GOOD... HELLO? MIU-MIU?
WAAAAAAAH!♥
FWOOSH
FINE!! I'M GOING IN WITHOUT YOU!!
GOD~~~!♥

MAGICAL GIRL APOCALYPSE

6

Kentaro Sato

Emergency Situation

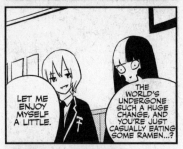

THE WORLD'S UNDERGONE SUCH A HUGE CHANGE, AND YOU'RE JUST CASUALLY EATING SOME RAMEN...?
LET ME ENJOY MYSELF A LITTLE.
THIS ISN'T THE TIME TO BE SAYING THAT!
THIS IS AN EMERGENCY SITUATION...
HUH?
UGH... THE SMELL OF GARLIC IS TOO MUCH... I'M GOING TO BARF...
PWAAAF...
OH, SORRY. I ADDED A TON~!

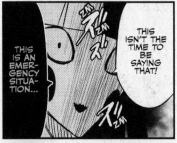

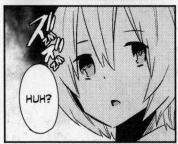

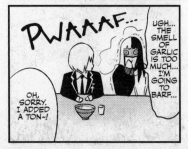

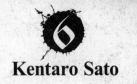

AKUTA RINTAROU

SEX: MALE   **AGE:** 23   **DATE OF BIRTH:** NOVEMBER 11 (SCORPIO)
HEIGHT: 175CM (~5'9")   **WEIGHT:** 65KG   **BLOODTYPE:** AB
BIRTHPLACE: TOKYO   **INTERESTS:** DVDS, DRIVING WHILE LUSTING
OVER GIRLS, 2-CHAN   **SPECIALTY:** SPORTS, SHOOTING, UNLIMITED
MASTURBATING.   **LIKES:** HIGH SCHOOL GIRLS, BIG BOOBS, RAMEN,
OMELET RICE, BATHS, TRAINING **DISLIKES:** CHORES, GREEN PEPPERS

WOO-HOO!

- AN EXTREME PERVERT.
- HE GIVES GIRLS BAD VIBES JUST BY TALKING
  TO THEM.
- WHEN HE WAS YOUNG, HE WAS UNUSUALLY
  TALENTED AND QUITE SMART, BUT HE FELL
  INTO IDIOSYNCRASY AND STAYED THERE.
- HIS MOTTO IS, "ONCE YOU DECIDE ON SOMETHING,
  DON'T STRAY, DON'T BREAK, STAND TALL!"

ANAI MIU

SEX: FEMALE   **AGE:** 28   **DATE OF BIRTH:** AUGUST 24 (VIRGO)
HEIGHT: 160CM (~5'3")   **WEIGHT:** 52KG   **BLOODTYPE:** B
3 SIZES: B: 95 (G) / W: 53 / H: 89   **BIRTHPLACE:** KANAGAWA
PREFECTURE   **INTERESTS:** YOGA **SPECIALTY:** KENDO (JAPANESE
SWORDSMANSHIP). SURFING   **LIKES:** AKUTA RINTAROU, FRIED
CHICKEN, SEAWATER BATHING
DISLIKES: CHORES, COOKING, VEGETABLES

- SINCE SHE WORSHIPS AKUTA, SHE KEPT
  HER BANGS THE SAME AS HIS.
- HER PERSONALITY IS A LITTLE AFFECTED
  BY AKUTA RINTAROU.
- NATURALLY DARK SKINNED.
- HAS A STRONG DESIRE TO GET MARRIED
  AND WANTS TO HAVE FIVE CHILDREN.

HANZAWA YORUKA

SEX: FEMALE   AGE: 16   DATE OF BIRTH: JULY 21 (CANCER)
HEIGHT: 162CM (~5'4")   WEIGHT: 54KG   BLOODTYPE: A
3 SIZES: B: 102 (K) / W: 56 / H: 90   BIRTHPLACE: TOKYO
INTERESTS: COOKING, SLEEPING, DANCE.   SPECIALTY: SINGING,
CHORES, BASKETBALL   LIKES: BARBECUE, EATING AND WALKING,
SHOUJO COMICS.   DISLIKES: PERVERTS, FORTUNETELLERS, BUGS

• SHE HAS A STRONG MINDED, BOYISH PERSONALITY,
BUT OCCASIONALLY SHOWS A MORE FEMININE SIDE.
• HER PREEMINENT PROPORTIONS HAVE GIVEN HER A
BIT OF A COMPLEX ABOUT HERSELF.
• SHE HAS BEEN SCOUTED SEVERAL TIMES FOR
GRAVURE IDOLING, BUT HAS REFUSED THEM ALL.
• ONCE SHE WAS ATTACKED BY A PERVERT AT NIGHT,
AND EVER SINCE SHE CARRIES A STUN GUN. SHE HAS
ARGUED ABOUT IT AT TIMES WITH THE POLICE.

KUSHIRO REN

SEX: MALE   AGE: 22   DATE OF BIRTH: MAY 3 (TAURUS)
HEIGHT: 182CM (~5'11")   WEIGHT: 62KG   BLOODTYPE: AB
BIRTHPLACE: TOKYO   INTERESTS: SLEEPING, GUITAR, CAMERAS,
RUIN EXPLORATION   SPECIALTY: TAE KWAN DO, BASKETBALL,
BILLIARDS   LIKES: TAPIOCA, TRAVELING, COFFEE
DISLIKES: JOB HUNTING, CILANTRO (CORIANDER)

• EXTREME "DOING THINGS AT MY OWN PACE"
PERSONALITY.

• HE HAS TROUBLE DEALING WITH PEOPLE
AND OFTEN GOES OFF ON HIS OWN WAY.

• HE SEEMS TO CATCH A COLD ONCE A MONTH.

SAYANO KAEDE

SEX: FEMALE **AGE:** 15 **DATE OF BIRTH:** JULY 20 (CANCER)
HEIGHT: 154CM (~5'1") **WEIGHT:** 45KG **BLOODTYPE:** O
3 SIZES: B: 78 (C) / W: 49 / H: 82 **BIRTHPLACE:** TOKYO
INTERESTS: KARAOKE, MUSIC (ALL TYPES), BATHS
SPECIALTY: SNOWBOARDING **LIKES:** SHOPPING, CLOTHES, SWEETS, PASTRIES, STEW **DISLIKES:** COFFEE

- SHE LOOKS LIKE A TOUGH GIRL ON THE OUTSIDE, BUT INSIDE SHE'S ACTUALLY VERY KIND.
- SHE HAS SOME EXPERIENCE AS A MODEL WHEN SHE WAS VERY YOUNG.
- SHE'S THE KIND OF GIRL WHO COULD EXHAUST A GUY (JUST A GUESS).

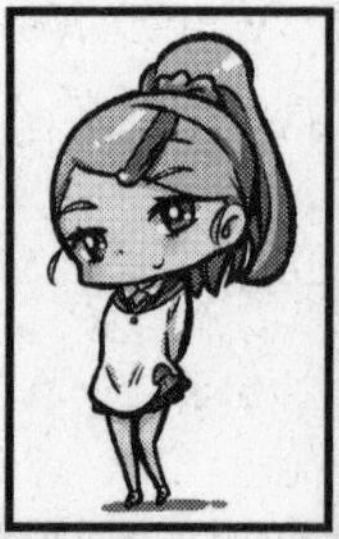

OOTSUKI MIKI

SEX: FEMALE **AGE:** 15 **DATE OF BIRTH:** FEBRUARY 23 (PISCES)
HEIGHT: 157CM (~5'2") **WEIGHT:** 45KG 3 **BLOODTYPE:** B
3 SIZES: B: 68 (B) / W: 48 / H: 80 **BIRTHPLACE:** CHIBA PREFECTURE
INTERESTS: PRINT CLUBS, SELFIES, MUSIC PROGRAMS (ALL KINDS), KARAOKE, BLOGS **SPECIALTY:** BALLET **LIKES:** KOREAN IDOLS, K-POP, FAMILY RESTAURANTS **DISLIKES:** HORROR MOVIES

- THE KIND OF HIGH SCHOOL GIRL YOU WOULD SEE ANYWHERE, ANY TIME.
- SHE SPENDS A LOT ON KOREAN IDOLS, SO SHE IS CONSTANTLY THINKING OF WORKING PART TIME TO EARN MONEY.
- HER BODY IS EXTREMELY SOFT.

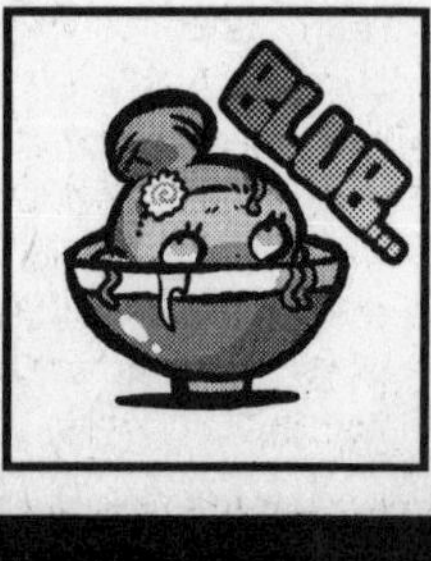
BLUB.

KOGAMI KII

SEX: MALE   **AGE:** 16   **DATE OF BIRTH:** APRIL 2 (ARIES)
HEIGHT: 168CM (5'6")   **WEIGHT:** 49KG   **BLOODTYPE:** O
BIRTHPLACE: TOKYO   **SPECIALTY:** SPRINTING
INTERESTS: GAMES, VARIETY SHOWS (ALL FORMS)
LIKES: COMEDY PROGRAMS, MOVIES, GAMES, CURRY RICE,
WATERMELON   **DISLIKES:** BOTHERSOME THINGS.

- HE ABSOLUTELY HATES DOING ANYTHING THAT'S A
  BOTHER TO HIM. HOWEVER, IN TIMES LIKE THESE,
  HE IS EXTREMELY ACTIVE.
- HE IS A LITTLE NERVOUS AROUND GIRLS.
- WHEN HE'S ALONE, HE'S OFTEN VERY LAZY
  AND SLUGGISH.
- HE HAS ABOVE AVERAGE ENDURANCE.

FUKUMOTO TSUKUNE

SEX: FEMALE   **AGE:** 15   **DATE OF BIRTH:** JUNE 6 (GEMINI)
HEIGHT: 148CM (4'10")   **WEIGHT:** 43KG 3   **BLOODTYPE:** A
3 SIZES: B: 70 (B) / W: 55 / H: 83   **BIRTHPLACE:** TOKYO
INTERESTS: PLAYING THE PIANO, DRAWING **SPECIALTIES:** SEWING,
HANDICRAFTS, CALLIGRAPHY   **LIKES:** SMALL ANIMALS, PEACHES,
NAPS, ALL SORTS OF DRINKS, SWEETS   **DISLIKES:** SPORTS, BUGS

- SHE KEEPS HER THOUGHTS TO HERSELF AND IS QUITE DOCILE.
- SHE IS GOOD AT ALL HOUSEHOLD CHORES AND IS
  QUITE FAMILY CENTRIC.
- SHE LIKES TO DRAW, AND REALLY LIKES GIVING HER
  DRAWINGS TO FRIENDS AS PRESENTS.
- SHE LIKES TO DRINK THINGS, AND OFTEN HAS
  SOME SORT OF BEVERAGE, SO SOMETIMES SHE
  GETS BLOATED WHEN SHE WAKES UP IN THE
  MORNING.

To Be Continued...

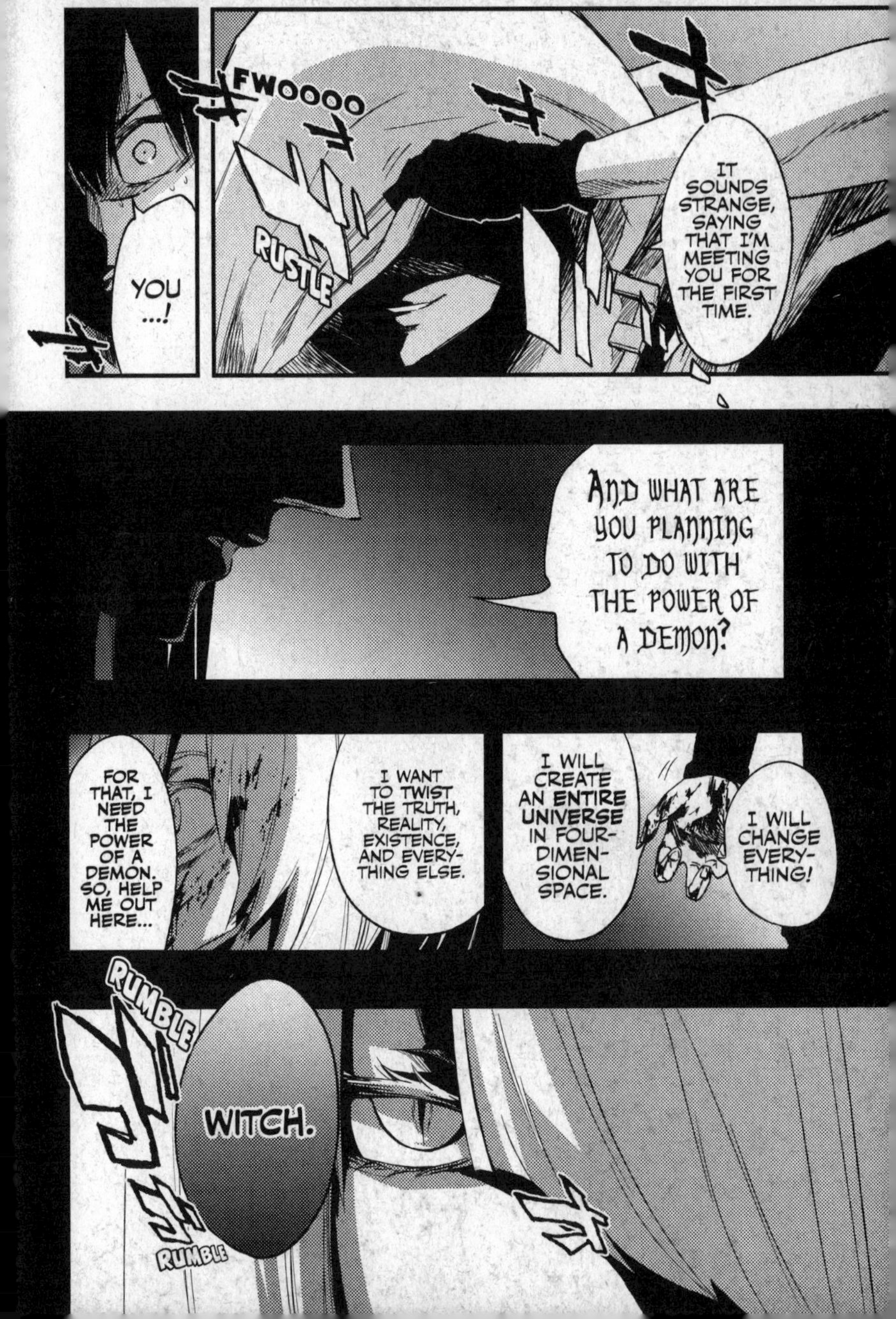
FWOOOO
RUSTLE
IT SOUNDS STRANGE, SAYING THAT I'M MEETING YOU FOR THE FIRST TIME.
YOU ...!
AND WHAT ARE YOU PLANNING TO DO WITH THE POWER OF A DEMON?
I WILL CHANGE EVERYTHING!
I WILL CREATE AN ENTIRE UNIVERSE IN FOUR-DIMENSIONAL SPACE.
I WANT TO TWIST THE TRUTH, REALITY, EXISTENCE, AND EVERYTHING ELSE.
FOR THAT, I NEED THE POWER OF A DEMON. SO, HELP ME OUT HERE...
RUMBLE
WITCH.
RUMBLE

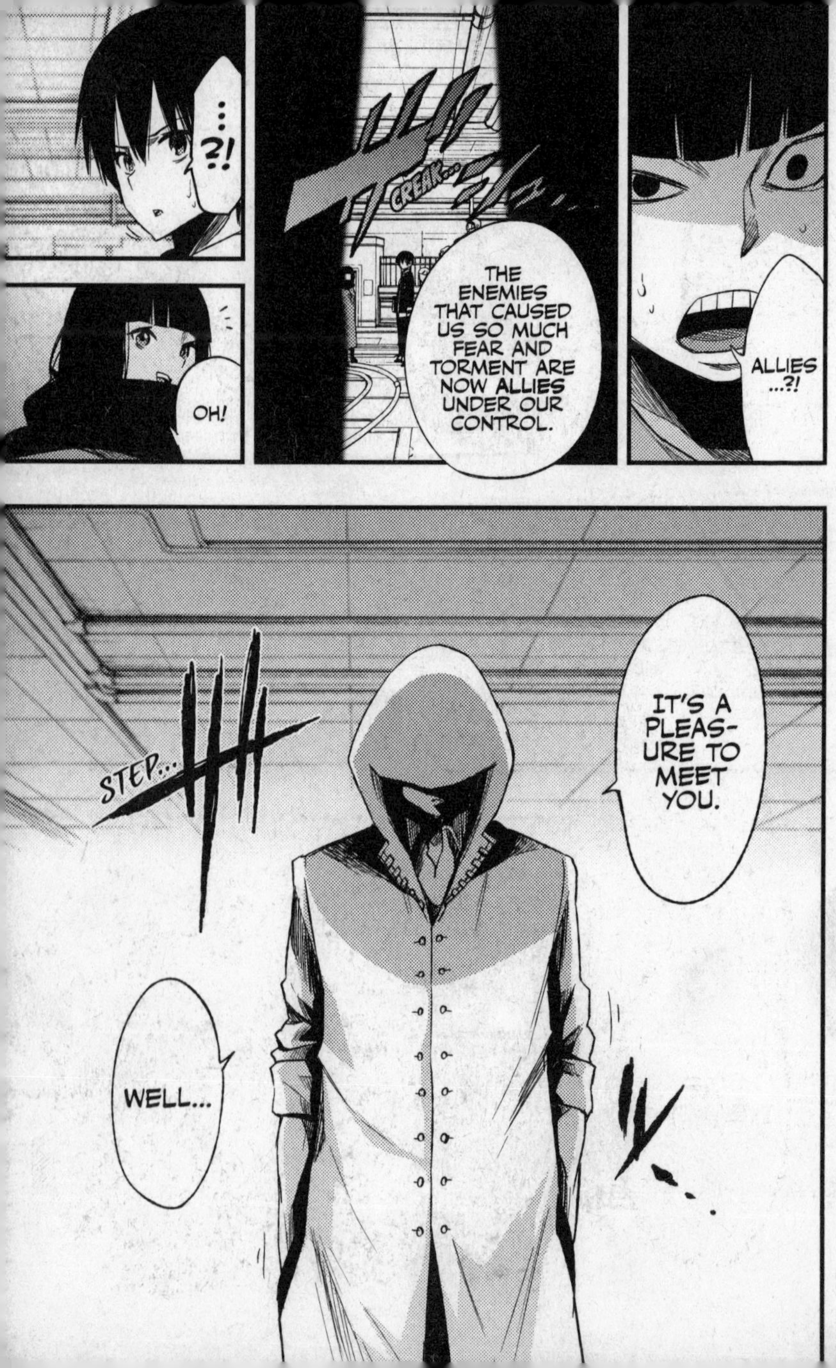
CREAK...
THE ENEMIES THAT CAUSED US SO MUCH FEAR AND TORMENT ARE NOW ALLIES UNDER OUR CONTROL.
ALLIES ...?!
...?!
OH!
IT'S A PLEAS-URE TO MEET YOU.
STEP...
WELL...

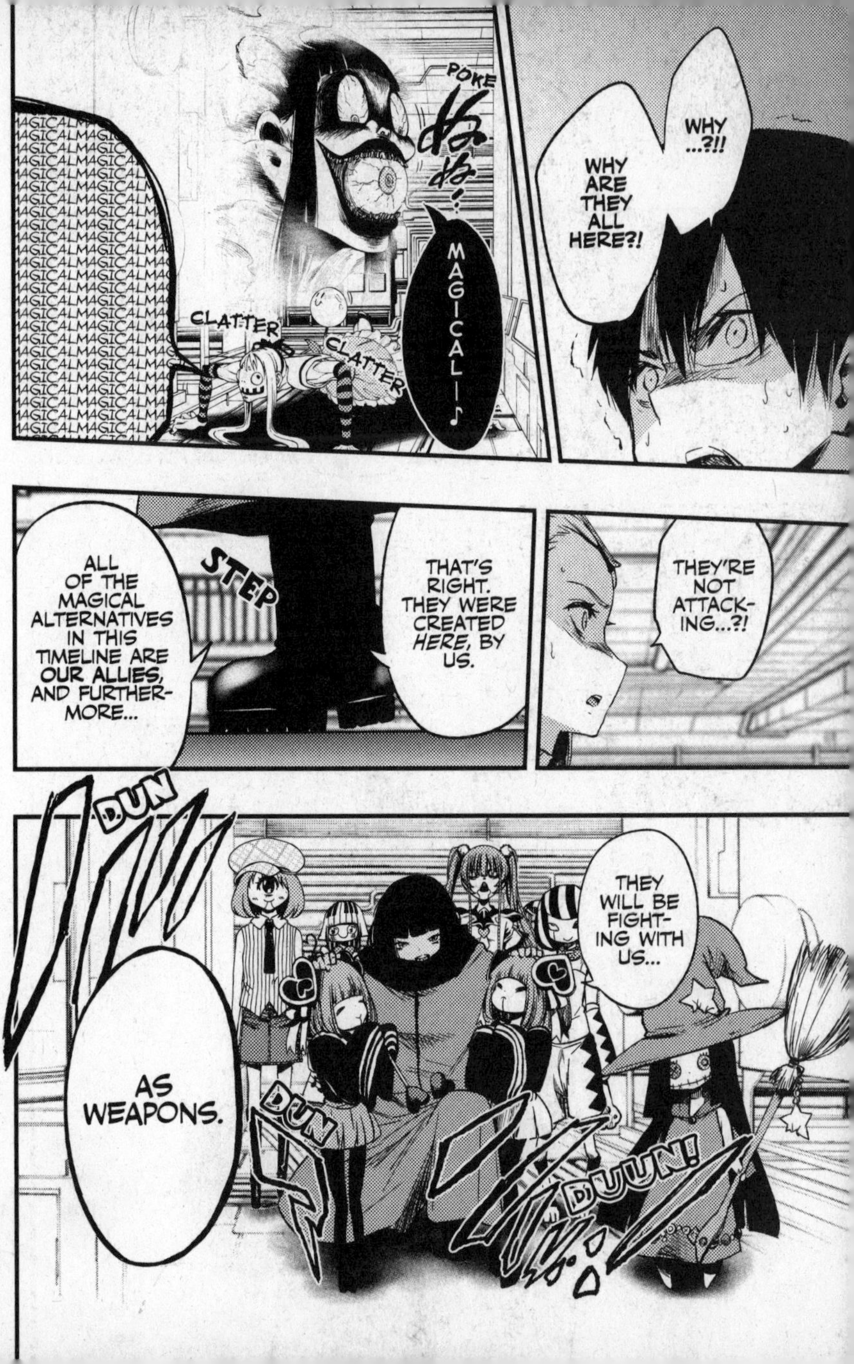
WHY ...?!!
WHY ARE THEY ALL HERE?!
POKE
ぬぬ…!
MAGICAL!♪
CLATTER
CLATTER
THEY'RE NOT ATTACKING...?!
THAT'S RIGHT. THEY WERE CREATED *HERE*, BY US.
STEP
ALL OF THE MAGICAL ALTERNATIVES IN THIS TIMELINE ARE OUR ALLIES, AND FURTHERMORE...
THEY WILL BE FIGHTING WITH US...
DUN
AS WEAPONS.
DUN
DUUN!

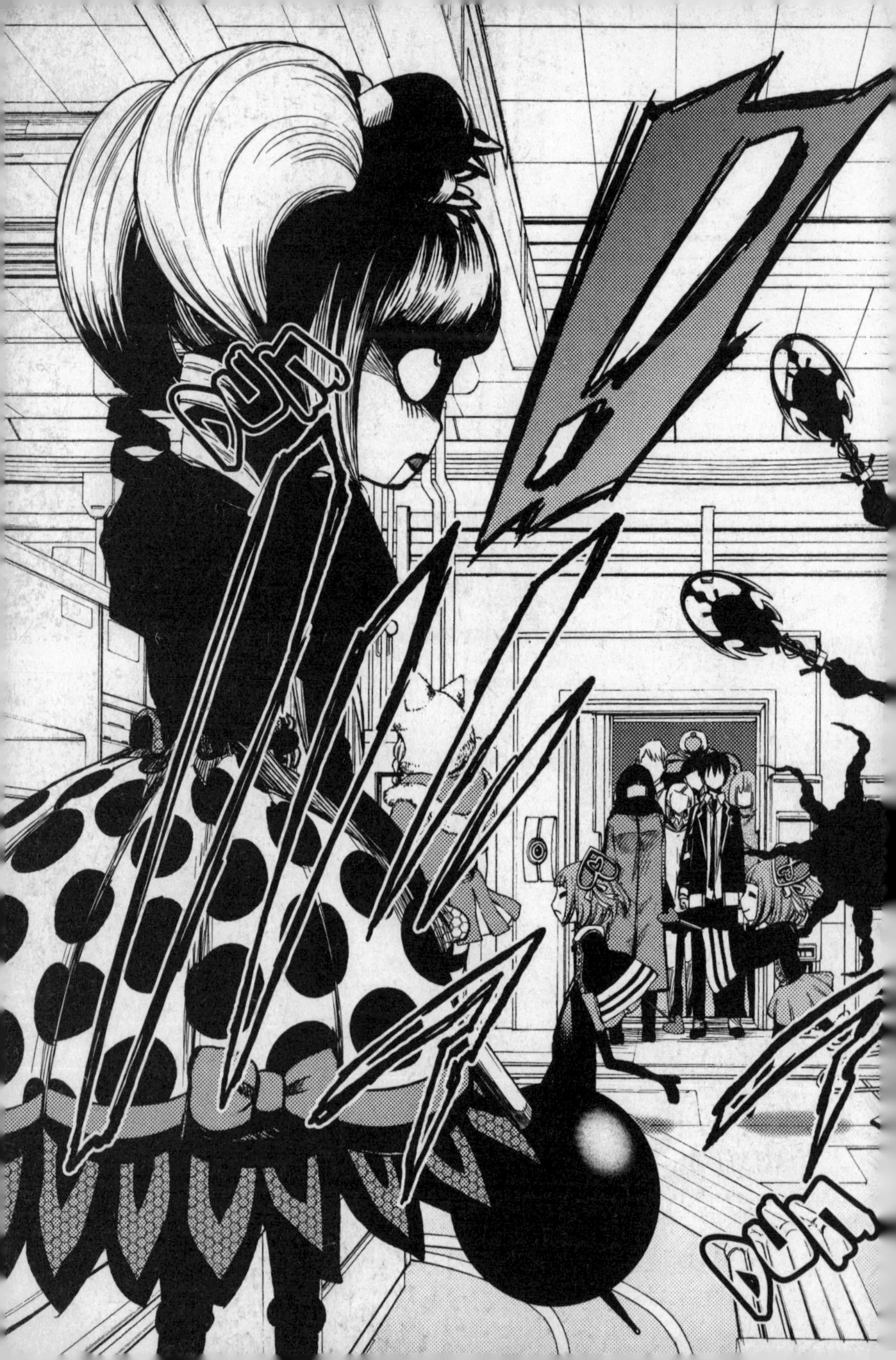
DUN
DUN

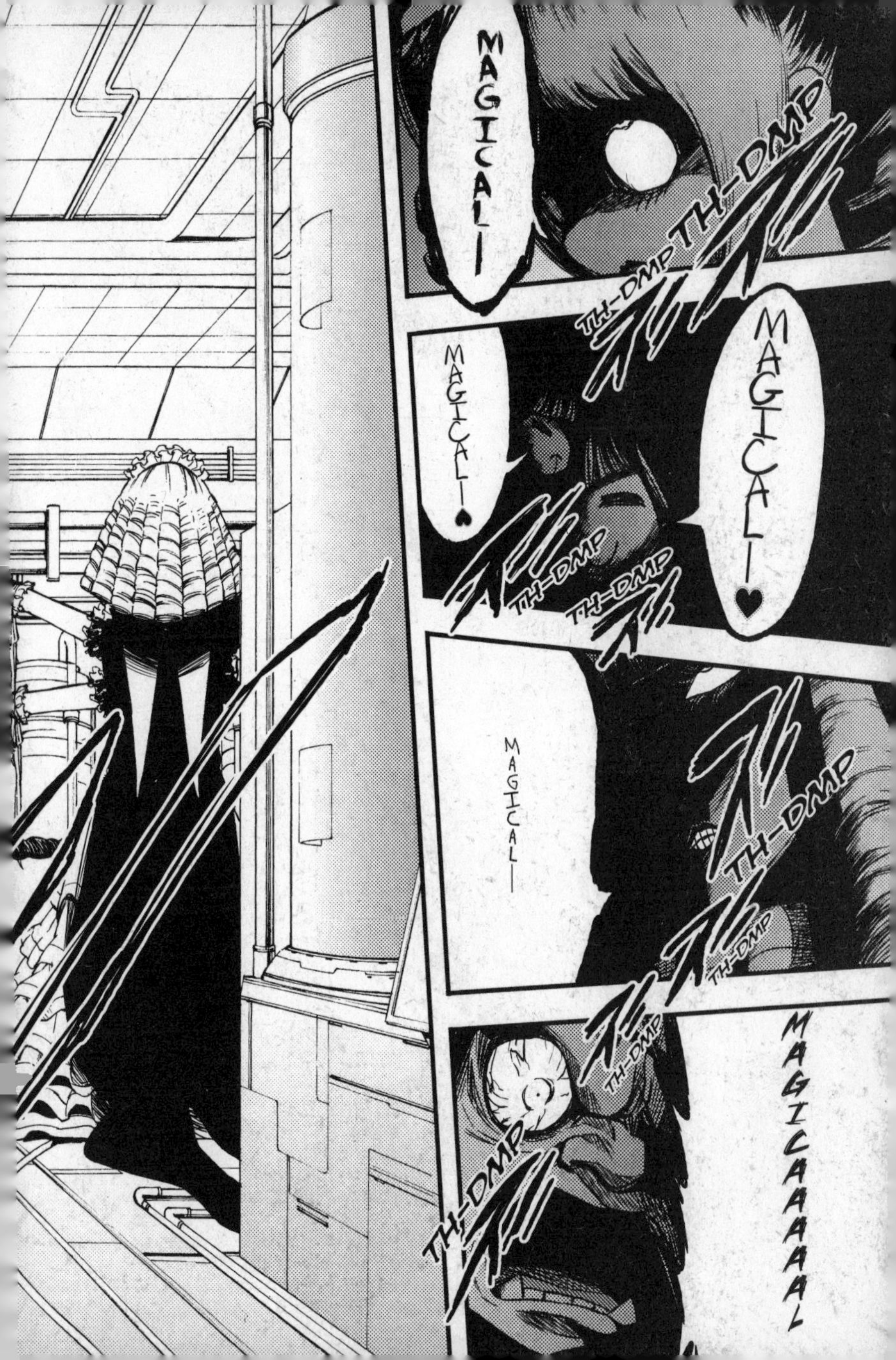

MAGICAL!
TH-DMP TH-DMP
TH-DMP
MAGICAL!♥
MAGICAL!♥
TH-DMP
TH-DMP
MAGICAL!
TH-DMP
TH-DMP
MAGICAAAAAAAL
TH-DMP
TH-DMP

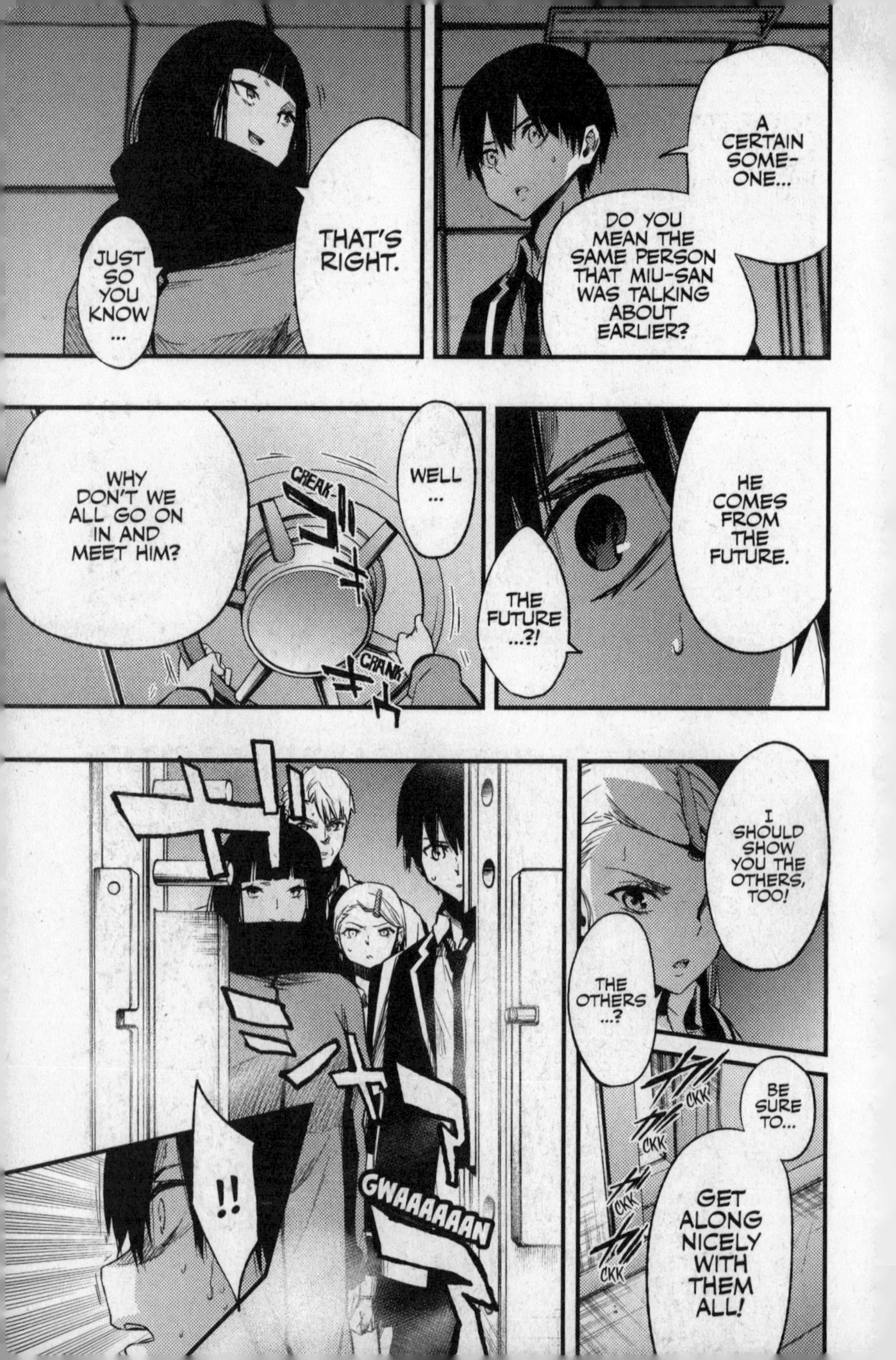
A CERTAIN SOMEONE...
DO YOU MEAN THE SAME PERSON THAT MIU-SAN WAS TALKING ABOUT EARLIER?
THAT'S RIGHT.
JUST SO YOU KNOW ...
HE COMES FROM THE FUTURE.
THE FUTURE ...?!
WELL ...
CREAK
WHY DON'T WE ALL GO ON IN AND MEET HIM?
CRANK
I SHOULD SHOW YOU THE OTHERS, TOO!
THE OTHERS ...?
BE SURE TO...
CKK
CKK
CKK
CKK
GET ALONG NICELY WITH THEM ALL!
GWAAAAAAAN
!!

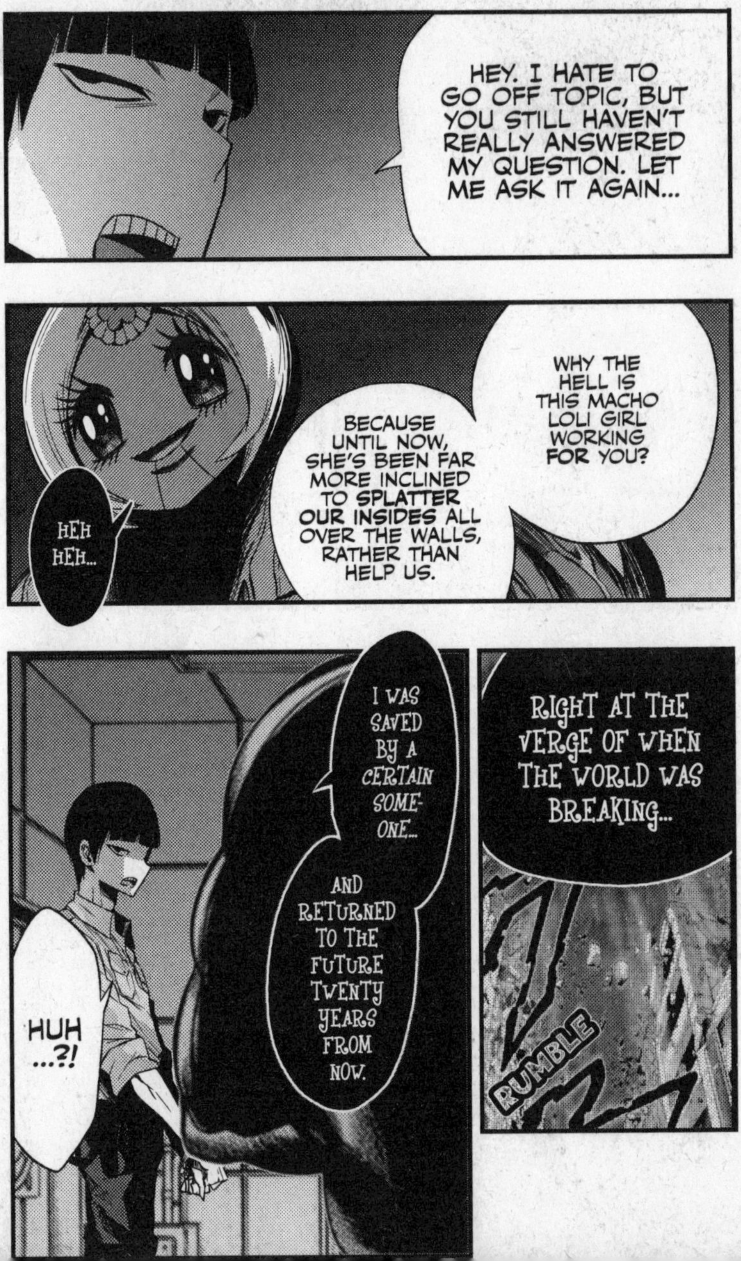
HEY. I HATE TO GO OFF TOPIC, BUT YOU STILL HAVEN'T REALLY ANSWERED MY QUESTION. LET ME ASK IT AGAIN...
WHY THE HELL IS THIS MACHO LOLI GIRL WORKING FOR YOU?
BECAUSE UNTIL NOW, SHE'S BEEN FAR MORE INCLINED TO **SPLATTER OUR INSIDES** ALL OVER THE WALLS, RATHER THAN HELP US.
HEH HEH...
RIGHT AT THE VERGE OF WHEN THE WORLD WAS BREAKING...
RUMBLE
I WAS SAVED BY A CERTAIN SOME-ONE...
AND RETURNED TO THE FUTURE TWENTY YEARS FROM NOW.
HUH ...?!

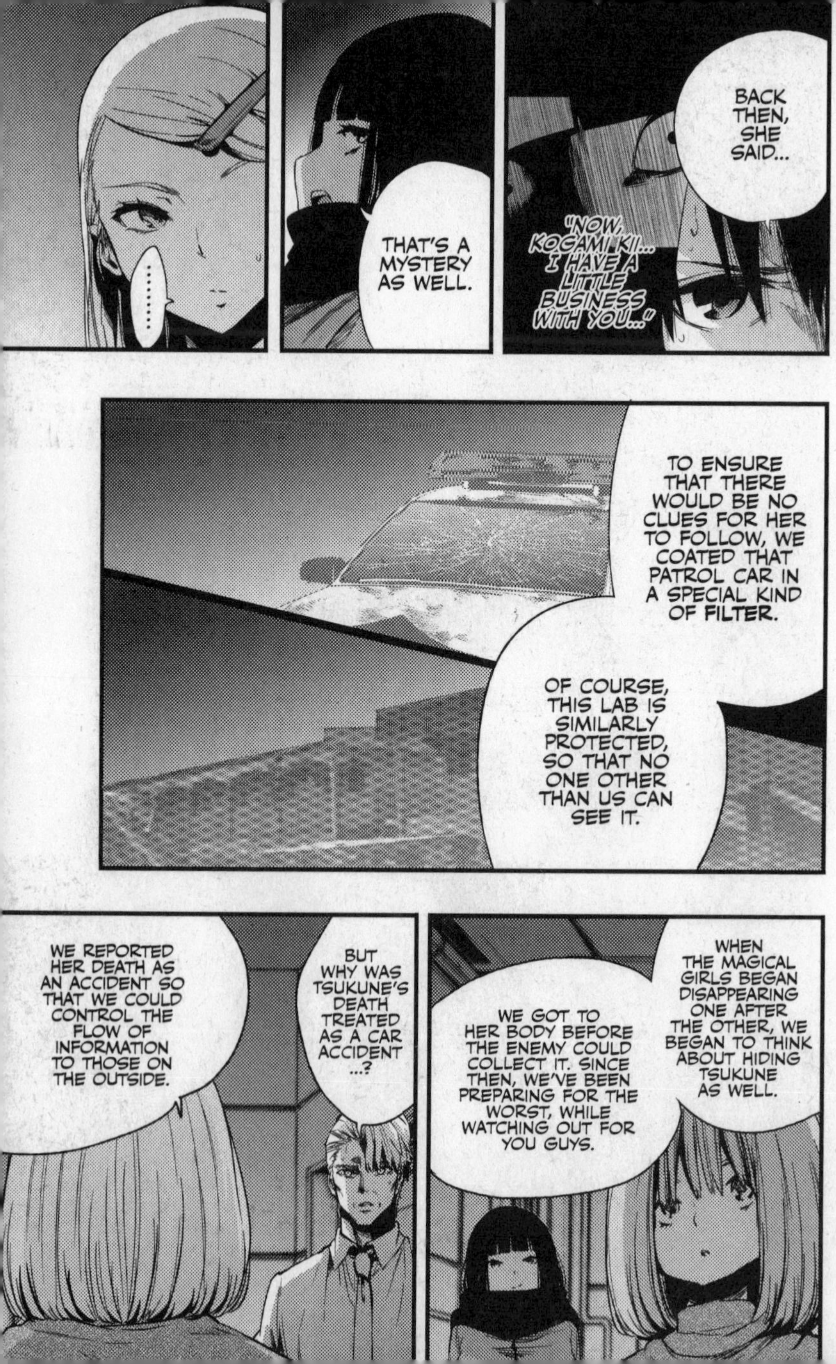
BACK THEN, SHE SAID...
"NOW, KOGAMI KI... I HAVE A LITTLE BUSINESS WITH YOU..."
THAT'S A MYSTERY AS WELL.
......
TO ENSURE THAT THERE WOULD BE NO CLUES FOR HER TO FOLLOW, WE COATED THAT PATROL CAR IN A SPECIAL KIND OF FILTER.
OF COURSE, THIS LAB IS SIMILARLY PROTECTED, SO THAT NO ONE OTHER THAN US CAN SEE IT.
WHEN THE MAGICAL GIRLS BEGAN DISAPPEARING ONE AFTER THE OTHER, WE BEGAN TO THINK ABOUT HIDING TSUKUNE AS WELL.
WE GOT TO HER BODY BEFORE THE ENEMY COULD COLLECT IT. SINCE THEN, WE'VE BEEN PREPARING FOR THE WORST, WHILE WATCHING OUT FOR YOU GUYS.
BUT WHY WAS TSUKUNE'S DEATH TREATED AS A CAR ACCIDENT ...?
WE REPORTED HER DEATH AS AN ACCIDENT SO THAT WE COULD CONTROL THE FLOW OF INFORMATION TO THOSE ON THE OUTSIDE.

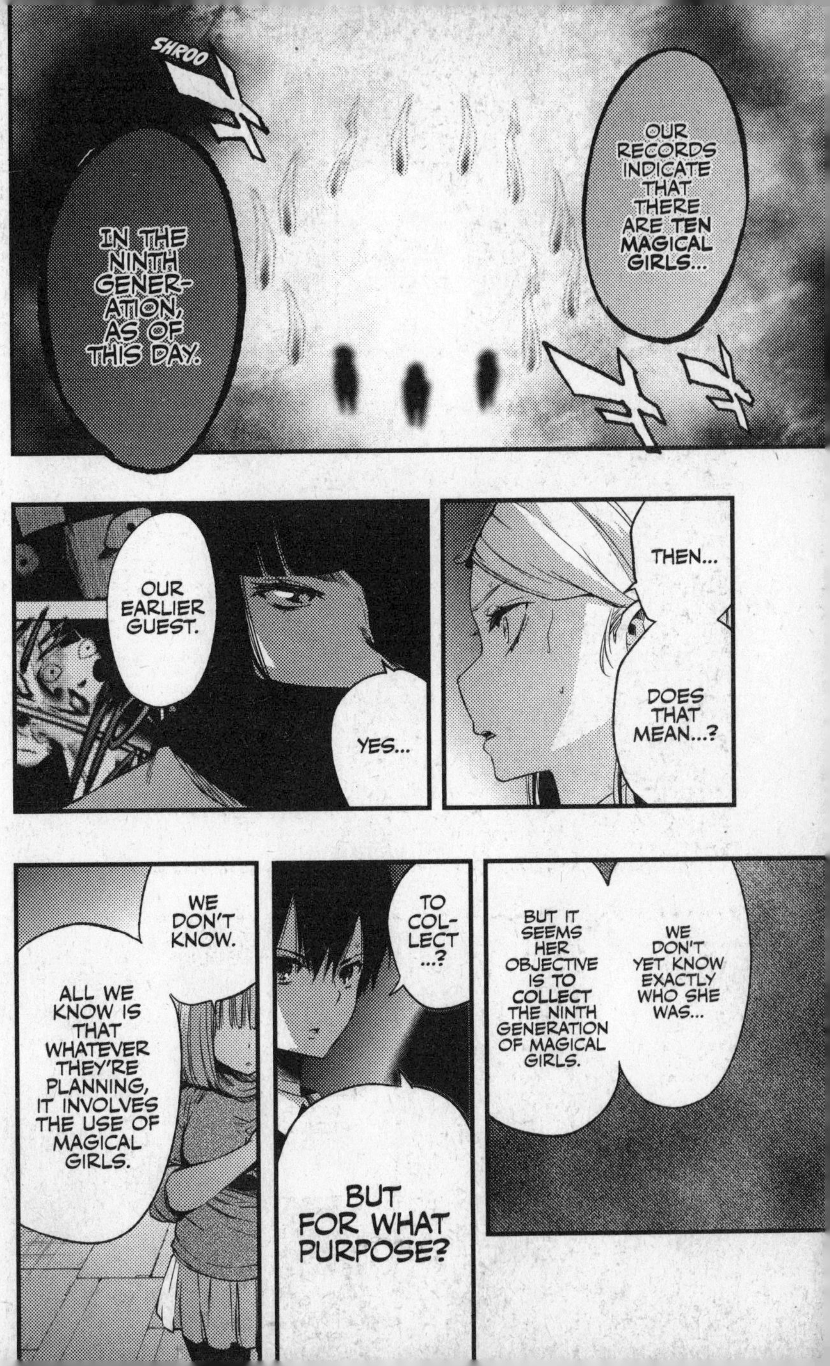
OUR RECORDS INDICATE THAT THERE ARE TEN MAGICAL GIRLS...
SHROO
IN THE NINTH GENERATION, AS OF THIS DAY.
THEN...
DOES THAT MEAN...?
YES...
OUR EARLIER GUEST.
WE DON'T YET KNOW EXACTLY WHO SHE WAS...
BUT IT SEEMS HER OBJECTIVE IS TO COLLECT THE NINTH GENERATION OF MAGICAL GIRLS.
TO COLLECT...?
BUT FOR WHAT PURPOSE?
WE DON'T KNOW.
ALL WE KNOW IS THAT WHATEVER THEY'RE PLANNING, IT INVOLVES THE USE OF MAGICAL GIRLS.

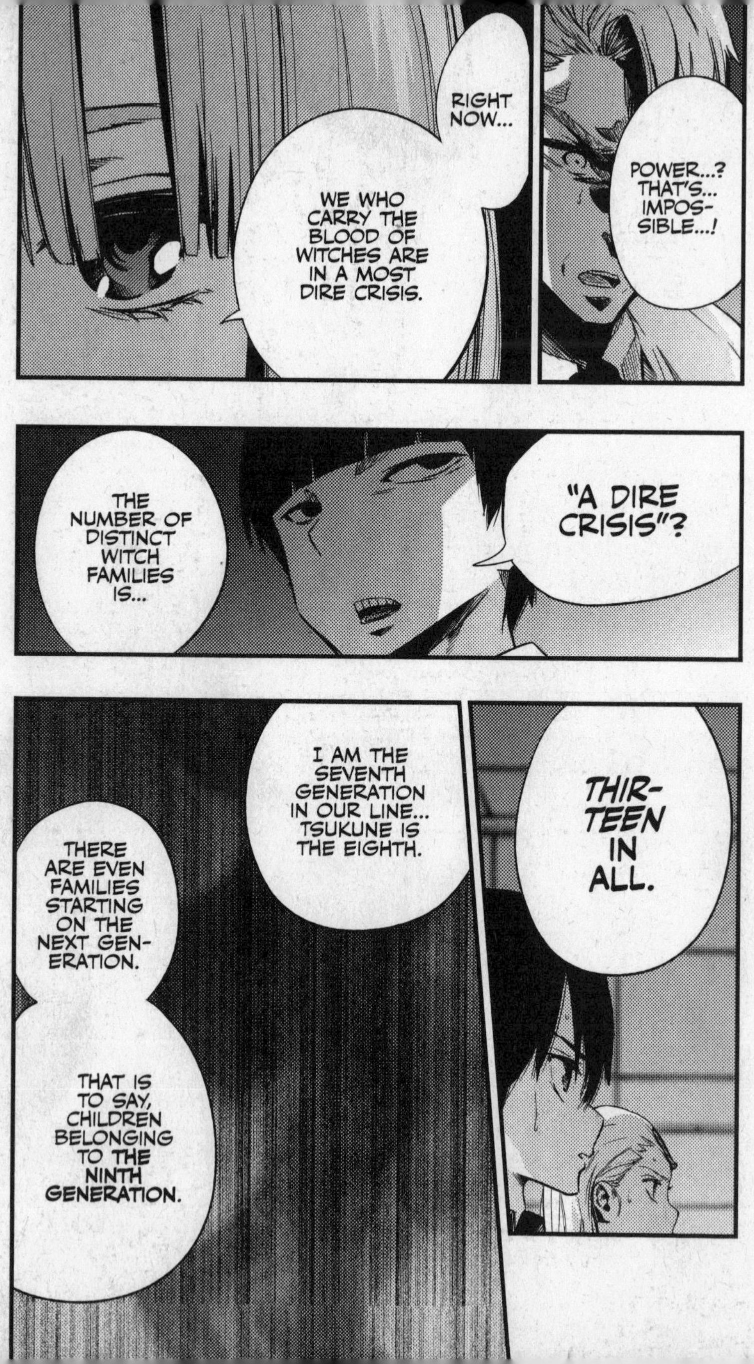
POWER...? THAT'S... IMPOS-SIBLE...!
RIGHT NOW...
WE WHO CARRY THE BLOOD OF WITCHES ARE IN A MOST DIRE CRISIS.
"A DIRE CRISIS"?
THE NUMBER OF DISTINCT WITCH FAMILIES IS...
THIR-TEEN IN ALL.
I AM THE SEVENTH GENERATION IN OUR LINE... TSUKUNE IS THE EIGHTH.
THERE ARE EVEN FAMILIES STARTING ON THE NEXT GEN-ERATION.
THAT IS TO SAY, CHILDREN BELONGING TO THE NINTH GENERATION.

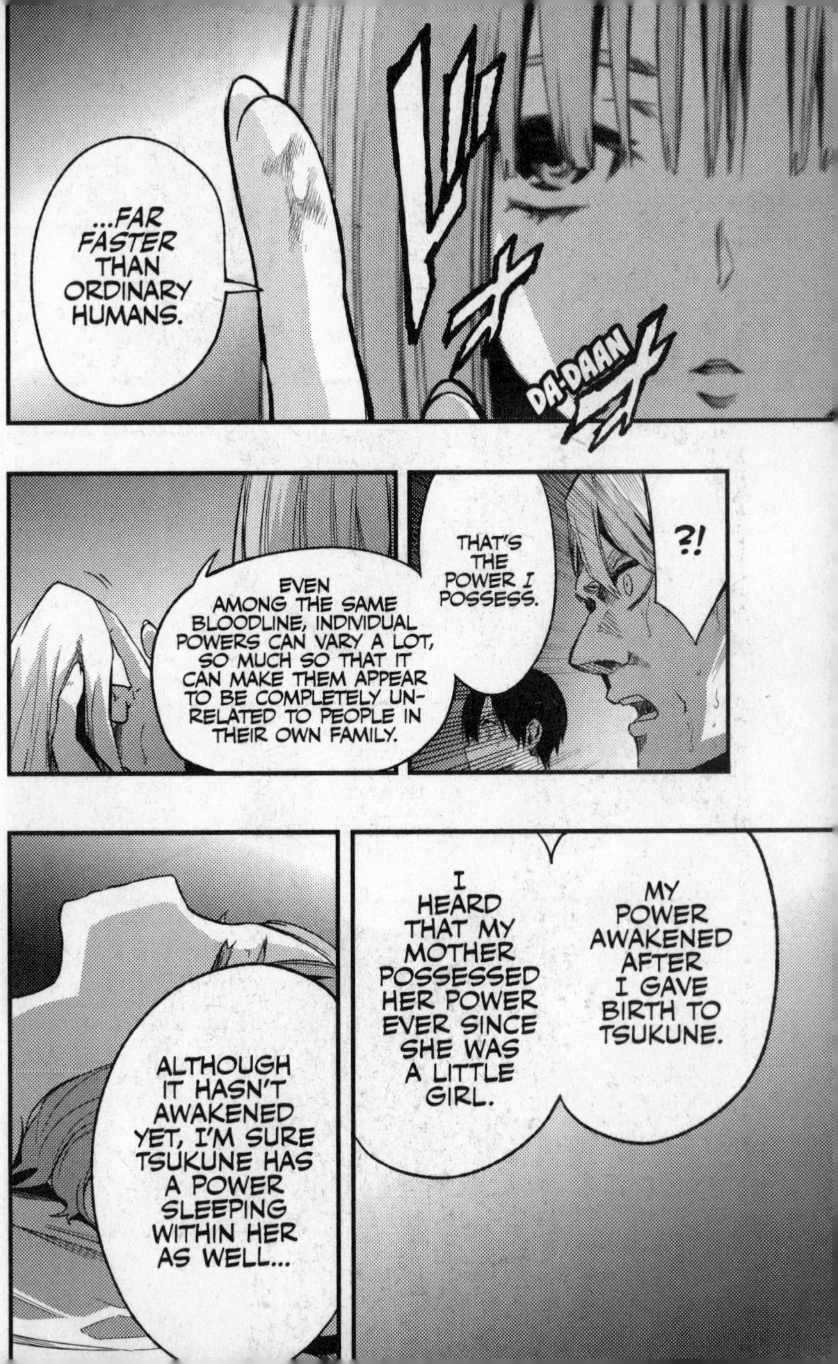

...FAR FASTER THAN ORDINARY HUMANS.
DA-DAAN
THAT'S THE POWER I POSSESS.
?!
EVEN AMONG THE SAME BLOODLINE, INDIVIDUAL POWERS CAN VARY A LOT, SO MUCH SO THAT IT CAN MAKE THEM APPEAR TO BE COMPLETELY UN-RELATED TO PEOPLE IN THEIR OWN FAMILY.
MY POWER AWAKENED AFTER I GAVE BIRTH TO TSUKUNE.
I HEARD THAT MY MOTHER POSSESSED HER POWER EVER SINCE SHE WAS A LITTLE GIRL.
ALTHOUGH IT HASN'T AWAKENED YET, I'M SURE TSUKUNE HAS A POWER SLEEPING WITHIN HER AS WELL...

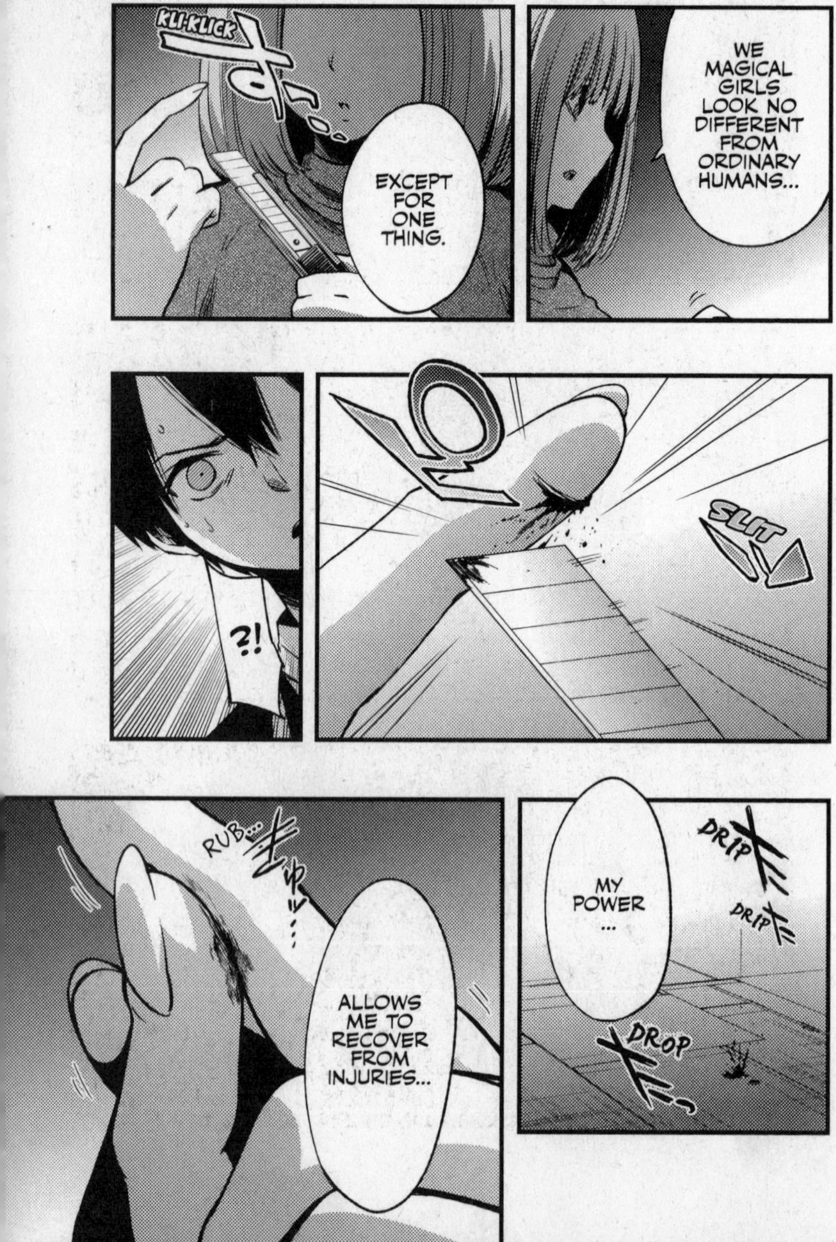
WE MAGICAL GIRLS LOOK NO DIFFERENT FROM ORDINARY HUMANS...
KLI-KLICK
EXCEPT FOR ONE THING.
SLIT
?!
DRIP
DRIP
MY POWER ...
DROP
RUB...
ALLOWS ME TO RECOVER FROM INJURIES...

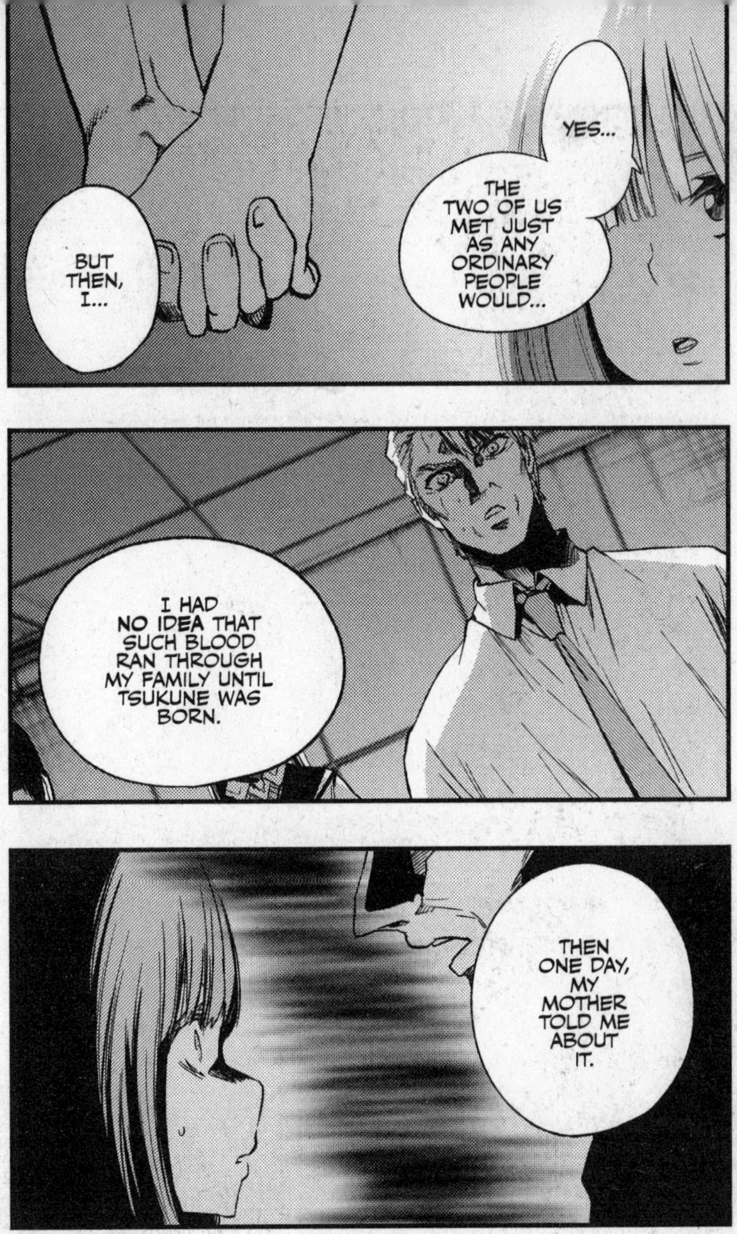
YES...
THE TWO OF US MET JUST AS ANY ORDINARY PEOPLE WOULD...
BUT THEN, I...
I HAD NO IDEA THAT SUCH BLOOD RAN THROUGH MY FAMILY UNTIL TSUKUNE WAS BORN.
THEN ONE DAY, MY MOTHER TOLD ME ABOUT IT.

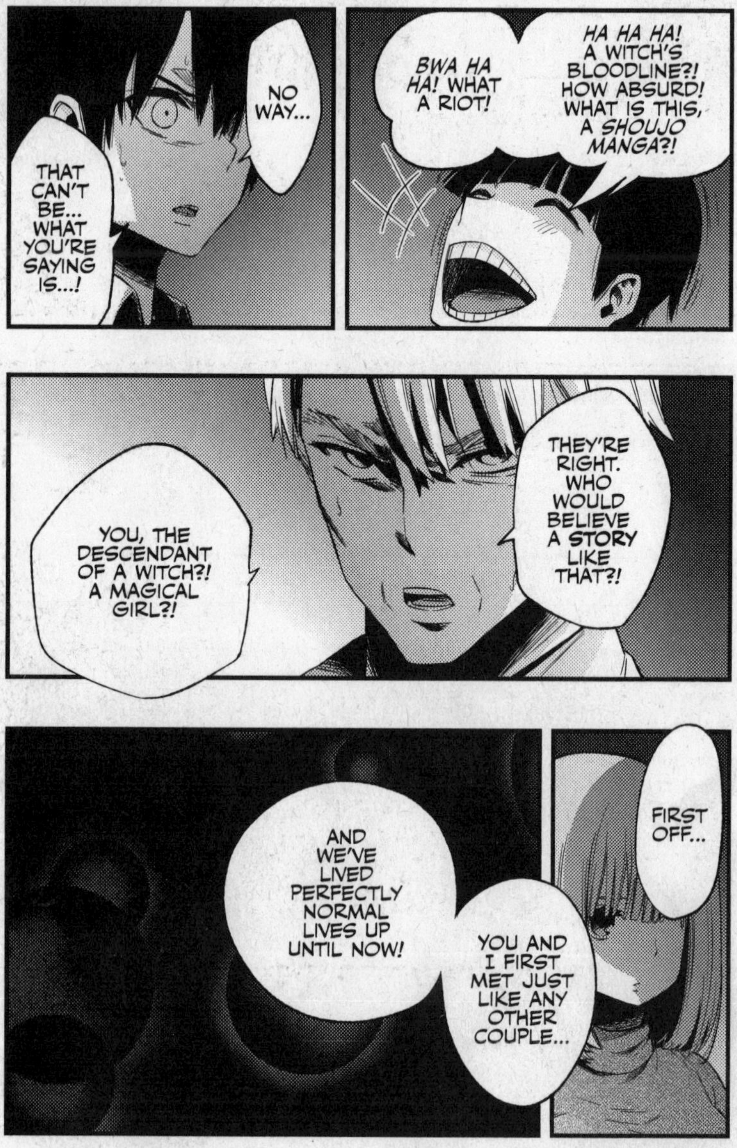
HA HA HA! A WITCH'S BLOODLINE?! HOW ABSURD! WHAT IS THIS, A *SHOUJO MANGA*?!
BWA HA HA! WHAT A RIOT!
NO WAY...
THAT CAN'T BE... WHAT YOU'RE SAYING IS...!
THEY'RE RIGHT. WHO WOULD BELIEVE A **STORY** LIKE THAT?!
YOU, THE DESCENDANT OF A WITCH?! A MAGICAL GIRL?!
FIRST OFF...
YOU AND I FIRST MET JUST LIKE ANY OTHER COUPLE...
AND WE'VE LIVED PERFECTLY NORMAL LIVES UP UNTIL NOW!

THE CHILD BORN BETWEEN A MAGICAL GIRL AND A HUMAN WILL ALWAYS BE A GIRL, AND SHE WILL ALWAYS BE A MAGICAL GIRL.
AND SO, THIS BLOODLINE HAS CONTINUED ON FOR MANY GENERATIONS.
DEMON
HUMAN
WITCH
HUMAN
MAGICAL GIRL
HUM
MAGICAL GIRL
ONE OF THE DESCENDANTS OF THAT FAMILY TREE...
IS ME...
ASANO KAORU
MASAKI KINYA
MASAKI KOTONE
FUKUMOTO SEIICHI
FUKUMOTO TSUKUNE
AND ANOTHER LIES SLEEPING BEFORE YOU.
TSUKUNE.

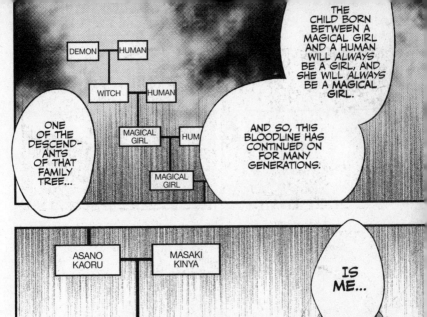

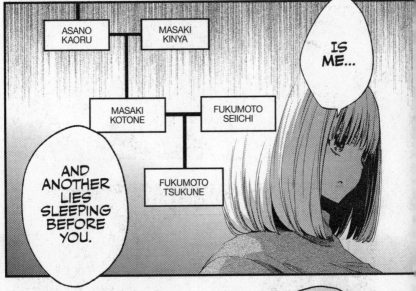

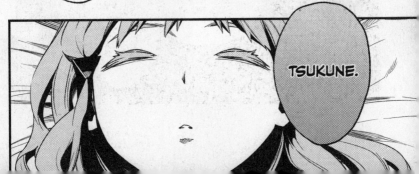

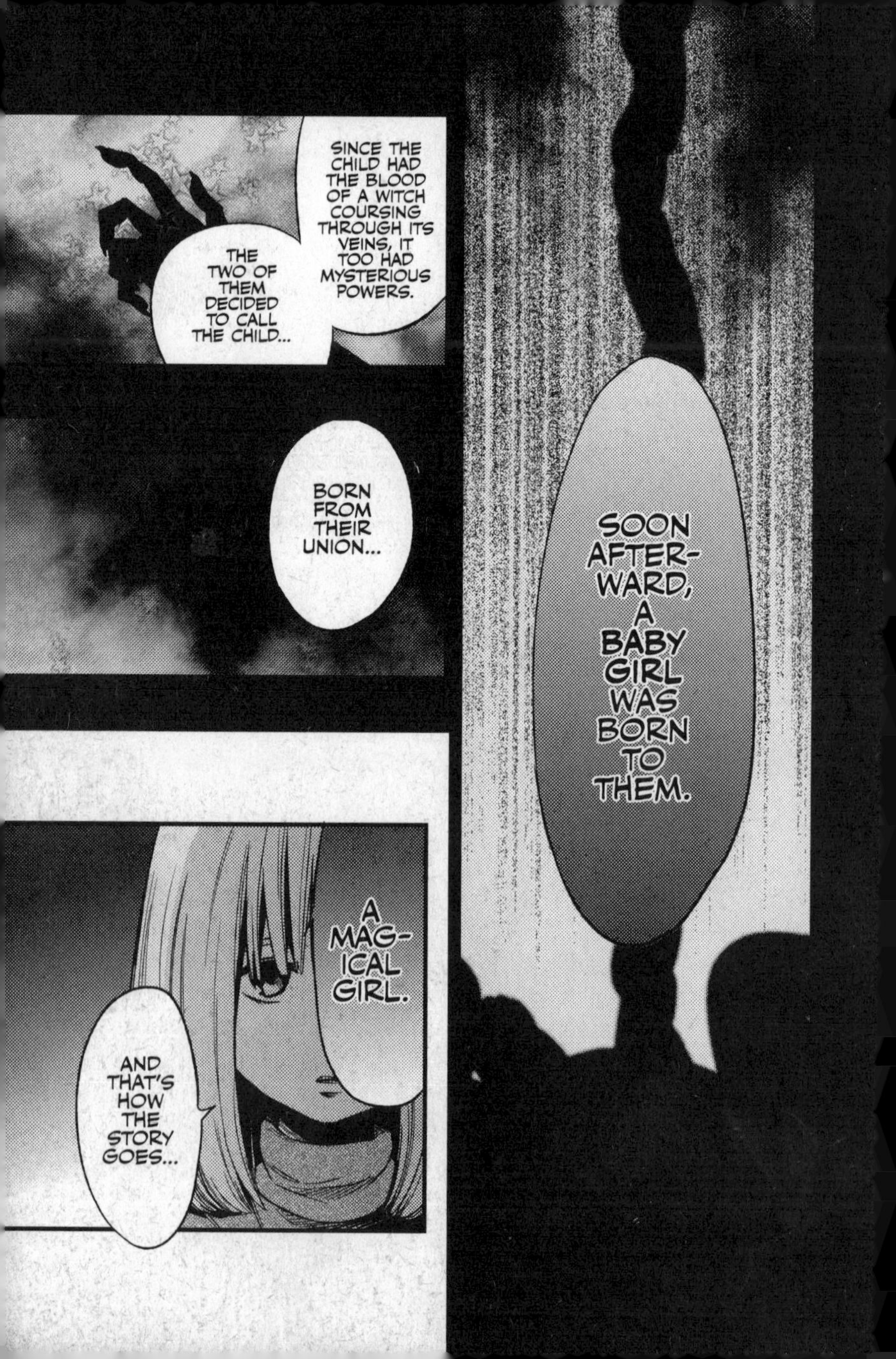
SOON AFTERWARD, A BABY GIRL WAS BORN TO THEM.
SINCE THE CHILD HAD THE BLOOD OF A WITCH COURSING THROUGH ITS VEINS, IT TOO HAD MYSTERIOUS POWERS.
THE TWO OF THEM DECIDED TO CALL THE CHILD...
BORN FROM THEIR UNION...
A MAGICAL GIRL.
AND THAT'S HOW THE STORY GOES...

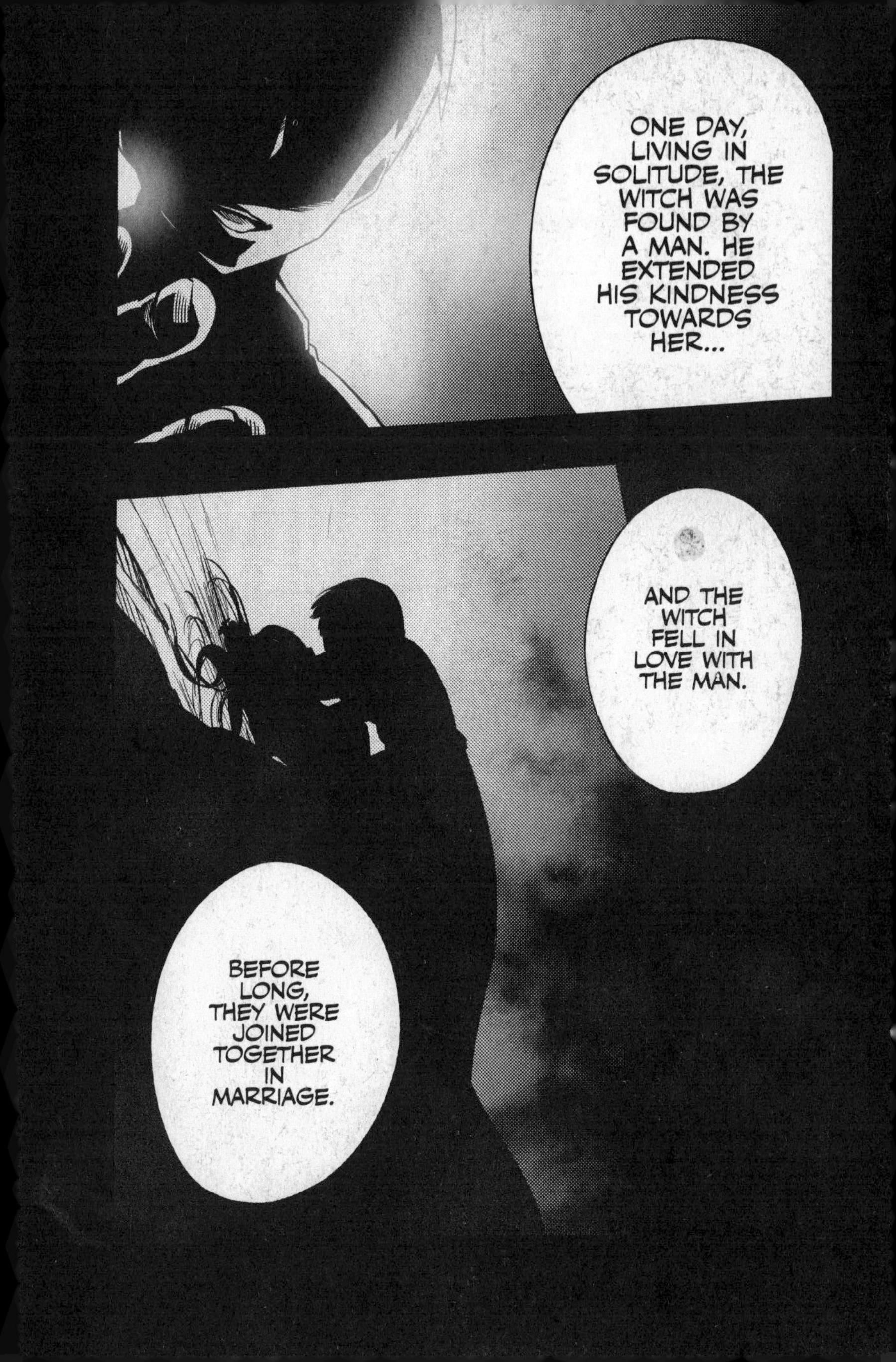
ONE DAY, LIVING IN SOLITUDE, THE WITCH WAS FOUND BY A MAN. HE EXTENDED HIS KINDNESS TOWARDS HER...
AND THE WITCH FELL IN LOVE WITH THE MAN.
BEFORE LONG, THEY WERE JOINED TOGETHER IN MARRIAGE.

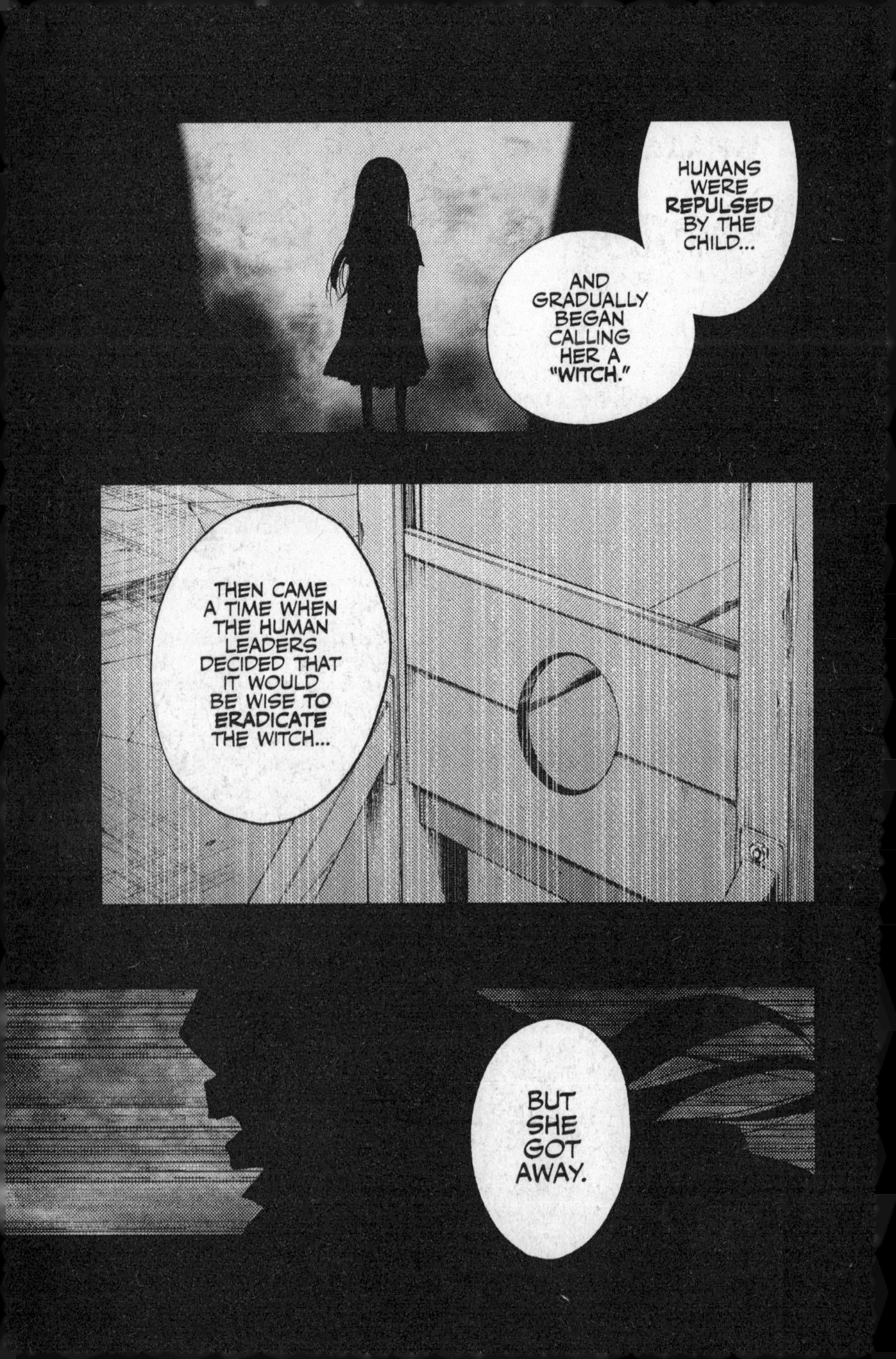
HUMANS WERE REPULSED BY THE CHILD...
AND GRADUALLY BEGAN CALLING HER A "WITCH."
THEN CAME A TIME WHEN THE HUMAN LEADERS DECIDED THAT IT WOULD BE WISE TO ERADICATE THE WITCH...
BUT SHE GOT AWAY.

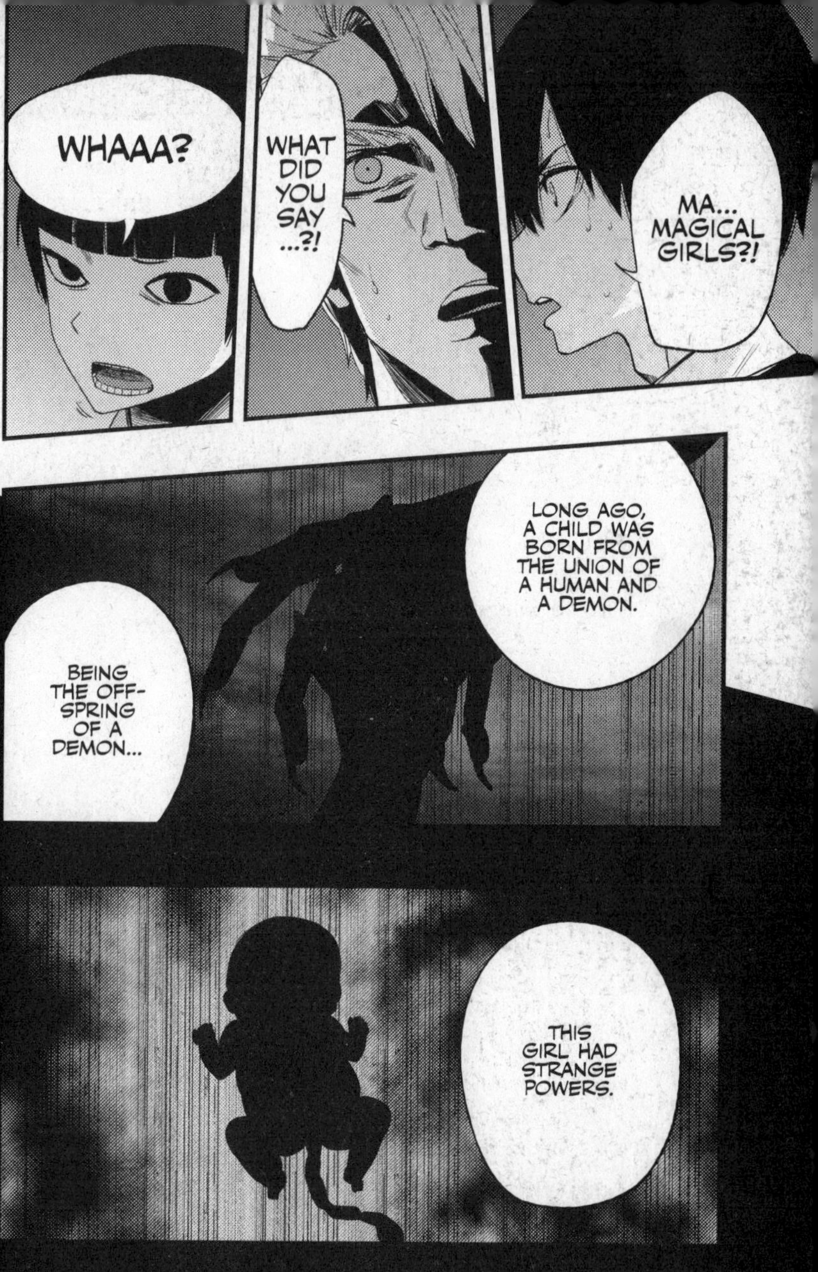
MA... MAGICAL GIRLS?!
WHAT DID YOU SAY ...?!
WHAAA?
LONG AGO, A CHILD WAS BORN FROM THE UNION OF A HUMAN AND A DEMON.
BEING THE OFF-SPRING OF A DEMON...
THIS GIRL HAD STRANGE POWERS.

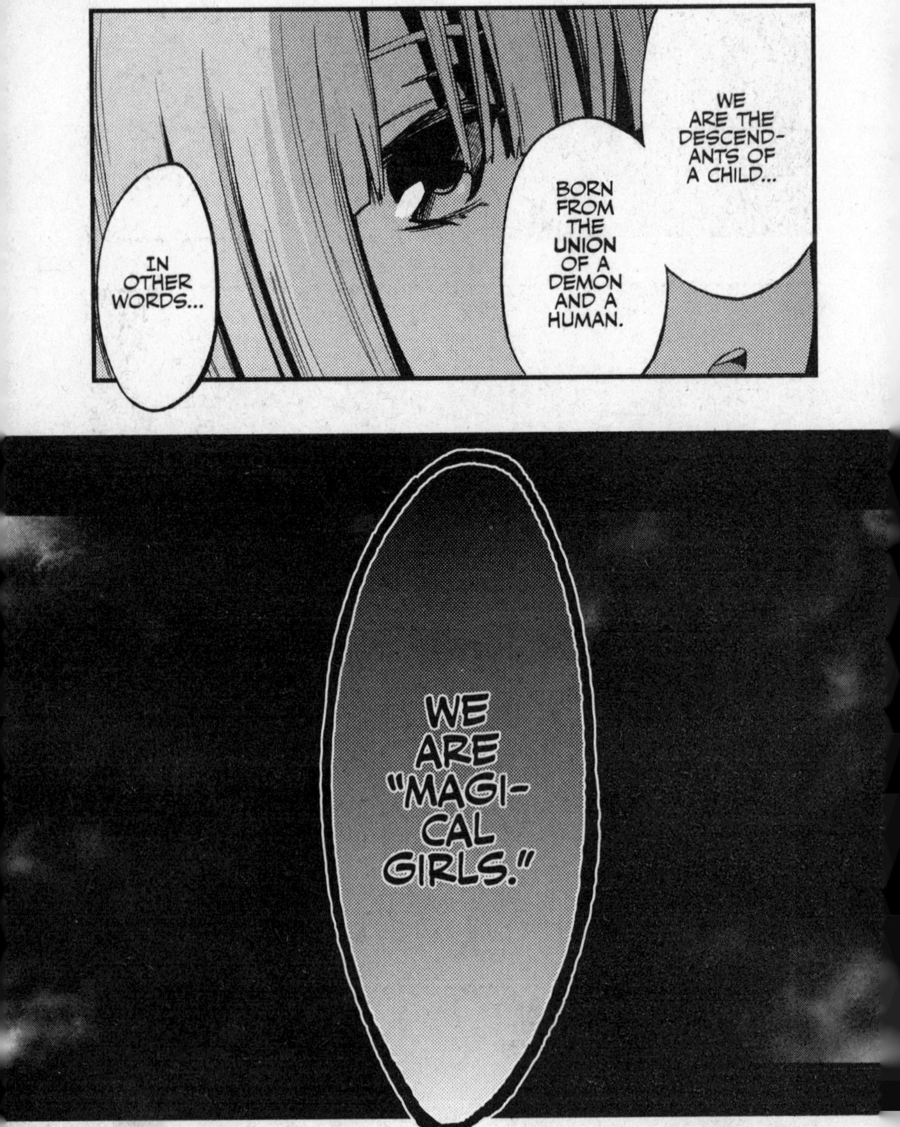
WE ARE THE DESCENDANTS OF A CHILD...
BORN FROM THE UNION OF A DEMON AND A HUMAN.
IN OTHER WORDS...
WE ARE "MAGICAL GIRLS."

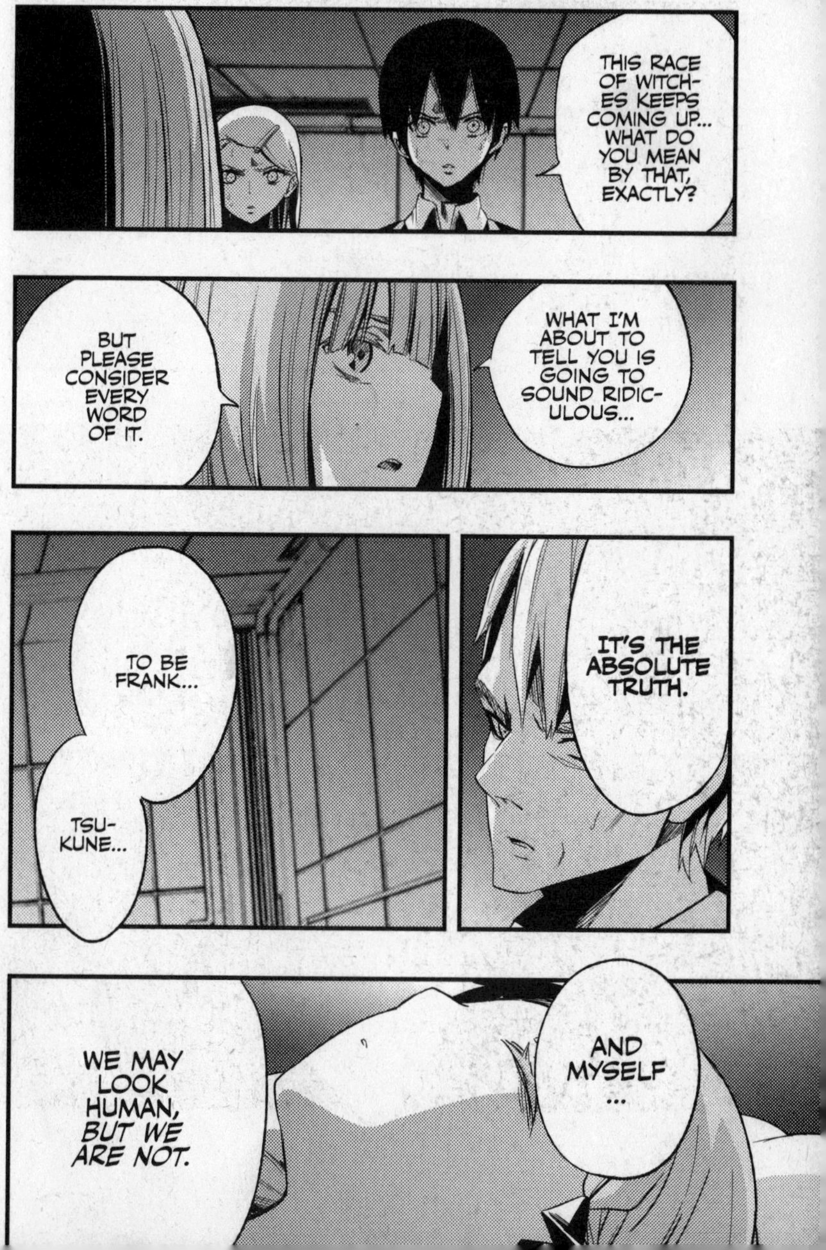
THIS RACE OF WITCHES KEEPS COMING UP... WHAT DO YOU MEAN BY THAT, EXACTLY?
WHAT I'M ABOUT TO TELL YOU IS GOING TO SOUND RIDICULOUS...
BUT PLEASE CONSIDER EVERY WORD OF IT.
IT'S THE ABSOLUTE TRUTH.
TO BE FRANK...
TSUKUNE...
AND MYSELF ...
WE MAY LOOK HUMAN, *BUT WE ARE NOT.*

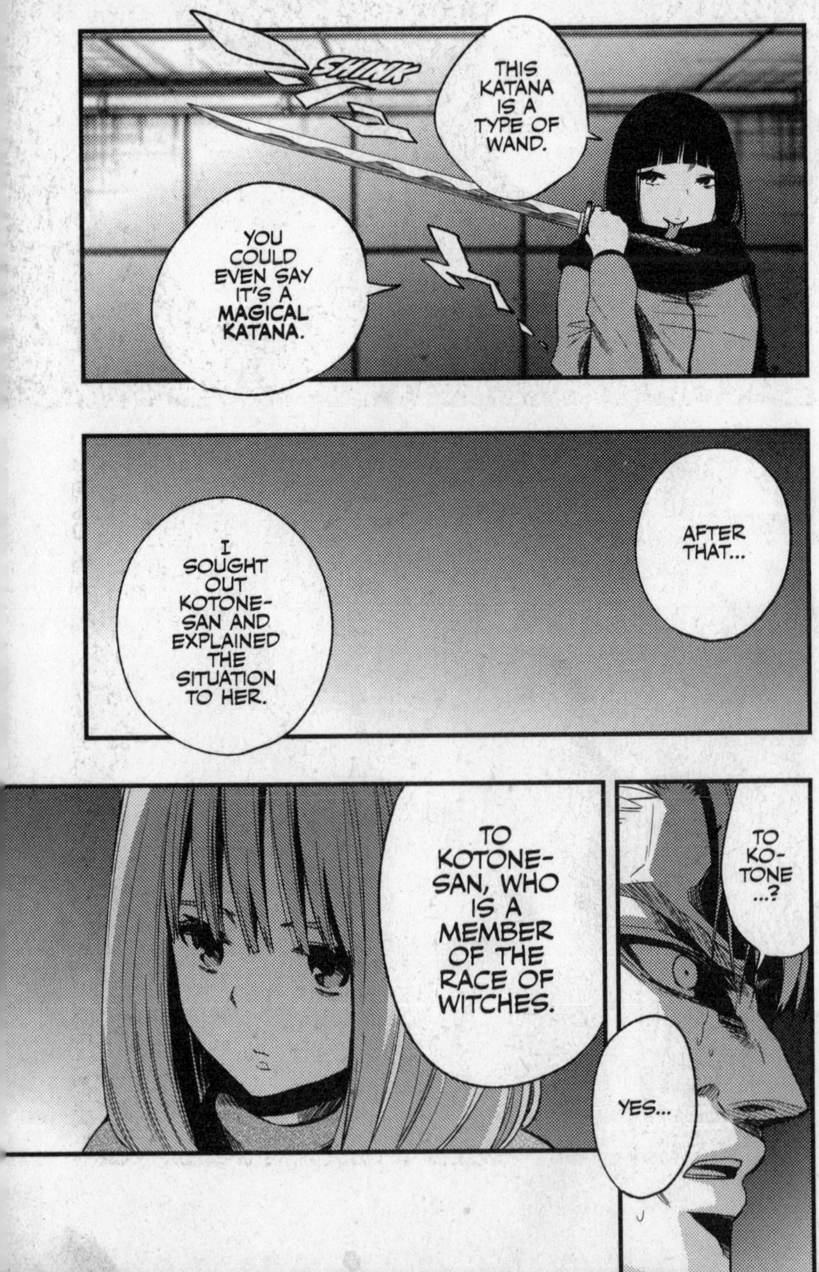
THIS KATANA IS A TYPE OF WAND.
SHINK
YOU COULD EVEN SAY IT'S A MAGICAL KATANA.
AFTER THAT...
I SOUGHT OUT KOTONE-SAN AND EXPLAINED THE SITUATION TO HER.
TO KO-TONE ...?
YES...
TO KOTONE-SAN, WHO IS A MEMBER OF THE RACE OF WITCHES.

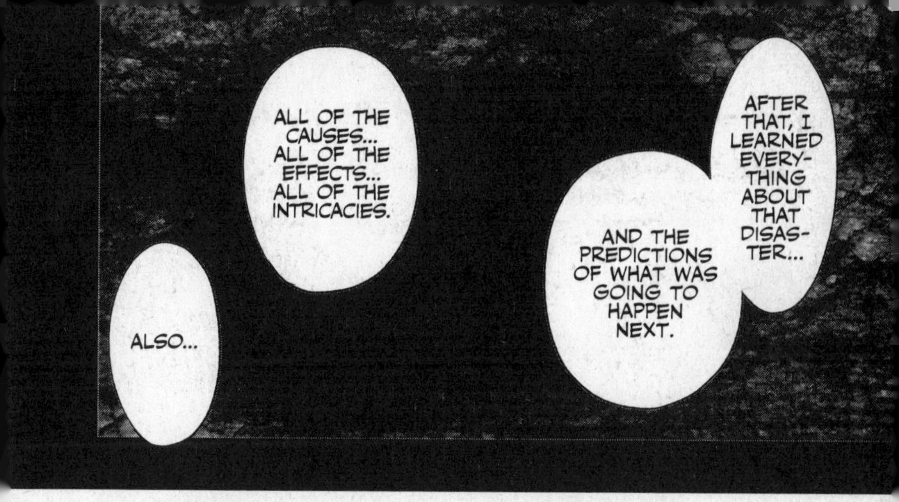
AFTER THAT, I LEARNED EVERY-THING ABOUT THAT DISAS-TER...
AND THE PREDICTIONS OF WHAT WAS GOING TO HAPPEN NEXT.
ALL OF THE CAUSES... ALL OF THE EFFECTS... ALL OF THE INTRICACIES.
ALSO...
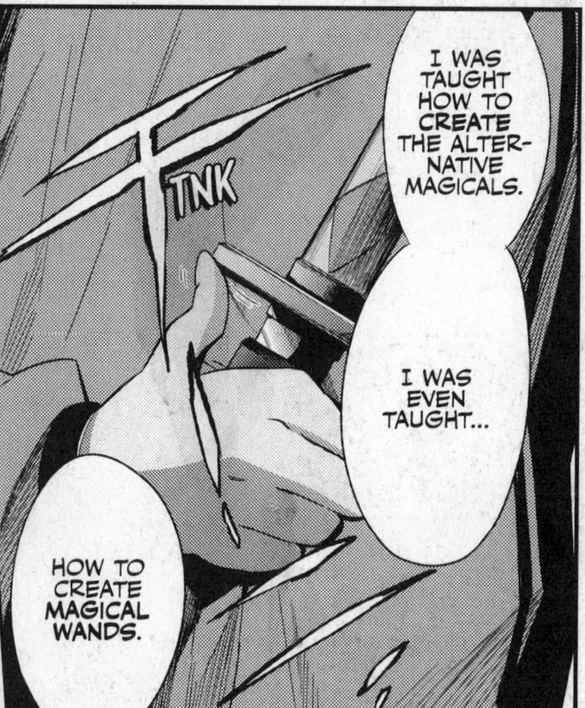
I WAS TAUGHT HOW TO CREATE THE ALTER-NATIVE MAGICALS.
TNK
I WAS EVEN TAUGHT...
HOW TO CREATE MAGICAL WANDS.
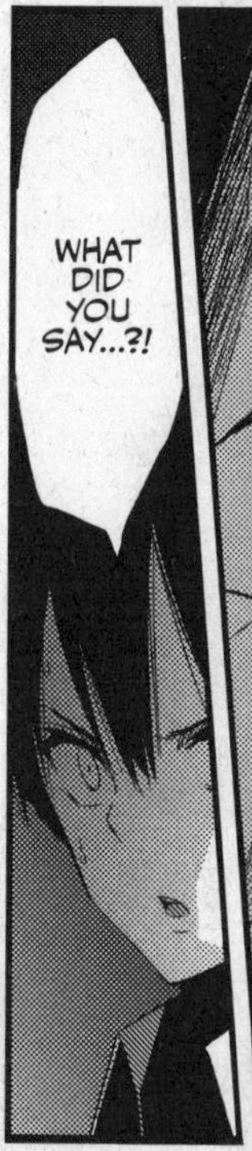
WHAT DID YOU SAY...?!

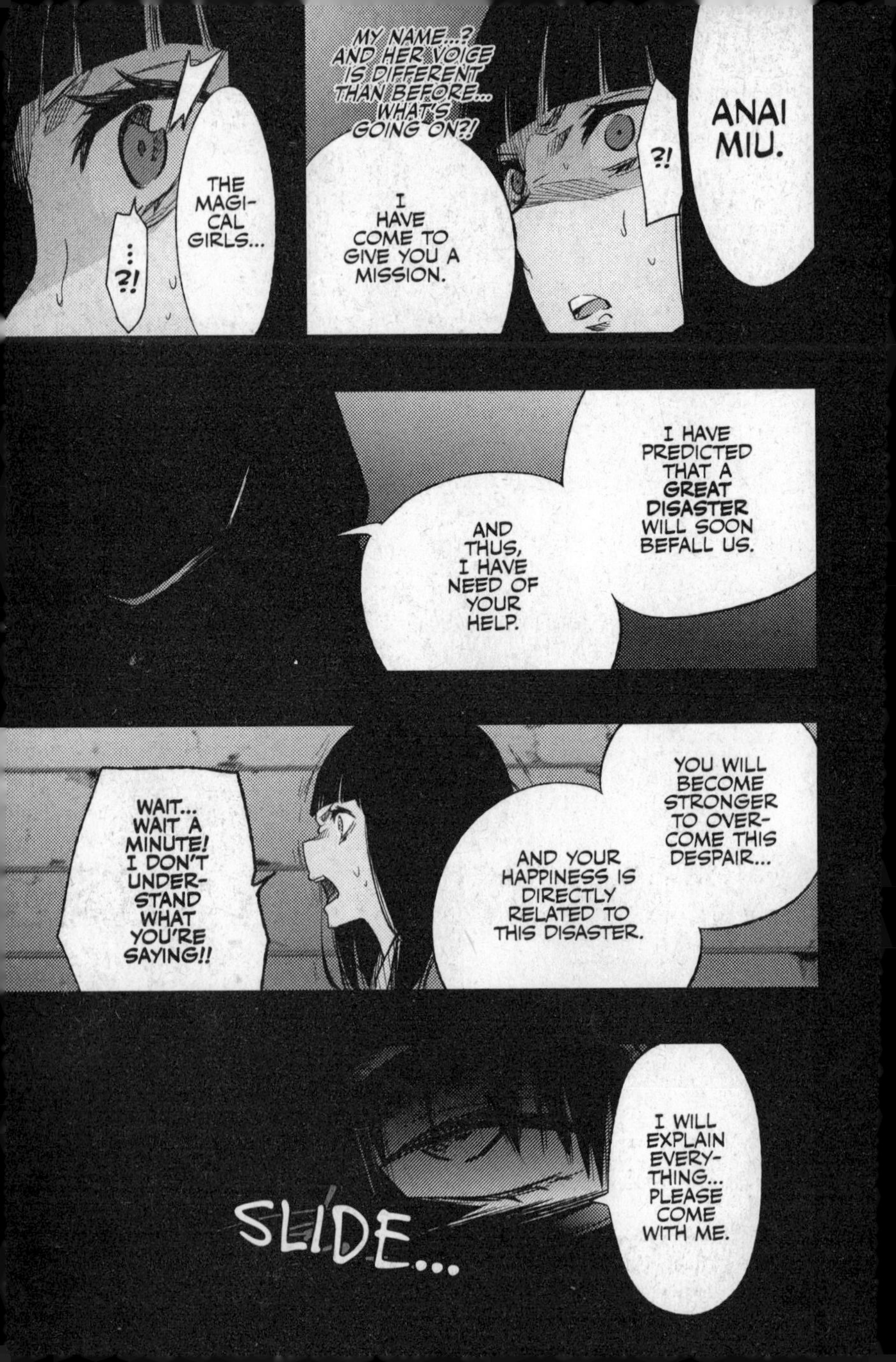
ANAI MIU.
?!
MY NAME...? AND HER VOICE IS DIFFERENT THAN BEFORE... WHAT'S GOING ON?!
I HAVE COME TO GIVE YOU A MISSION.
THE MAGICAL GIRLS...
...?!
I HAVE PREDICTED THAT A GREAT DISASTER WILL SOON BEFALL US.
AND THUS, I HAVE NEED OF YOUR HELP.
YOU WILL BECOME STRONGER TO OVERCOME THIS DESPAIR...
AND YOUR HAPPINESS IS DIRECTLY RELATED TO THIS DISASTER.
WAIT... WAIT A MINUTE! I DON'T UNDERSTAND WHAT YOU'RE SAYING!!
I WILL EXPLAIN EVERYTHING... PLEASE COME WITH ME.
SLIDE...

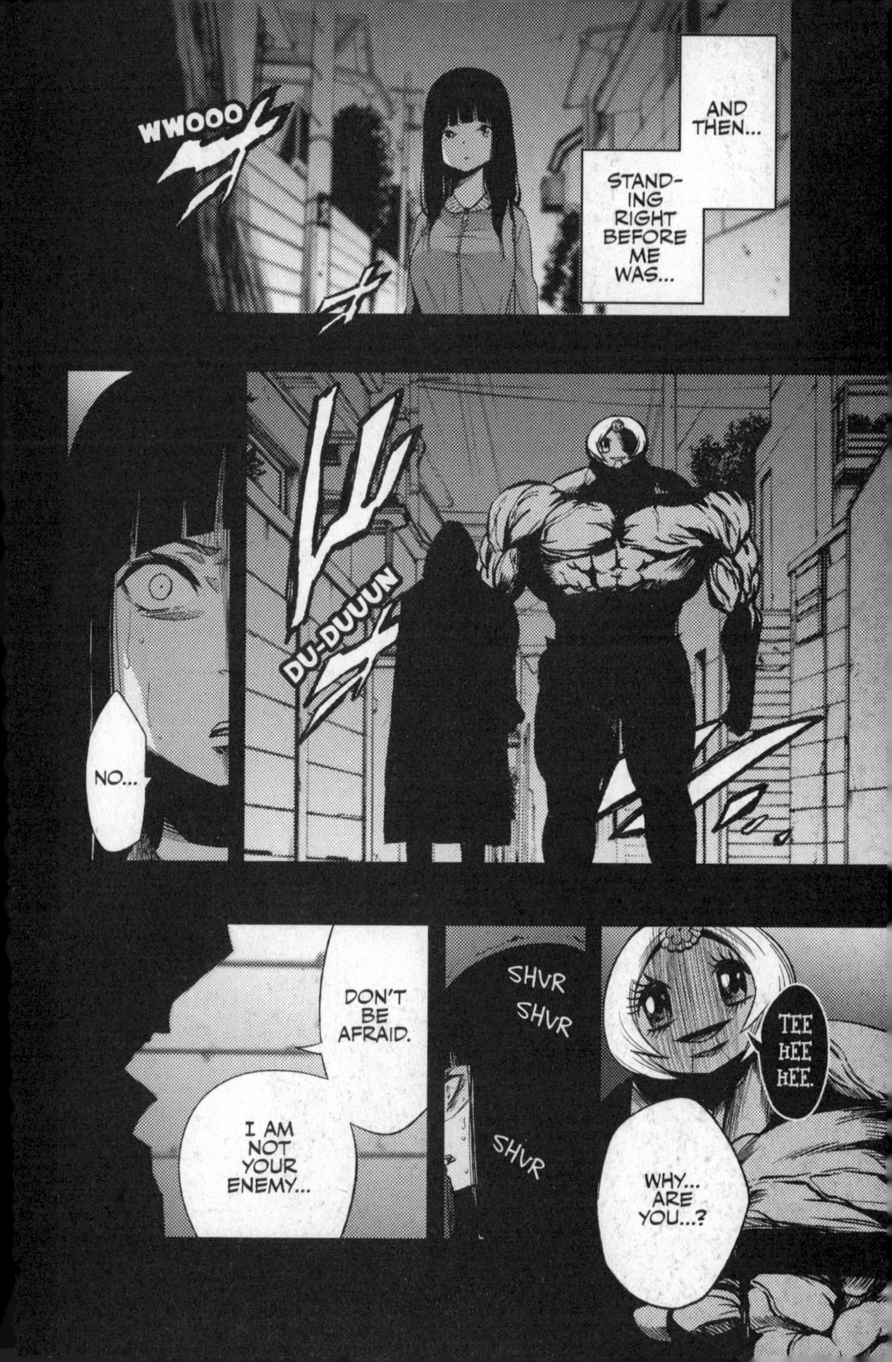
AND THEN...
STAND-ING RIGHT BEFORE ME WAS...
WWOOO
DU-DUUUN
NO...
TEE HEE HEE.
WHY... ARE YOU...?
SHVR SHVR
SHVR
DON'T BE AFRAID.
I AM NOT YOUR ENEMY...

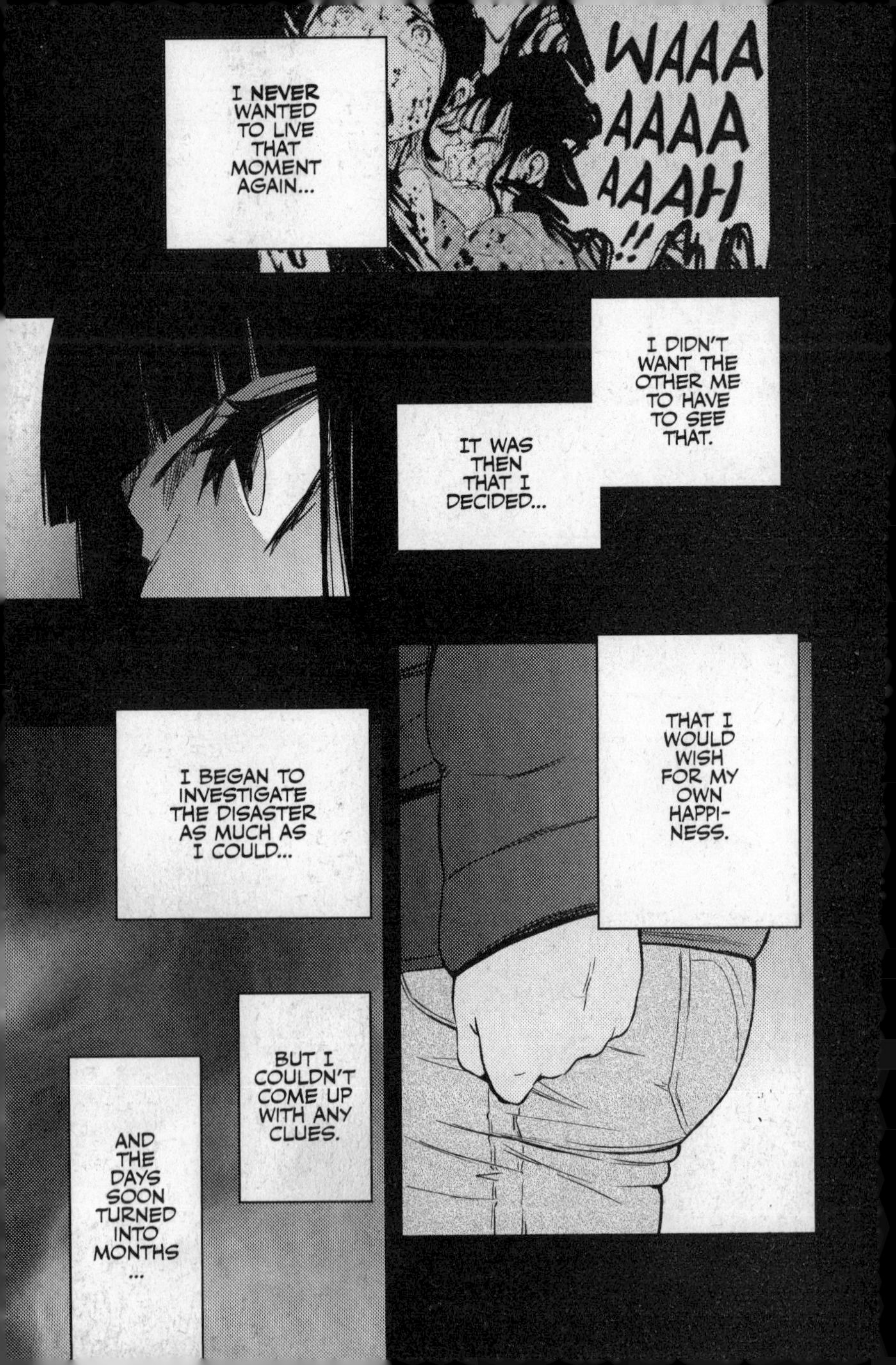

WAAA
AAAA
AAAH
!!

I NEVER
WANTED
TO LIVE
THAT
MOMENT
AGAIN...

I DIDN'T
WANT THE
OTHER ME
TO HAVE
TO SEE
THAT.

IT WAS
THEN
THAT I
DECIDED...

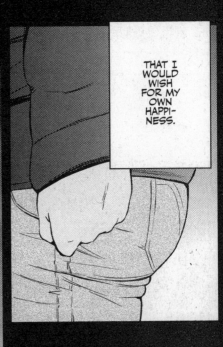

THAT I
WOULD
WISH
FOR MY
OWN
HAPPI-
NESS.

I BEGAN TO
INVESTIGATE
THE DISASTER
AS MUCH AS
I COULD...

BUT I
COULDN'T
COME UP
WITH ANY
CLUES.

AND
THE
DAYS
SOON
TURNED
INTO
MONTHS
...

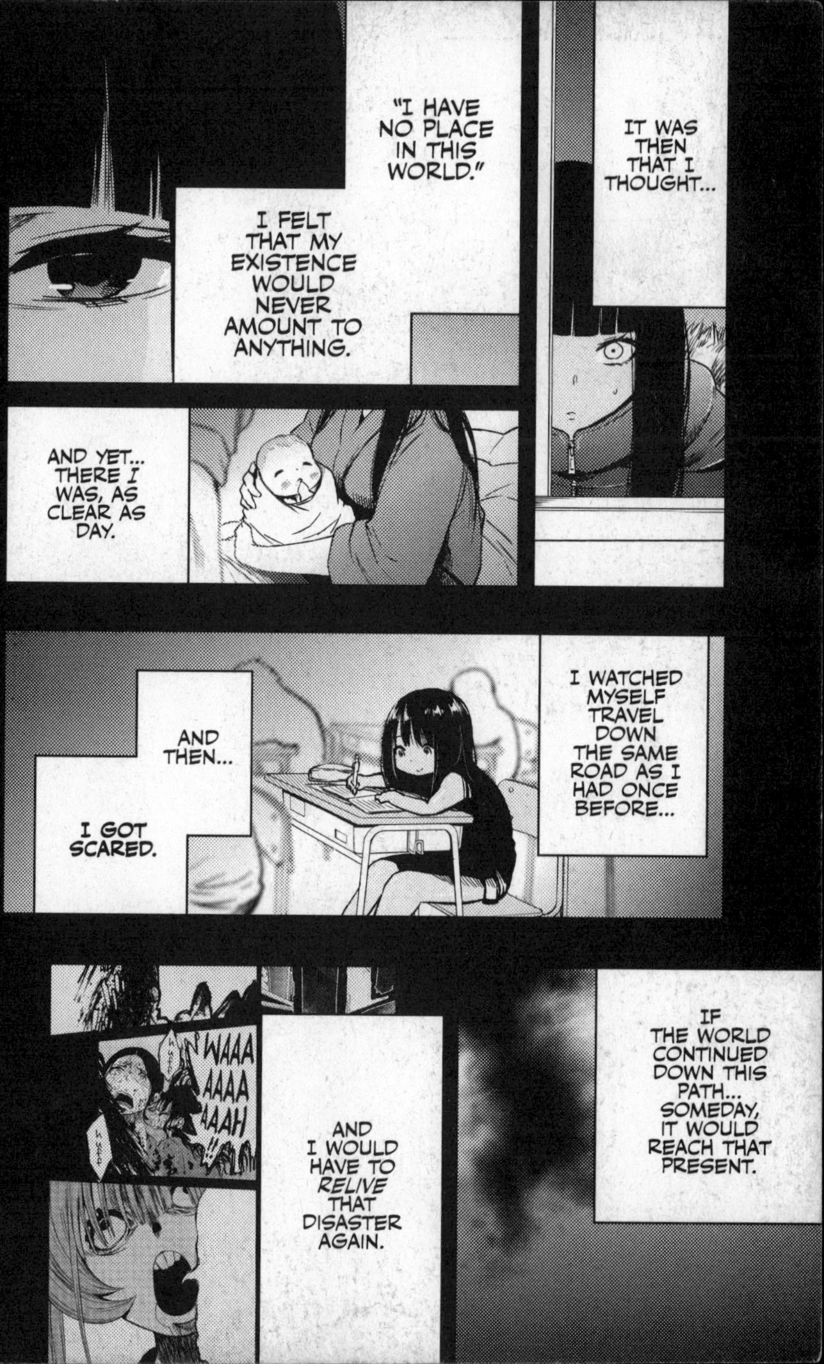
IT WAS THEN THAT I THOUGHT...
"I HAVE NO PLACE IN THIS WORLD."
I FELT THAT MY EXISTENCE WOULD NEVER AMOUNT TO ANYTHING.
AND YET... THERE *I* WAS, AS CLEAR AS DAY.
I WATCHED MYSELF TRAVEL DOWN THE SAME ROAD AS I HAD ONCE BEFORE...
AND THEN...
I GOT SCARED.
IF THE WORLD CONTINUED DOWN THIS PATH... SOMEDAY, IT WOULD REACH THAT PRESENT.
AND I WOULD HAVE TO *RELIVE* THAT DISASTER AGAIN.
WAAAAAAAAAAH!!

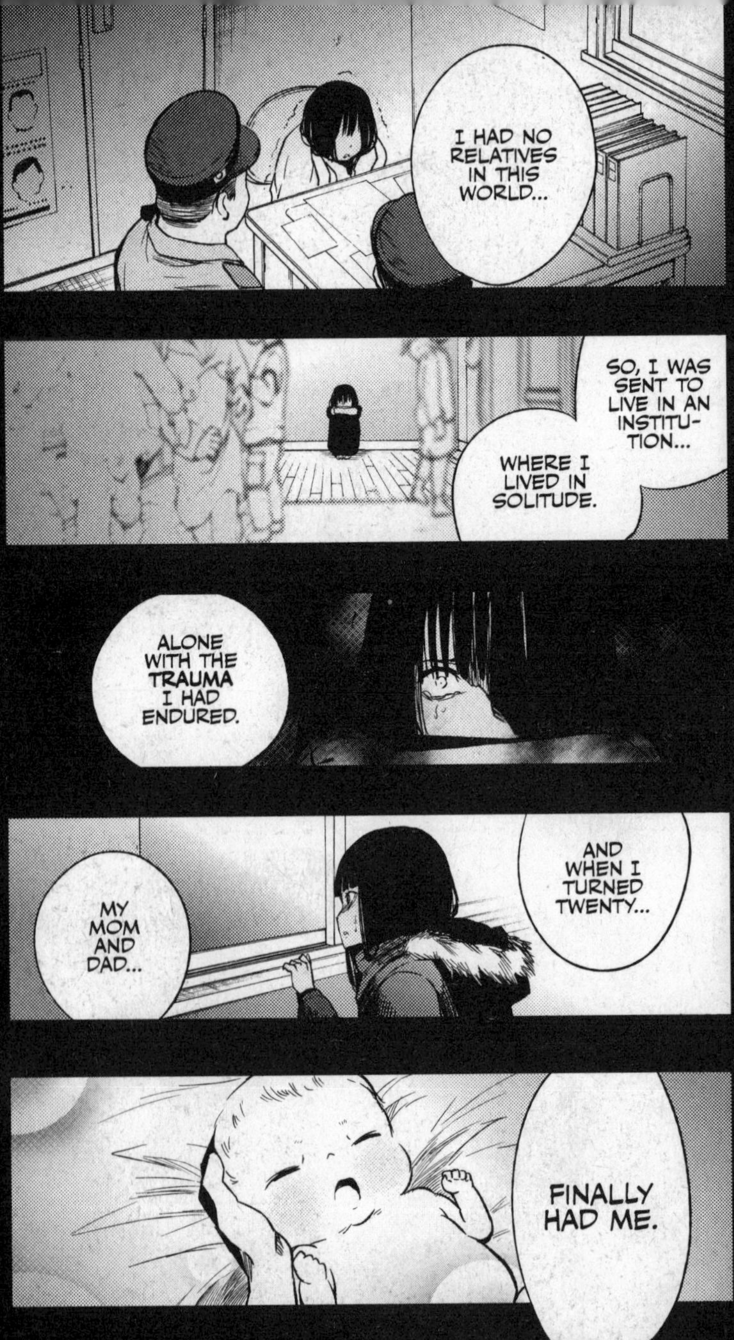
I HAD NO RELATIVES IN THIS WORLD...
SO, I WAS SENT TO LIVE IN AN INSTITUTION...
WHERE I LIVED IN SOLITUDE.
ALONE WITH THE TRAUMA I HAD ENDURED.
AND WHEN I TURNED TWENTY...
MY MOM AND DAD...
FINALLY HAD ME.

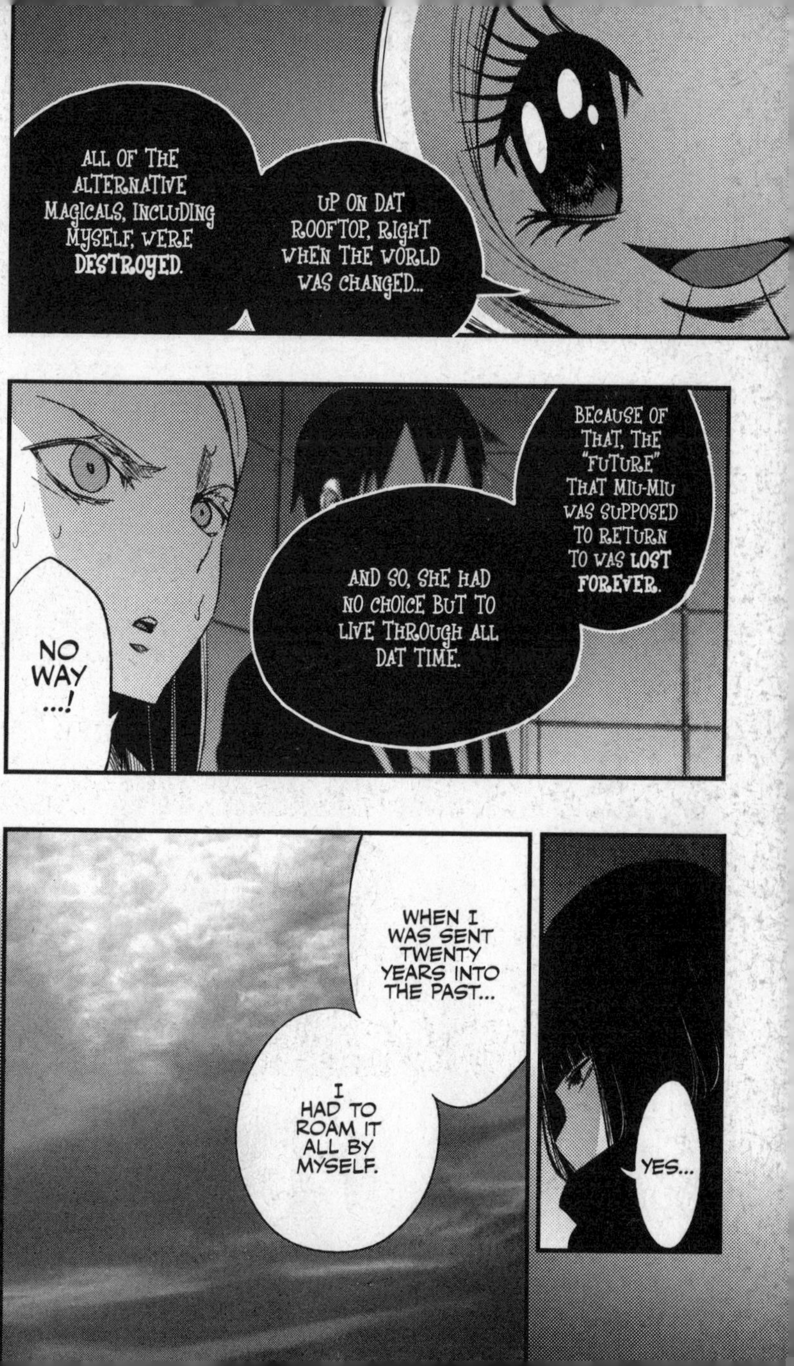
UP ON DAT ROOFTOP, RIGHT WHEN THE WORLD WAS CHANGED...
ALL OF THE ALTERNATIVE MAGICALS, INCLUDING MYSELF, WERE DESTROYED.
BECAUSE OF THAT, THE "FUTURE" THAT MIU-MIU WAS SUPPOSED TO RETURN TO WAS LOST FOREVER.
AND SO, SHE HAD NO CHOICE BUT TO LIVE THROUGH ALL DAT TIME.
NO WAY ...!
YES...
WHEN I WAS SENT TWENTY YEARS INTO THE PAST...
I HAD TO ROAM IT ALL BY MYSELF.

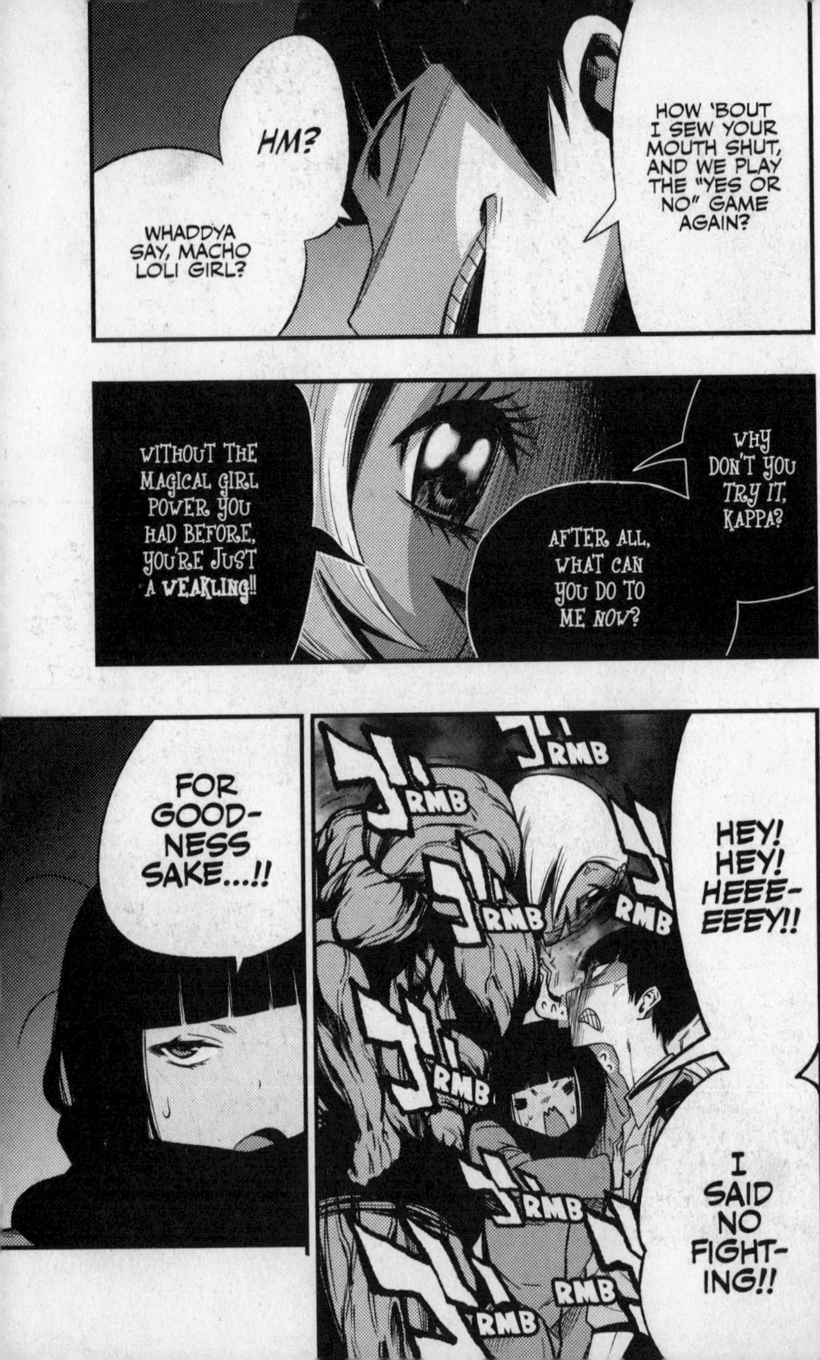
HOW 'BOUT I SEW YOUR MOUTH SHUT, AND WE PLAY THE "YES OR NO" GAME AGAIN?
HM?
WHADDYA SAY, MACHO LOLI GIRL?
WHY DON'T YOU TRY IT, KAPPA?
AFTER ALL, WHAT CAN YOU DO TO ME NOW?
WITHOUT THE MAGICAL GIRL POWER YOU HAD BEFORE, YOU'RE JUST A WEAKLING!!
RMB
HEY! HEY! HEEEE-EEEY!!
I SAID NO FIGHT-ING!!
FOR GOOD-NESS SAKE...!!

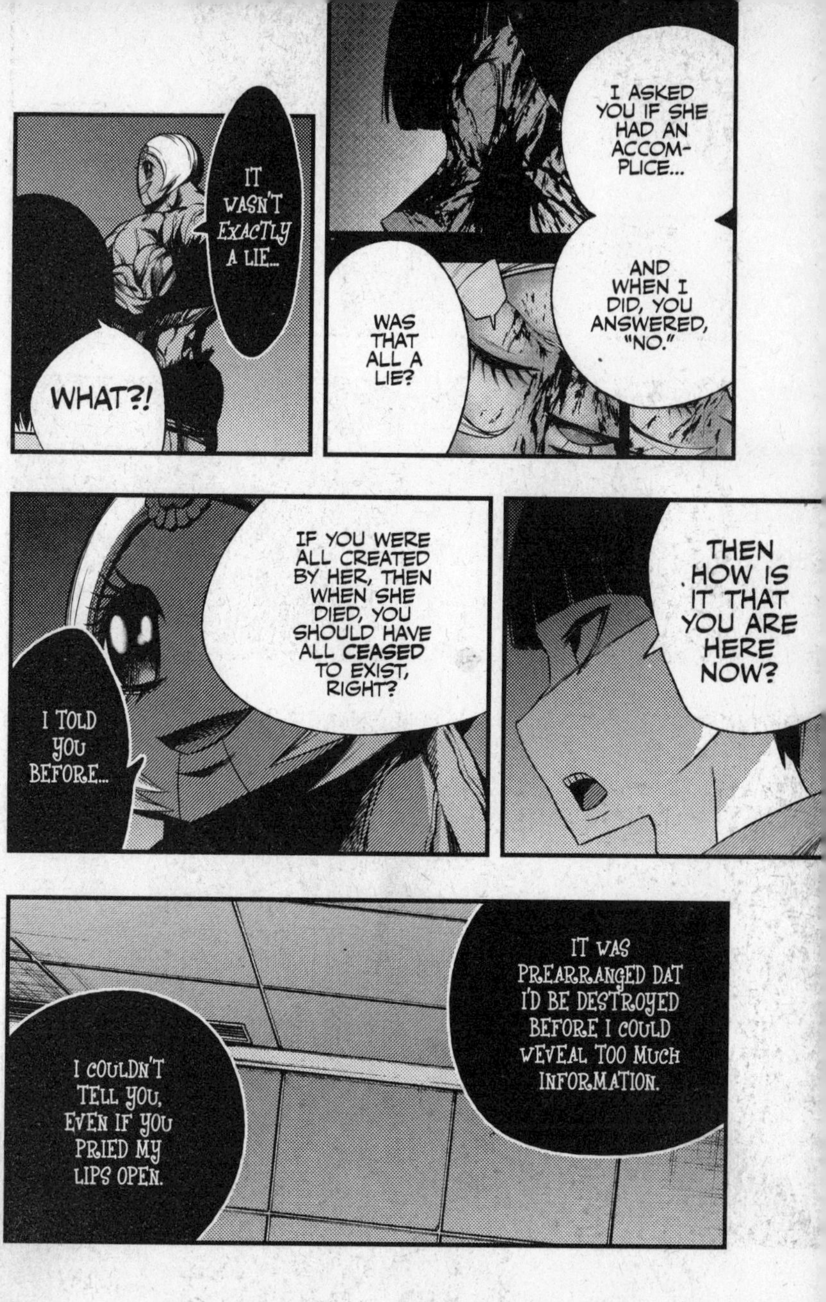
I ASKED YOU IF SHE HAD AN ACCOM-PLICE...
AND WHEN I DID, YOU ANSWERED, "NO."
WAS THAT ALL A LIE?
IT WASN'T EXACTLY A LIE...
WHAT?!
THEN HOW IS IT THAT YOU ARE HERE NOW?
IF YOU WERE ALL CREATED BY HER, THEN WHEN SHE DIED, YOU SHOULD HAVE ALL CEASED TO EXIST, RIGHT?
I TOLD YOU BEFORE...
IT WAS PREARRANGED DAT I'D BE DESTROYED BEFORE I COULD WEVEAL TOO MUCH INFORMATION.
I COULDN'T TELL YOU, EVEN IF YOU PRIED MY LIPS OPEN.

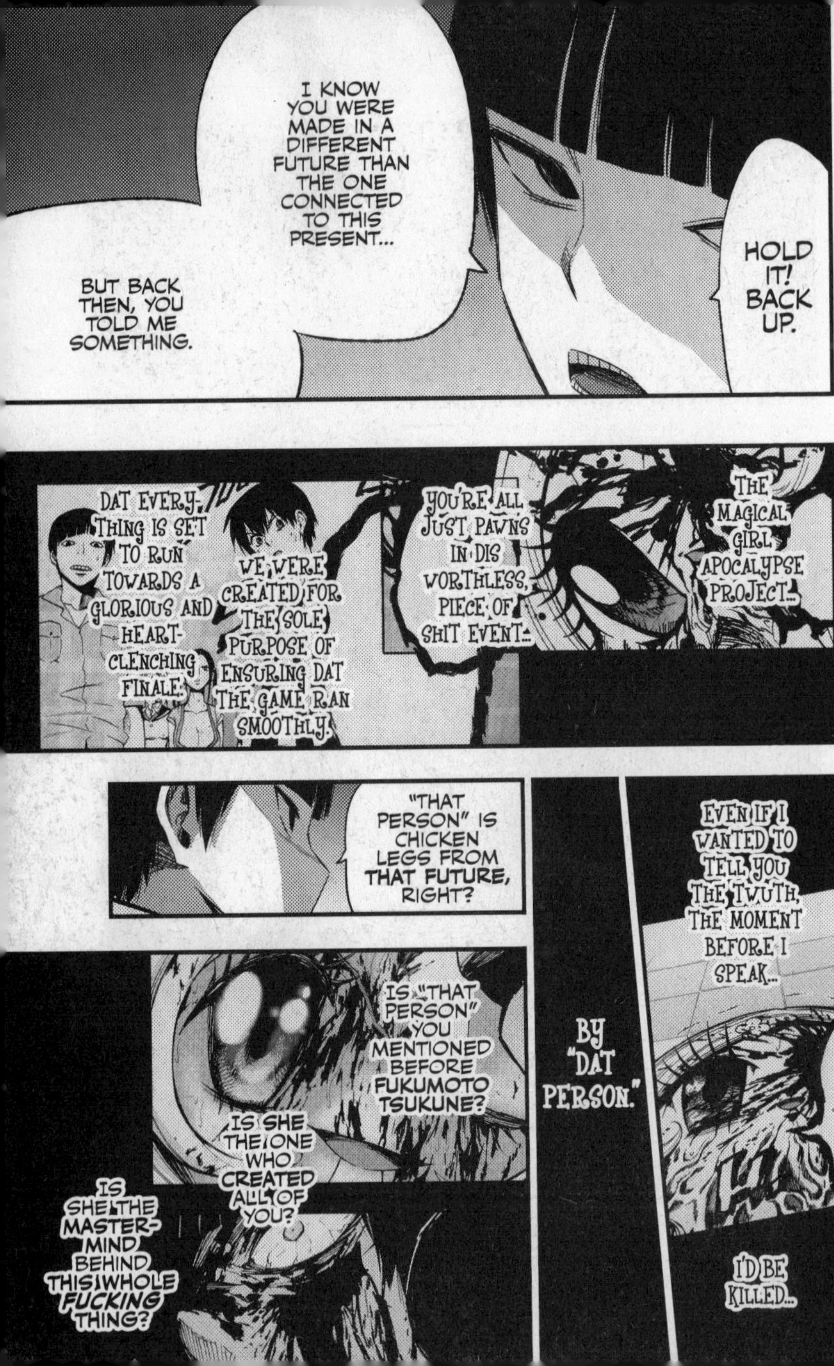
HOLD IT! BACK UP.
I KNOW YOU WERE MADE IN A DIFFERENT FUTURE THAN THE ONE CONNECTED TO THIS PRESENT...
BUT BACK THEN, YOU TOLD ME SOMETHING.
THE MAGICAL GIRL APOCALYPSE PROJECT...
YOU'RE ALL JUST PAWNS IN DIS WORTHLESS, PIECE OF SHIT EVENT...
WE WERE CREATED FOR THE SOLE PURPOSE OF ENSURING DAT THE GAME RAN SMOOTHLY.
DAT EVERYTHING IS SET TO RUN TOWARDS A GLORIOUS AND HEART-CLENCHING FINALE.
EVEN IF I WANTED TO TELL YOU THE TWUTH, THE MOMENT BEFORE I SPEAK...
I'D BE KILLED...
BY "DAT PERSON."
"THAT PERSON" IS CHICKEN LEGS FROM THAT FUTURE, RIGHT?
IS "THAT PERSON" YOU MENTIONED BEFORE FUKUMOTO TSUKUNE?
IS SHE THE ONE WHO CREATED ALL OF YOU?
IS SHE THE MASTERMIND BEHIND THIS WHOLE *FUCKING* THING?

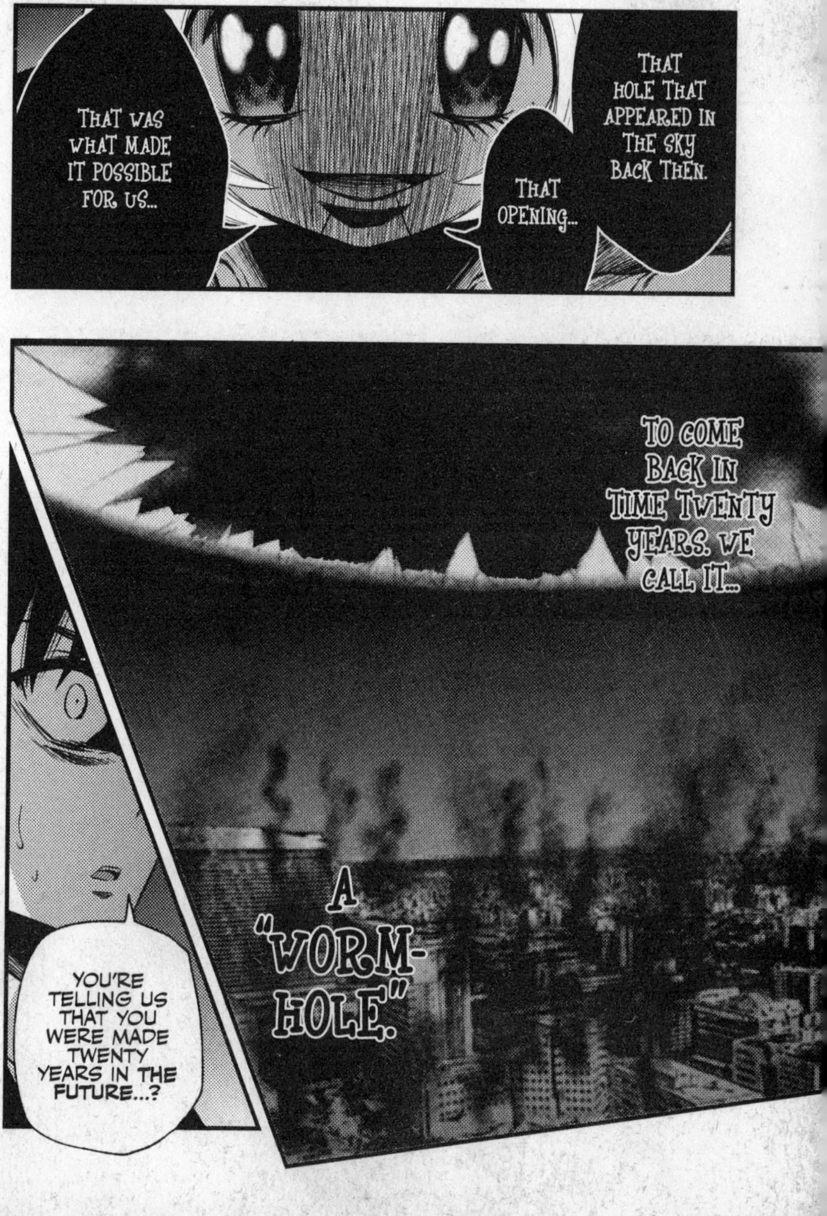
THAT HOLE THAT APPEARED IN THE SKY BACK THEN.
THAT OPENING...
THAT WAS WHAT MADE IT POSSIBLE FOR US...
TO COME BACK IN TIME TWENTY YEARS. WE CALL IT...
A "WORM-HOLE."
YOU'RE TELLING US THAT YOU WERE MADE TWENTY YEARS IN THE FUTURE...?

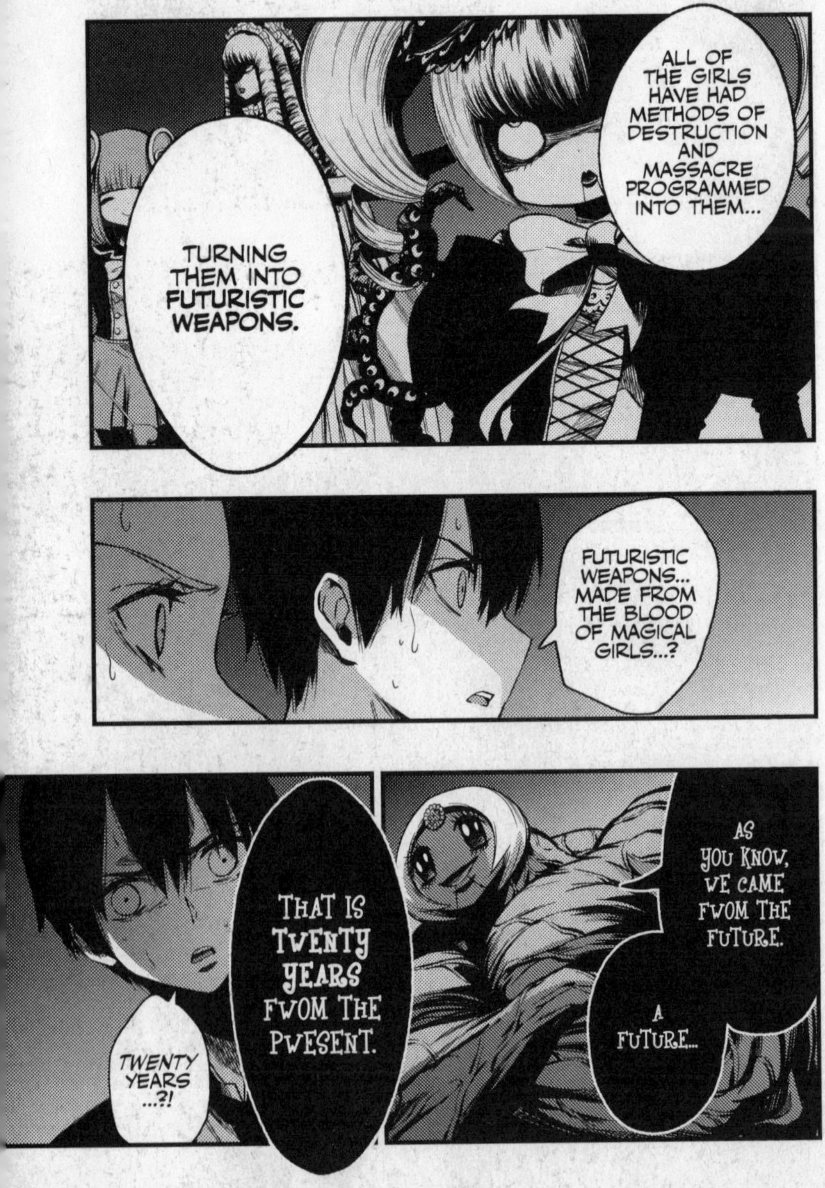
ALL OF THE GIRLS HAVE HAD METHODS OF DESTRUCTION AND MASSACRE PROGRAMMED INTO THEM...
TURNING THEM INTO FUTURISTIC WEAPONS.
FUTURISTIC WEAPONS... MADE FROM THE BLOOD OF MAGICAL GIRLS...?
AS YOU KNOW, WE CAME FWOM THE FUTURE.
A FUTURE...
THAT IS TWENTY YEARS FWOM THE PWESENT.
TWENTY YEARS ...?!

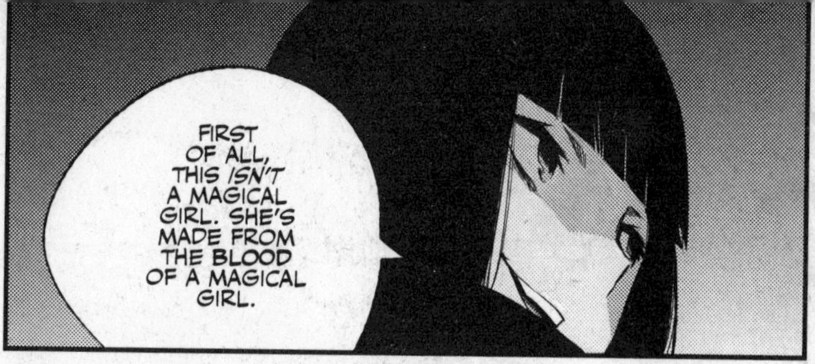
FIRST OF ALL, THIS *ISN'T* A MAGICAL GIRL. SHE'S MADE FROM THE BLOOD OF A MAGICAL GIRL.

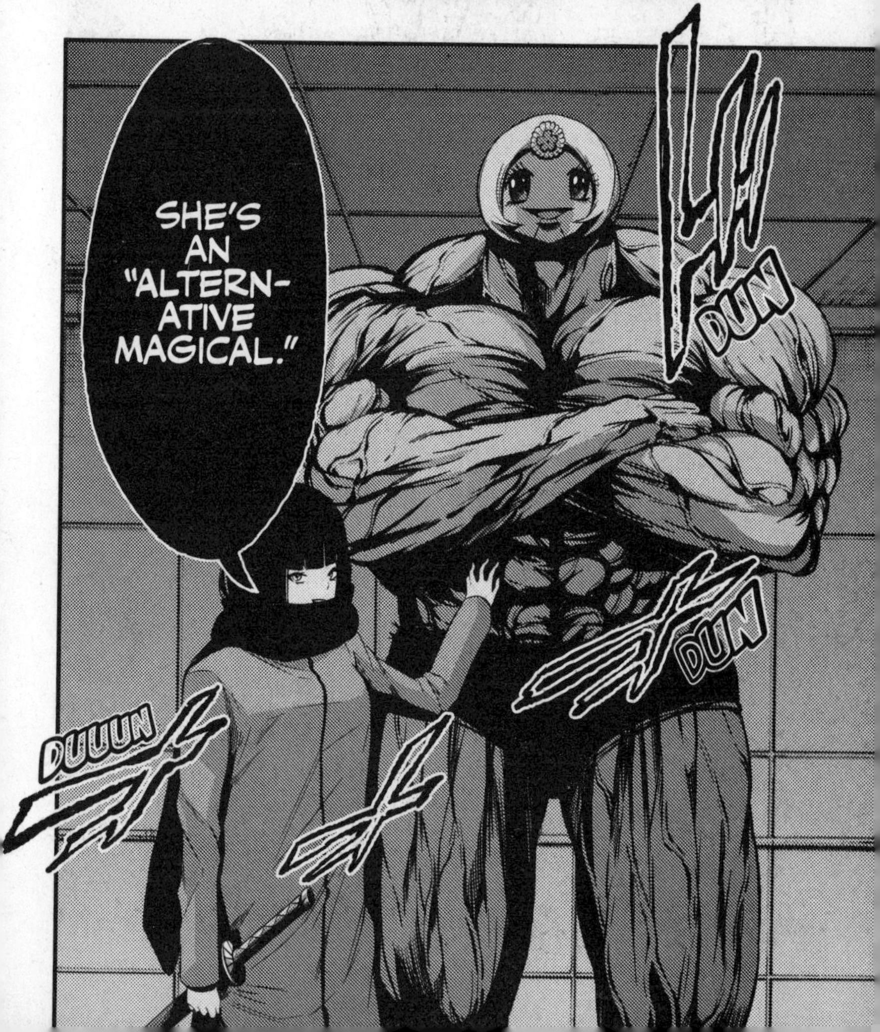
SHE'S AN "ALTERN-ATIVE MAGICAL."
DUN
DUN
DUUUN

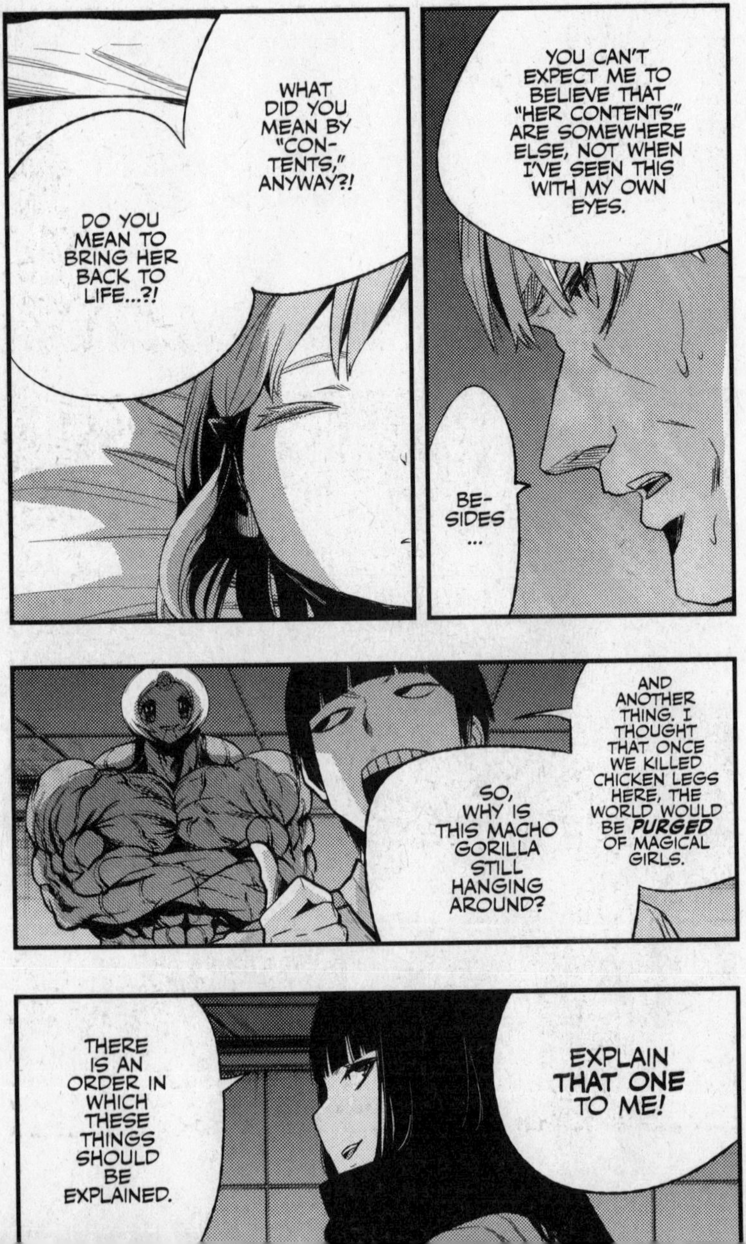
YOU CAN'T EXPECT ME TO BELIEVE THAT "HER CONTENTS" ARE SOMEWHERE ELSE, NOT WHEN I'VE SEEN THIS WITH MY OWN EYES.
BE-SIDES ...
WHAT DID YOU MEAN BY "CON-TENTS," ANYWAY?!
DO YOU MEAN TO BRING HER BACK TO LIFE...?!
AND ANOTHER THING. I THOUGHT THAT ONCE WE KILLED CHICKEN LEGS HERE, THE WORLD WOULD BE *PURGED* OF MAGICAL GIRLS.
SO, WHY IS THIS MACHO GORILLA STILL HANGING AROUND?
EXPLAIN THAT ONE TO ME!
THERE IS AN ORDER IN WHICH THESE THINGS SHOULD BE EXPLAINED.

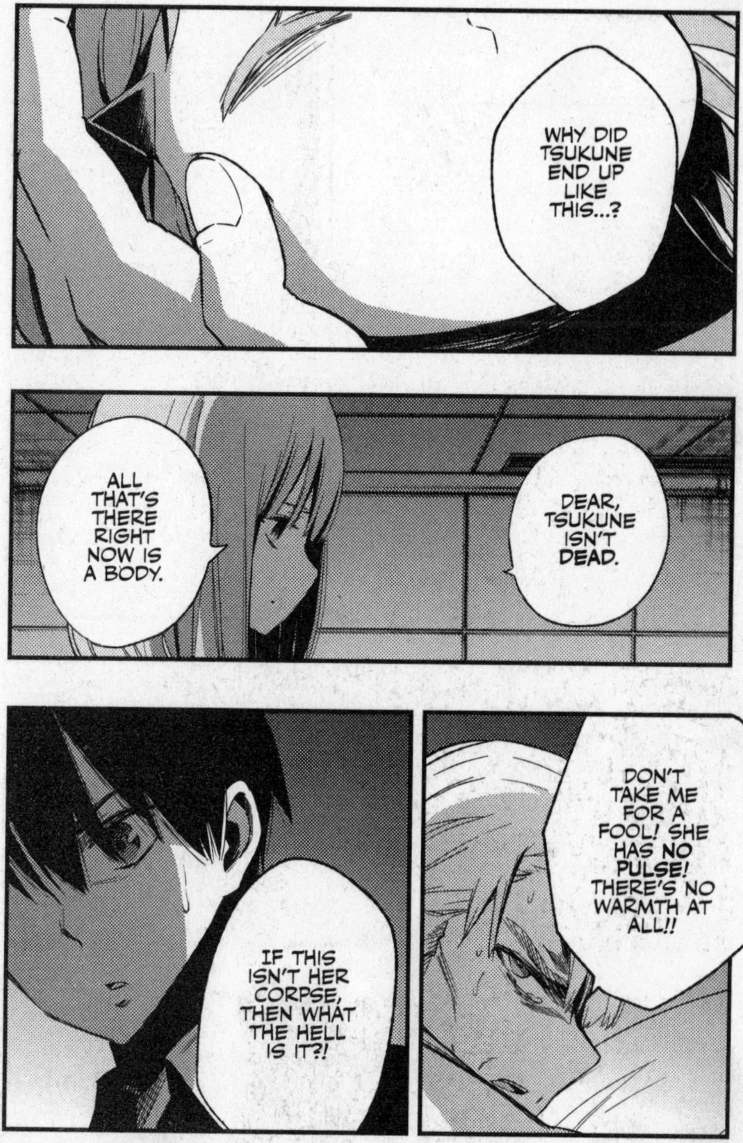
WHY DID TSUKUNE END UP LIKE THIS...?
DEAR, TSUKUNE ISN'T DEAD.
ALL THAT'S THERE RIGHT NOW IS A BODY.
DON'T TAKE ME FOR A FOOL! SHE HAS NO PULSE! THERE'S NO WARMTH AT ALL!!
IF THIS ISN'T HER CORPSE, THEN WHAT THE HELL IS IT?!

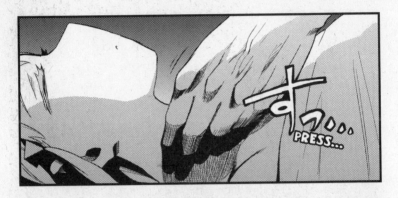

PRESS...

AND HER BODY IS COLD...!

NO PULSE ...

DAM- MIT...

THIS CAN'T ...!!

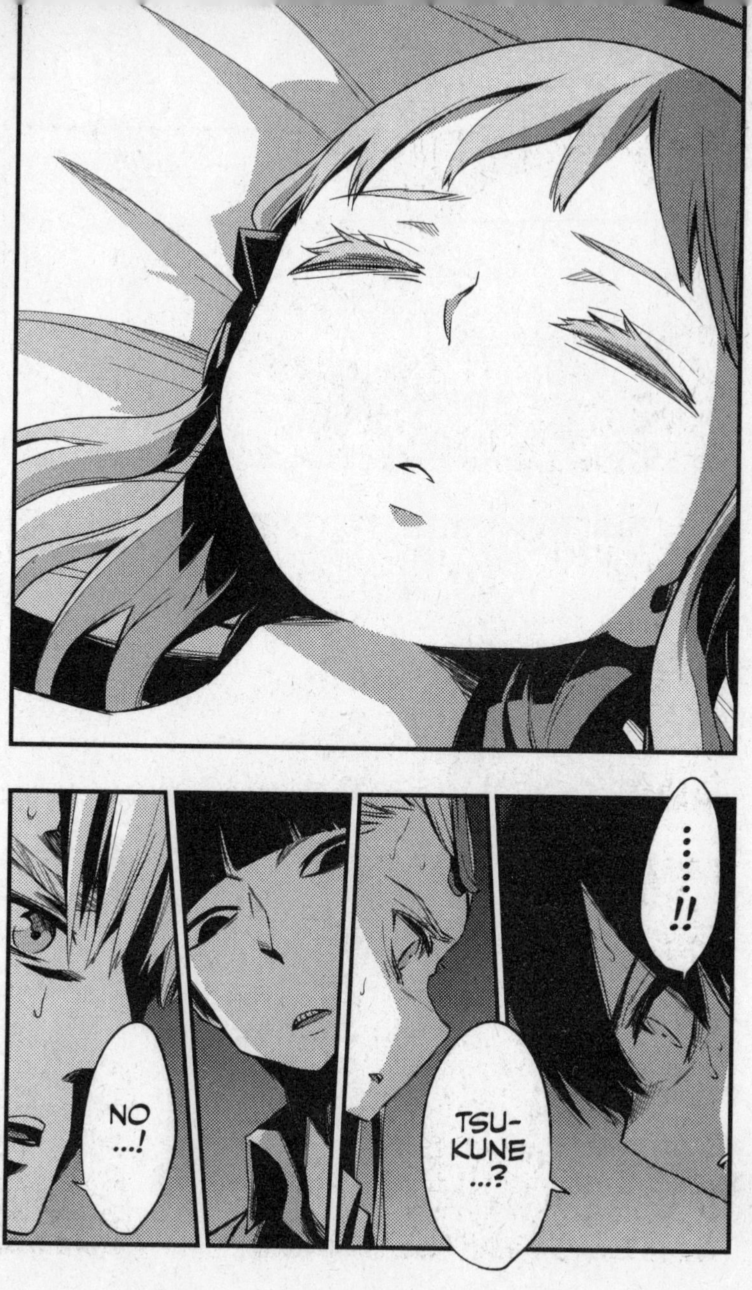
......!!
TSU-KUNE ...?
NO ...!

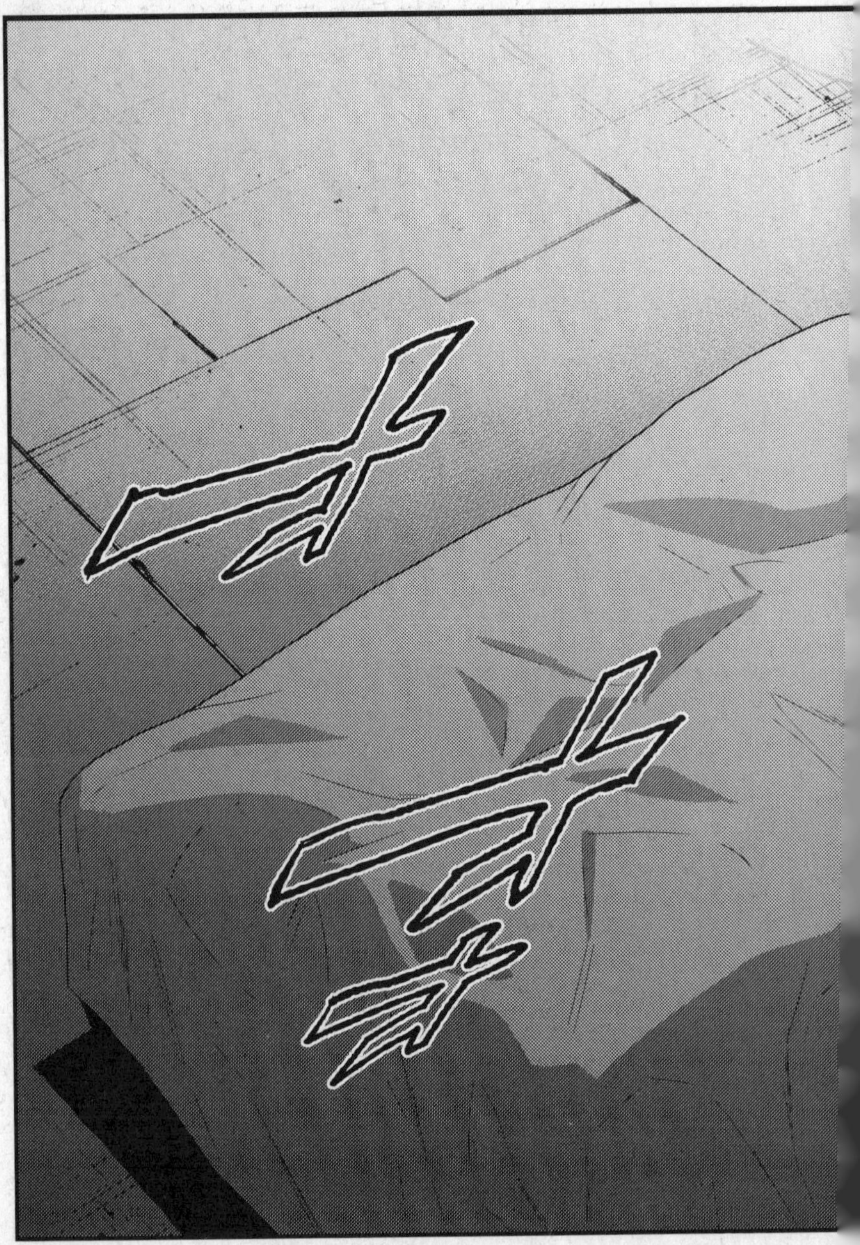

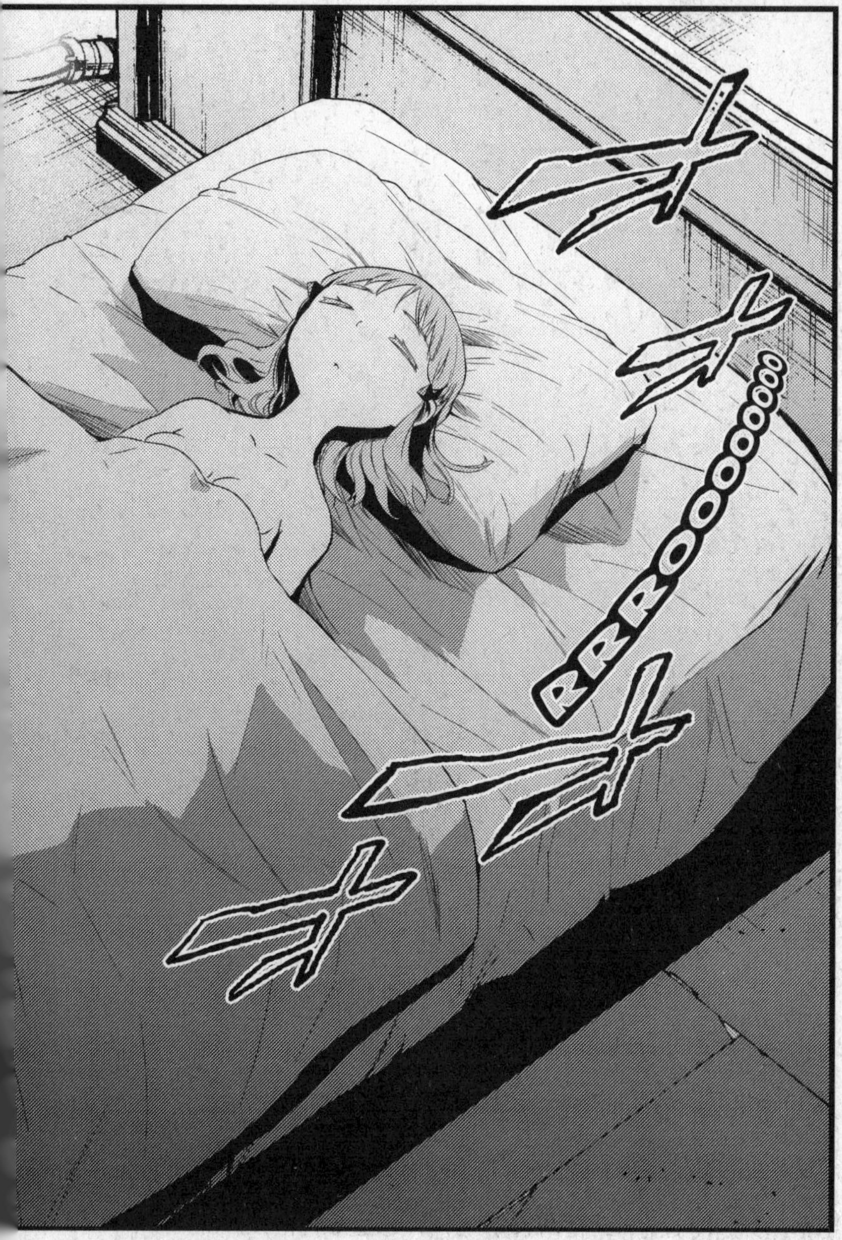
RRROOOOOOOO

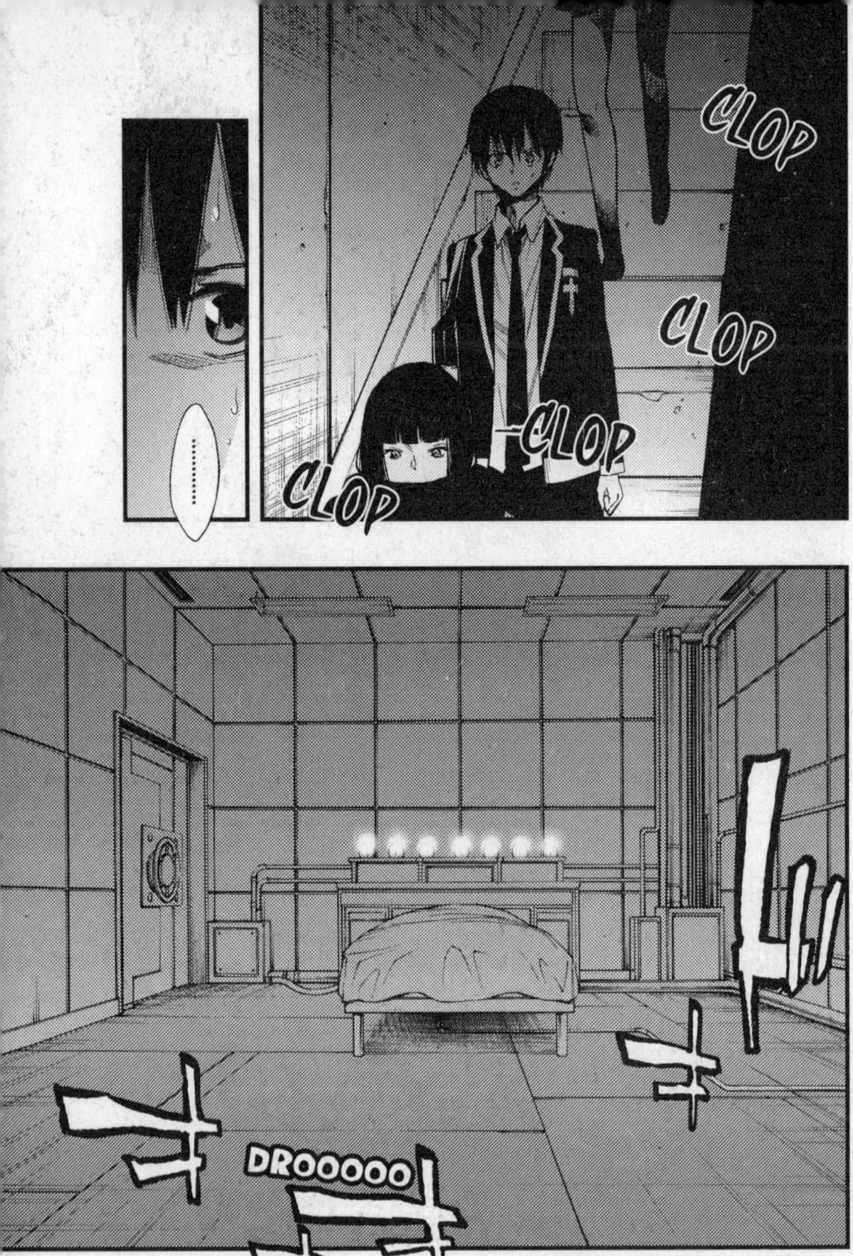
CLOP
CLOP
CLOP
CLOP
......
DROOOOO

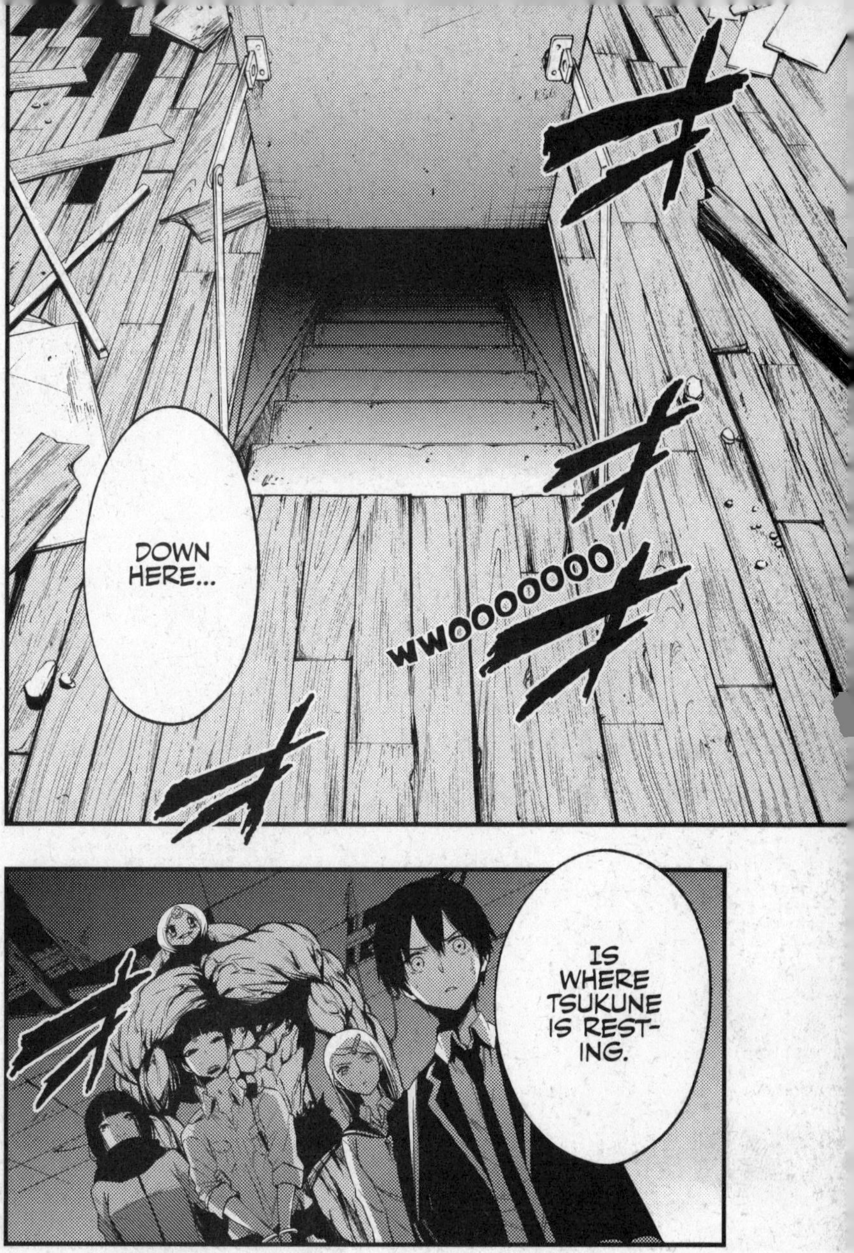
WWOOOOOOO
DOWN HERE...
IS WHERE TSUKUNE IS REST-ING.

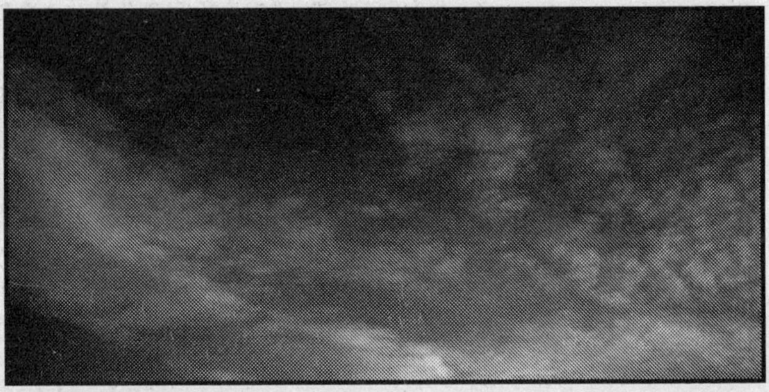

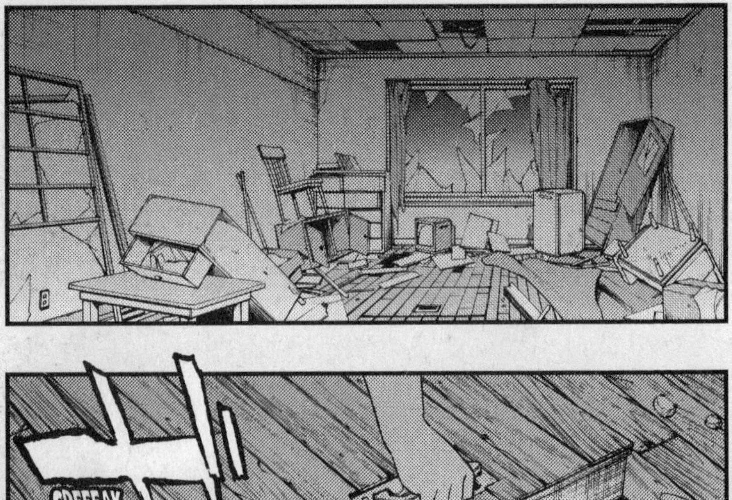

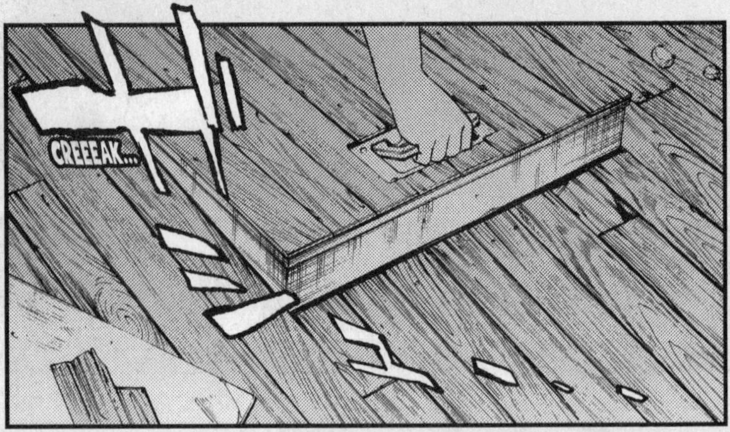
CREEEAK...

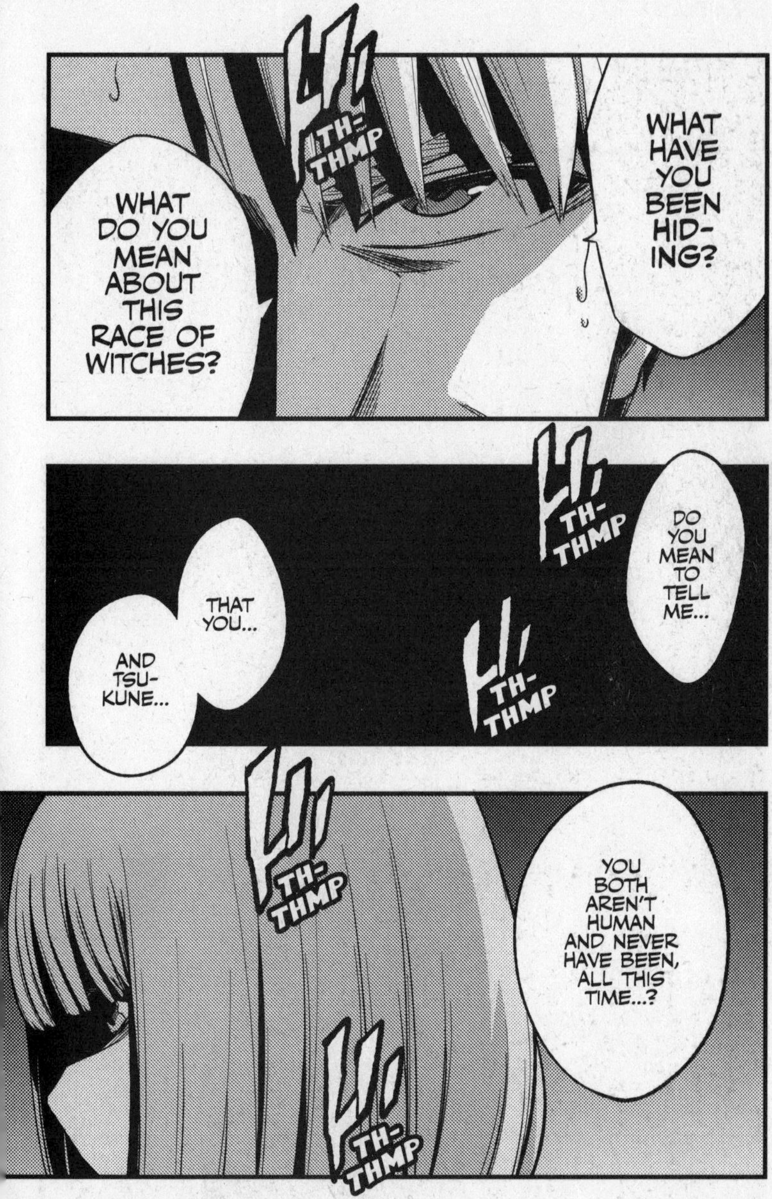
TH-THMP
WHAT HAVE YOU BEEN HID-ING?
WHAT DO YOU MEAN ABOUT THIS RACE OF WITCHES?
TH-THMP
DO YOU MEAN TO TELL ME...
TH-THMP
THAT YOU...
AND TSU-KUNE...
TH-THMP
YOU BOTH AREN'T HUMAN AND NEVER HAVE BEEN, ALL THIS TIME...?
TH-THMP

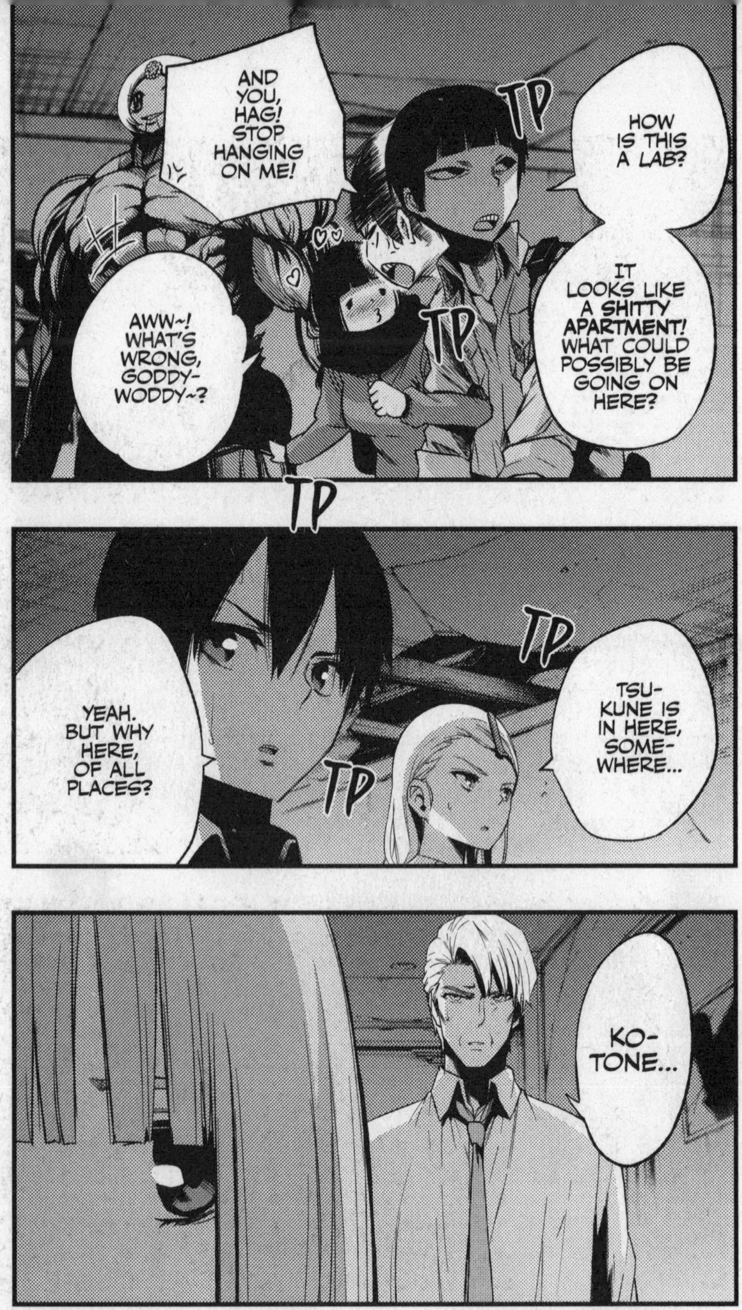
HOW IS THIS A LAB?
TP
AND YOU, HAG! STOP HANGING ON ME!
IT LOOKS LIKE A SHITTY APARTMENT! WHAT COULD POSSIBLY BE GOING ON HERE?
TP
AWW~! WHAT'S WRONG, GODDY-WODDY~?
TP
TP
TSU-KUNE IS IN HERE, SOME-WHERE...
TP
YEAH. BUT WHY HERE, OF ALL PLACES?
KO-TONE...

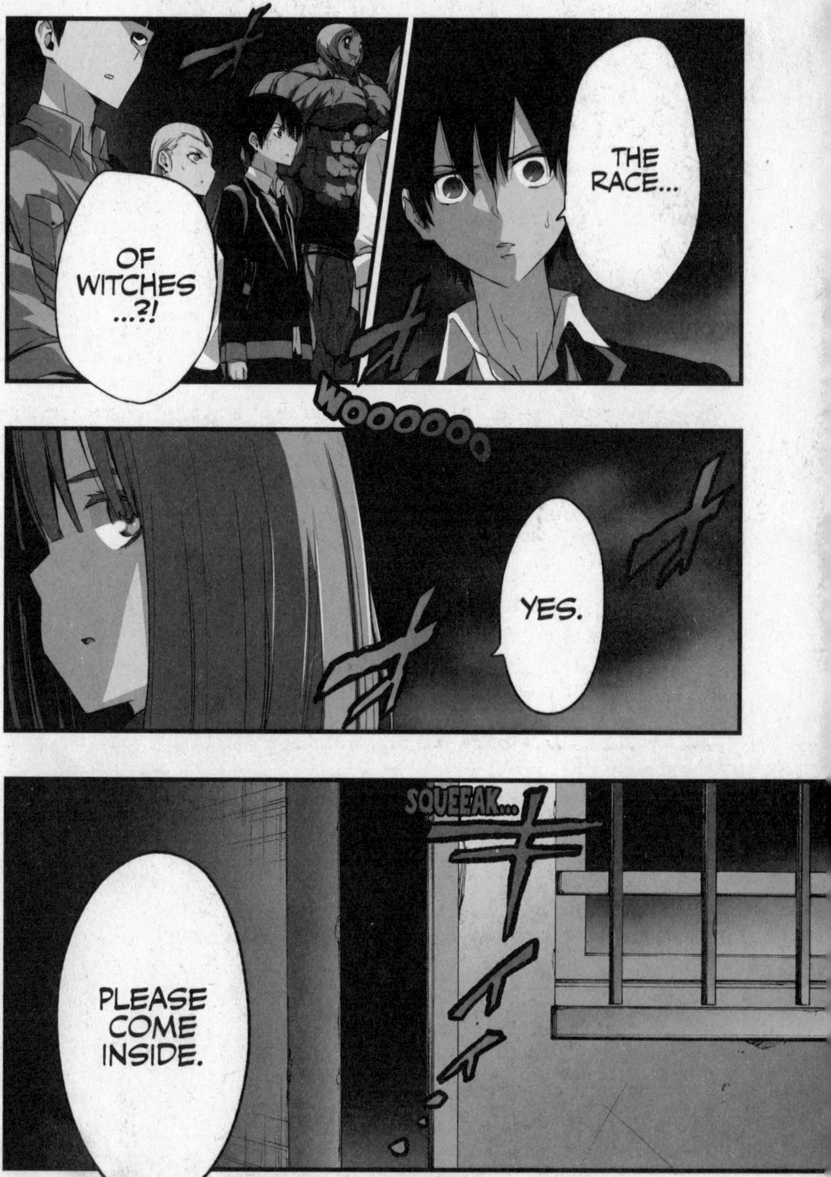
THE RACE...
OF WITCHES ...?!
WOOOOOO
YES.
SQUEEAK...
PLEASE COME INSIDE.

024.The Ninth

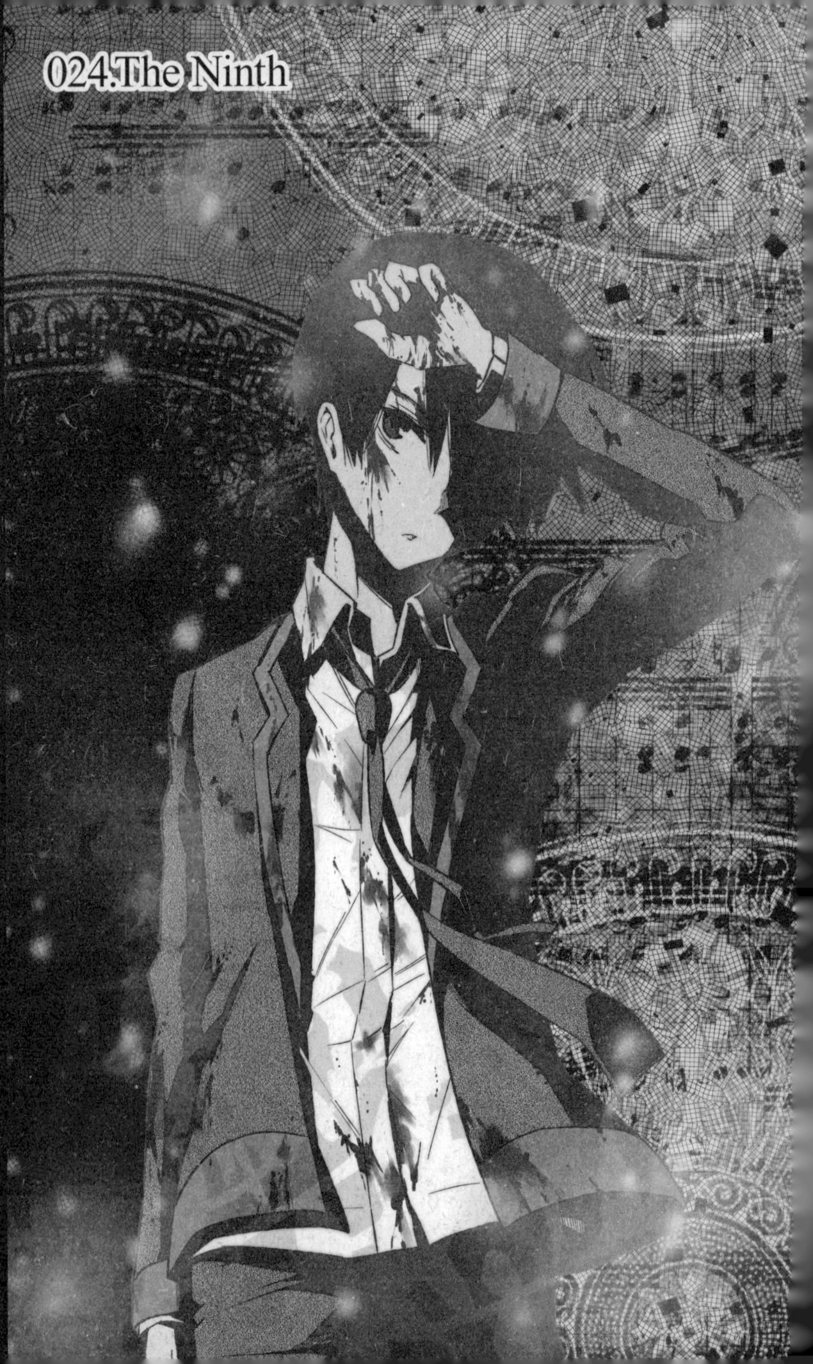

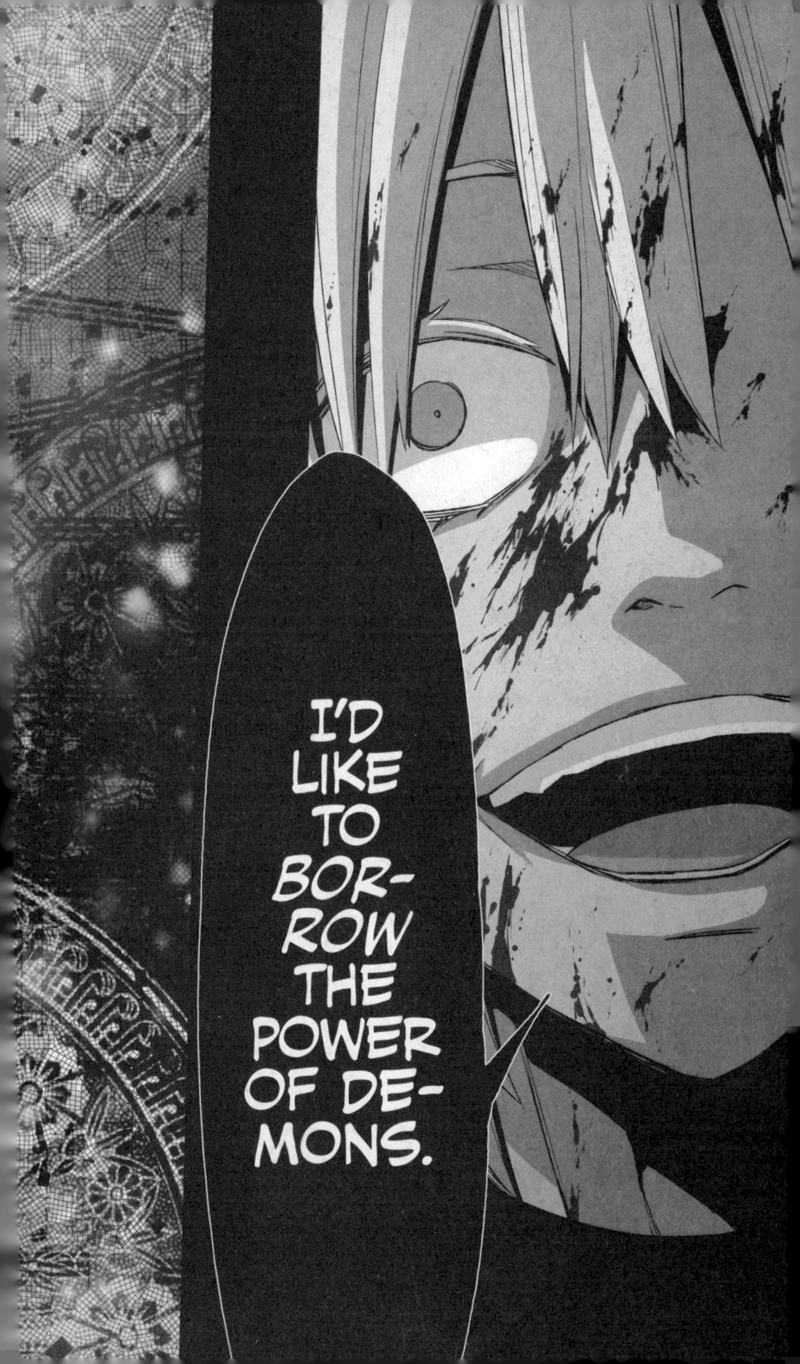
I'D LIKE TO BOR-ROW THE POWER OF DE-MONS.

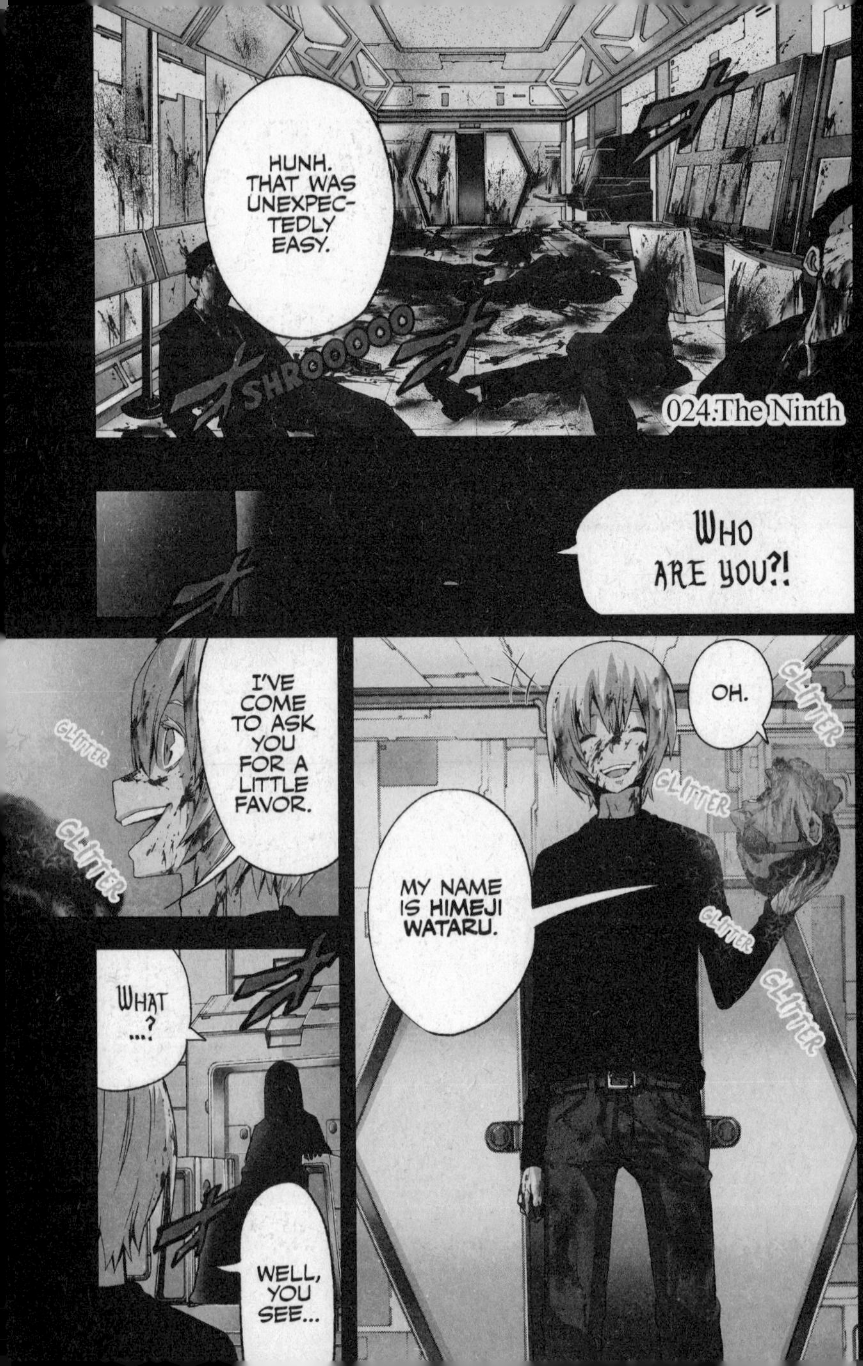
HUNH. THAT WAS UNEXPECTEDLY EASY.
SHROOOOO
024:The Ninth
WHO ARE YOU?!
OH.
GLITTER
GLITTER
MY NAME IS HIMEJI WATARU.
GLITTER
GLITTER
I'VE COME TO ASK YOU FOR A LITTLE FAVOR.
GLITTER
GLITTER
WHAT ...?
WELL, YOU SEE...

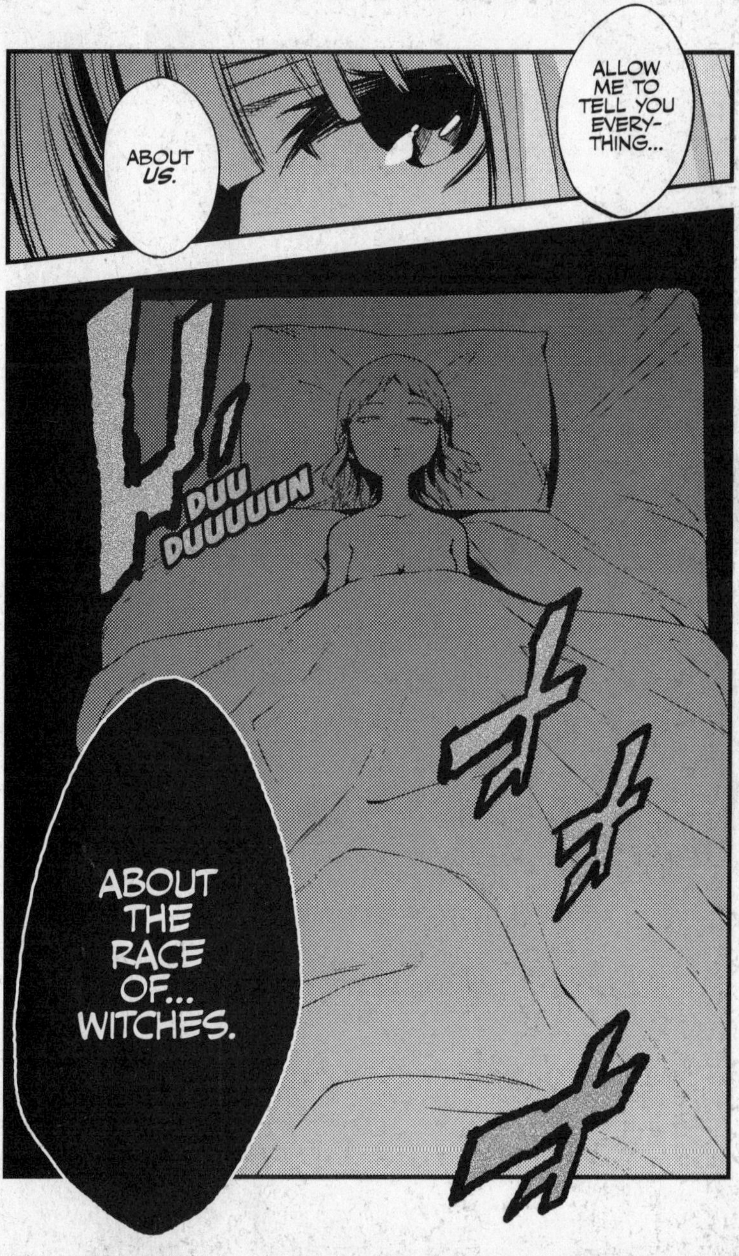
ALLOW ME TO TELL YOU EVERYTHING...
ABOUT US.
DUU DUUUUUN
ABOUT THE RACE OF... WITCHES.

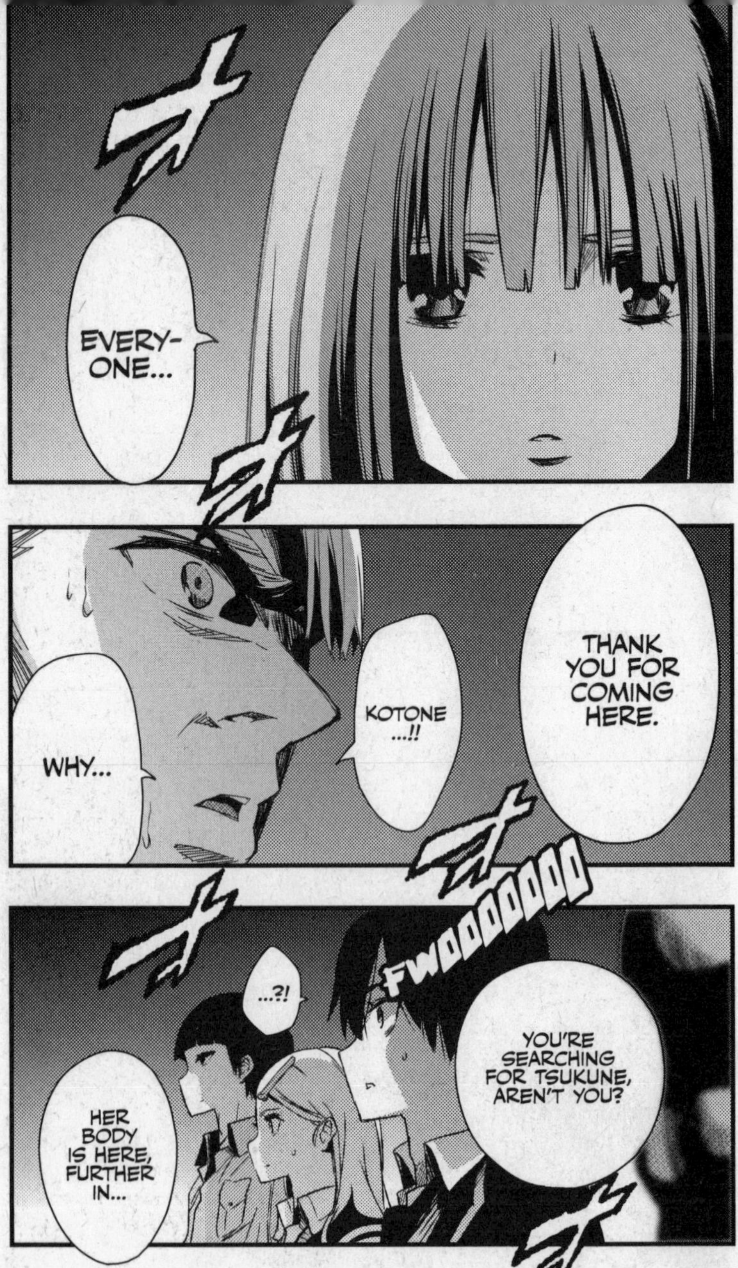
EVERY-ONE...
THANK YOU FOR COMING HERE.
KOTONE ...!!
WHY...
FWOOOOOOOO
YOU'RE SEARCHING FOR TSUKUNE, AREN'T YOU?
...?!
HER BODY IS HERE, FURTHER IN...

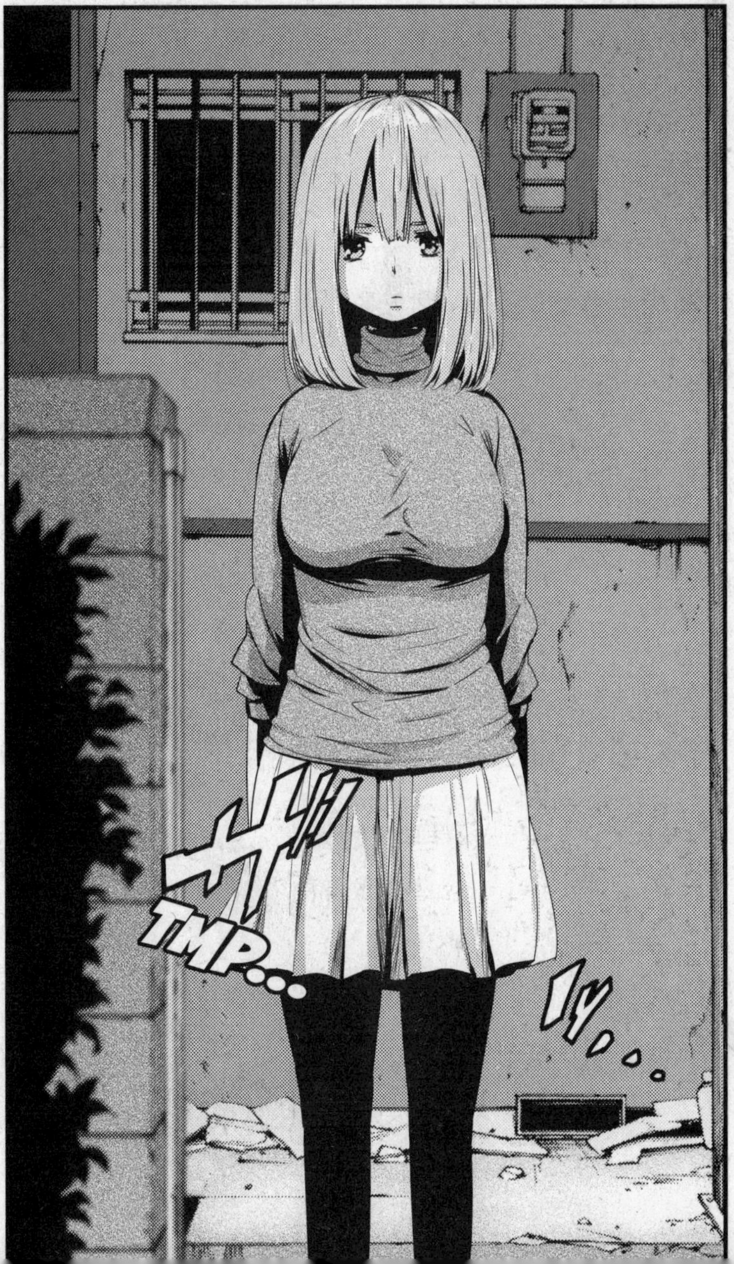
TMP...

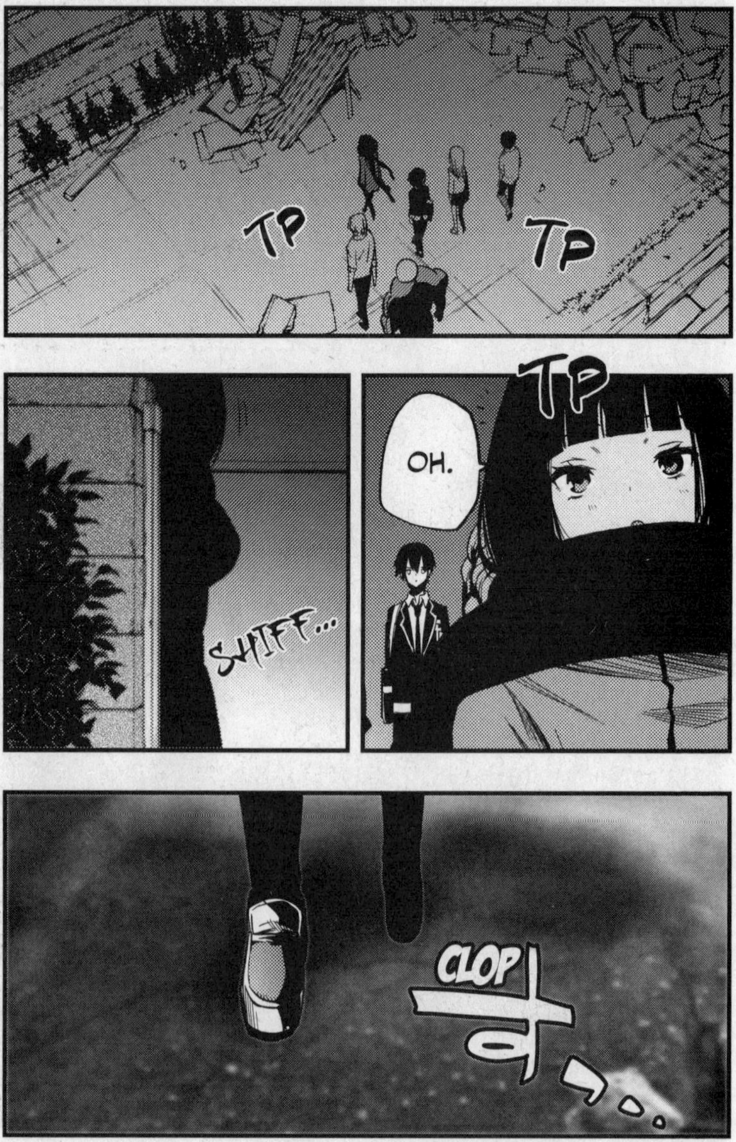
TP
TP
TP
OH.
SHIFF...
CLOP
すっ..

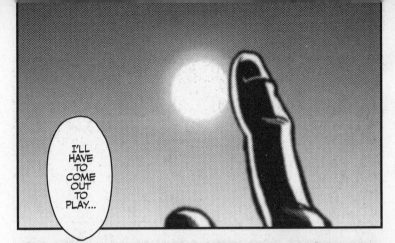

I'LL HAVE TO COME OUT TO PLAY...

SLIDE

NAH. JUST KID-DING.

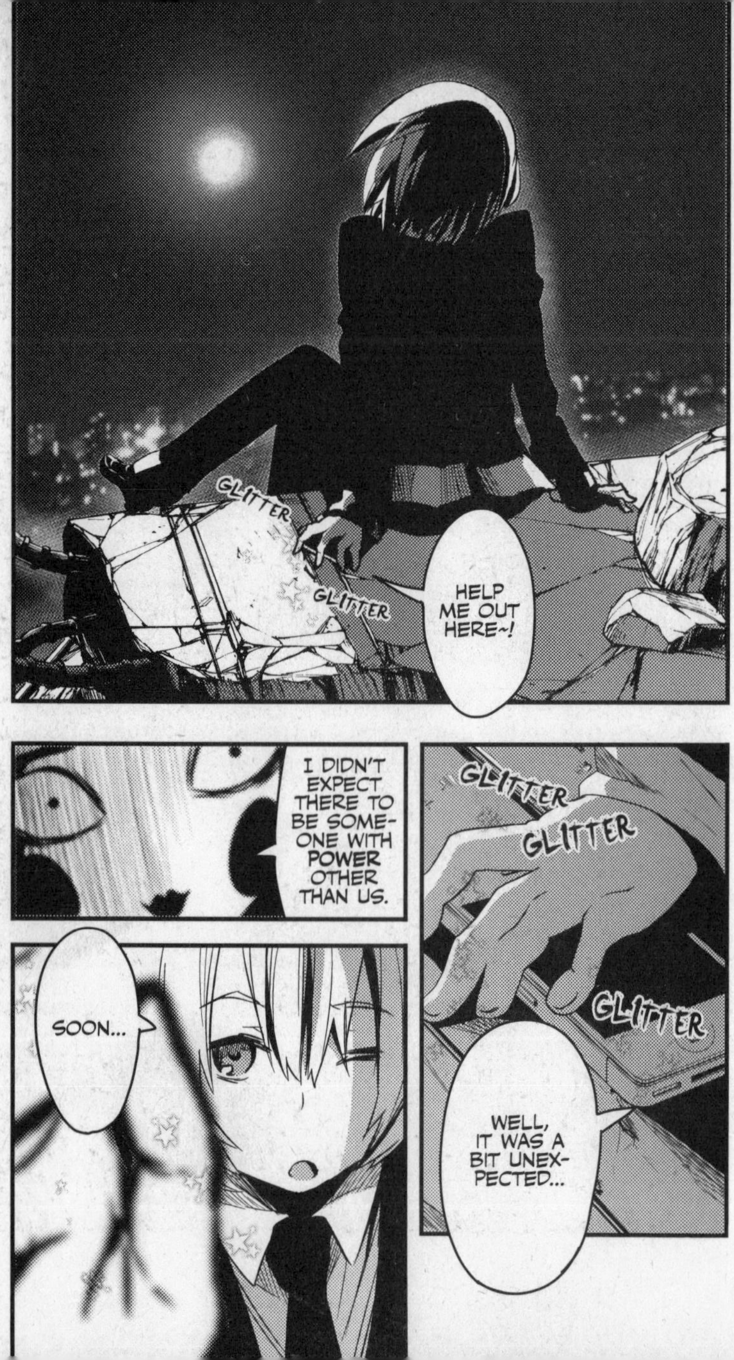
GLITTER
GLITTER
HELP ME OUT HERE~!
GLITTER
GLITTER
GLITTER
WELL, IT WAS A BIT UNEXPECTED...
I DIDN'T EXPECT THERE TO BE SOMEONE WITH POWER OTHER THAN US.
SOON...

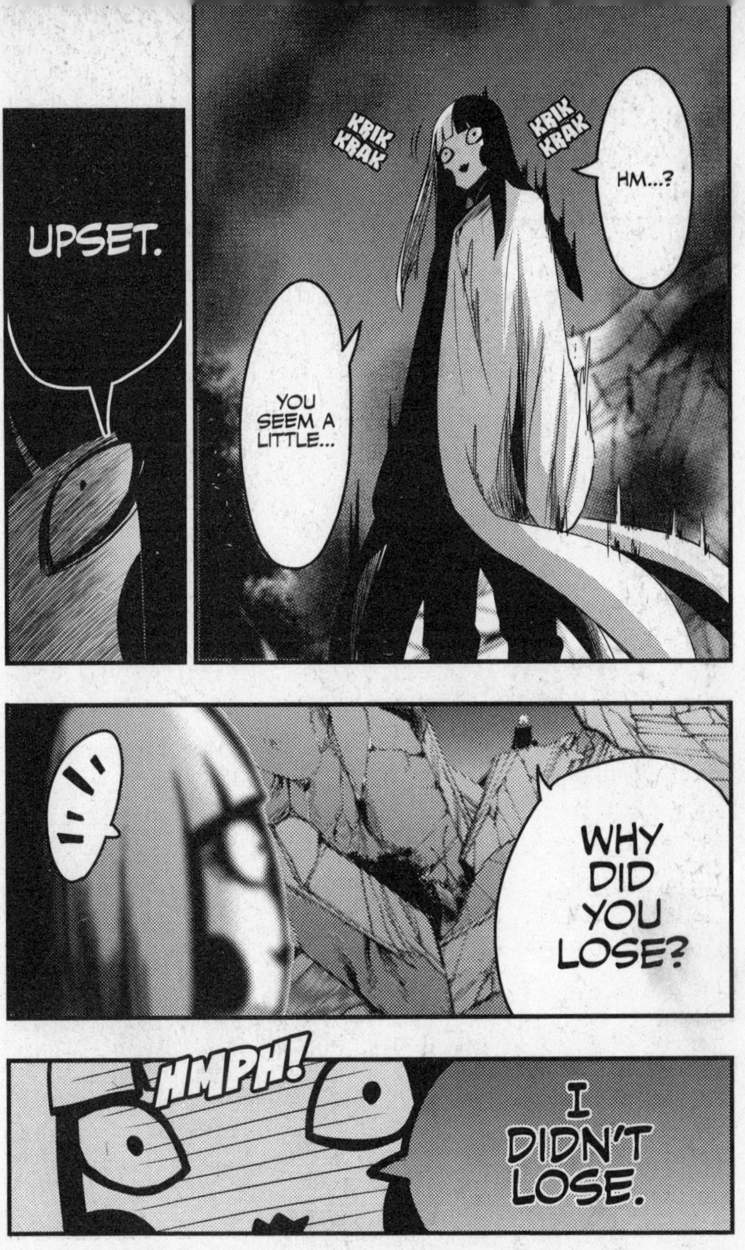
HM...?
KRIK KRAK
KRIK KRAK
YOU SEEM A LITTLE...
UPSET.
WHY DID YOU LOSE?
I DIDN'T LOSE.
HMPH!

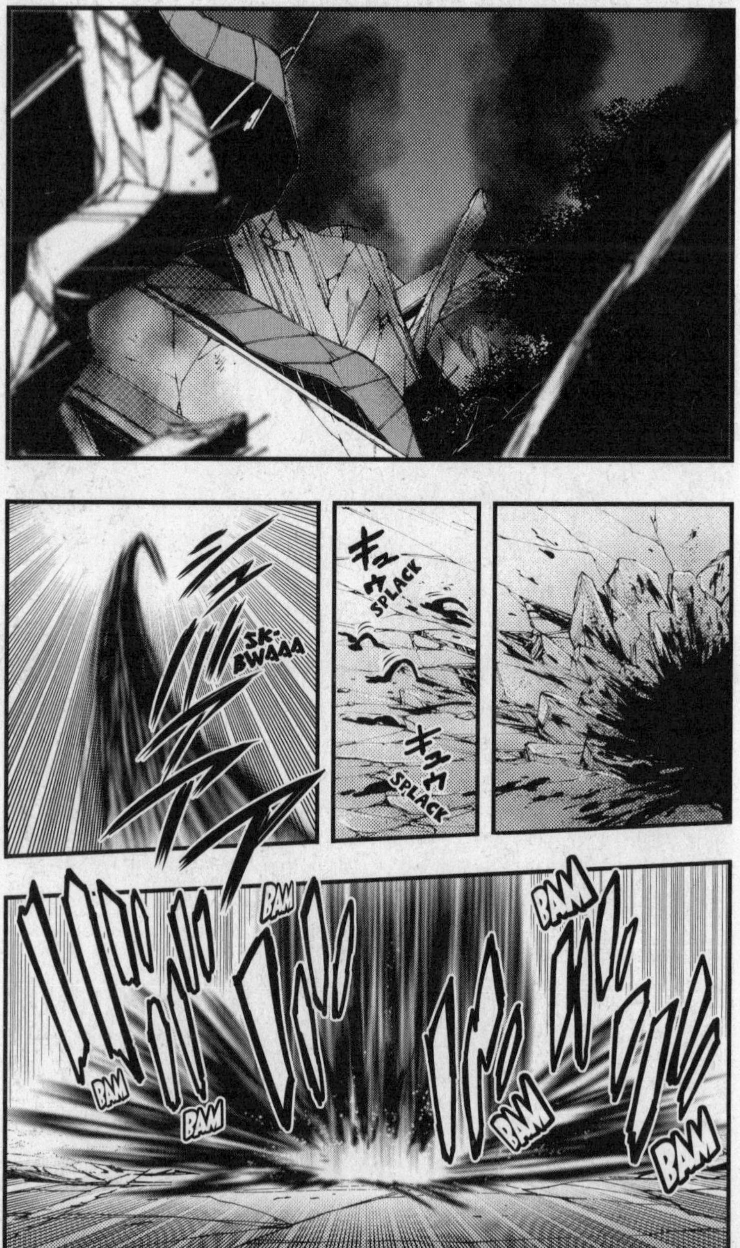
SPLACK
SPLACK
SK-BWAAA
BAM
BAM
BAM
BAM
BAM
BAM

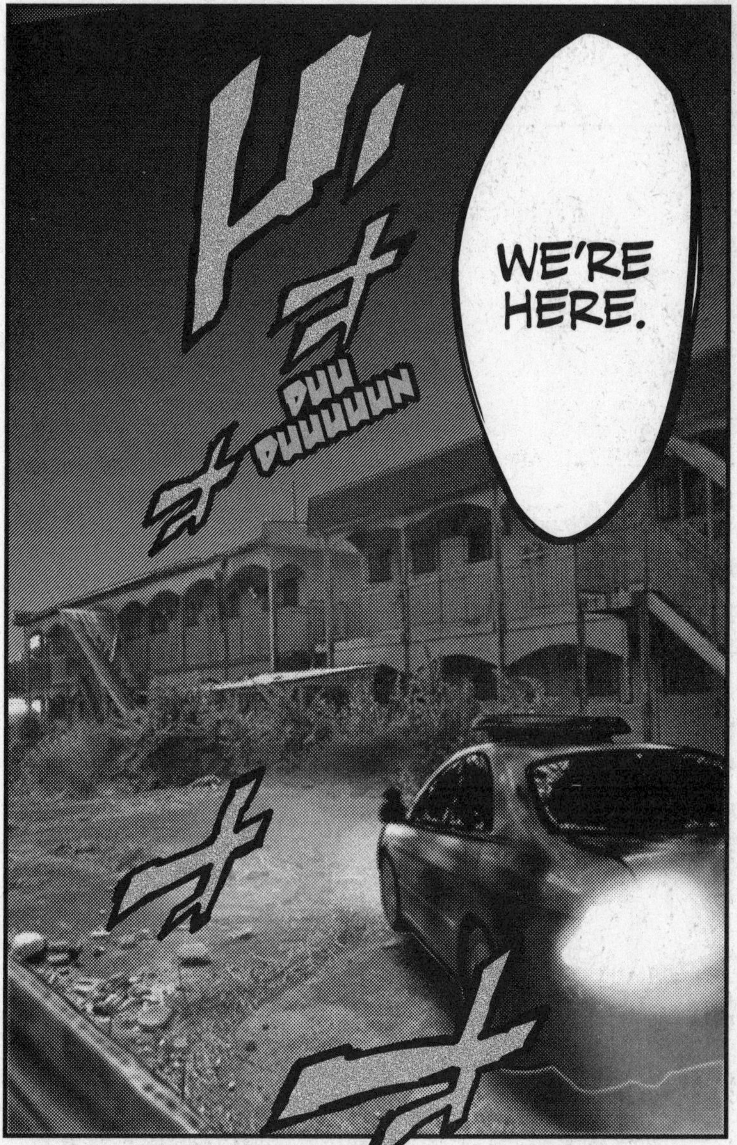
WE'RE HERE.
DUU DUUUUUN

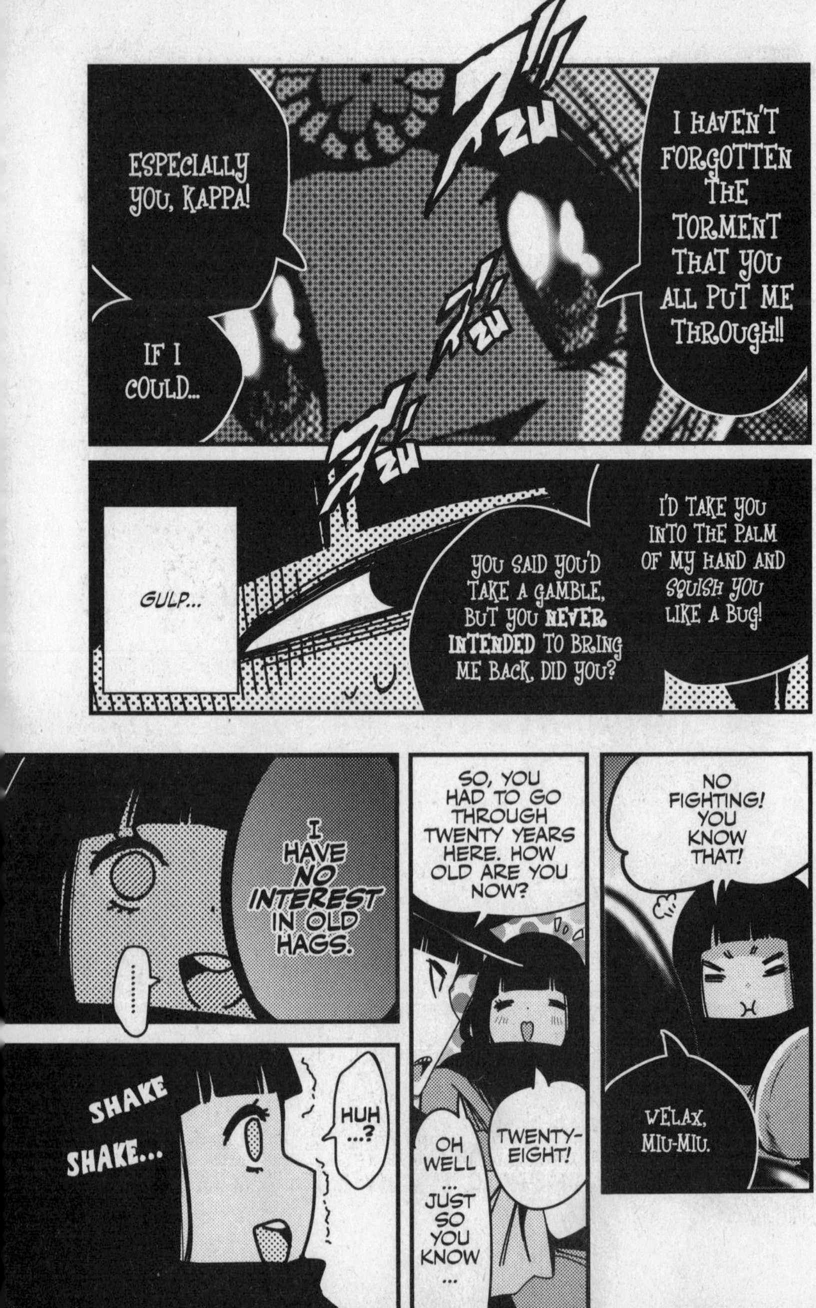
I HAVEN'T FORGOTTEN THE TORMENT THAT YOU ALL PUT ME THROUGH!!
ZU
ZU
ESPECIALLY YOU, KAPPA!
IF I COULD...
ZU
I'D TAKE YOU INTO THE PALM OF MY HAND AND SQUISH YOU LIKE A BUG!
YOU SAID YOU'D TAKE A GAMBLE, BUT YOU NEVER INTENDED TO BRING ME BACK, DID YOU?
GULP...
NO FIGHTING! YOU KNOW THAT!
WELAX, MIU-MIU.
SO, YOU HAD TO GO THROUGH TWENTY YEARS HERE. HOW OLD ARE YOU NOW?
TWENTY-EIGHT!
OH WELL ... JUST SO YOU KNOW ...
I HAVE NO INTEREST IN OLD HAGS.
......
HUH ...?
SHAKE SHAKE...

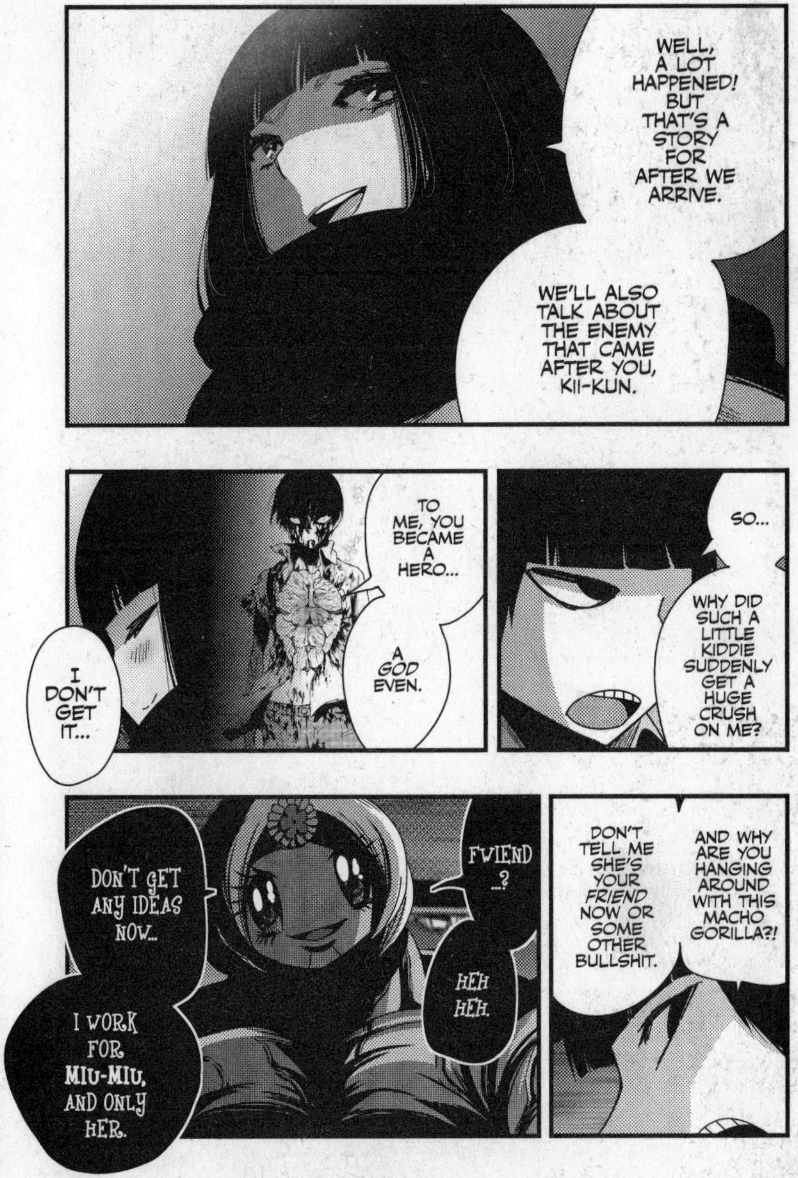
WELL, A LOT HAPPENED! BUT THAT'S A STORY FOR AFTER WE ARRIVE.
WE'LL ALSO TALK ABOUT THE ENEMY THAT CAME AFTER YOU, KII-KUN.
SO...
WHY DID SUCH A LITTLE KIDDIE SUDDENLY GET A HUGE CRUSH ON ME?
TO ME, YOU BECAME A HERO...
A *GOD* EVEN.
I DON'T GET IT...
AND WHY ARE YOU HANGING AROUND WITH THIS MACHO GORILLA?!
DON'T TELL ME SHE'S YOUR *FRIEND* NOW OR SOME OTHER BULLSHIT.
FWIEND ...?
HEH HEH.
DON'T GET ANY IDEAS NOW...
I WORK FOR **MIU-MIU,** AND ONLY HER.

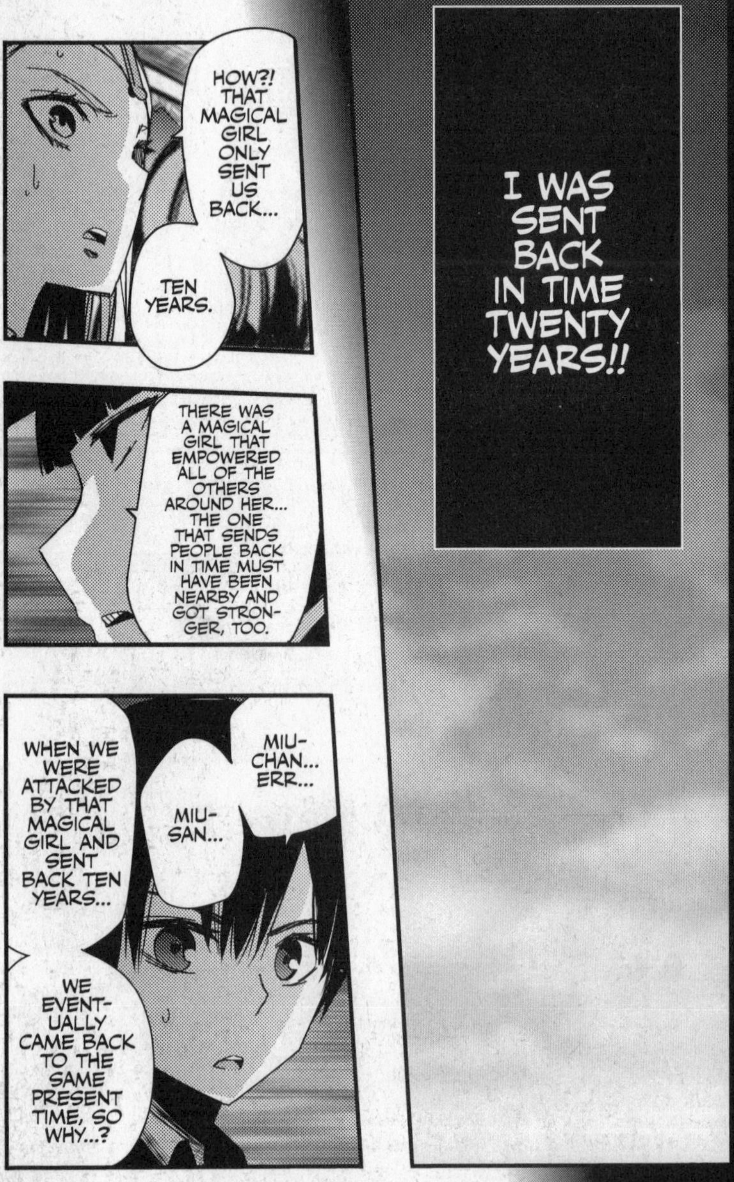
I WAS SENT BACK IN TIME TWENTY YEARS!!
HOW?! THAT MAGICAL GIRL ONLY SENT US BACK...
TEN YEARS.
THERE WAS A MAGICAL GIRL THAT EMPOWERED ALL OF THE OTHERS AROUND HER... THE ONE THAT SENDS PEOPLE BACK IN TIME MUST HAVE BEEN NEARBY AND GOT STRONGER, TOO.
MIU-CHAN... ERR...
MIU-SAN...
WHEN WE WERE ATTACKED BY THAT MAGICAL GIRL AND SENT BACK TEN YEARS...
WE EVENTUALLY CAME BACK TO THE SAME PRESENT TIME, SO WHY...?

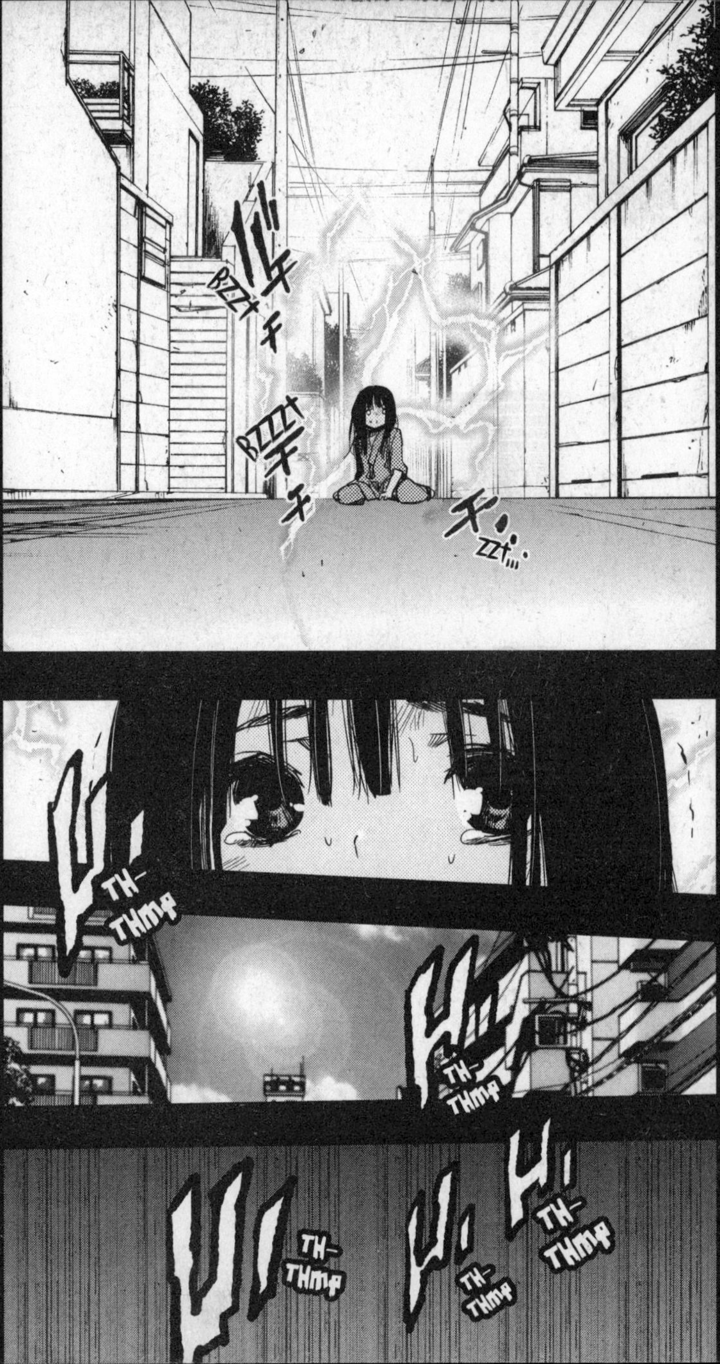
BZZZT
BZZZT
ZZT...
TH-THMP
TH-THMP
TH-THMP
TH-THMP
TH-THMP

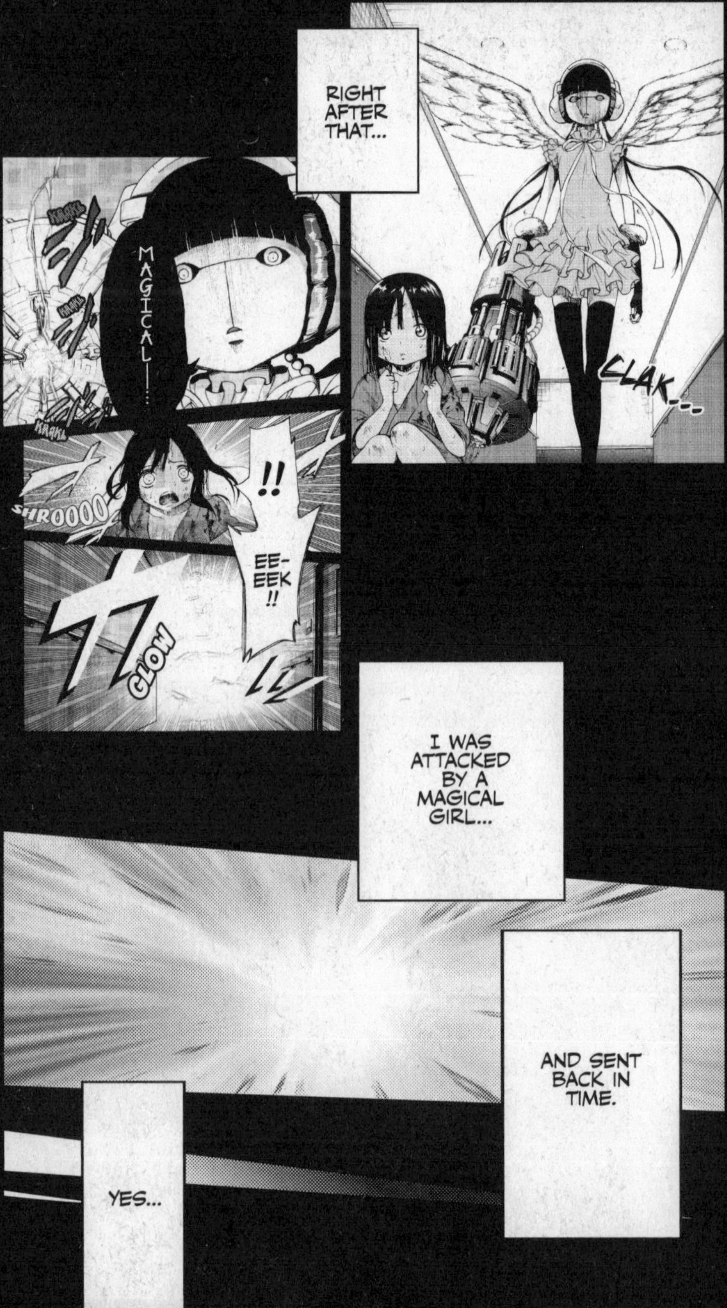
RIGHT AFTER THAT...
CLAK...
MAGICAL!!...
!!
SHROOOO
EE-EEK!!
GLOW
I WAS ATTACKED BY A MAGICAL GIRL...
AND SENT BACK IN TIME.
YES...

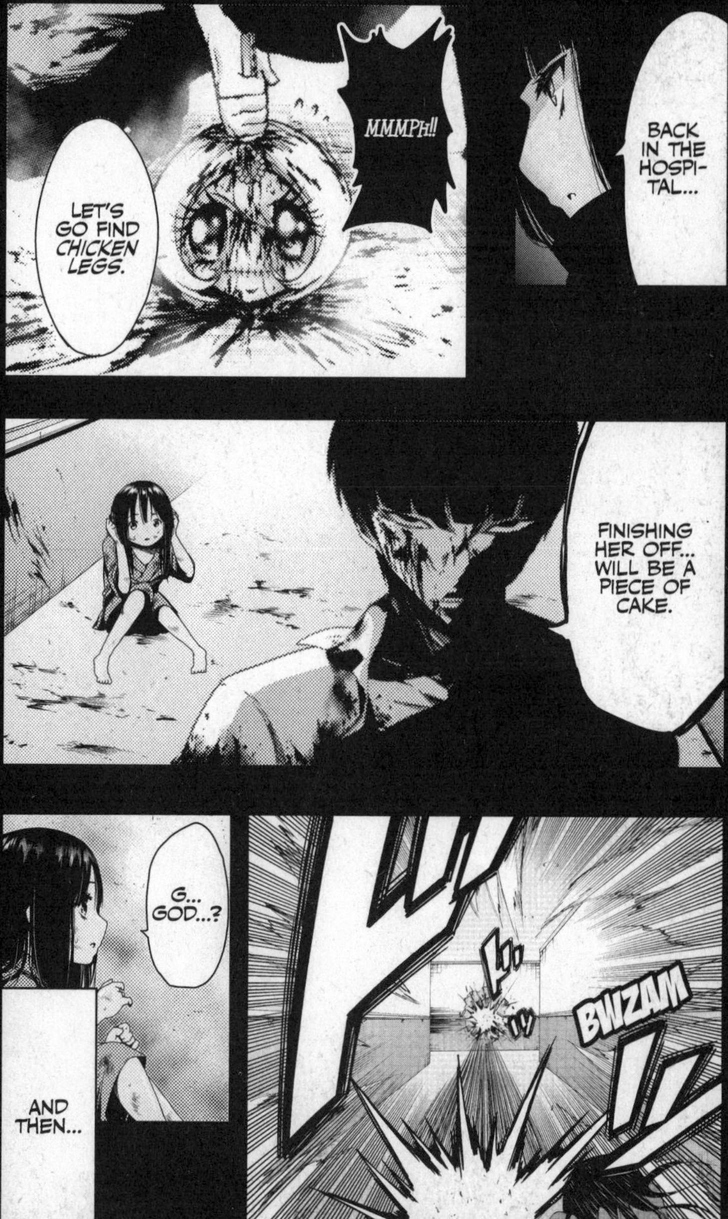
BACK IN THE HOSPITAL...
MMMPH!!
LET'S GO FIND CHICKEN LEGS.
FINISHING HER OFF... WILL BE A PIECE OF CAKE.
BWZAM
G... GOD...?
AND THEN...

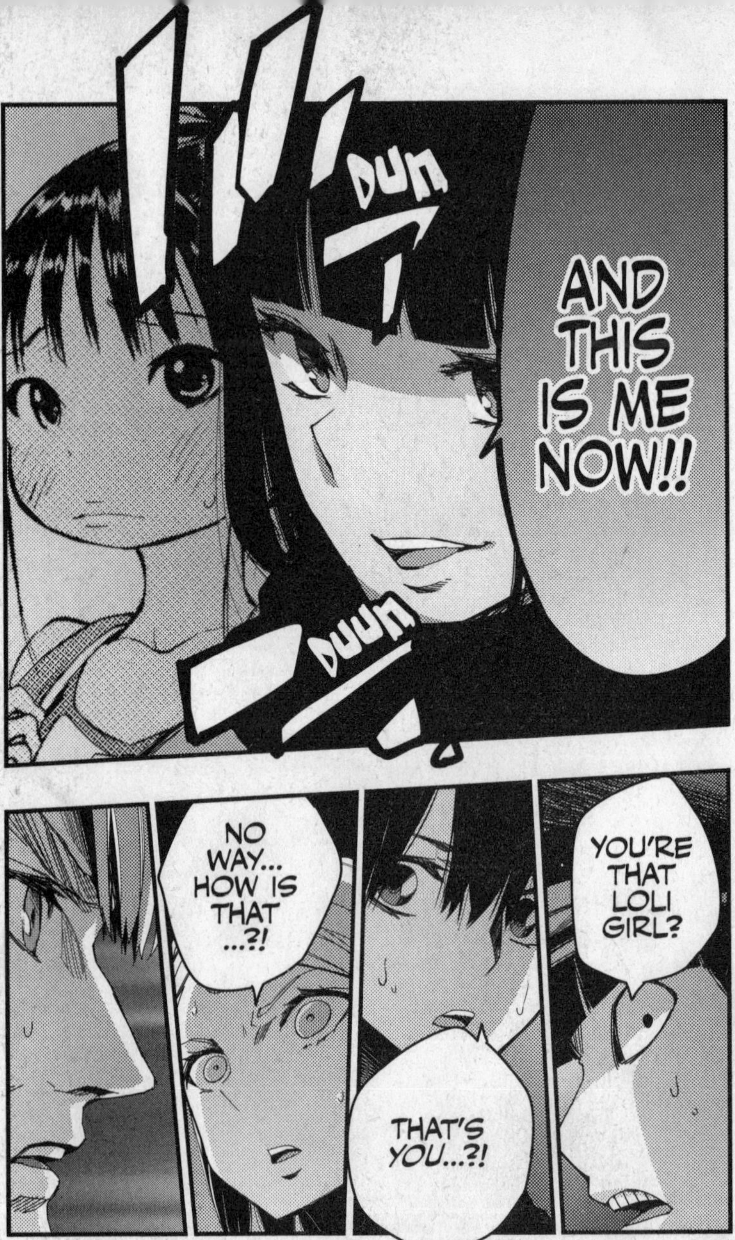
DUN
AND THIS IS ME NOW!!
DUUN
YOU'RE THAT LOLI GIRL?
THAT'S YOU...?!
NO WAY... HOW IS THAT ...?!

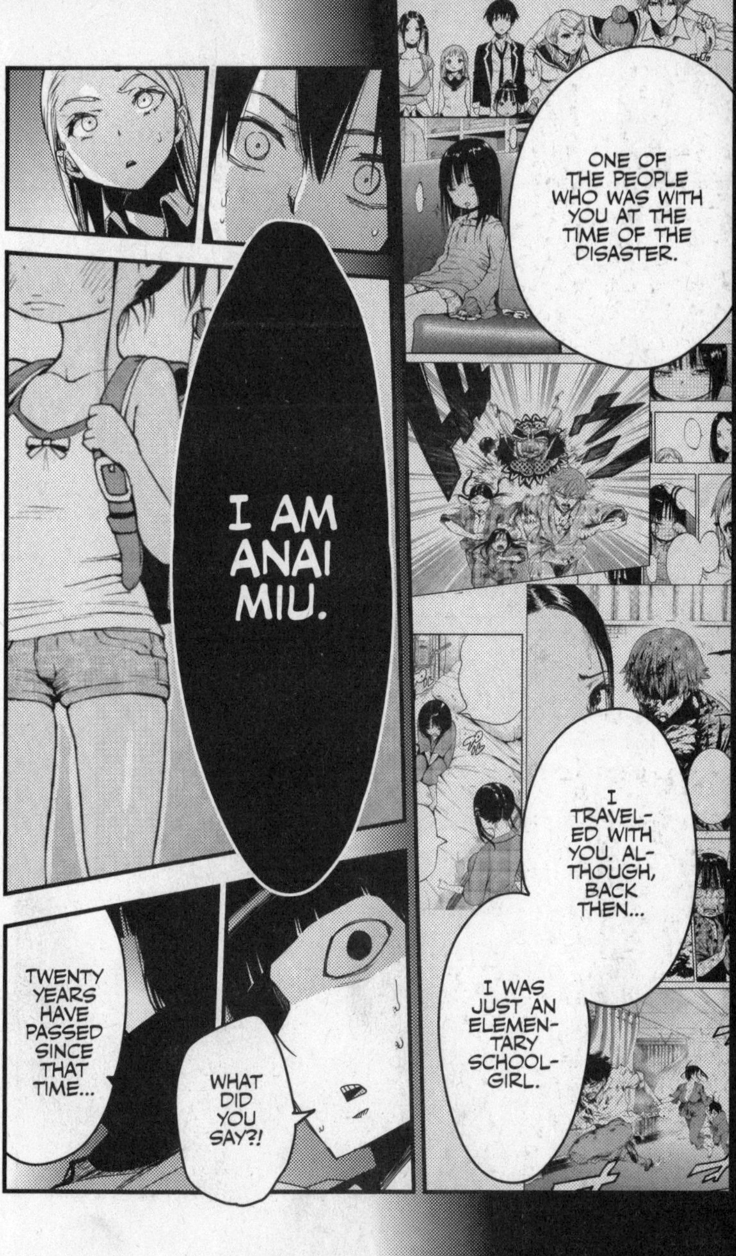
ONE OF THE PEOPLE WHO WAS WITH YOU AT THE TIME OF THE DISASTER.
I TRAVEL-ED WITH YOU. AL-THOUGH, BACK THEN...
I WAS JUST AN ELEMEN-TARY SCHOOL-GIRL.
I AM ANAI MIU.
WHAT DID YOU SAY?!
TWENTY YEARS HAVE PASSED SINCE THAT TIME...

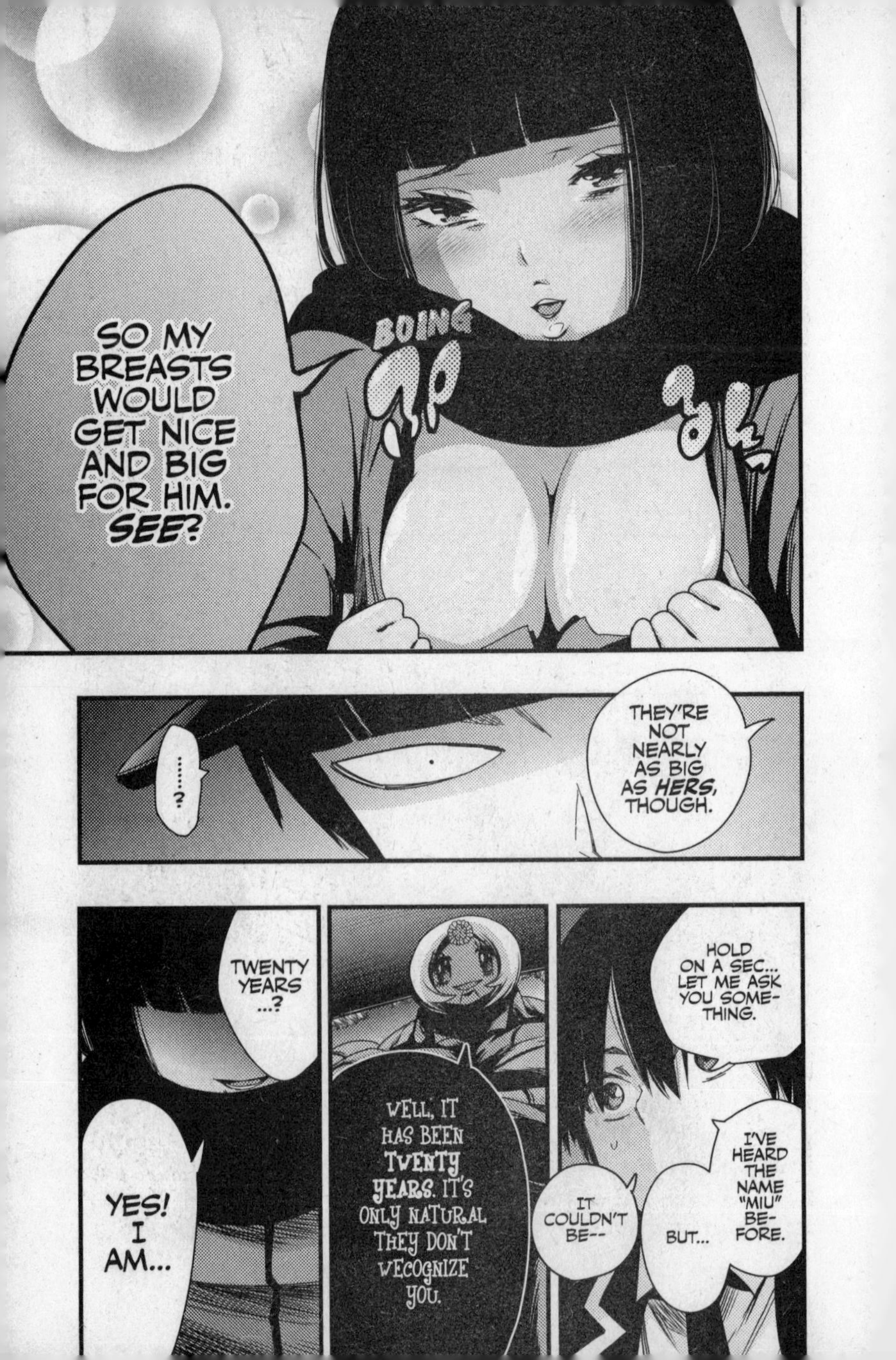
SO MY BREASTS WOULD GET NICE AND BIG FOR HIM. SEE?
BOING
THEY'RE NOT NEARLY AS BIG AS HERS, THOUGH.
......?
HOLD ON A SEC... LET ME ASK YOU SOMETHING.
I'VE HEARD THE NAME "MIU" BEFORE.
BUT...
IT COULDN'T BE--
WELL, IT HAS BEEN TWENTY YEARS. IT'S ONLY NATURAL THEY DON'T WECOGNIZE YOU.
TWENTY YEARS ...?
YES! I AM...

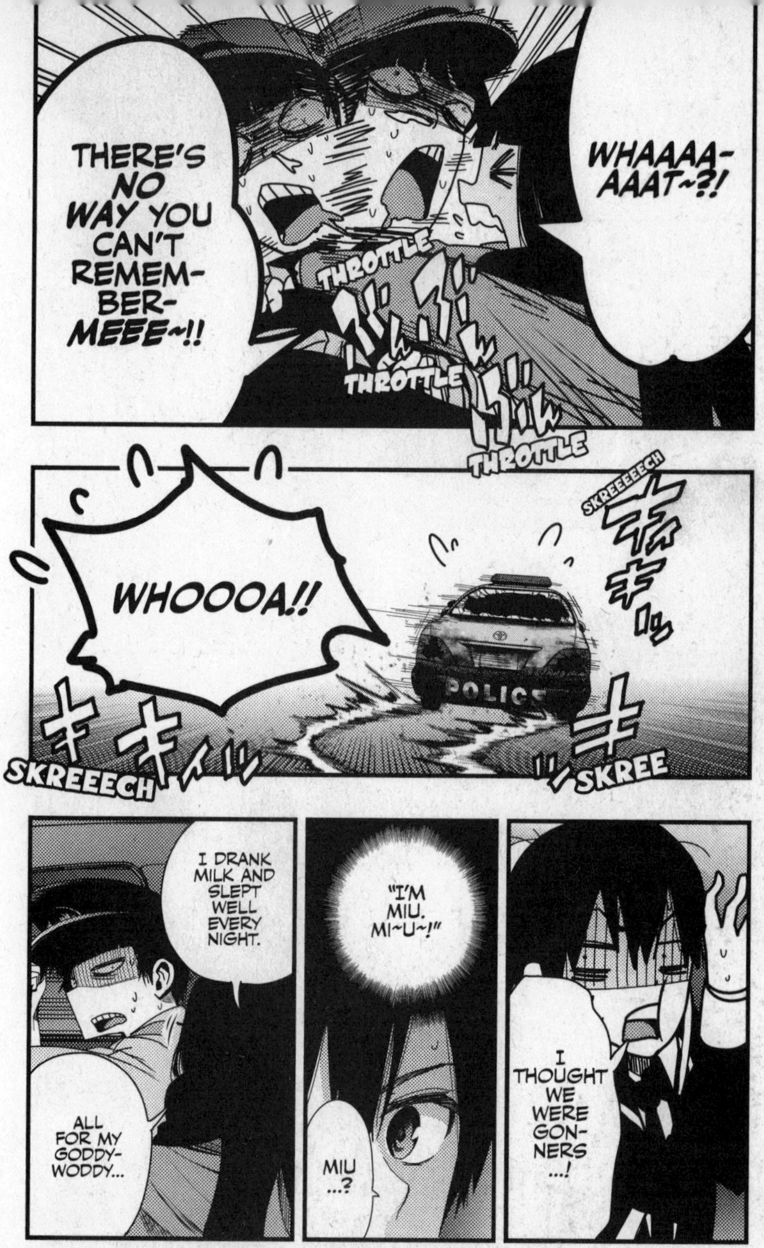
WHAAAA-AAAT~?!
THERE'S NO WAY YOU CAN'T REMEMBER-MEEE~!!
THROTTLE
THROTTLE
THROTTLE
SKREEEEECH
WHOOOA!!
SKREE
SKREEECH
I THOUGHT WE WERE GONNERS...!
"I'M MIU. MI~U~!"
MIU...?
I DRANK MILK AND SLEPT WELL EVERY NIGHT.
ALL FOR MY GODDY-WODDY...

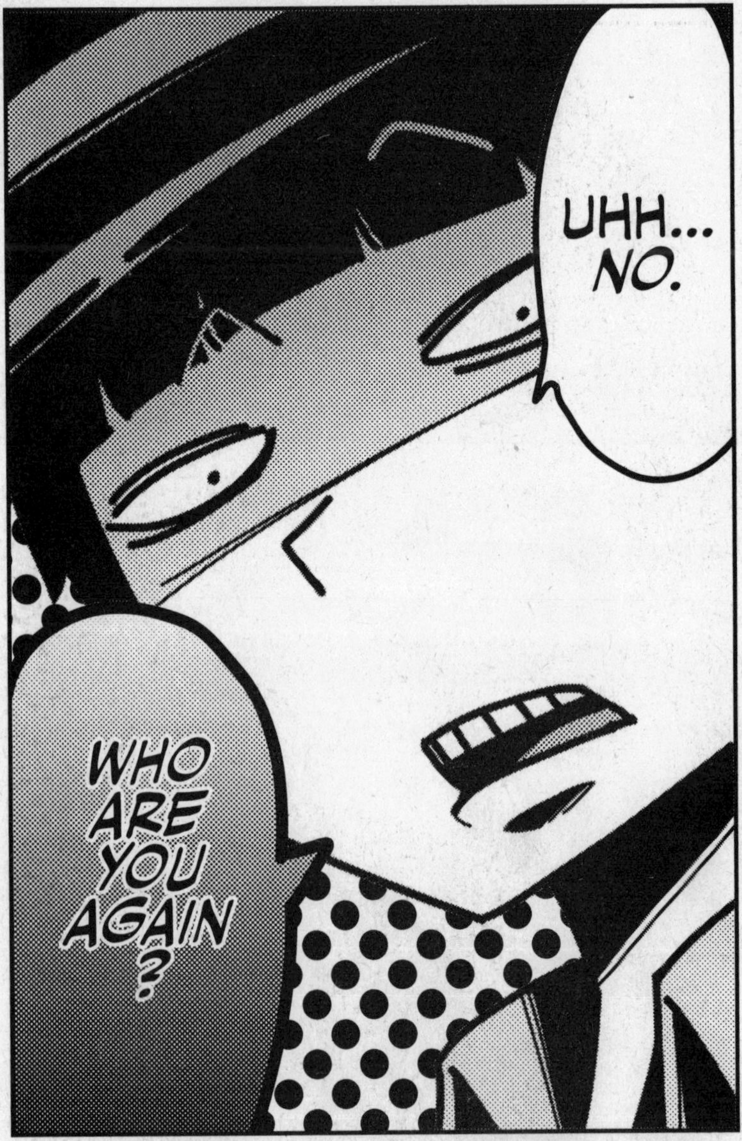
UHH... NO.
WHO ARE YOU AGAIN?

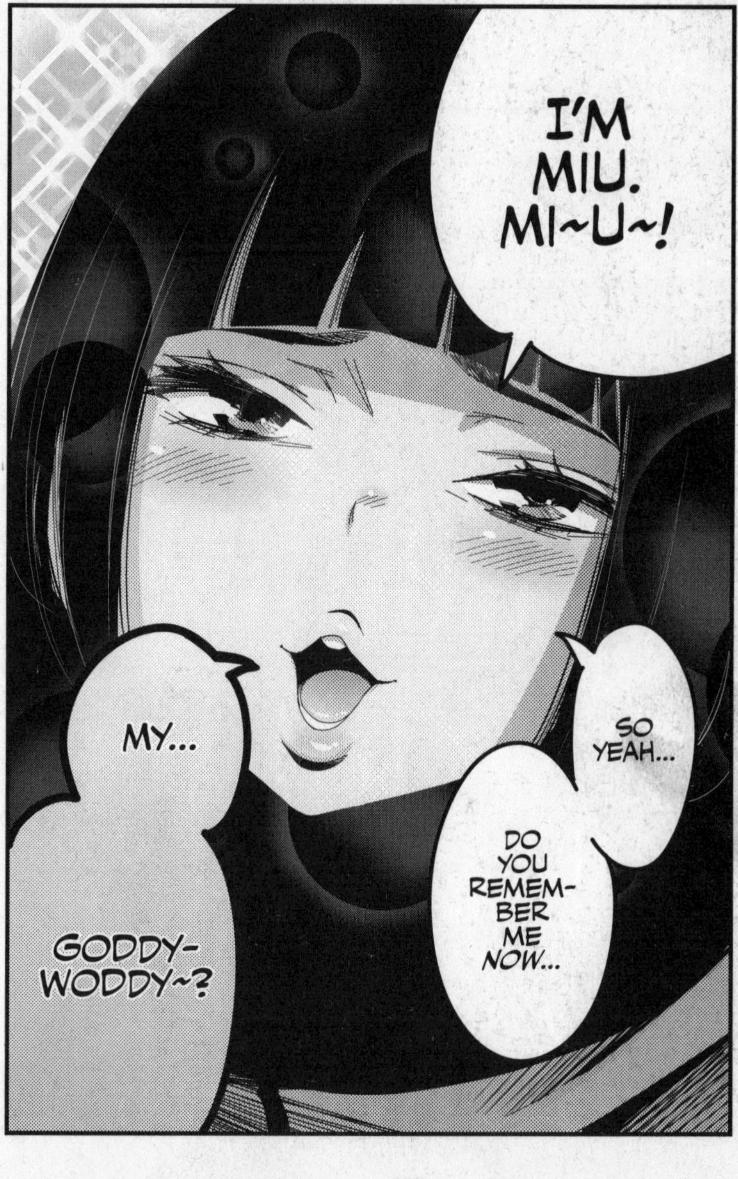
I'M MIU. MI~U~!
SO YEAH...
DO YOU REMEMBER ME NOW...
MY...
GODDY-WODDY~?

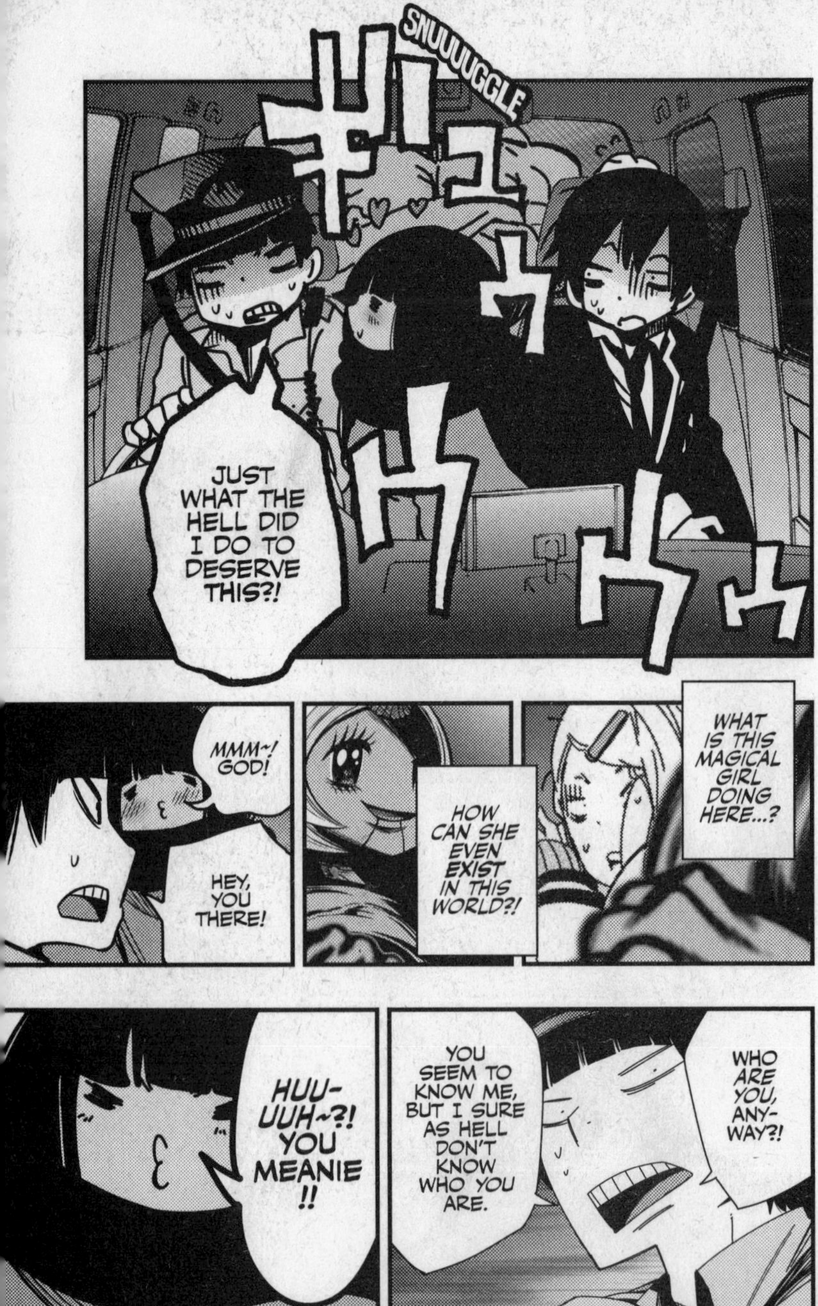
SNUUUUGGLE
JUST WHAT THE HELL DID I DO TO DESERVE THIS?!
WHAT IS THIS MAGICAL GIRL DOING HERE...?
HOW CAN SHE EVEN EXIST IN THIS WORLD?!
MMM~! GOD!
HEY, YOU THERE!
WHO ARE YOU, ANYWAY?!
YOU SEEM TO KNOW ME, BUT I SURE AS HELL DON'T KNOW WHO YOU ARE.
HUU-UUH~?! YOU MEANIE !!

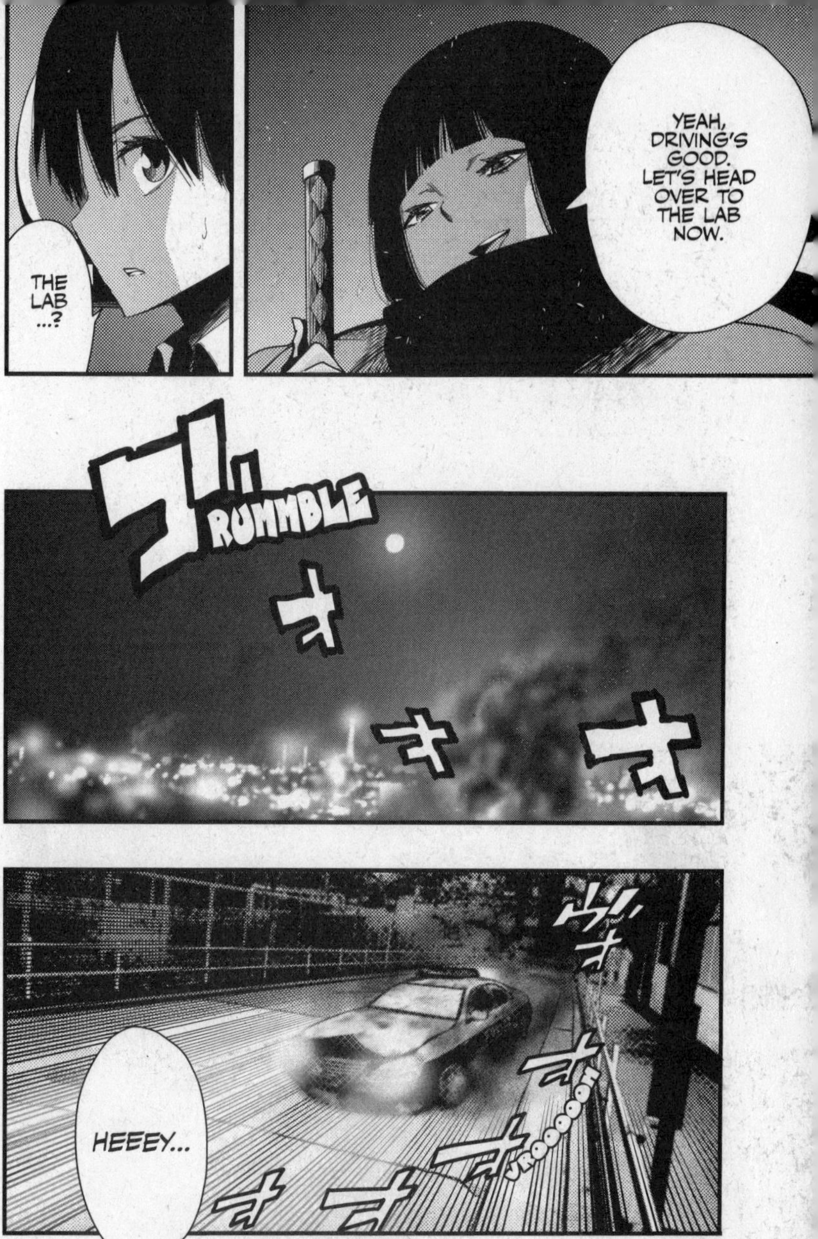
YEAH, DRIVING'S GOOD. LET'S HEAD OVER TO THE LAB NOW.
THE LAB ...?
RUMMBLE
VROOOOOM
HEEEY...

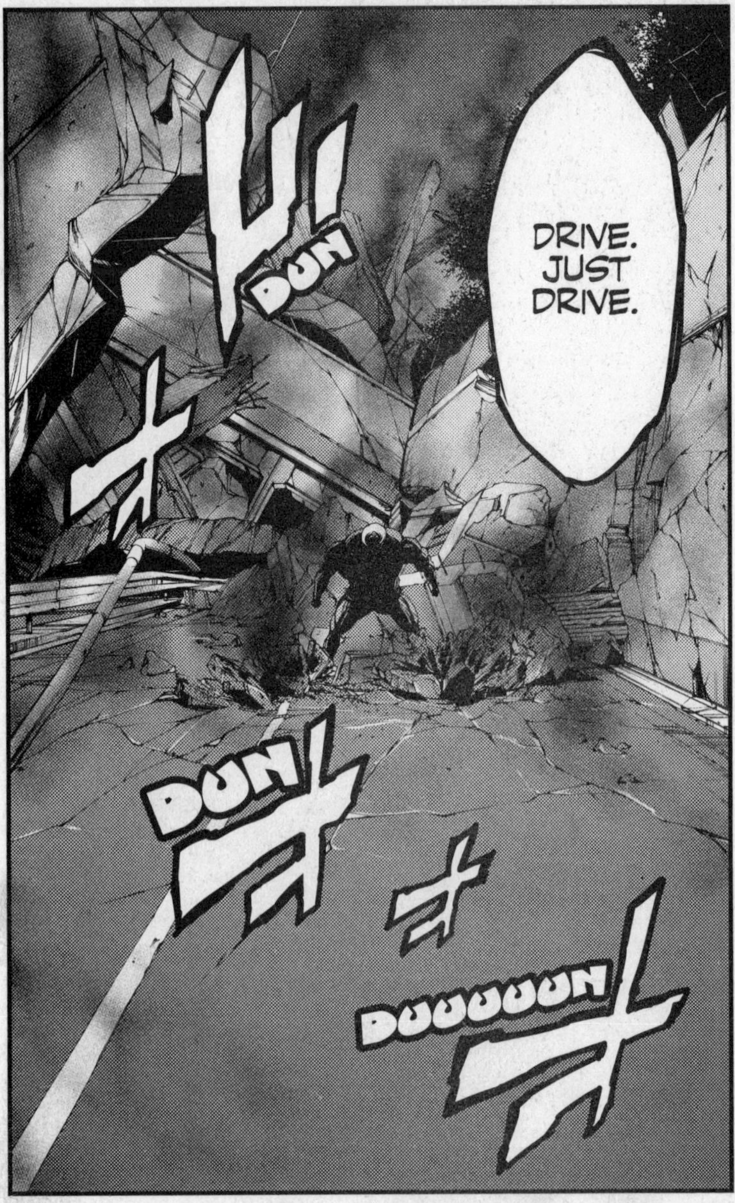
DRIVE. JUST DRIVE.
DUN
DUN
DUUUUUN

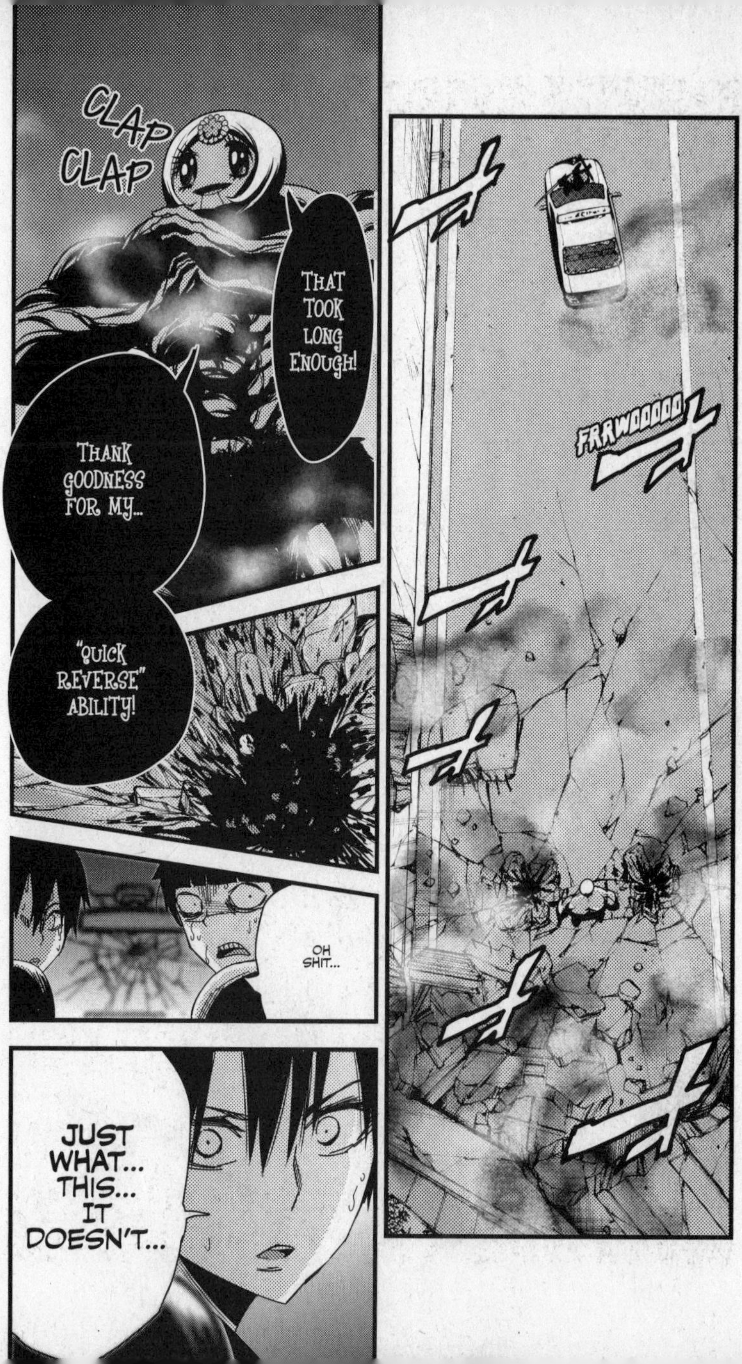
FRRWOOOOO
CLAP CLAP
THAT TOOK LONG ENOUGH!
THANK GOODNESS FOR MY...
"QUICK REVERSE" ABILITY!
OH SHIT...
JUST WHAT... THIS... IT DOESN'T...

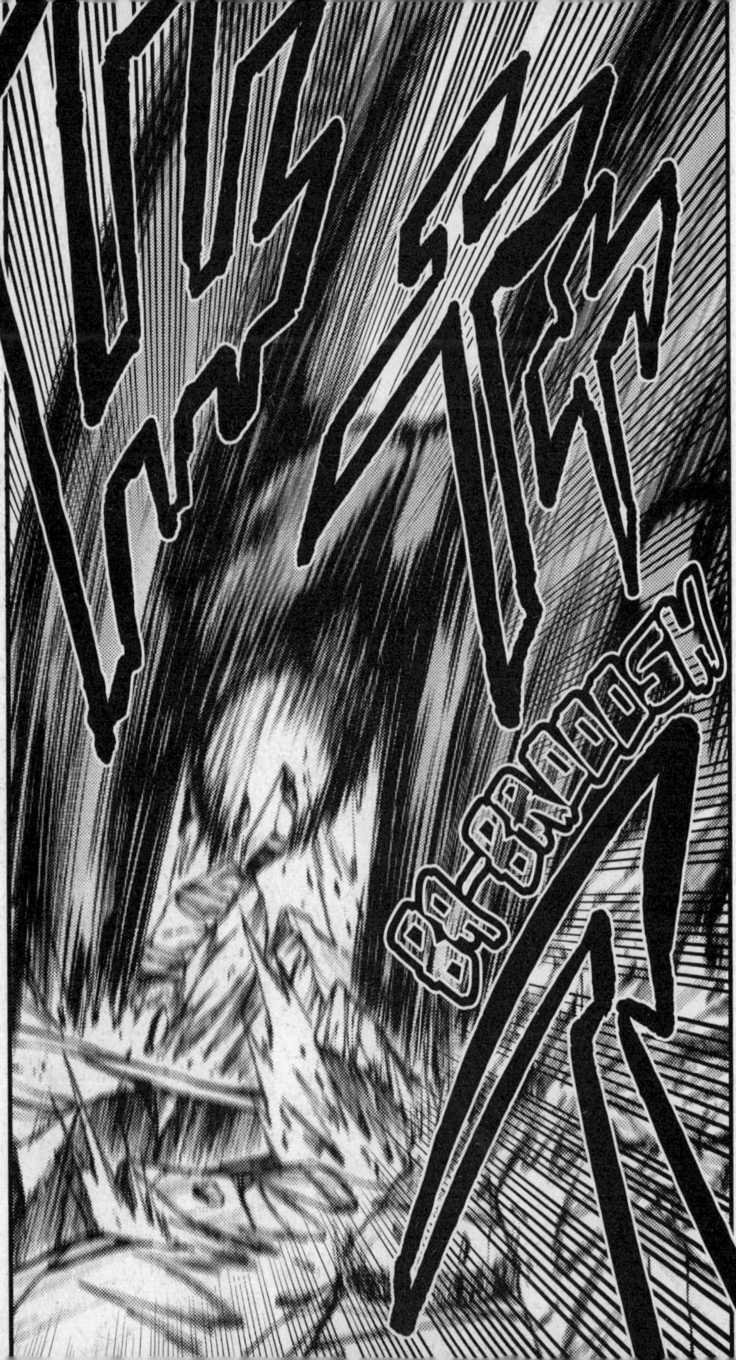

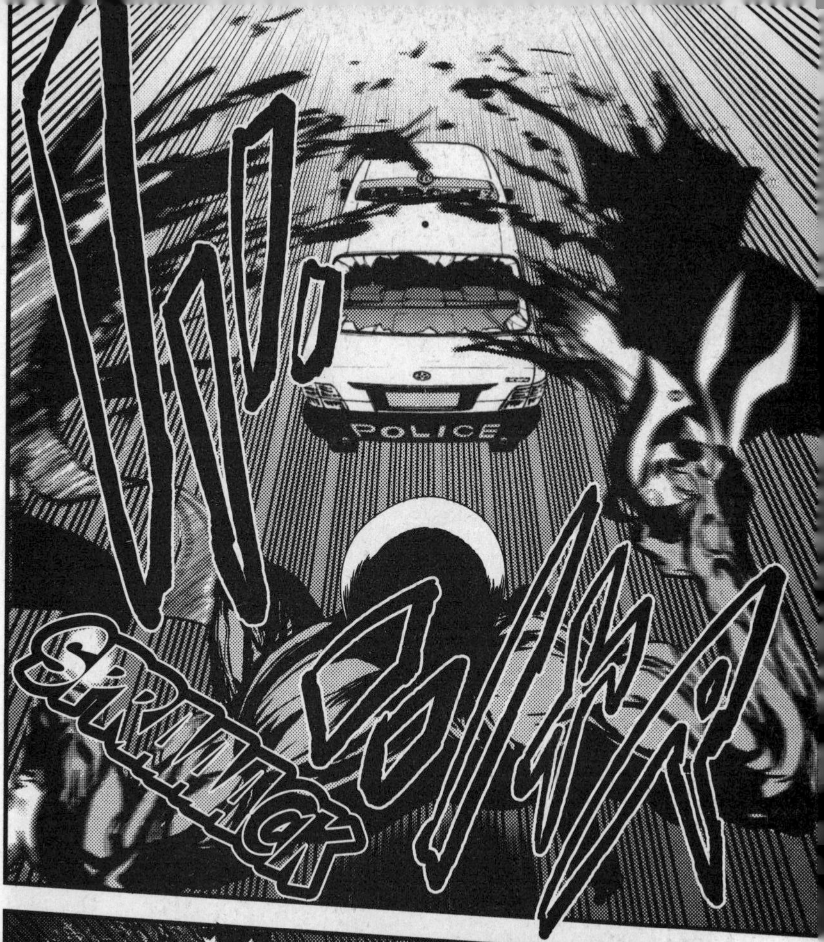

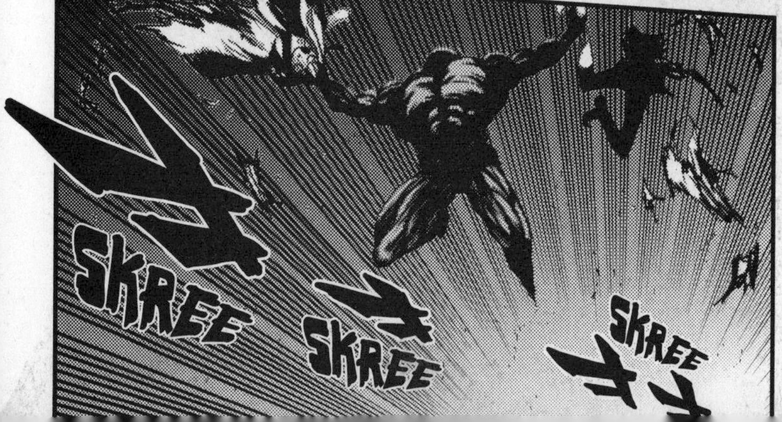
SKREE
SKREE
SKREE

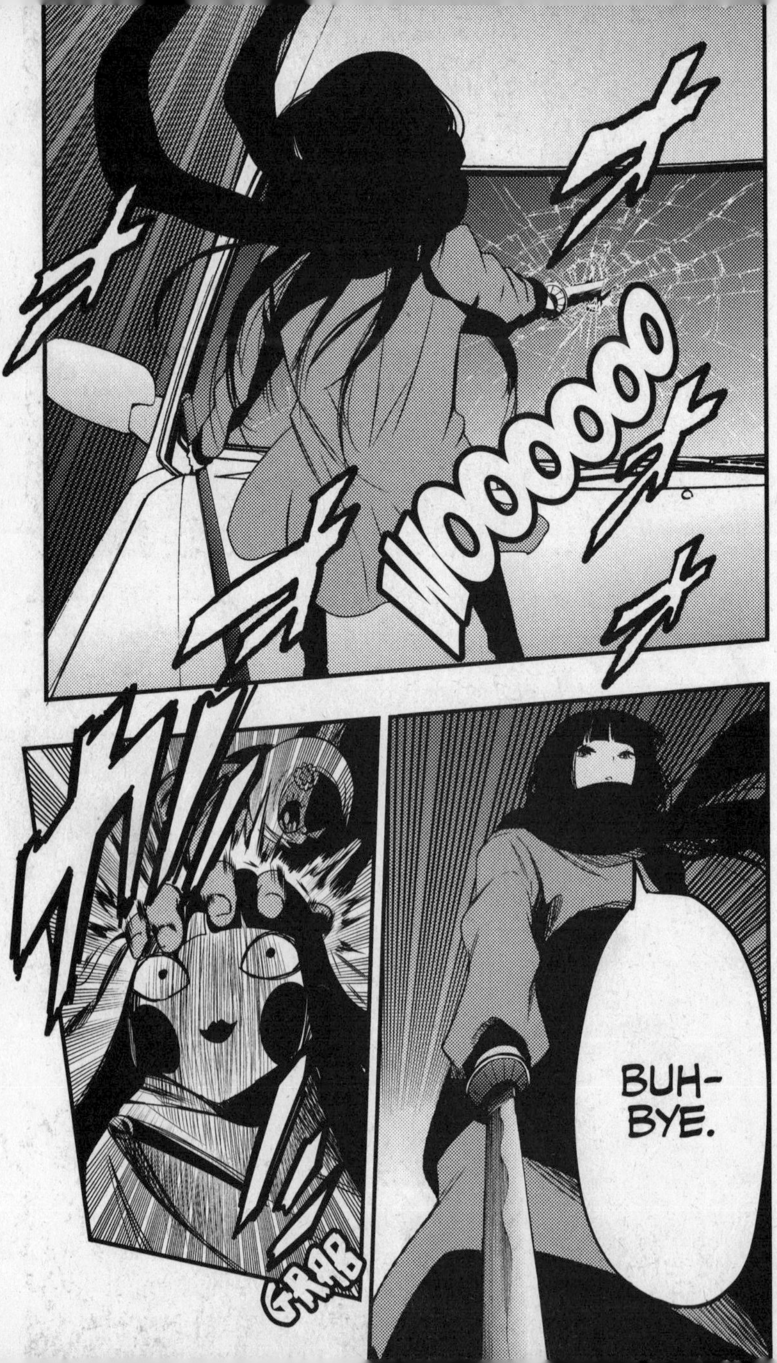
WOOOOOO
BUH-BYE.
GRAB

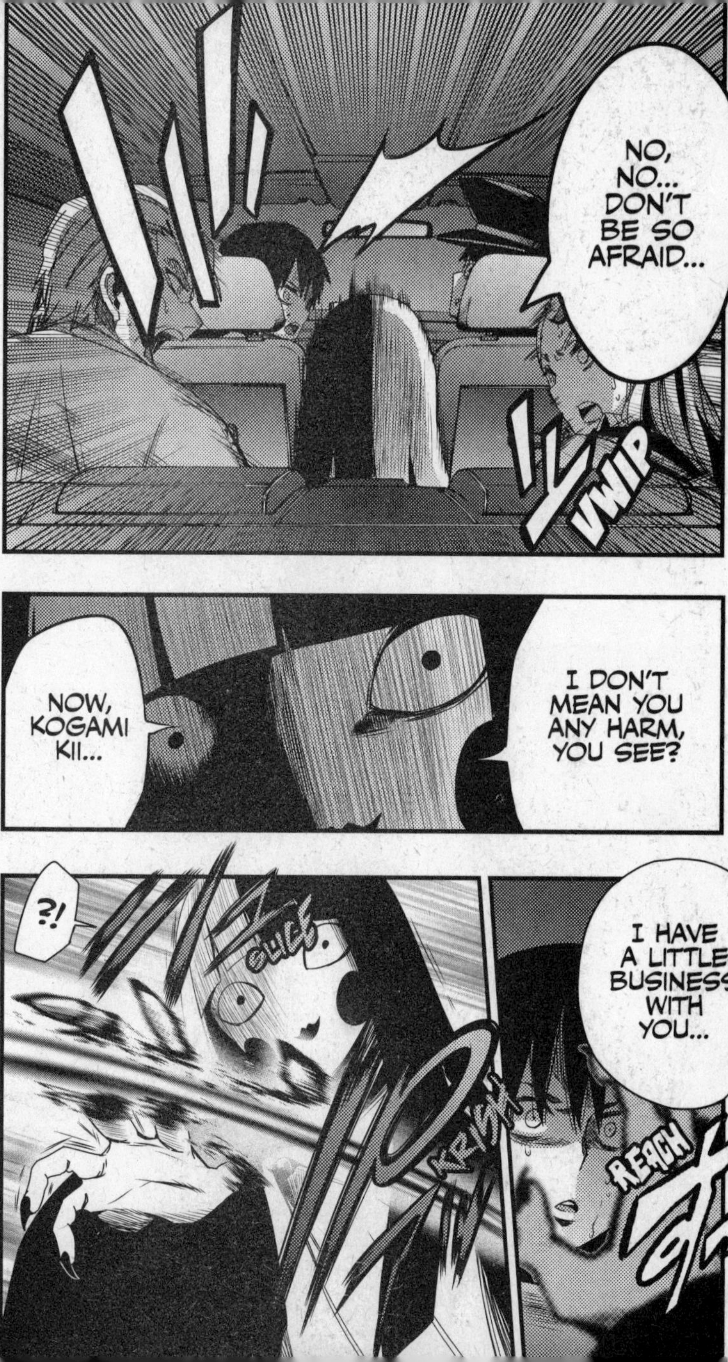
NO, NO... DON'T BE SO AFRAID...
VWIP
I DON'T MEAN YOU ANY HARM, YOU SEE?
NOW, KOGAMI KII...
I HAVE A LITTLE BUSINESS WITH YOU...
REACH
KRISH
SLICE
?!

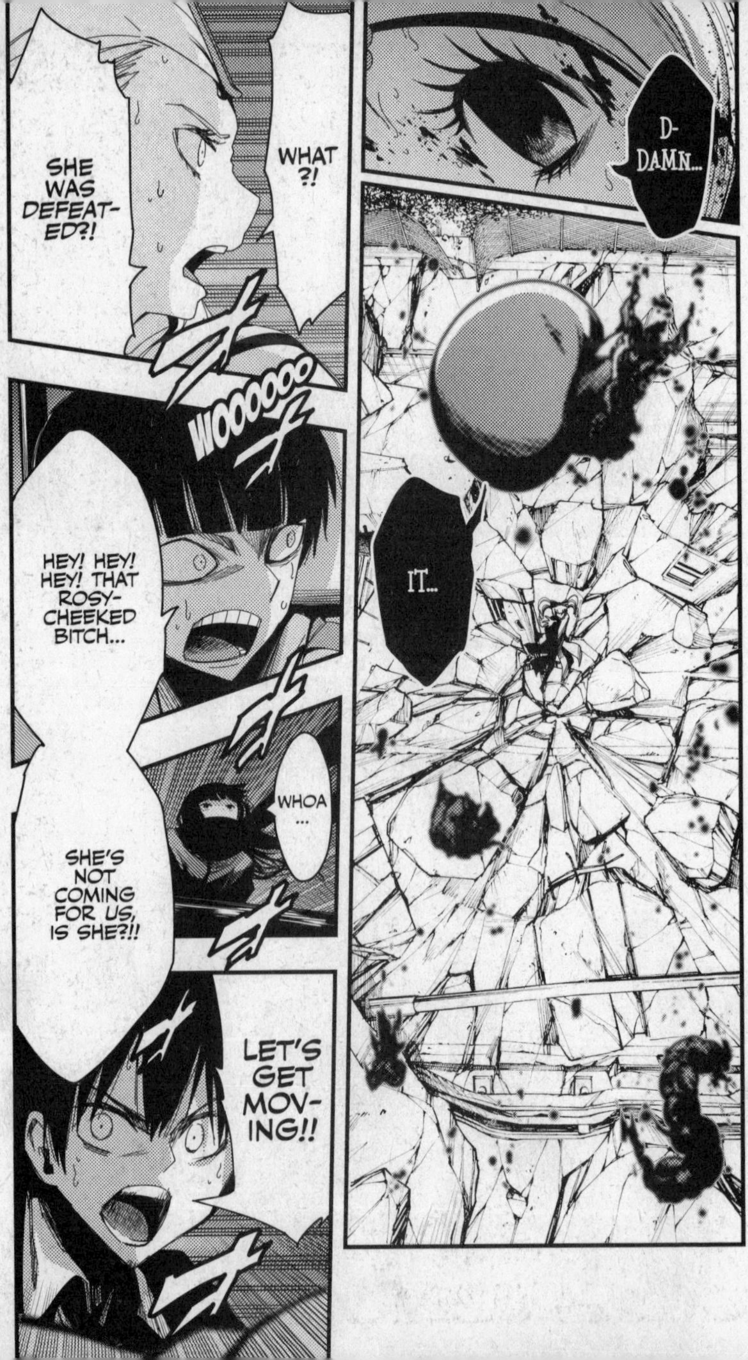
D-DAMN...
IT...
WHAT?!
SHE WAS DEFEATED?!
WOOOOOO
HEY! HEY! HEY! THAT ROSY-CHEEKED BITCH...
WHOA...
SHE'S NOT COMING FOR US, IS SHE?!!
LET'S GET MOVING!!

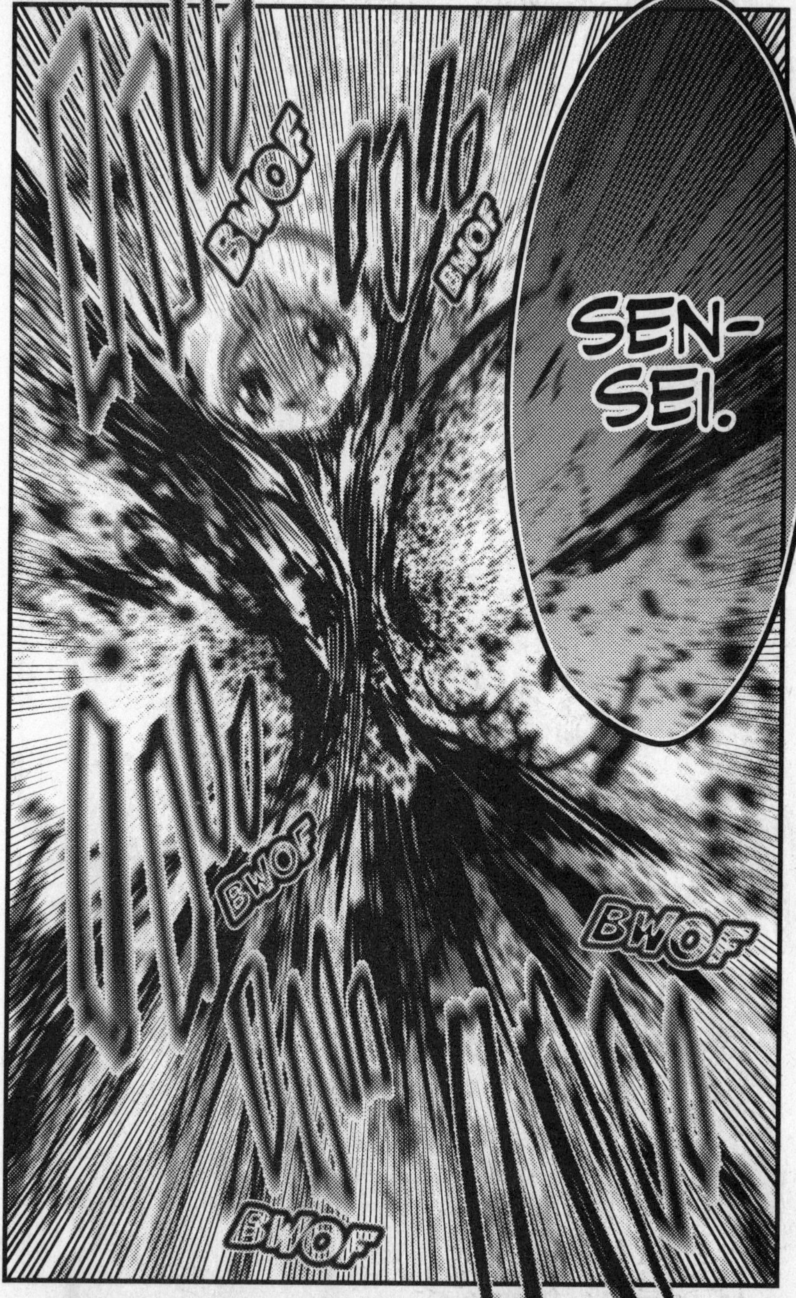
SEN-SEI.
BWOF
BWOF
BWOF
BWOF
BWOF

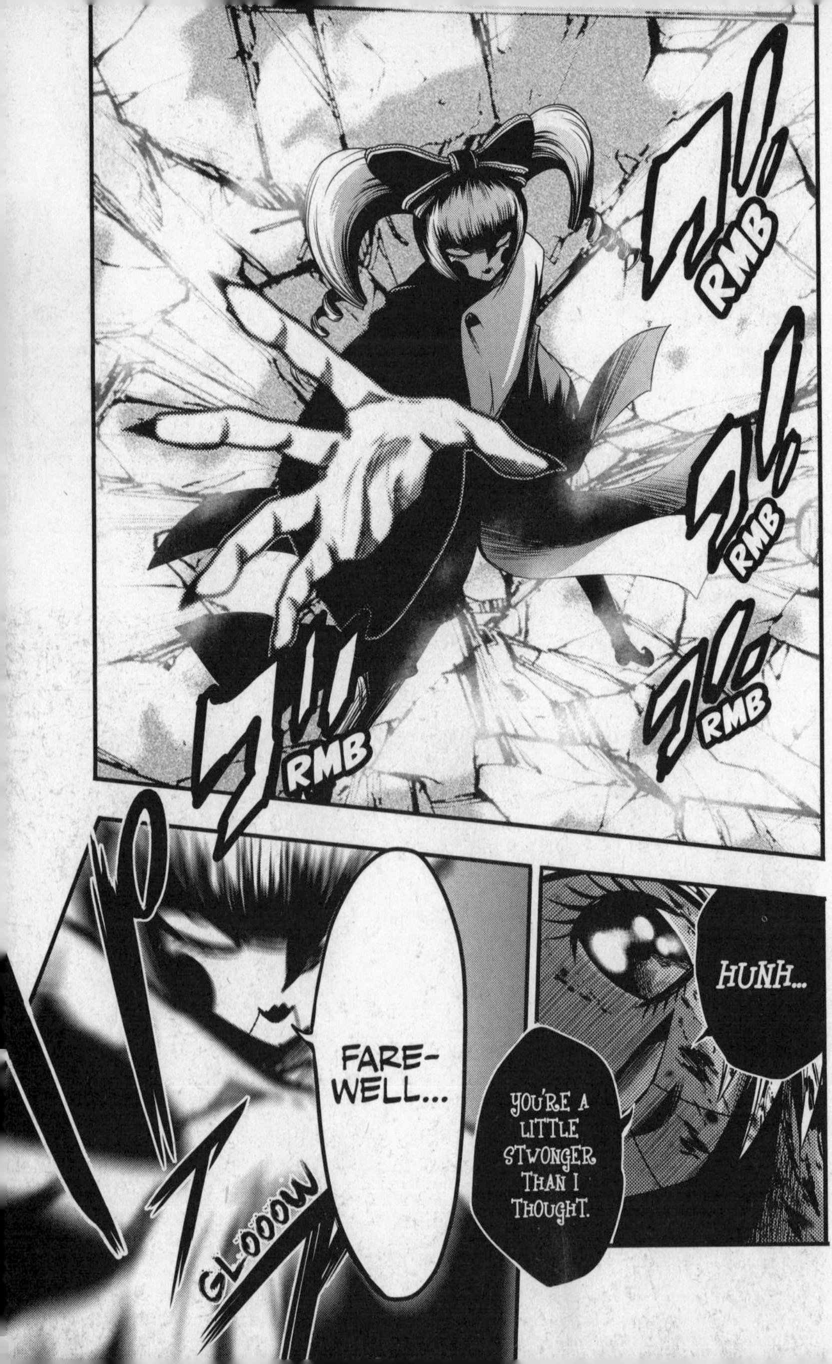
RMB
RMB
RMB
RMB
HUNH...
YOU'RE A LITTLE STWONGER THAN I THOUGHT.
FARE-WELL...
GLOOOW

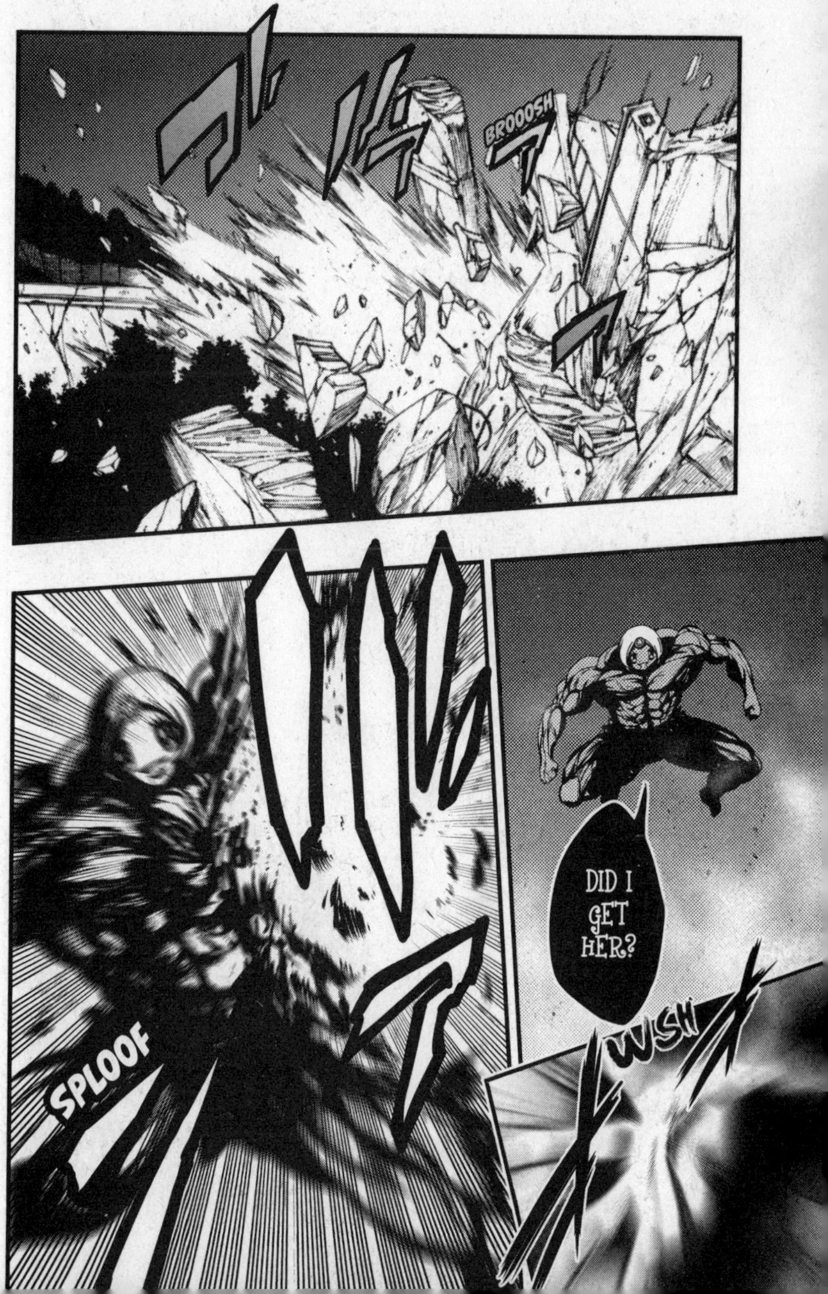
BROOOSH
DID I GET HER?
WUSH
SPLOOF

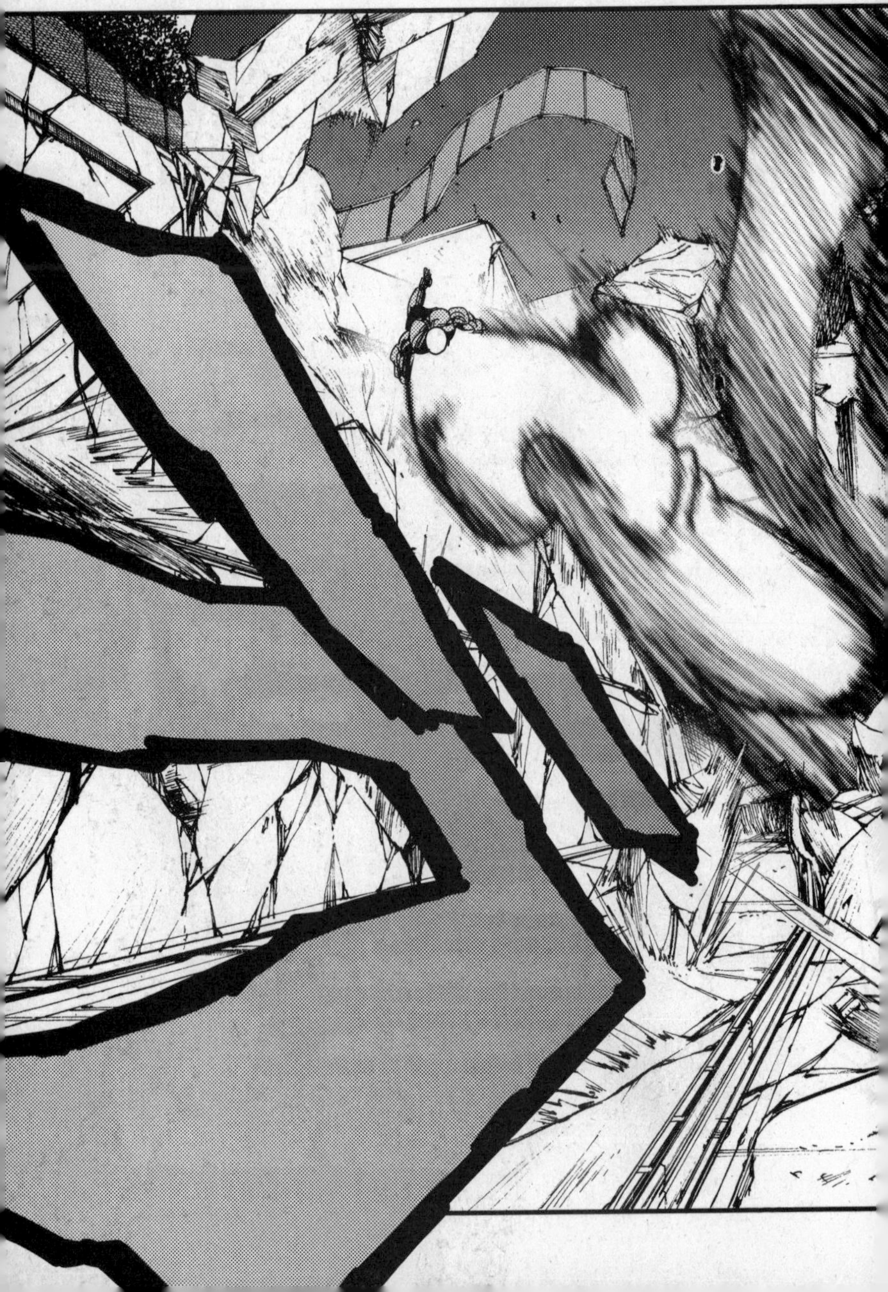

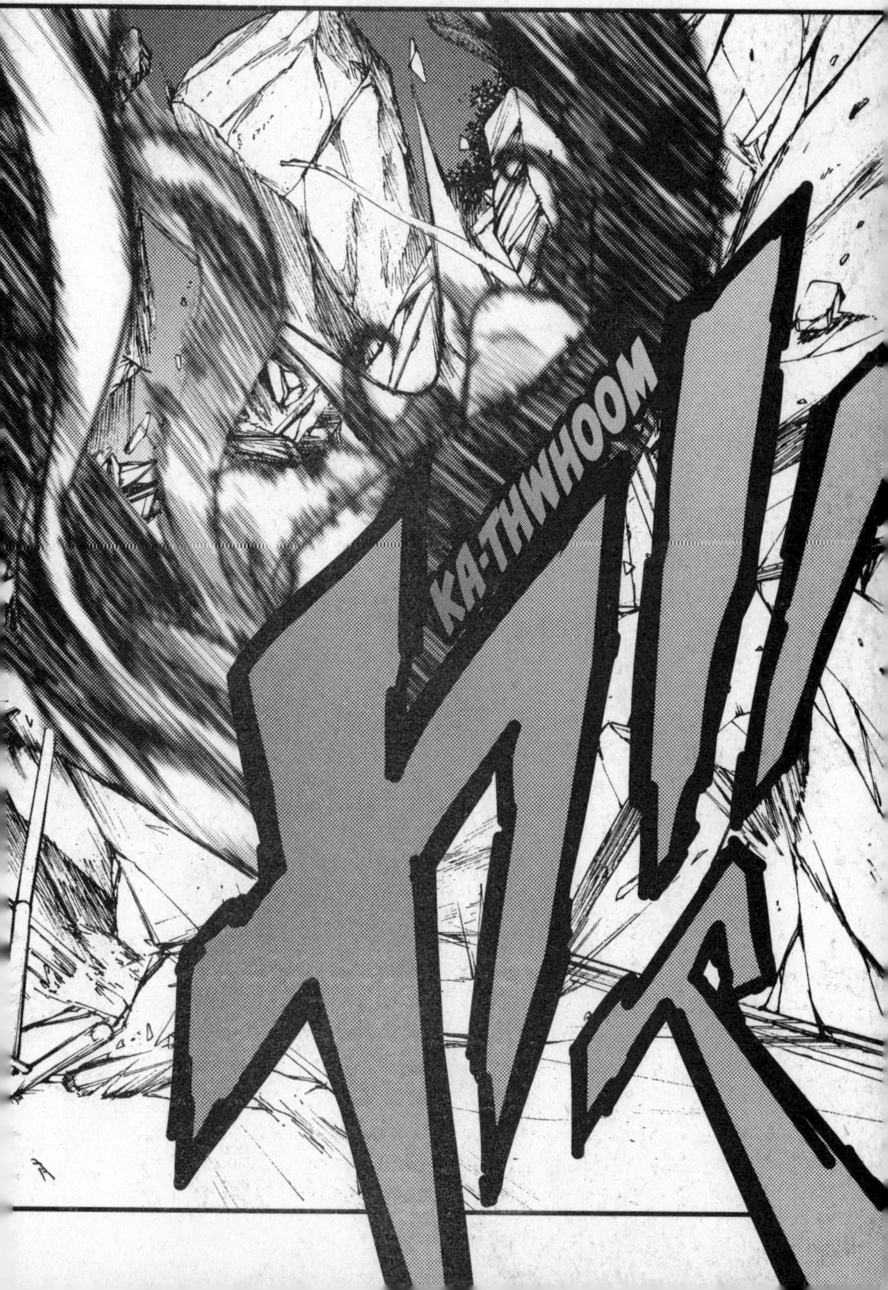
KA-THWHOOM

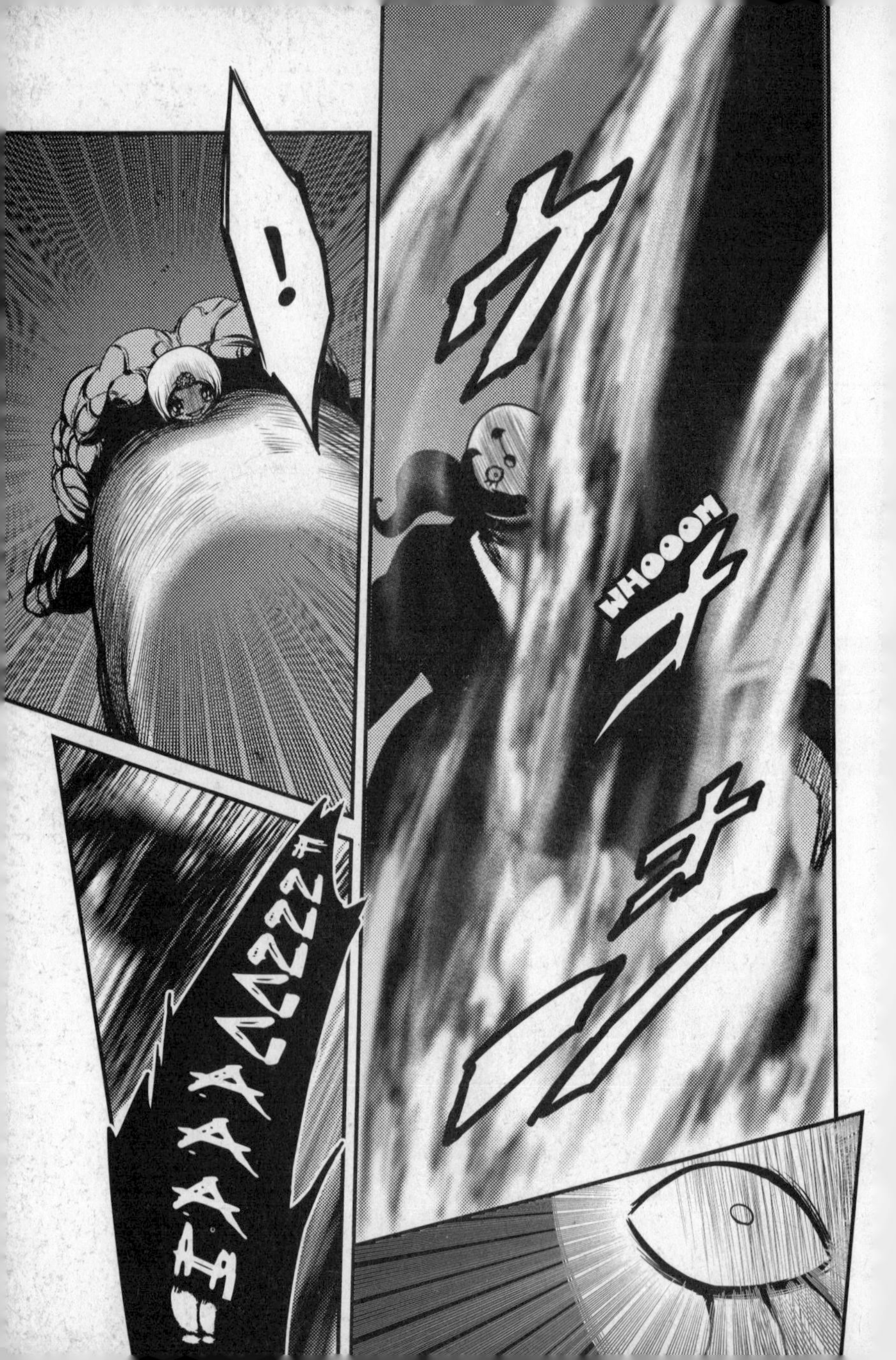
WHOOOM
!
FZZZVVAAAH!!

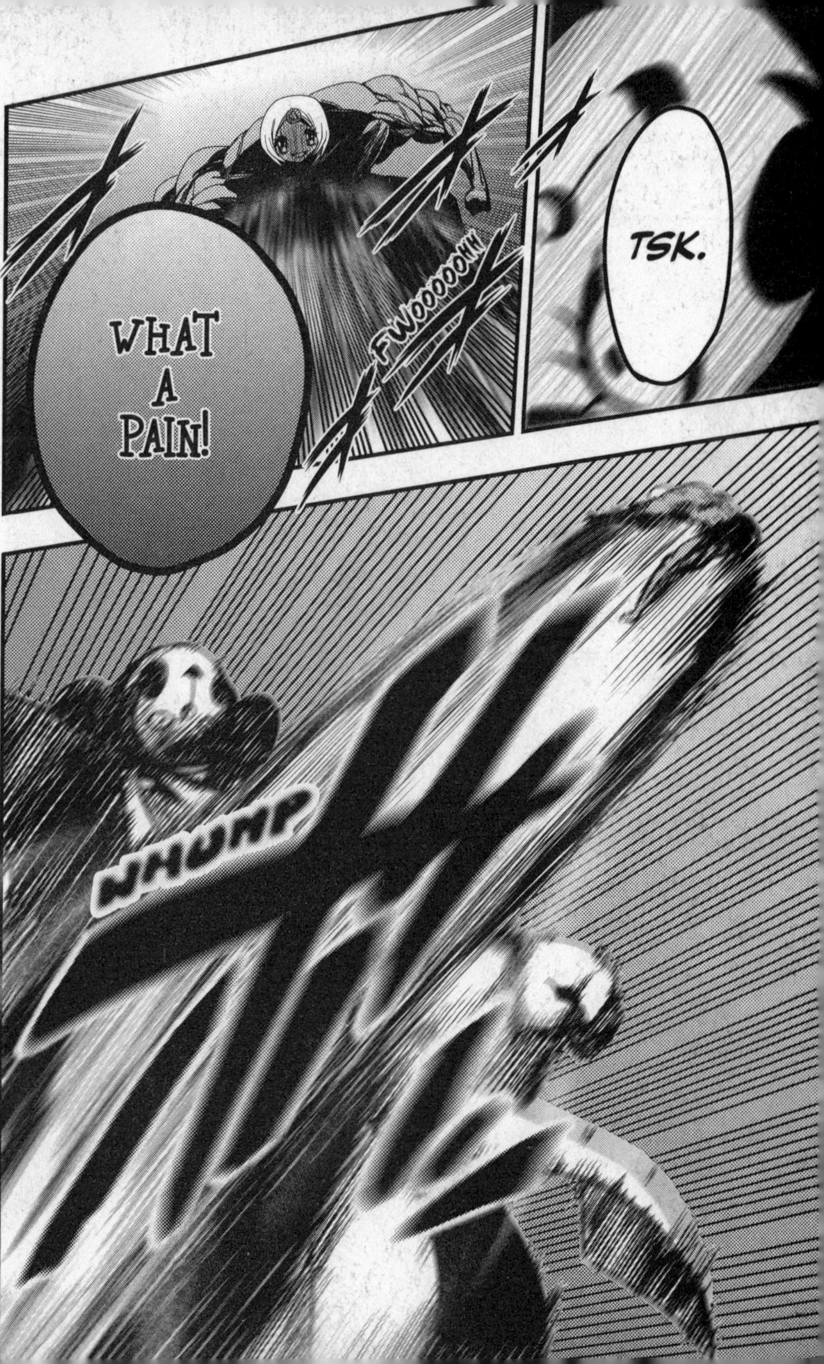
TSK.
WHAT A PAIN!
FWOOOOOHH
WHUMP

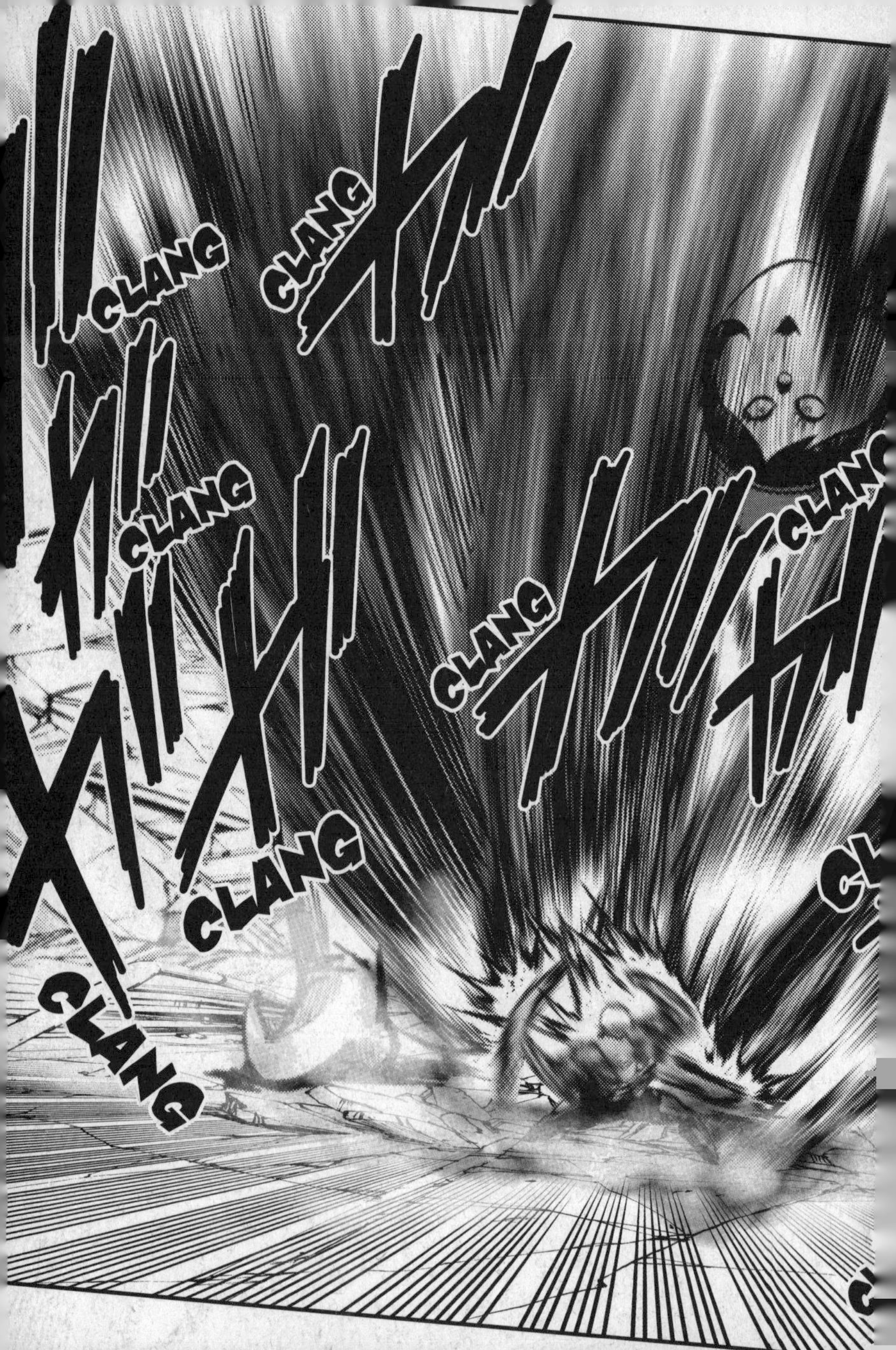
CLANG
CLANG
CLANG
CLANG
CLANG
CLANG

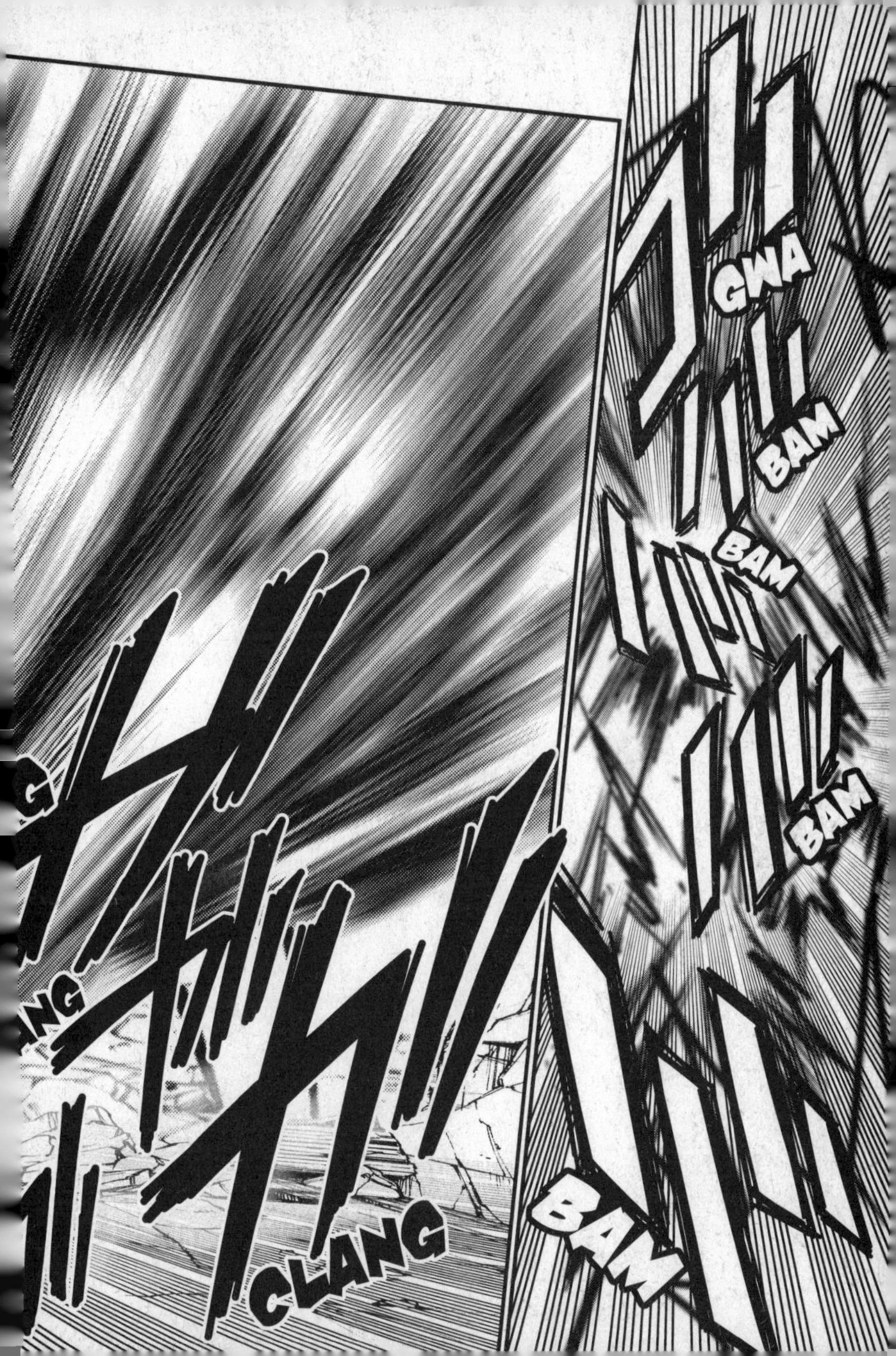
GWA
BAM
BAM
BAM
BAM
CLANG

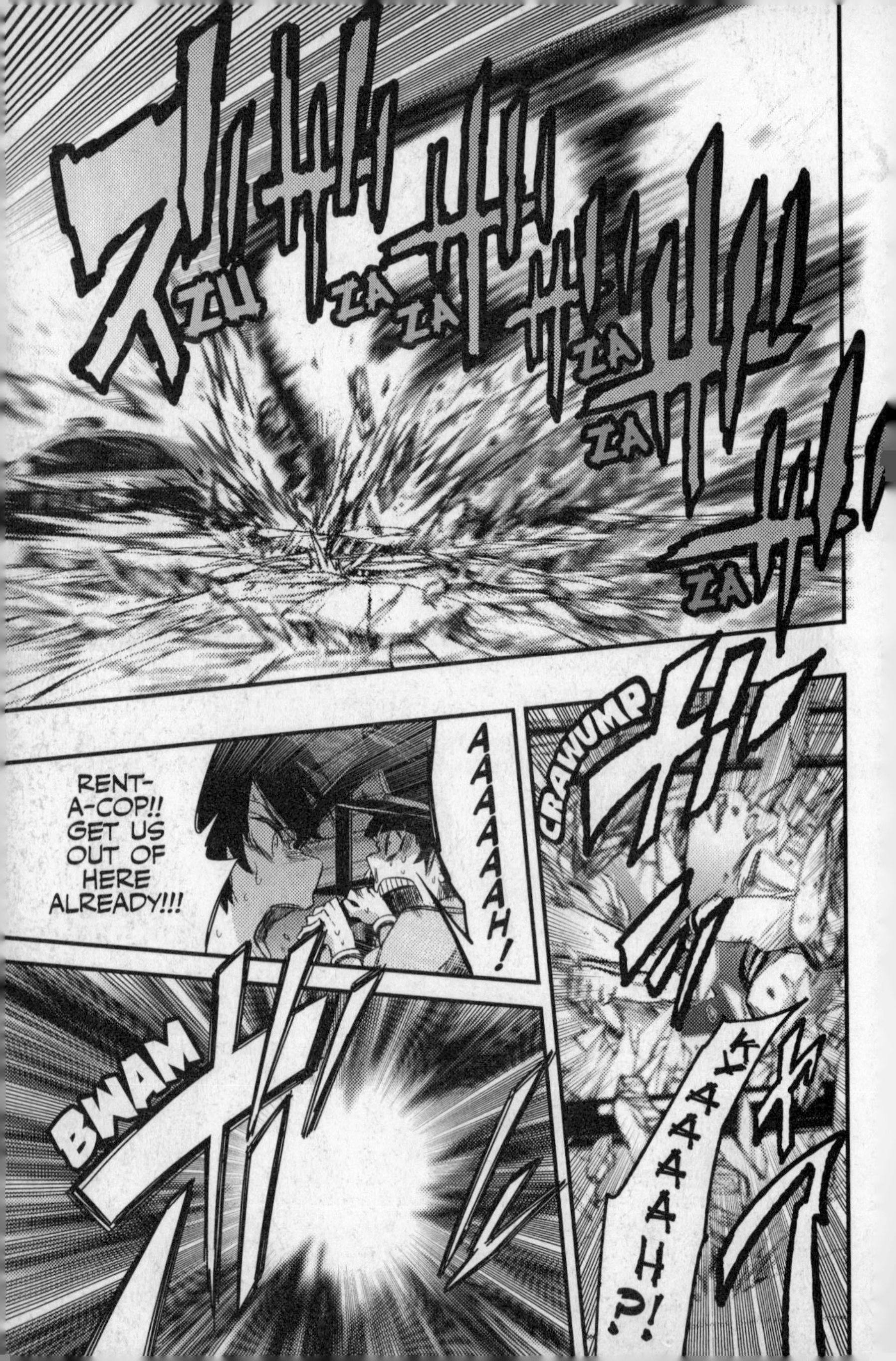
ZU
ZA
ZA
ZA
ZA
ZA
CRAWUMP
KYAAAAAH?!
AAAAAAAH!
RENT-A-COP!! GET US OUT OF HERE ALREADY!!!
BWAM

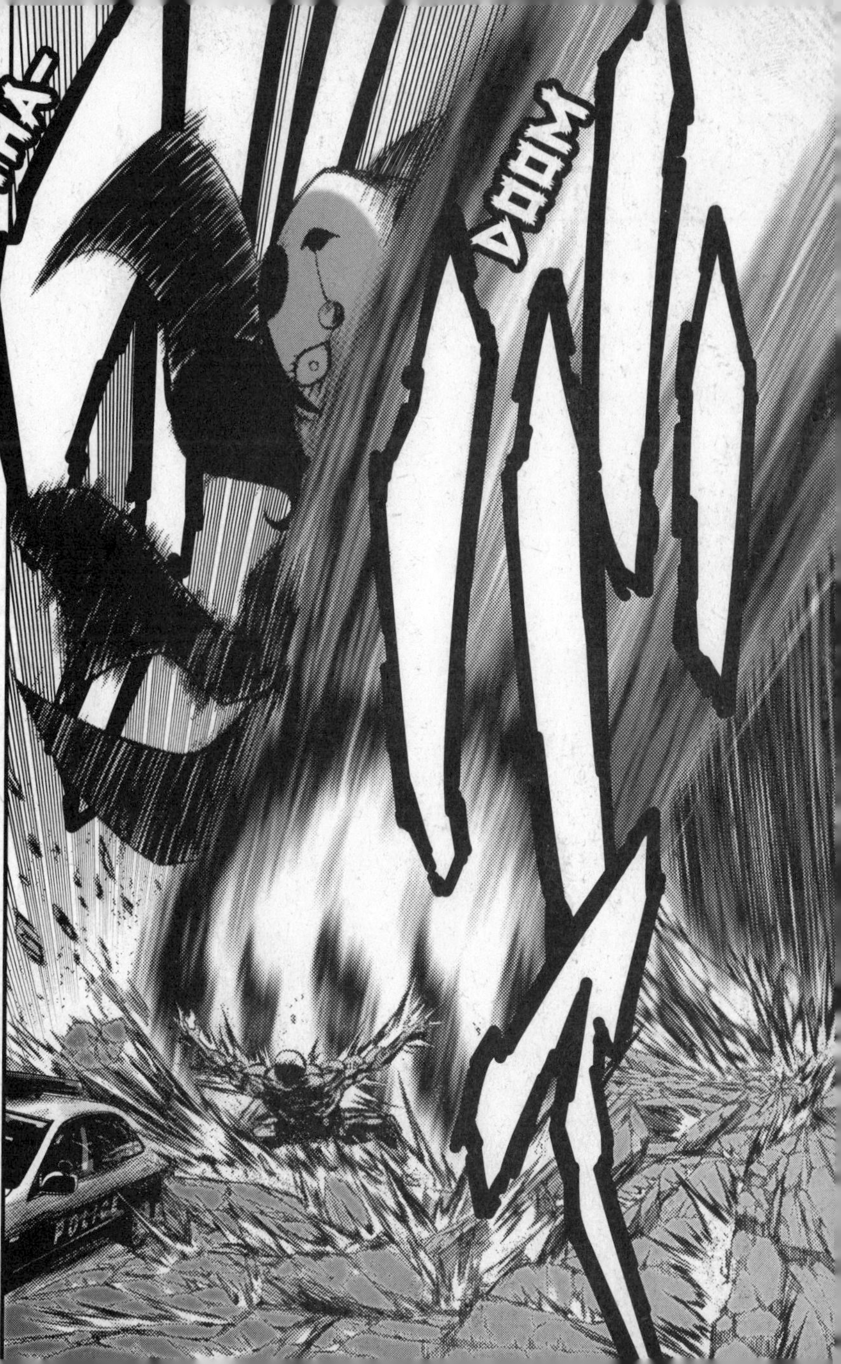
THA-
DOOM

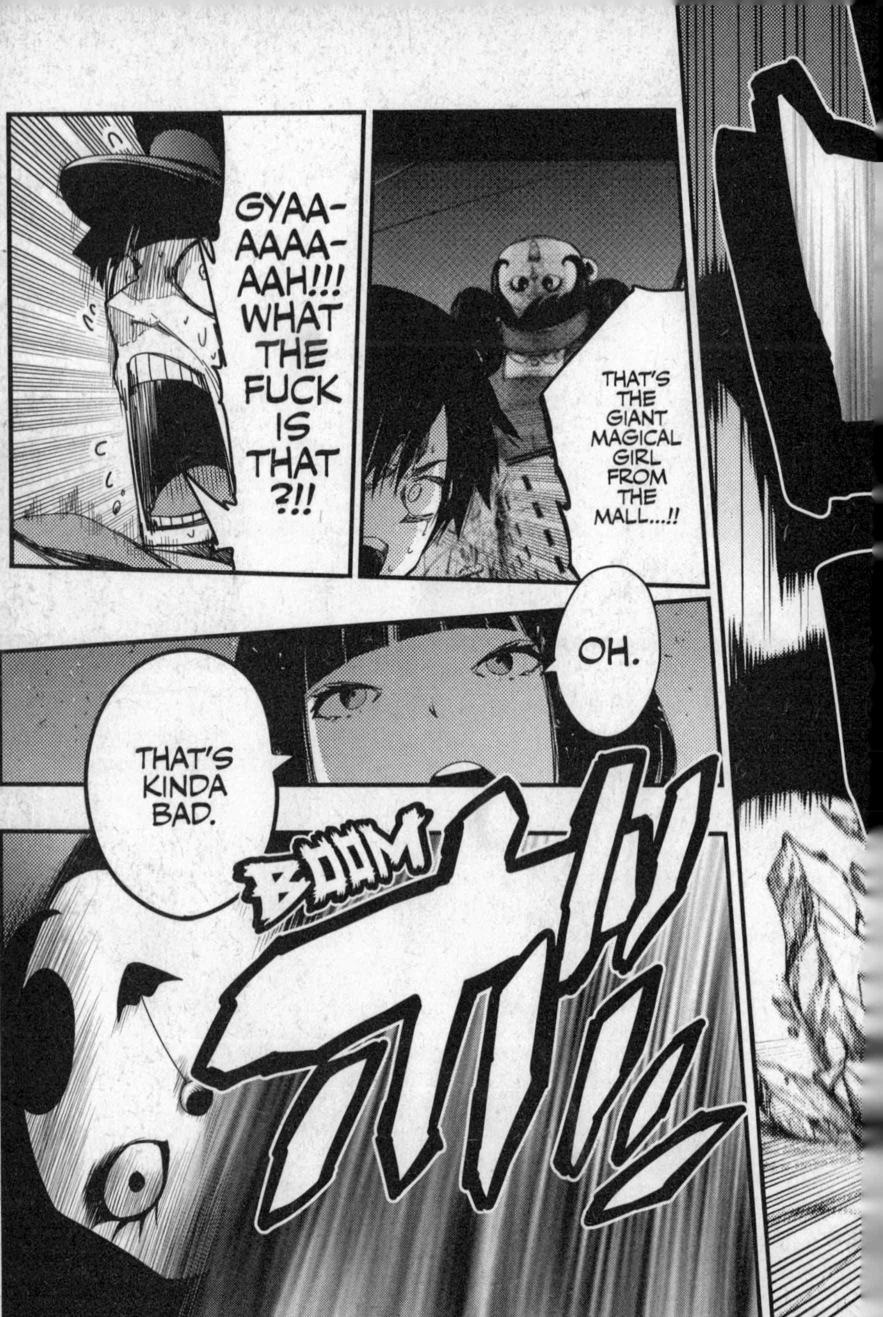
THAT'S THE GIANT MAGICAL GIRL FROM THE MALL...!!
GYAA-AAAA-AAH!!! WHAT THE FUCK IS THAT?!!
OH.
THAT'S KINDA BAD.
BOOM

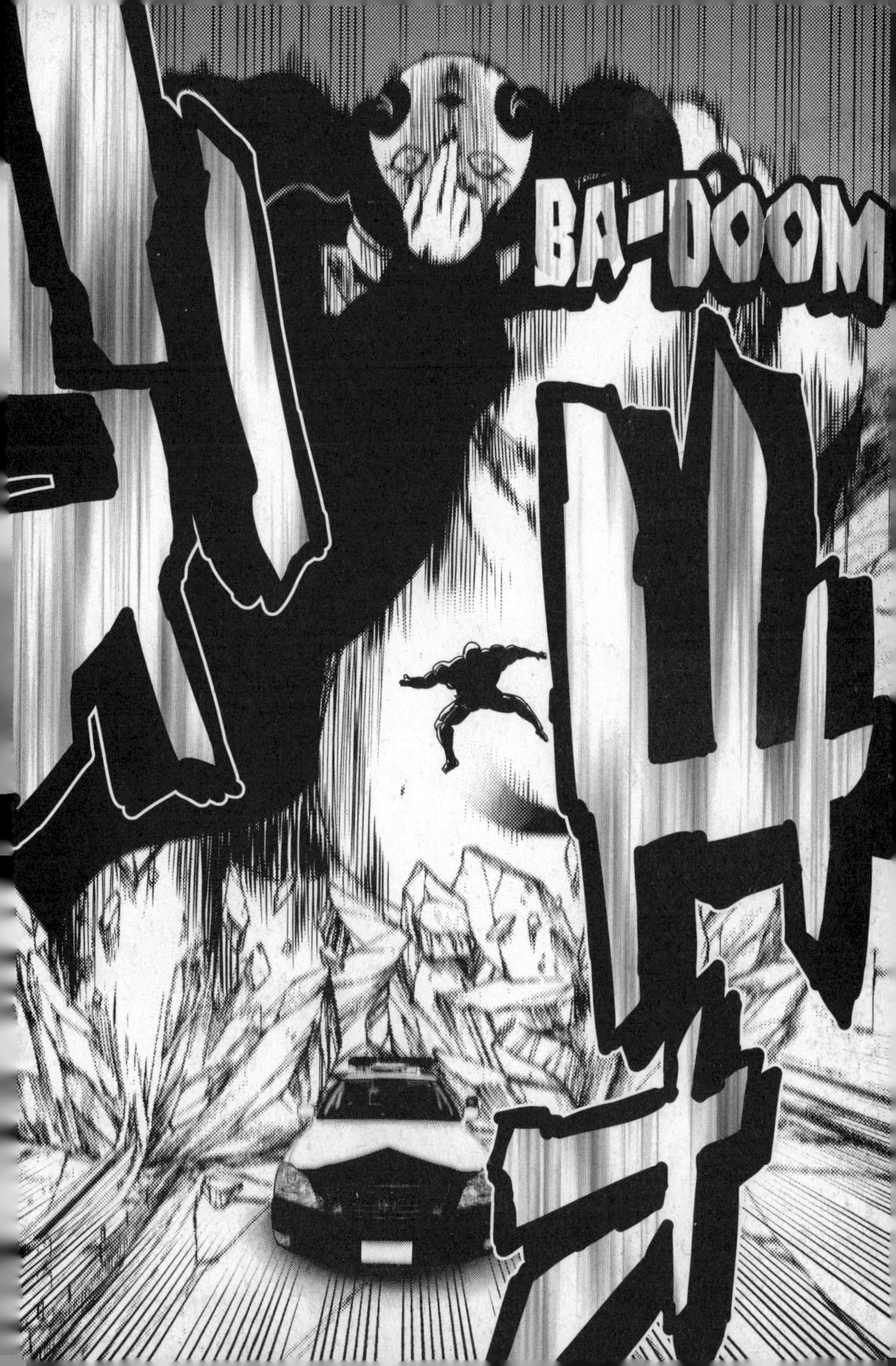
BA-DOOM

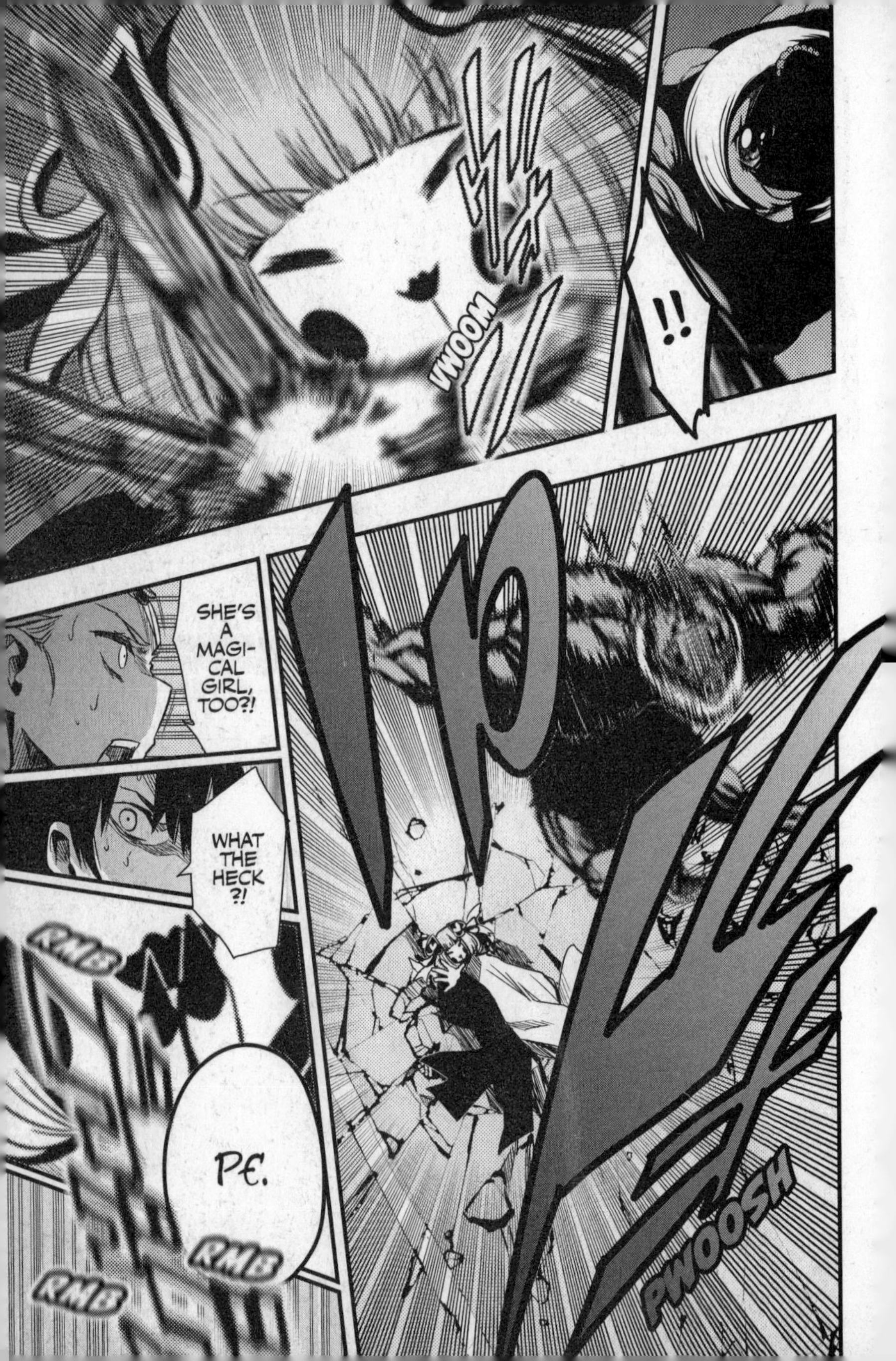
!!
VWOOM
PWOOSH
SHE'S A MAGICAL GIRL, TOO?!
WHAT THE HECK?!
RMB
PE.
RMB
RMB

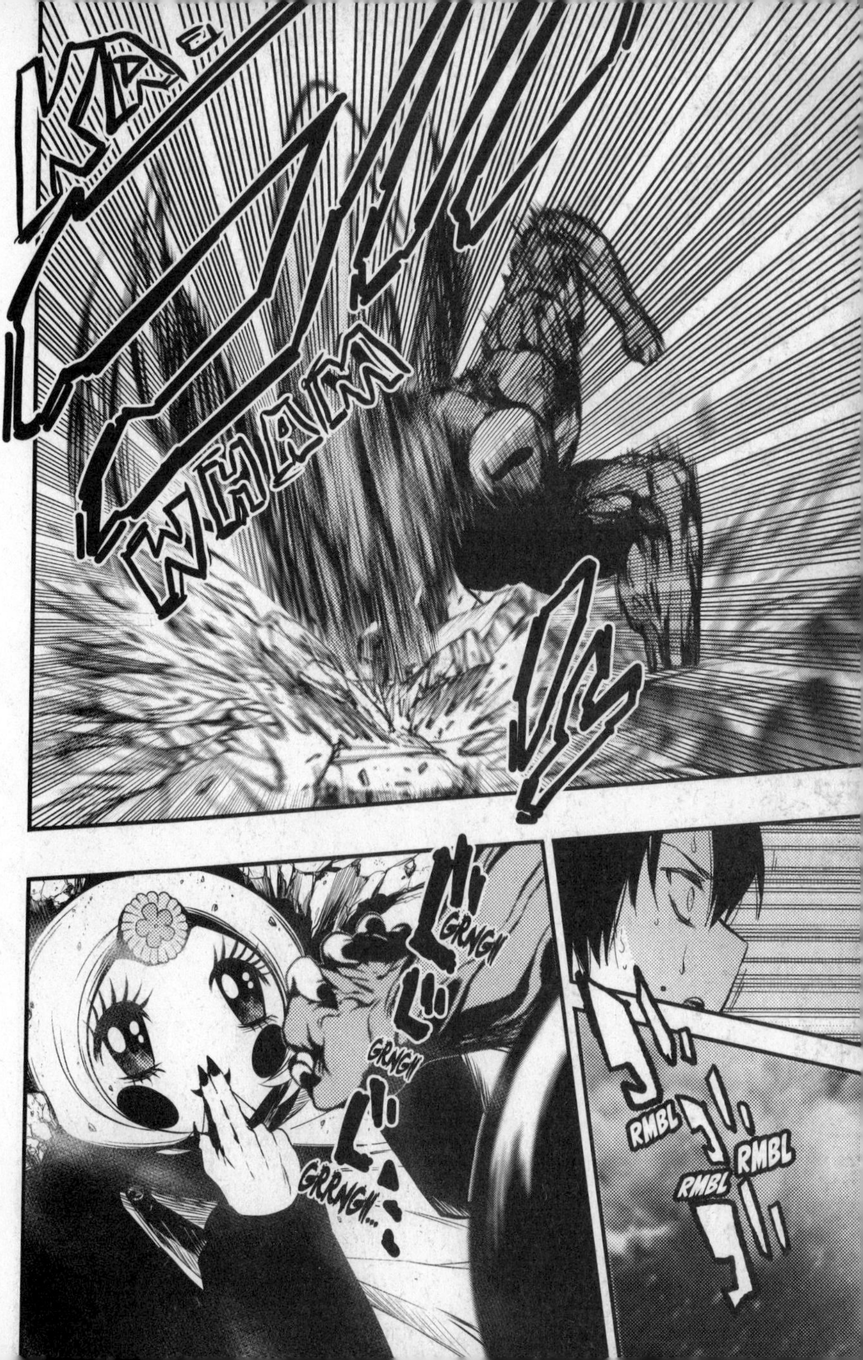
WHAM
RMBL
RMBL
RMBL
GRNGH
GRNGH
GRRNGH...

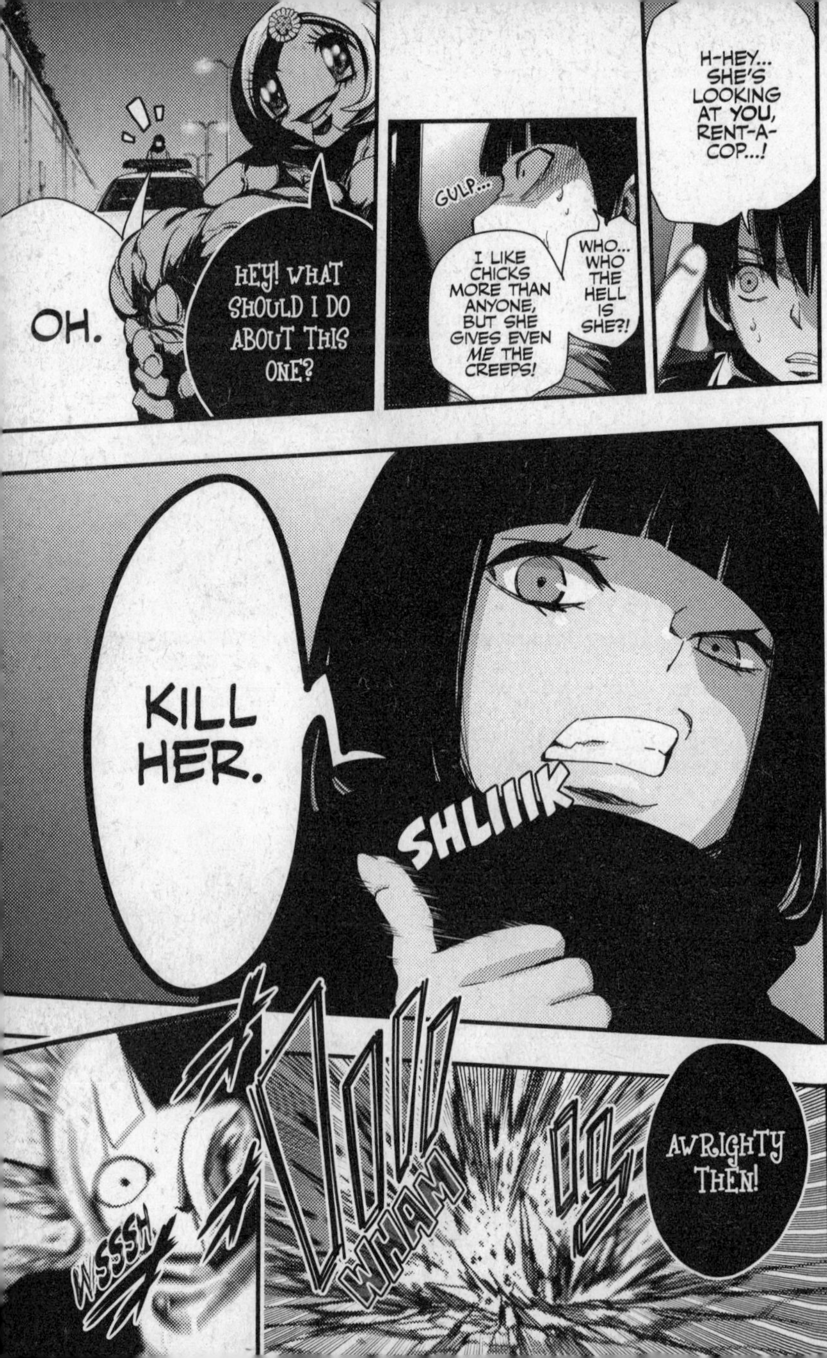
H-HEY... SHE'S LOOKING AT YOU, RENT-A-COP...!
GULP...
WHO... WHO THE HELL IS SHE?!
I LIKE CHICKS MORE THAN ANYONE, BUT SHE GIVES EVEN *ME* THE CREEPS!
HEY! WHAT SHOULD I DO ABOUT THIS ONE?
OH.
KILL HER.
SHLIIIK
AWRIGHTY THEN!
WHAM
WSSSH

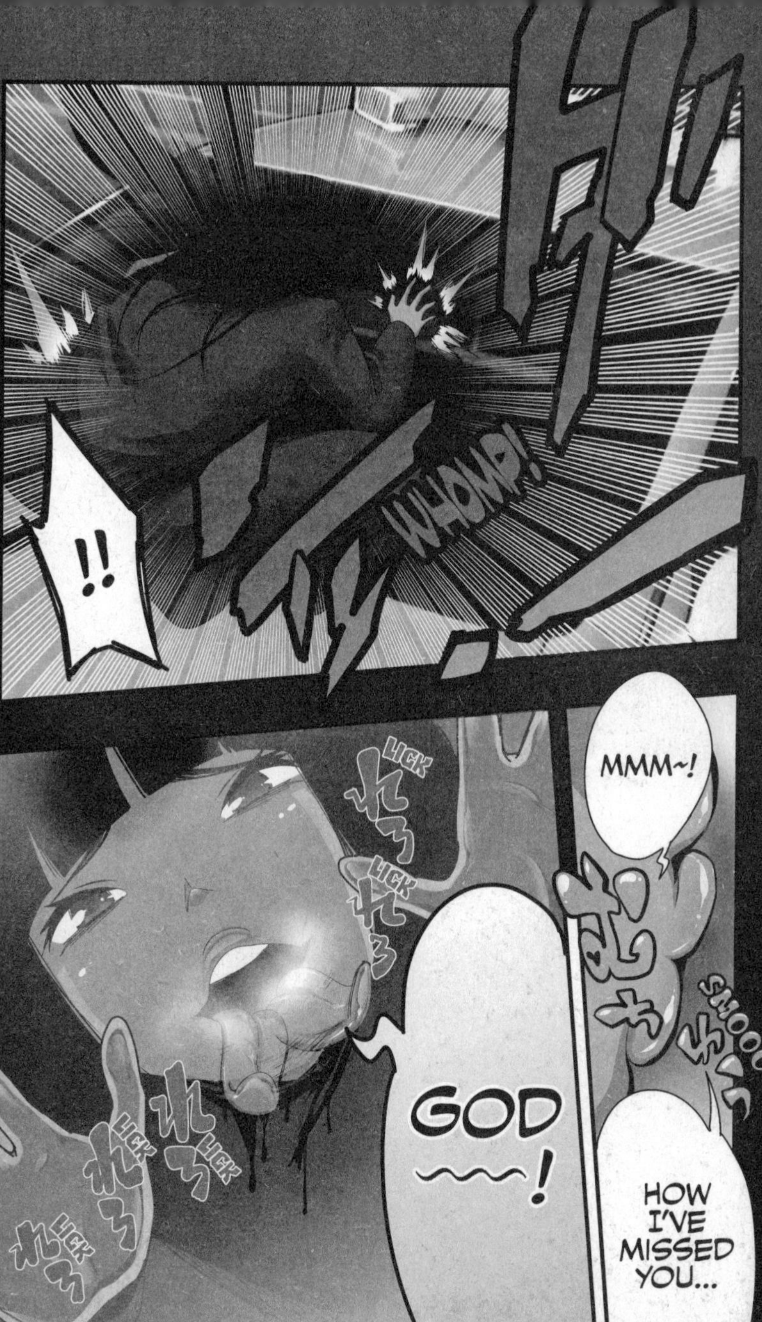

WHOMP!
!!
MMM~!
SMOOOCH
LICK
LICK
HOW I'VE MISSED YOU...
GOD ~~~!
LICK
LICK
LICK

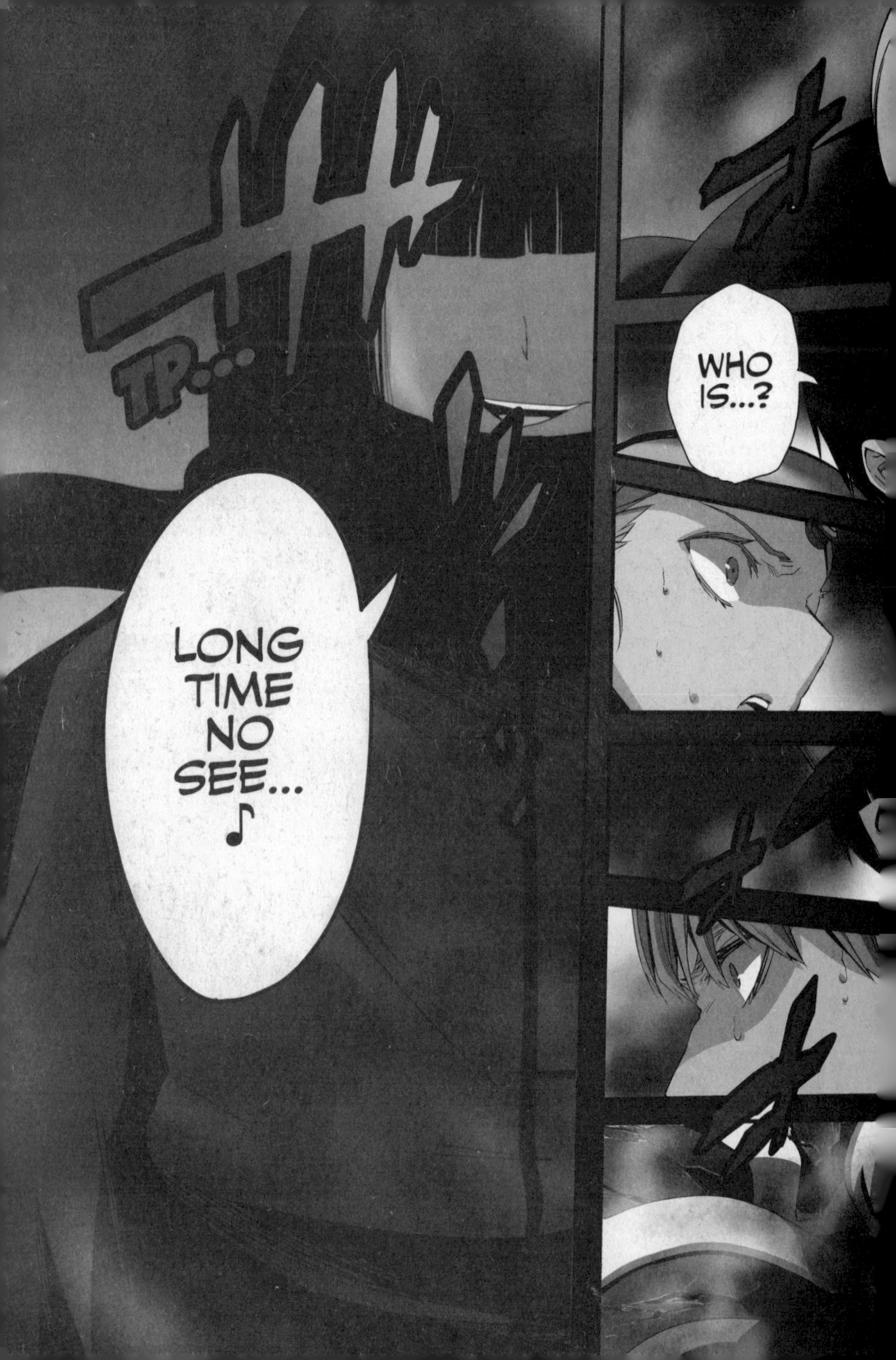
WHO IS...?
TP...
LONG TIME NO SEE... ♪

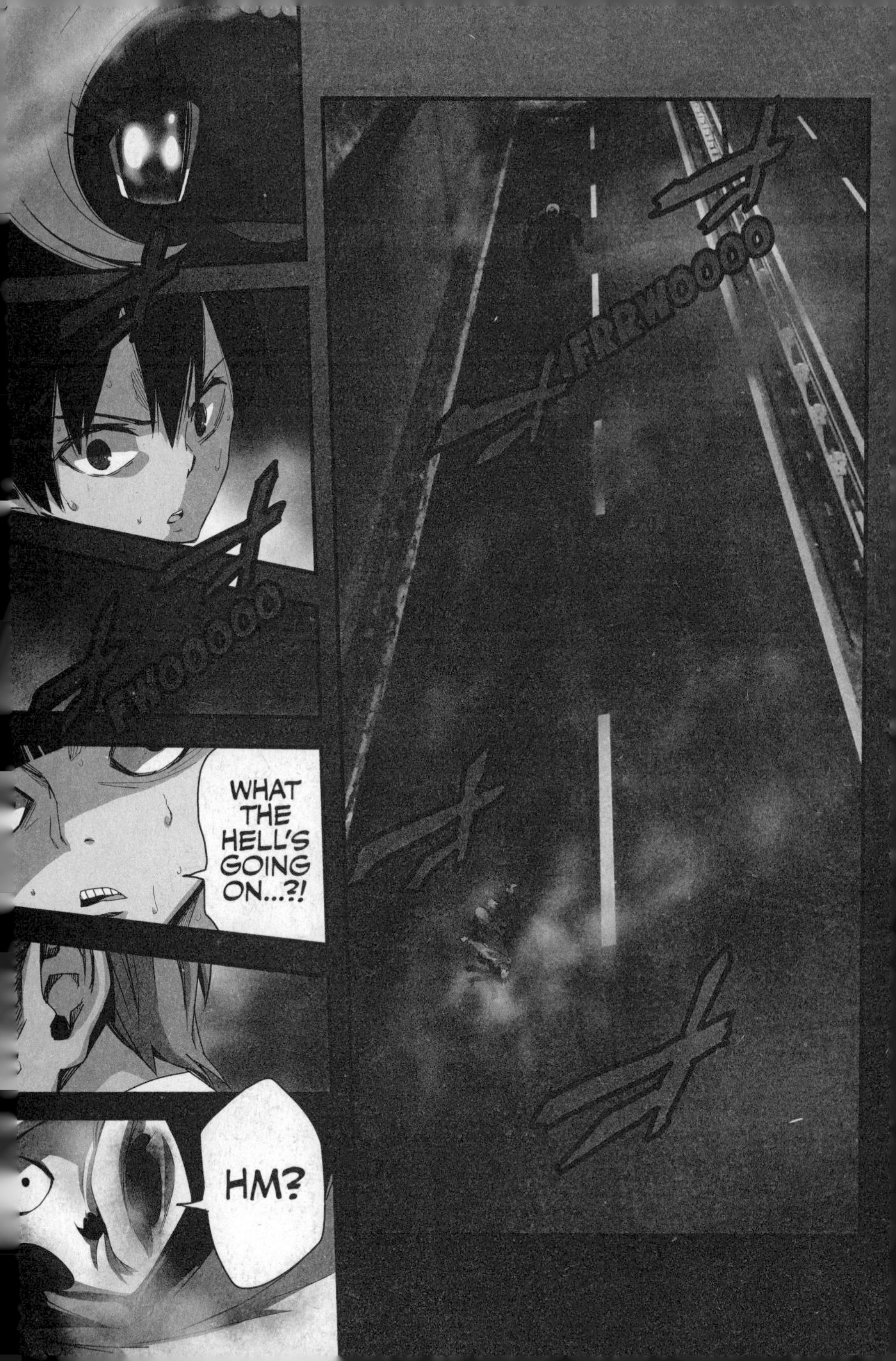
FRRWOOOO
WHAT THE HELL'S GOING ON...?!
HM?

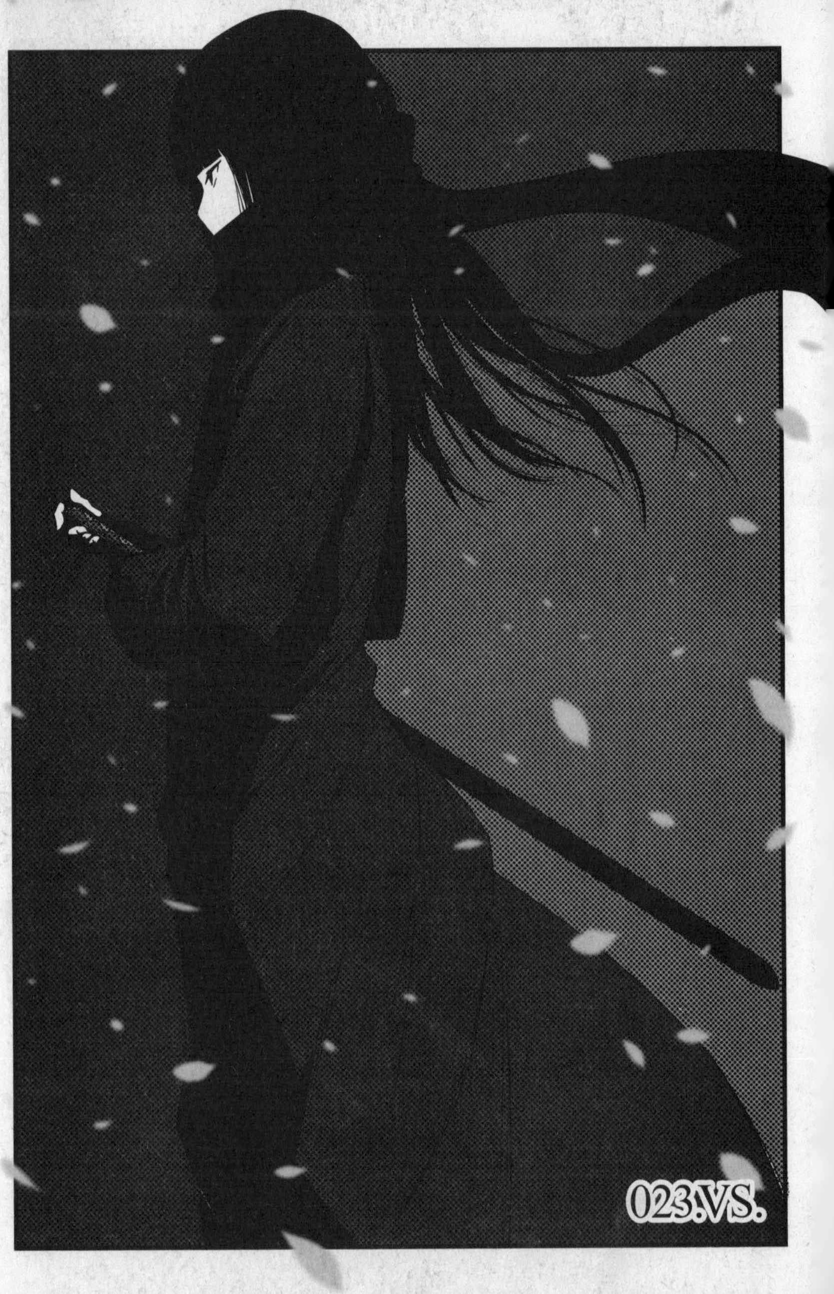
023.VS.

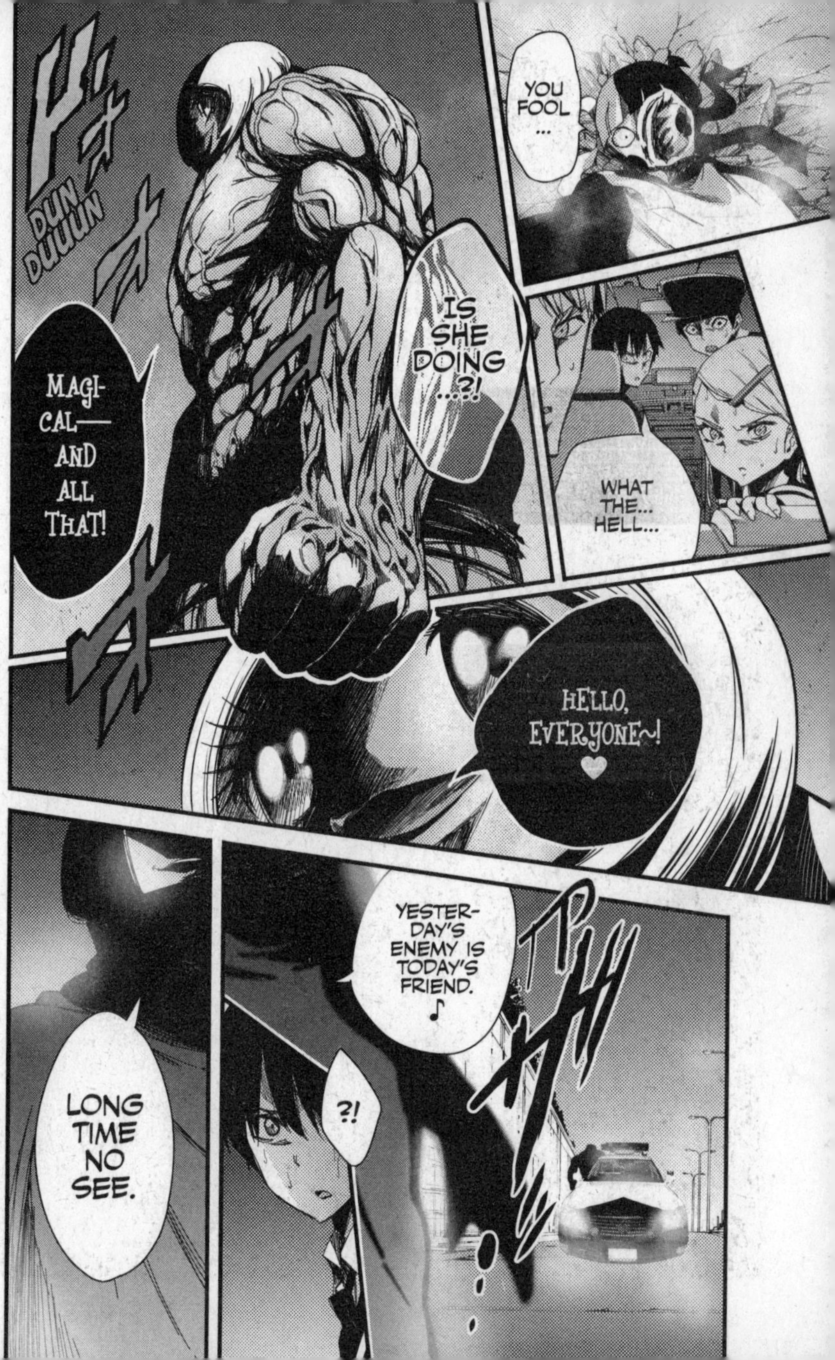
YOU FOOL ...
IS SHE DOING ...?!
WHAT THE... HELL...
DUN DUUUN
MAGI-CAL— AND ALL THAT!
HELLO, EVERYONE~! ♥
YESTER-DAY'S ENEMY IS TODAY'S FRIEND. ♪
?!
LONG TIME NO SEE.

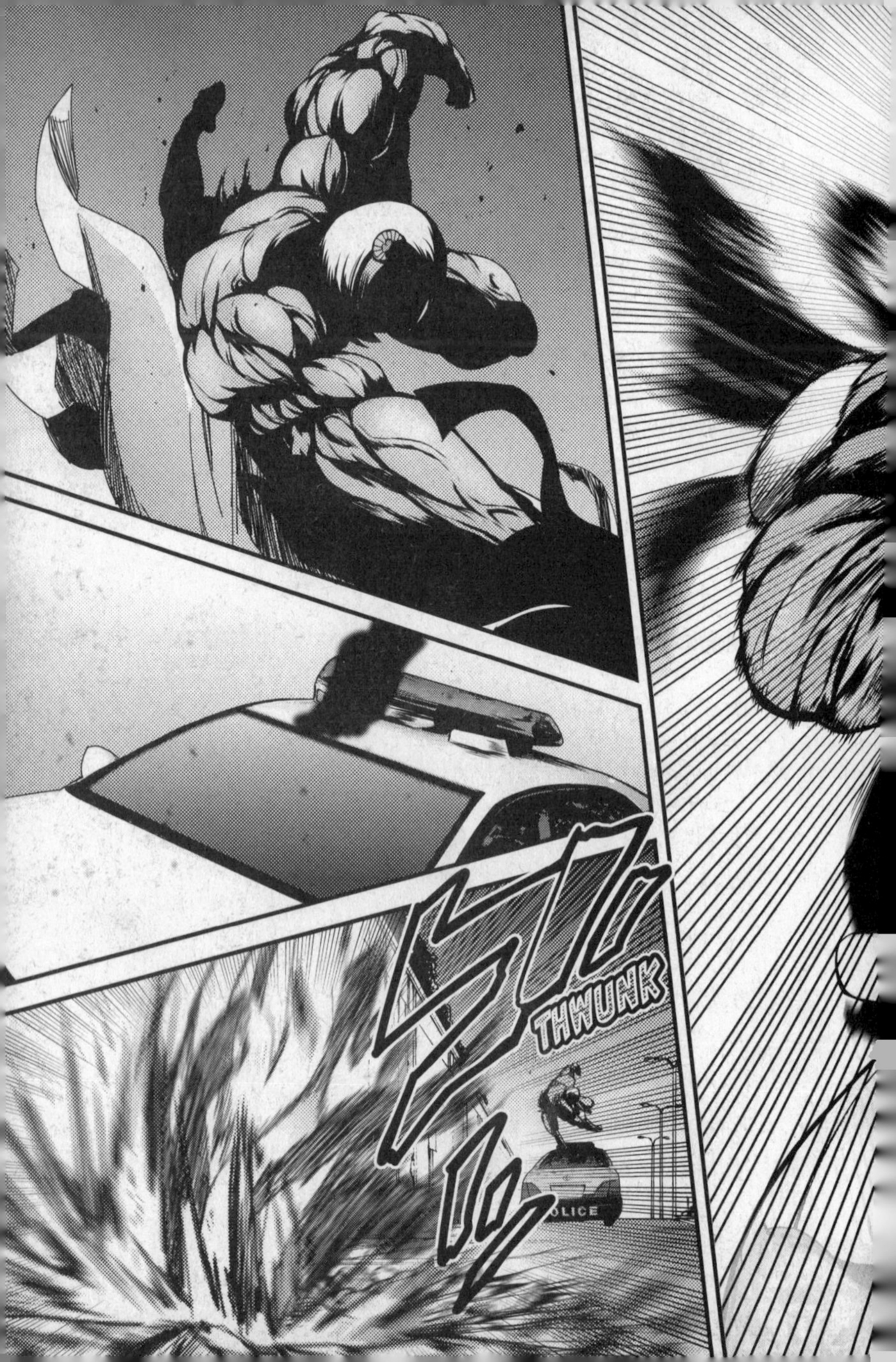
THWUNK
OLICE

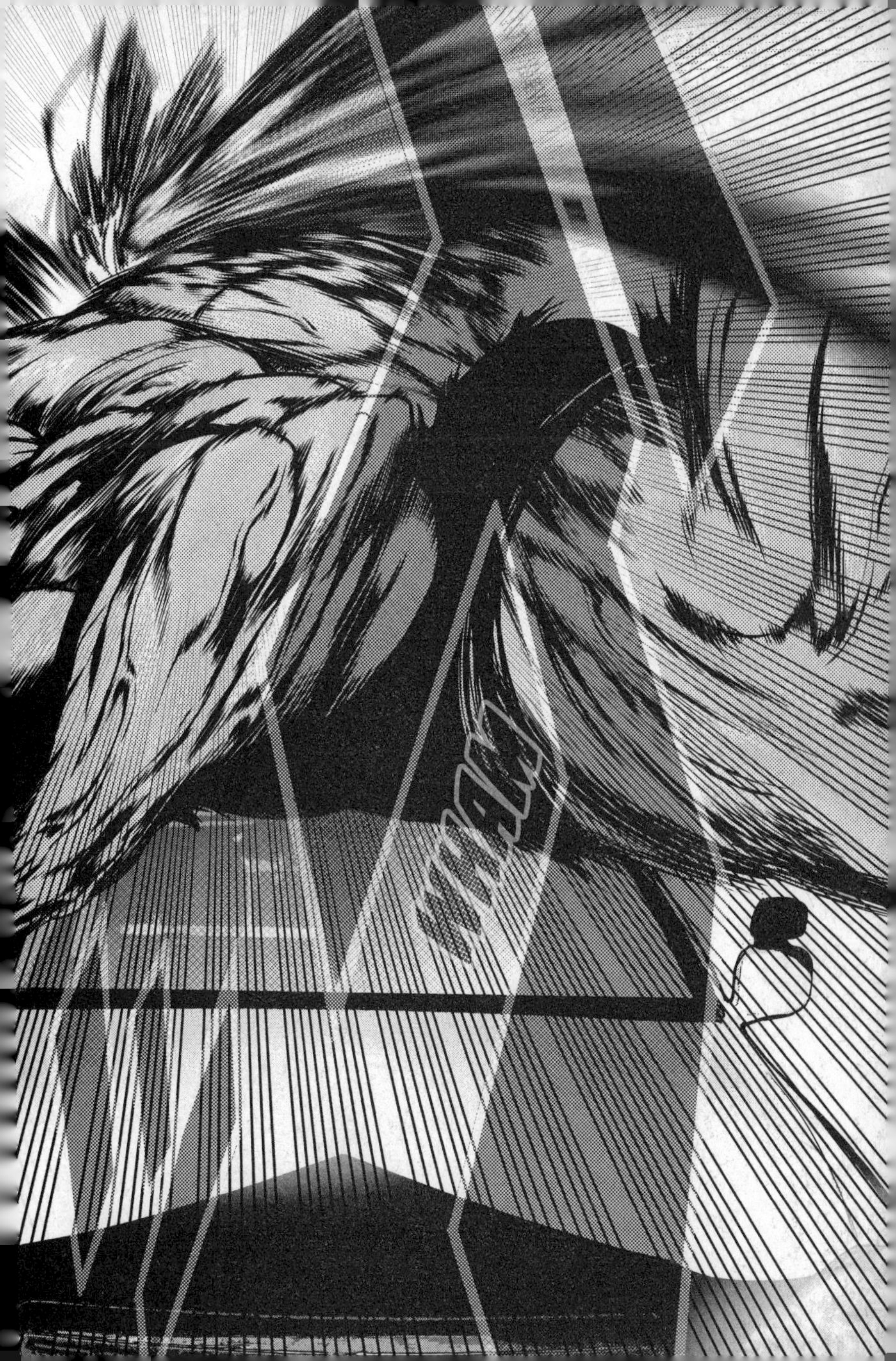

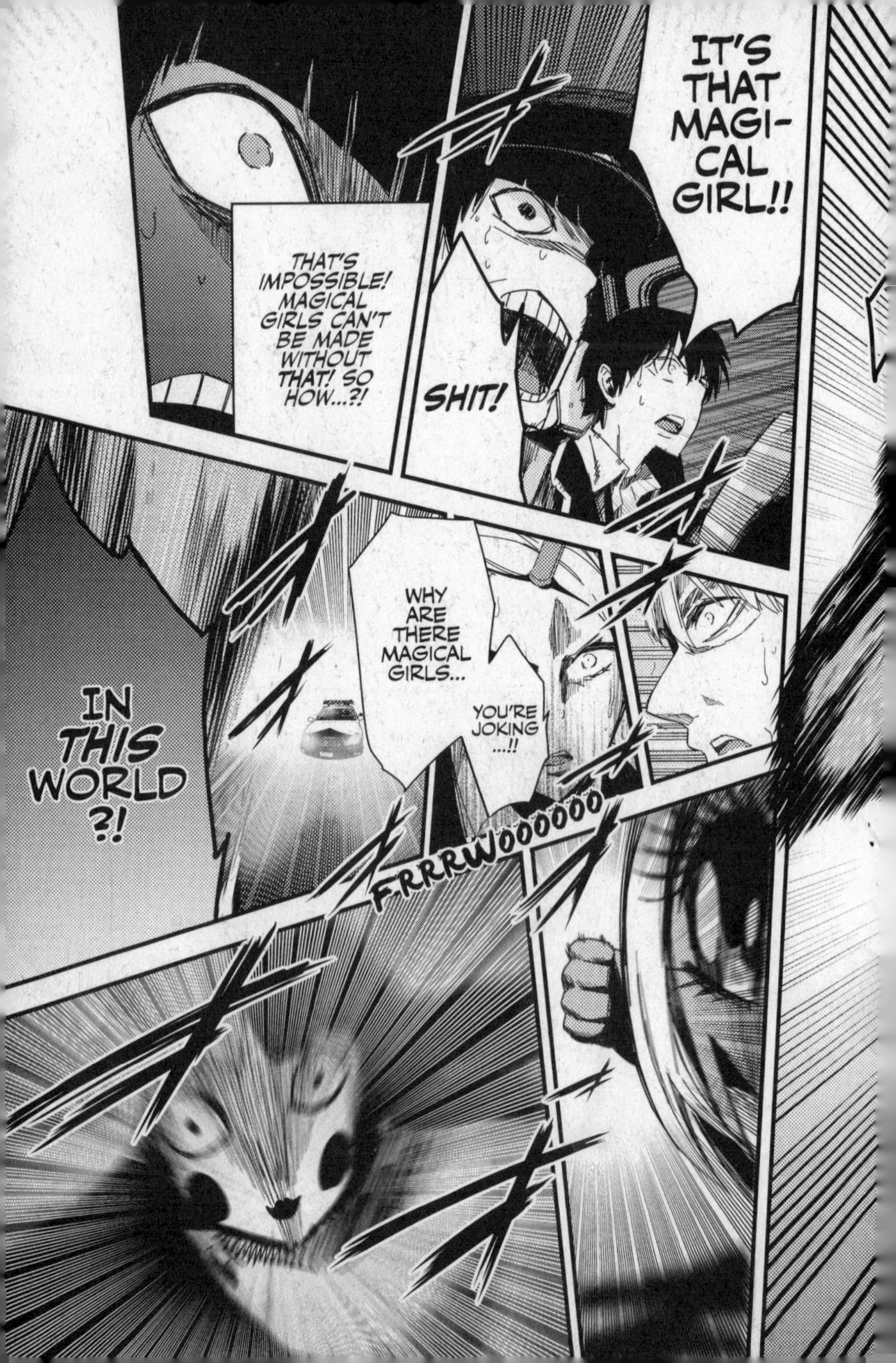
IT'S THAT MAGI-CAL GIRL!!
SHIT!
THAT'S IMPOSSIBLE! MAGICAL GIRLS CAN'T BE MADE WITHOUT THAT! SO HOW...?!
WHY ARE THERE MAGICAL GIRLS...
YOU'RE JOKING ...!!
IN THIS WORLD ?!
FRRRWOOOOOO

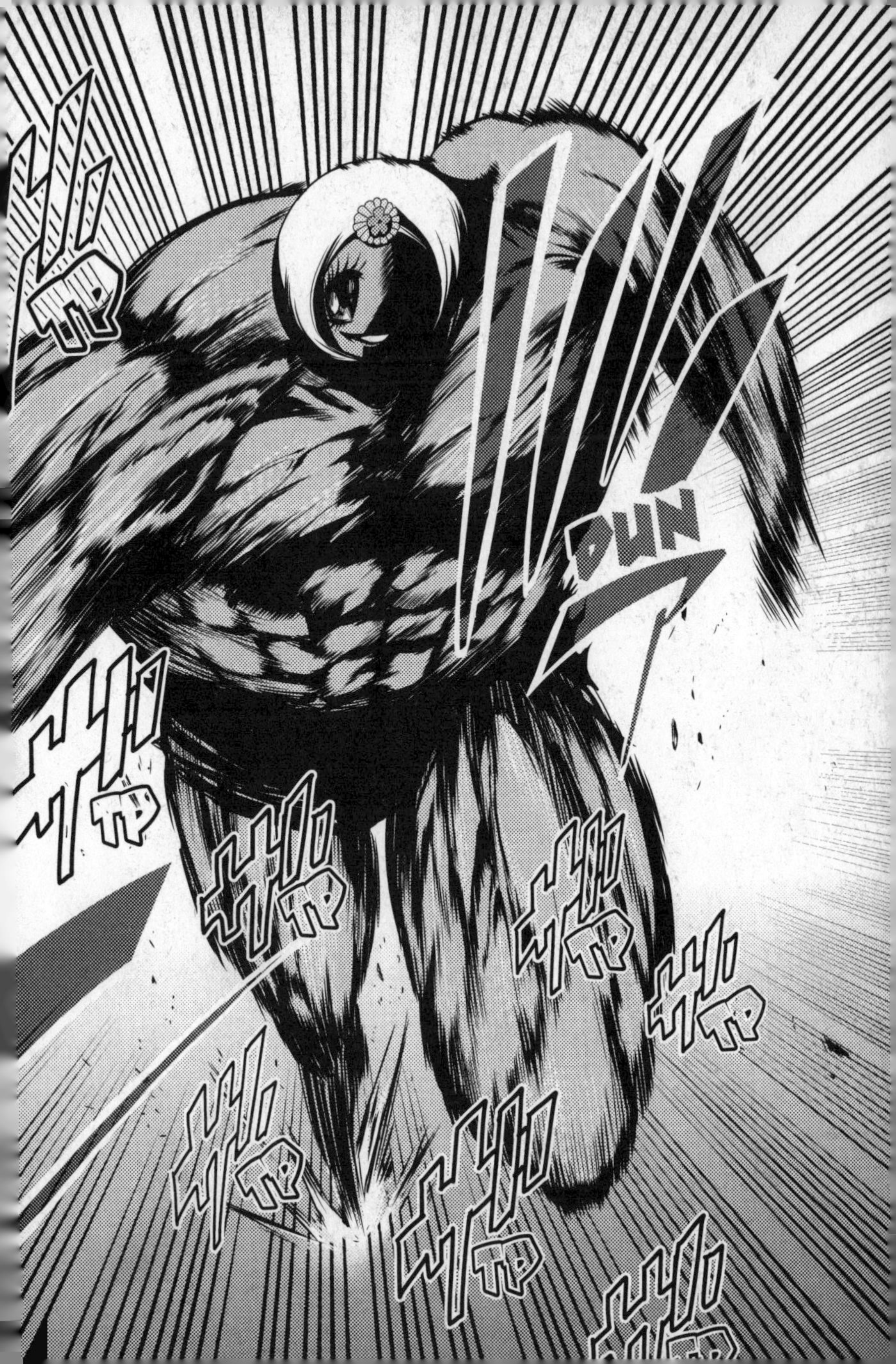

DUN
TP
TP
TP
TP
TP
TP
TP

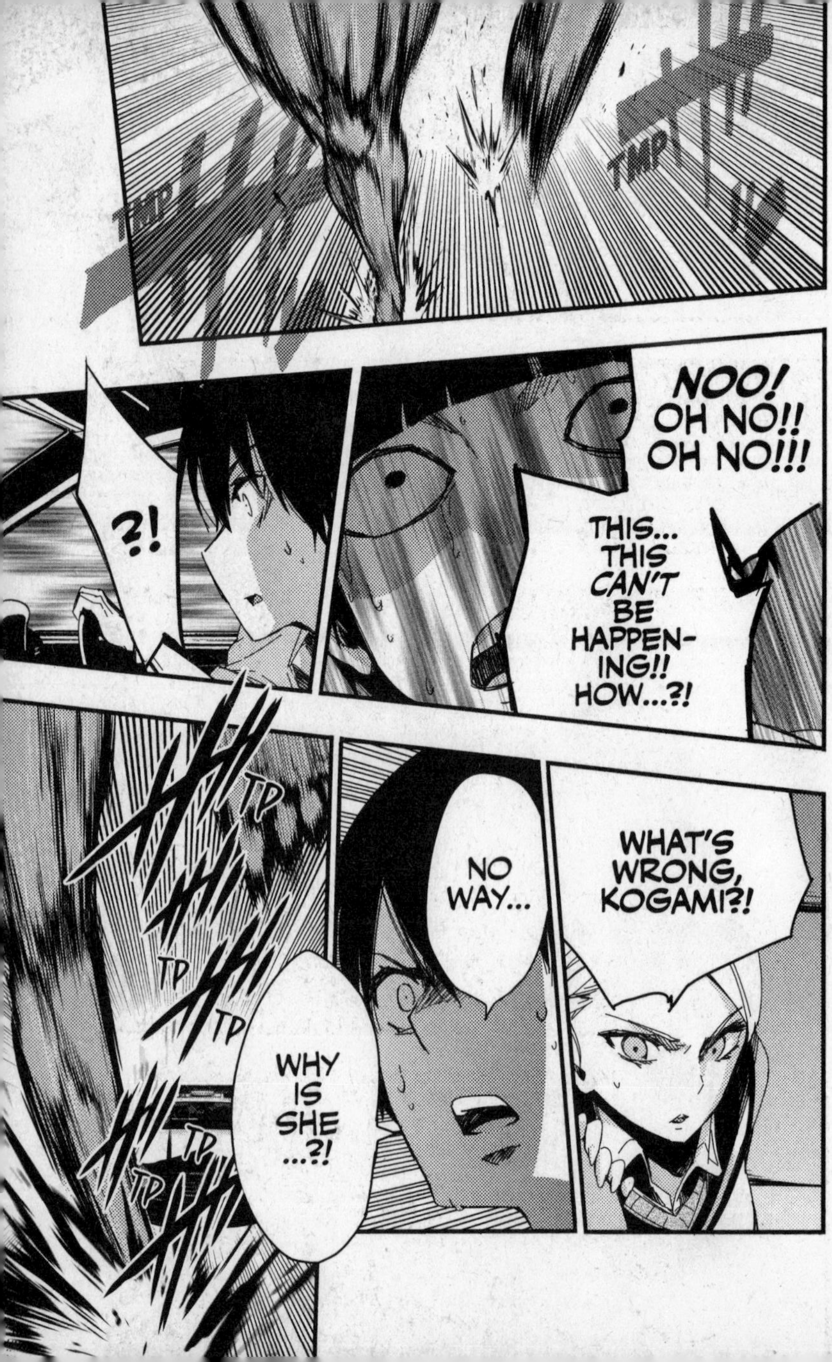
TMP
TMP
NOO! OH NO!! OH NO!!!
THIS... THIS CAN'T BE HAPPENING!! HOW...?!
?!
WHAT'S WRONG, KOGAMI?!
NO WAY...
WHY IS SHE ...?!
TP
TP
TP
TP
TP

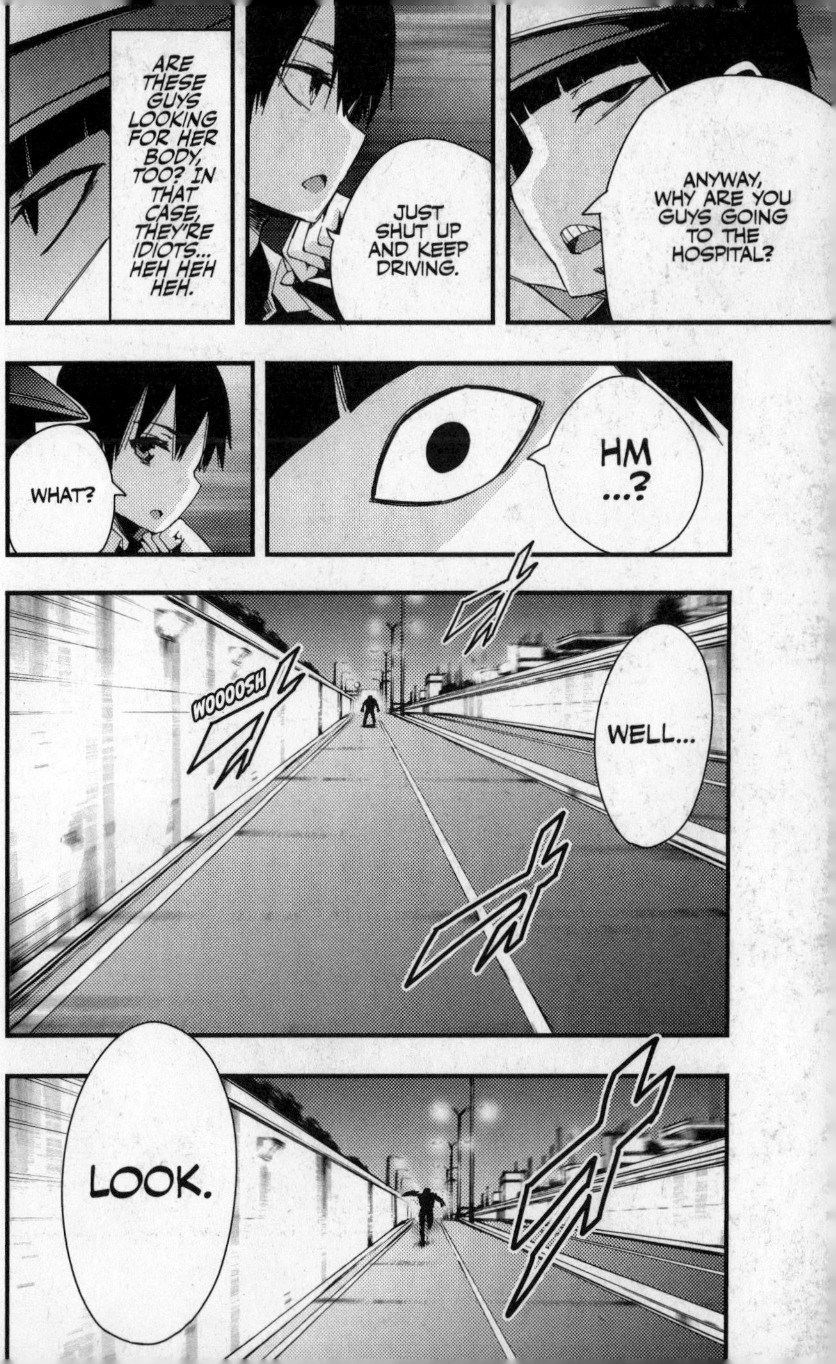
ANYWAY, WHY ARE YOU GUYS GOING TO THE HOSPITAL?
JUST SHUT UP AND KEEP DRIVING.
ARE THESE GUYS LOOKING FOR HER BODY, TOO? IN THAT CASE, THEY'RE IDIOTS... HEH HEH HEH.
HM ...?
WHAT?
WELL...
WOOOOSH
LOOK.

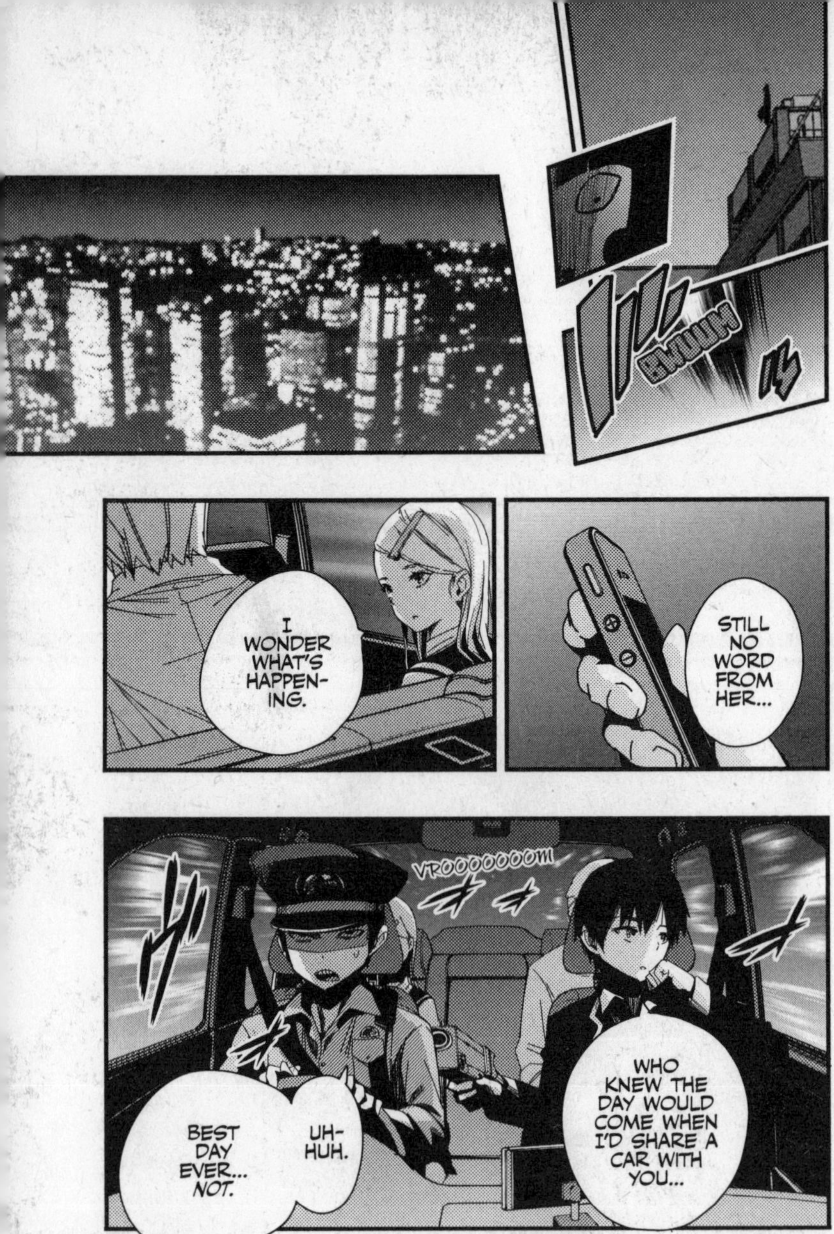
STILL NO WORD FROM HER...
I WONDER WHAT'S HAPPEN-ING.
VROOOOOOOOM
WHO KNEW THE DAY WOULD COME WHEN I'D SHARE A CAR WITH YOU...
UH-HUH.
BEST DAY EVER... *NOT.*

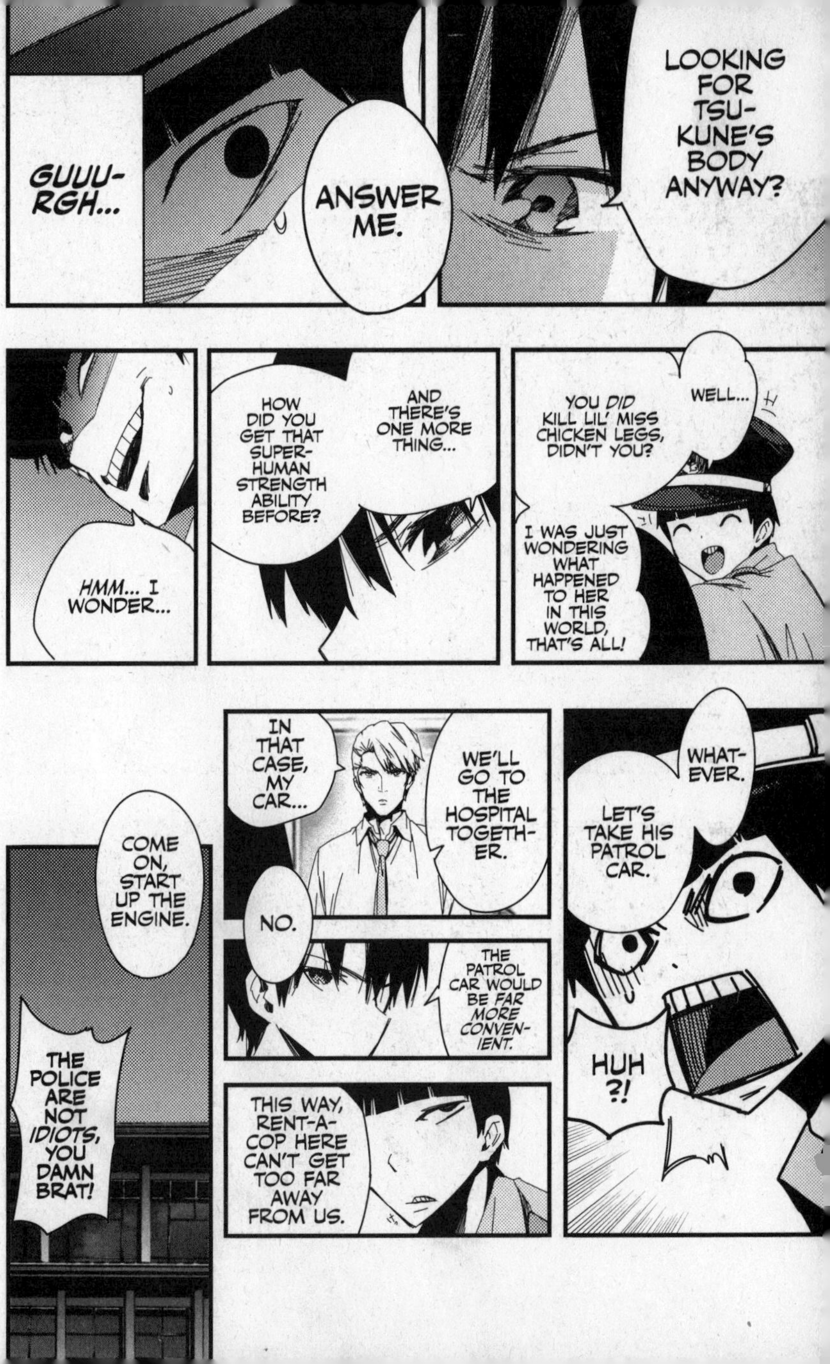
LOOKING FOR TSU-KUNE'S BODY ANYWAY?
ANSWER ME.
GUUU-RGH...
WELL...
YOU *DID* KILL LIL' MISS CHICKEN LEGS, DIDN'T YOU?
I WAS JUST WONDERING WHAT HAPPENED TO HER IN THIS WORLD, THAT'S ALL!
AND THERE'S ONE MORE THING...
HOW DID YOU GET THAT SUPER-HUMAN STRENGTH ABILITY BEFORE?
HMM... I WONDER...
WHAT-EVER.
LET'S TAKE HIS PATROL CAR.
HUH ?!
WE'LL GO TO THE HOSPITAL TOGETH-ER.
IN THAT CASE, MY CAR...
NO.
THE PATROL CAR WOULD BE *FAR MORE CONVEN-IENT.*
THIS WAY, RENT-A-COP HERE CAN'T GET TOO FAR AWAY FROM US.
COME ON, START UP THE ENGINE.
THE POLICE ARE NOT *IDIOTS,* YOU DAMN BRAT!

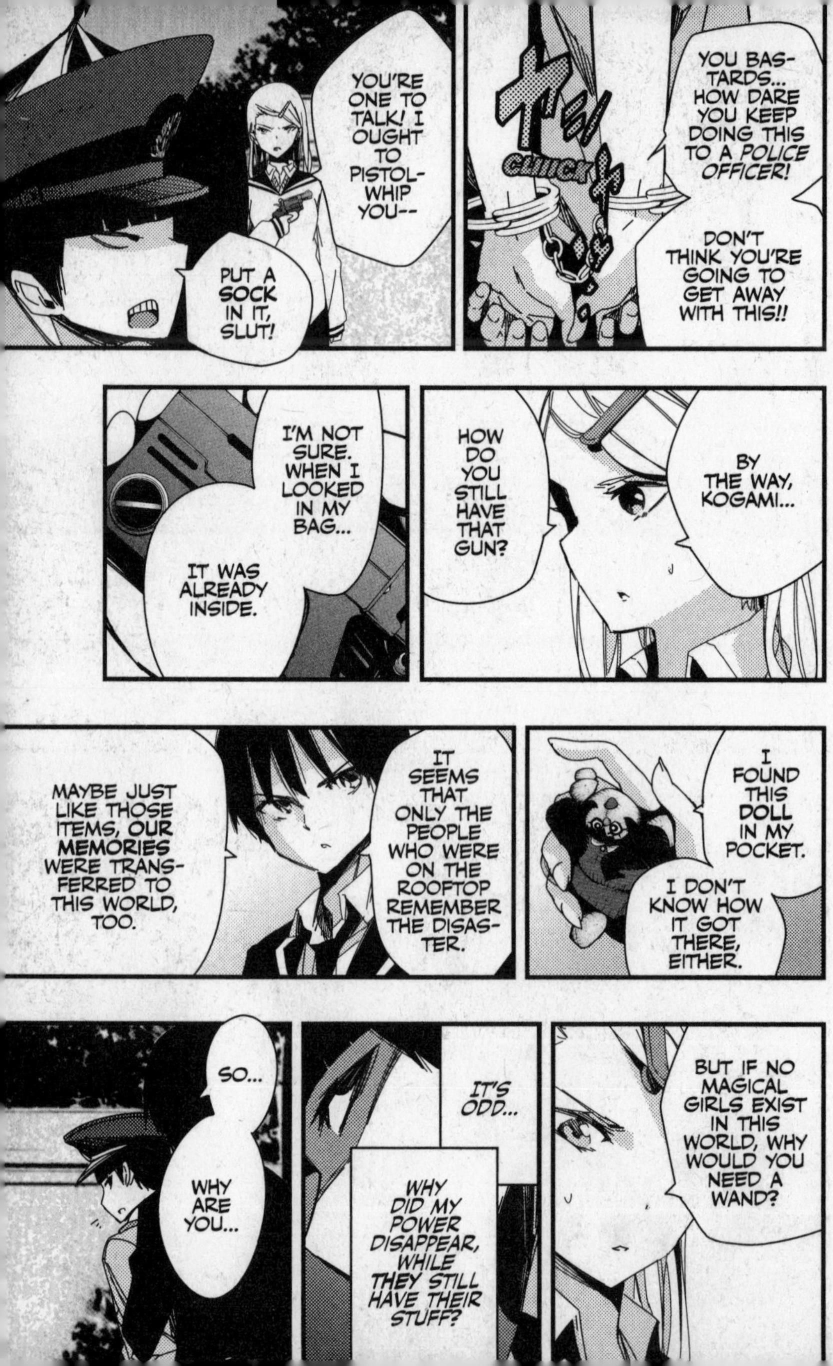

YOU BASTARDS... HOW DARE YOU KEEP DOING THIS TO A *POLICE OFFICER!*
CLICK
DON'T THINK YOU'RE GOING TO GET AWAY WITH THIS!!
YOU'RE ONE TO TALK! I OUGHT TO PISTOL-WHIP YOU--
PUT A SOCK IN IT, SLUT!
BY THE WAY, KOGAMI...
HOW DO YOU STILL HAVE THAT GUN?
I'M NOT SURE. WHEN I LOOKED IN MY BAG...
IT WAS ALREADY INSIDE.
I FOUND THIS **DOLL** IN MY POCKET.
I DON'T KNOW HOW IT GOT THERE, EITHER.
IT SEEMS THAT ONLY THE PEOPLE WHO WERE ON THE ROOFTOP REMEMBER THE DISASTER.
MAYBE JUST LIKE THOSE ITEMS, OUR **MEMORIES** WERE TRANSFERRED TO THIS WORLD, TOO.
BUT IF NO MAGICAL GIRLS EXIST IN THIS WORLD, WHY WOULD YOU NEED A WAND?
IT'S ODD...
*WHY DID MY POWER DISAPPEAR, WHILE **THEY** STILL HAVE THEIR STUFF?*
SO...
WHY ARE YOU...

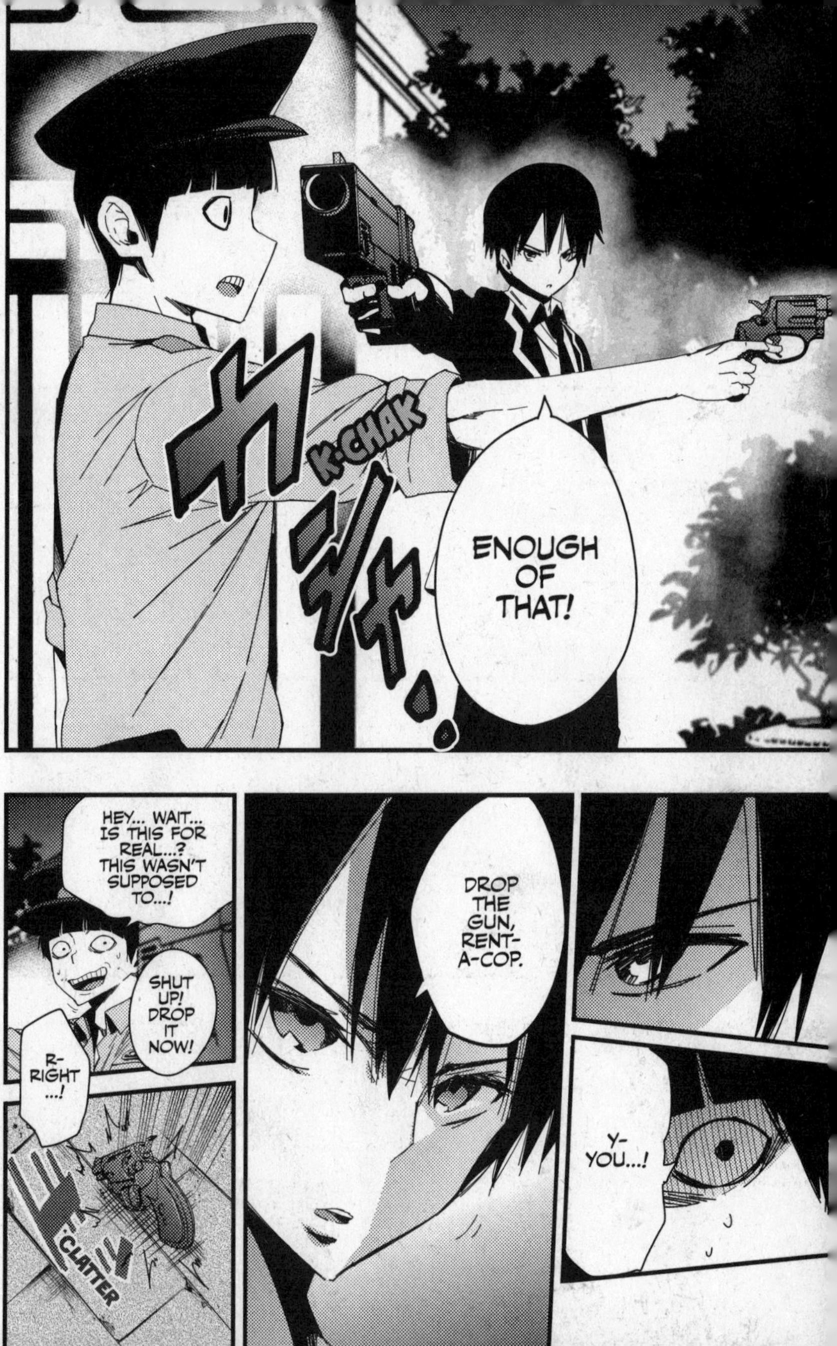
K-CHAK
ENOUGH OF THAT!
Y-YOU...!
DROP THE GUN, RENT-A-COP.
HEY... WAIT... IS THIS FOR REAL...? THIS WASN'T SUPPOSED TO...!
SHUT UP! DROP IT NOW!
R-RIGHT ...!
CLATTER

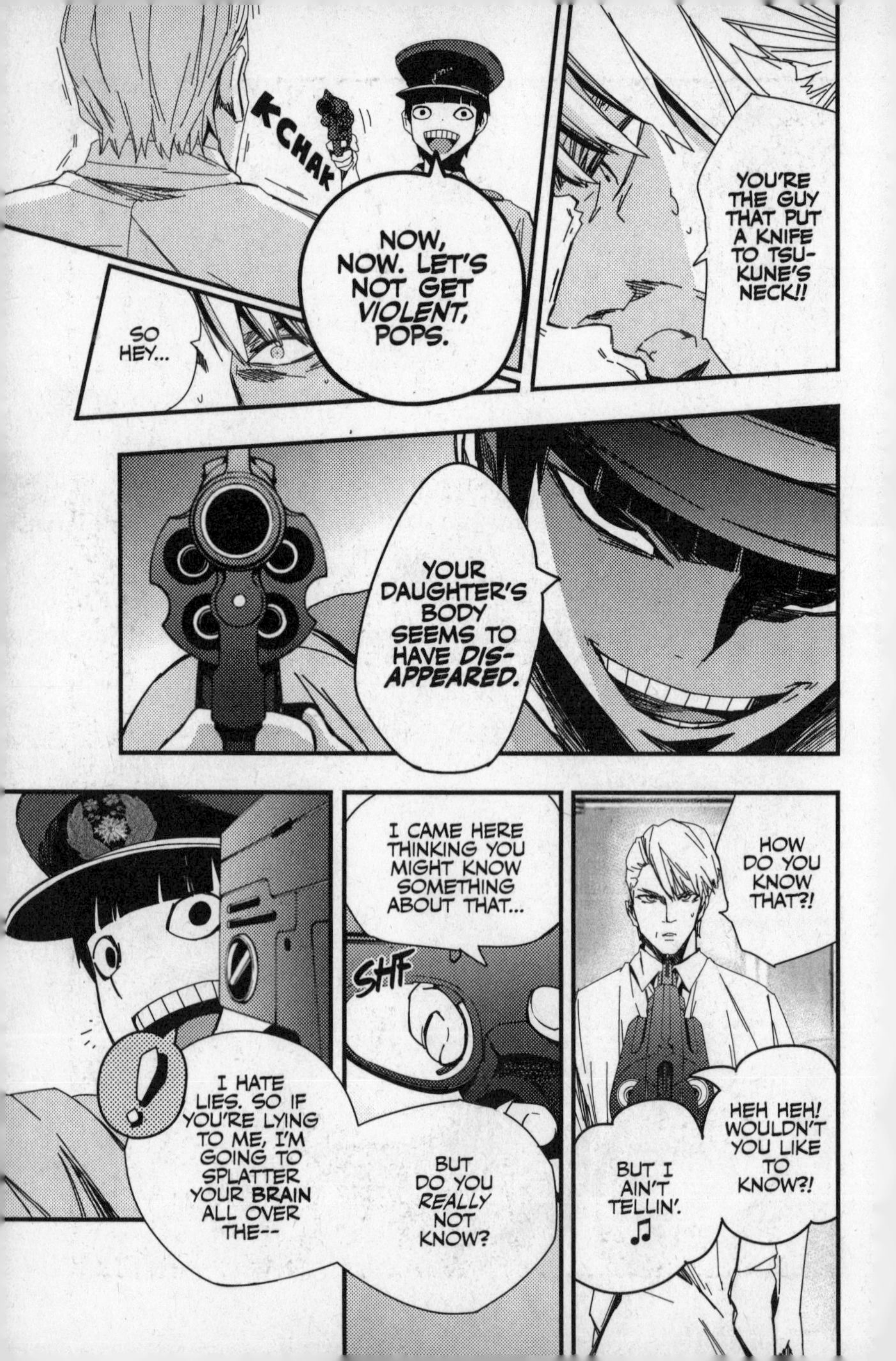
YOU'RE THE GUY THAT PUT A KNIFE TO TSU-KUNE'S NECK!!
KCHAK
NOW, NOW. LET'S NOT GET *VIOLENT*, POPS.
SO HEY...
YOUR DAUGHTER'S BODY SEEMS TO HAVE *DIS-APPEARED.*
HOW DO YOU KNOW THAT?!
HEH HEH! WOULDN'T YOU LIKE TO KNOW?!
BUT I AIN'T TELLIN'. ♫
I CAME HERE THINKING YOU MIGHT KNOW SOMETHING ABOUT THAT...
SHF
BUT DO YOU *REALLY* NOT KNOW?
!
I HATE LIES. SO IF YOU'RE LYING TO ME, I'M GOING TO SPLATTER YOUR **BRAIN** ALL OVER THE--

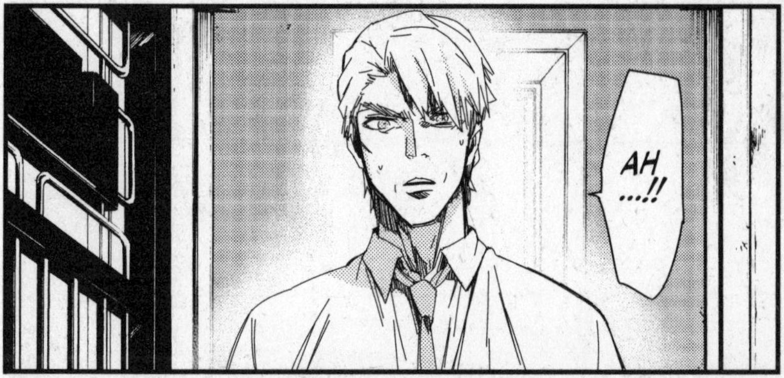
AH ...!!
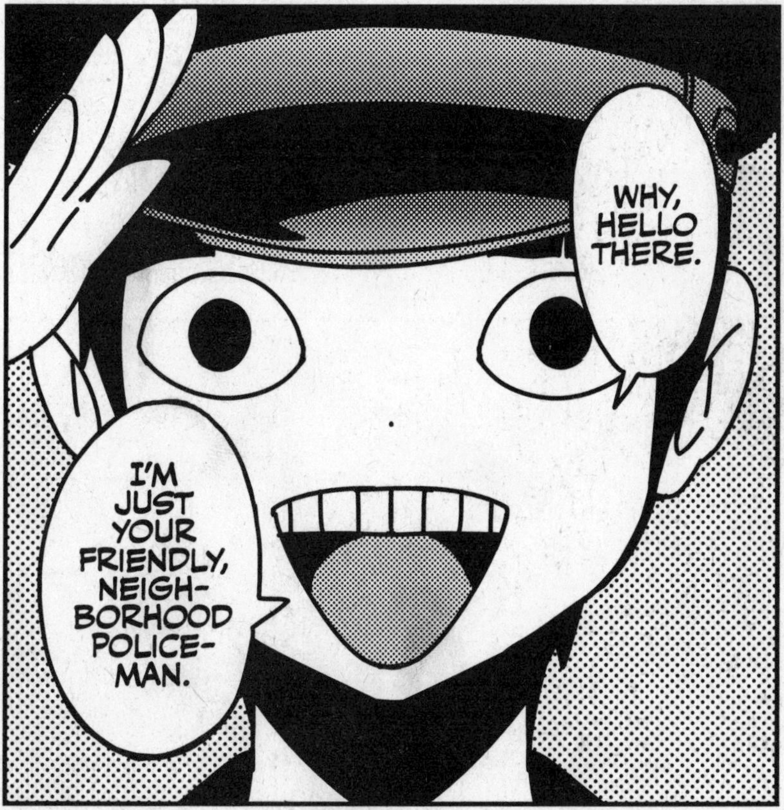
WHY, HELLO THERE.
I'M JUST YOUR FRIENDLY, NEIGH-BORHOOD POLICE-MAN.

IS THAT MRS. FUKUMO-TO...?

DING LO LO LO DOOONG

I'M WITH THE POLICE.

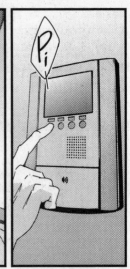

Pi

IT COULDN'T BE...!

A COP?

THE POLICE ...?

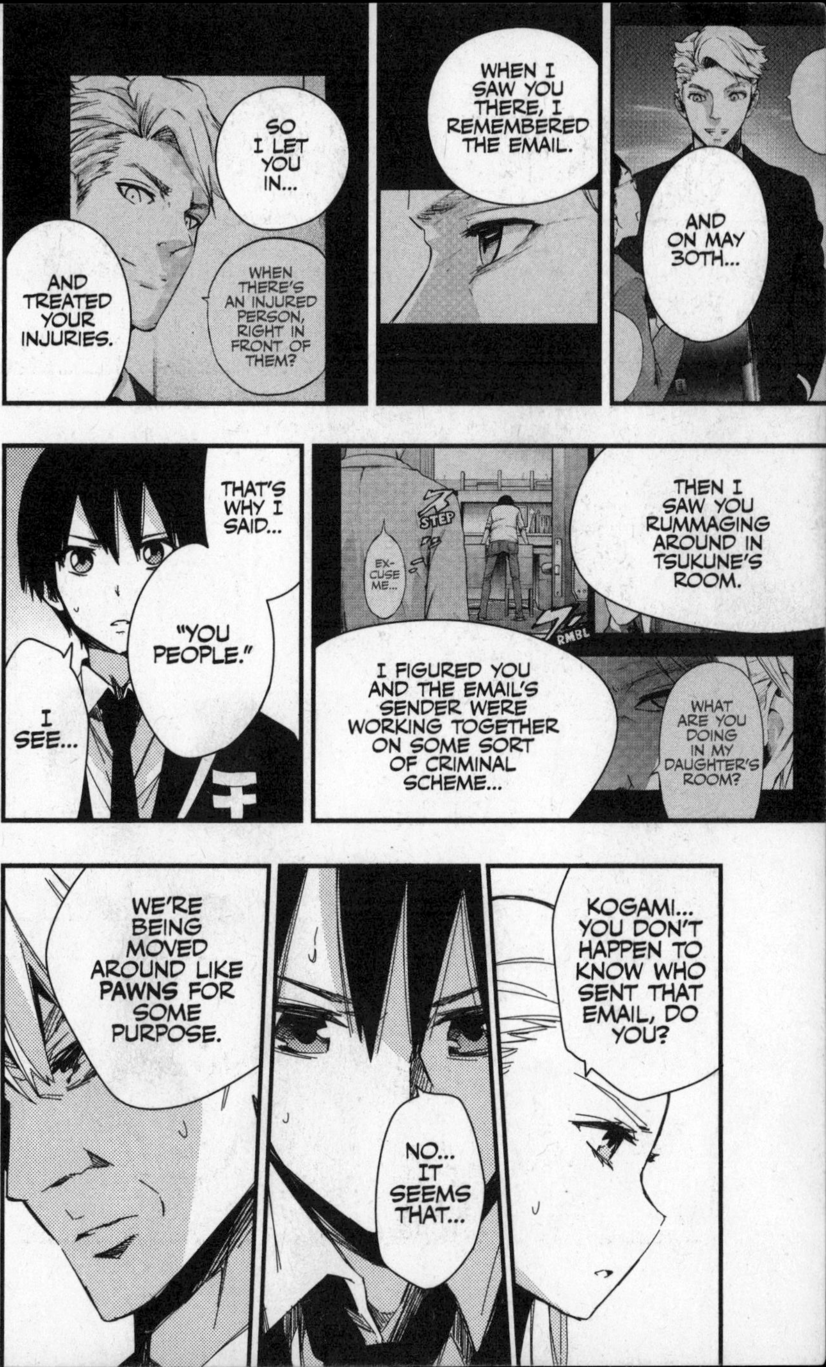
AND ON MAY 30TH...
WHEN I SAW YOU THERE, I REMEMBERED THE EMAIL.
SO I LET YOU IN...
WHEN THERE'S AN INJURED PERSON, RIGHT IN FRONT OF THEM?
AND TREATED YOUR INJURIES.
THEN I SAW YOU RUMMAGING AROUND IN TSUKUNE'S ROOM.
STEP
EX-CUSE ME...
RMBL
WHAT ARE YOU DOING IN MY DAUGHTER'S ROOM?
I FIGURED YOU AND THE EMAIL'S SENDER WERE WORKING TOGETHER ON SOME SORT OF CRIMINAL SCHEME...
THAT'S WHY I SAID...
"YOU PEOPLE."
I SEE...
KOGAMI... YOU DON'T HAPPEN TO KNOW WHO SENT THAT EMAIL, DO YOU?
NO... IT SEEMS THAT...
WE'RE BEING MOVED AROUND LIKE PAWNS FOR SOME PURPOSE.

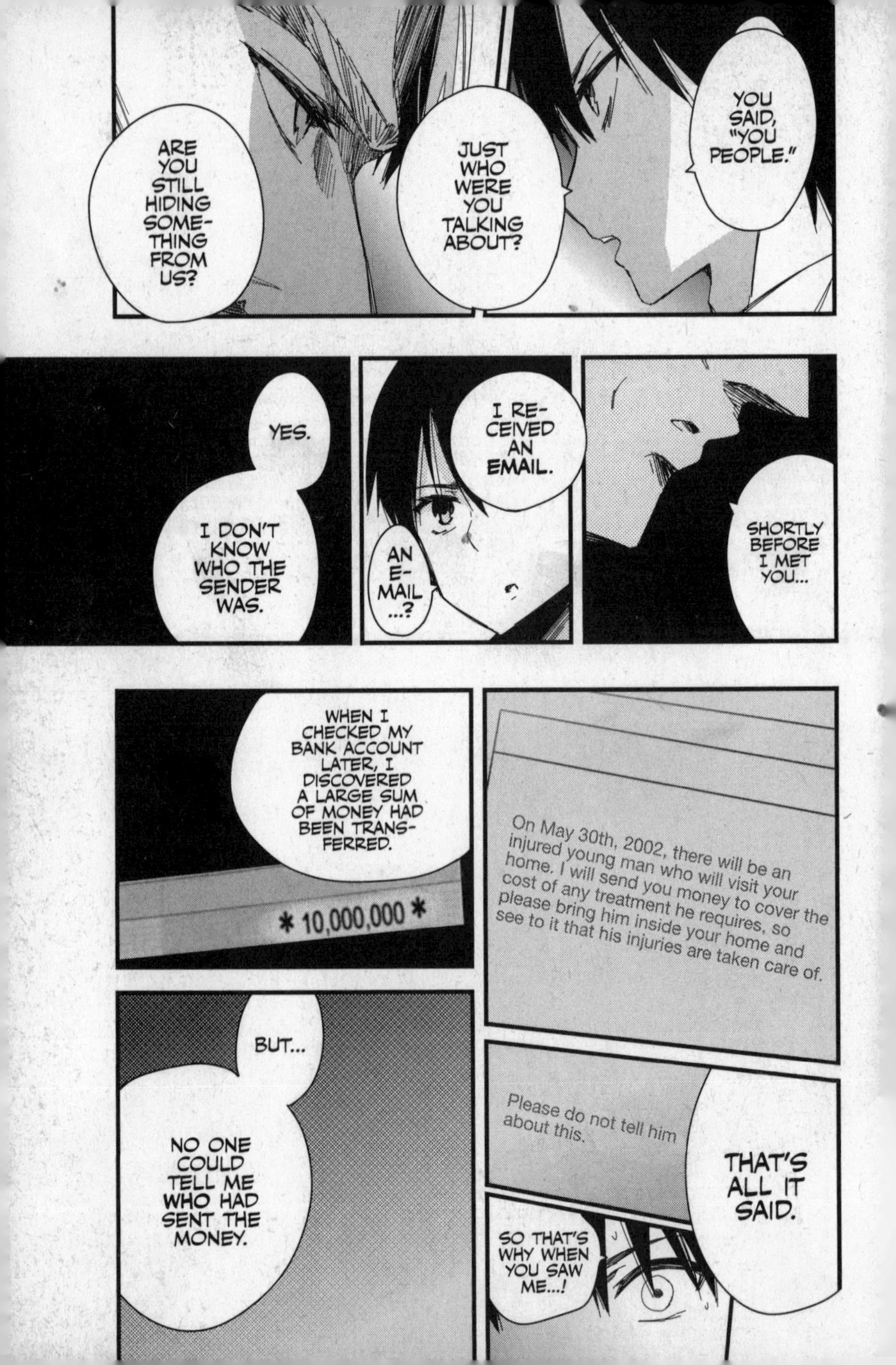
YOU SAID, "YOU PEOPLE."
JUST WHO WERE YOU TALKING ABOUT?
ARE YOU STILL HIDING SOME-THING FROM US?
SHORTLY BEFORE I MET YOU...
I RE-CEIVED AN EMAIL.
AN E-MAIL ...?
YES.
I DON'T KNOW WHO THE SENDER WAS.
On May 30th, 2002, there will be an injured young man who will visit your home. I will send you money to cover the cost of any treatment he requires, so please bring him inside your home and see to it that his injuries are taken care of.
WHEN I CHECKED MY BANK ACCOUNT LATER, I DISCOVERED A LARGE SUM OF MONEY HAD BEEN TRANS-FERRED.
* 10,000,000 *
Please do not tell him about this.
THAT'S ALL IT SAID.
SO THAT'S WHY WHEN YOU SAW ME...!
BUT...
NO ONE COULD TELL ME WHO HAD SENT THE MONEY.

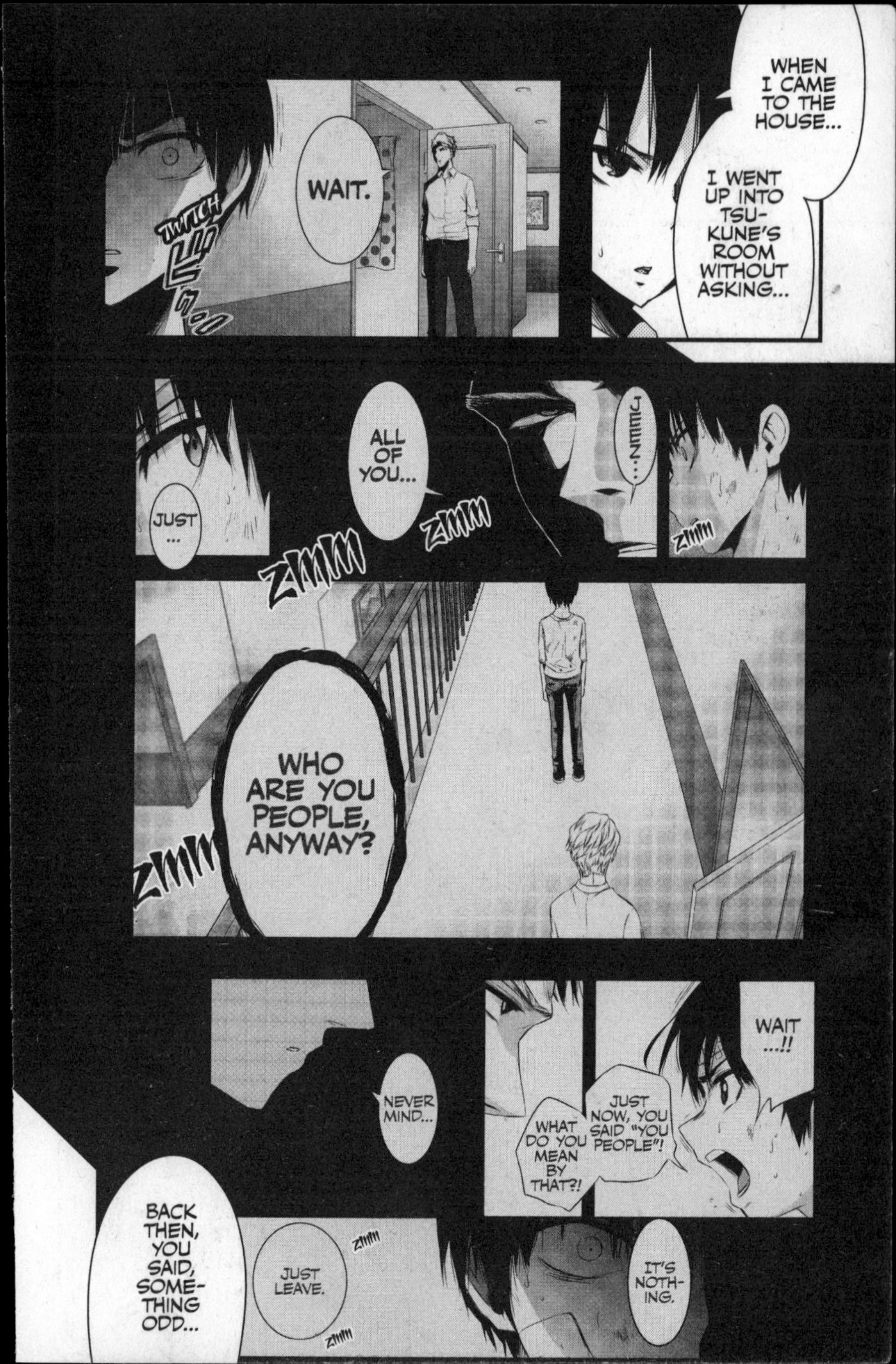
WHEN I CAME TO THE HOUSE...
I WENT UP INTO TSU-KUNE'S ROOM WITHOUT ASKING...
WAIT.
TWITCH
JEEZ...
ZMM
ALL OF YOU...
ZMM
JUST ...
ZMM
WHO ARE YOU PEOPLE, ANYWAY?
ZMM
WAIT ...!!
JUST NOW, YOU SAID "YOU PEOPLE"!
WHAT DO YOU MEAN BY THAT?!
NEVER MIND...
IT'S NOTHING.
ZMM
JUST LEAVE.
ZMM
BACK THEN, YOU SAID, SOME-THING ODD...

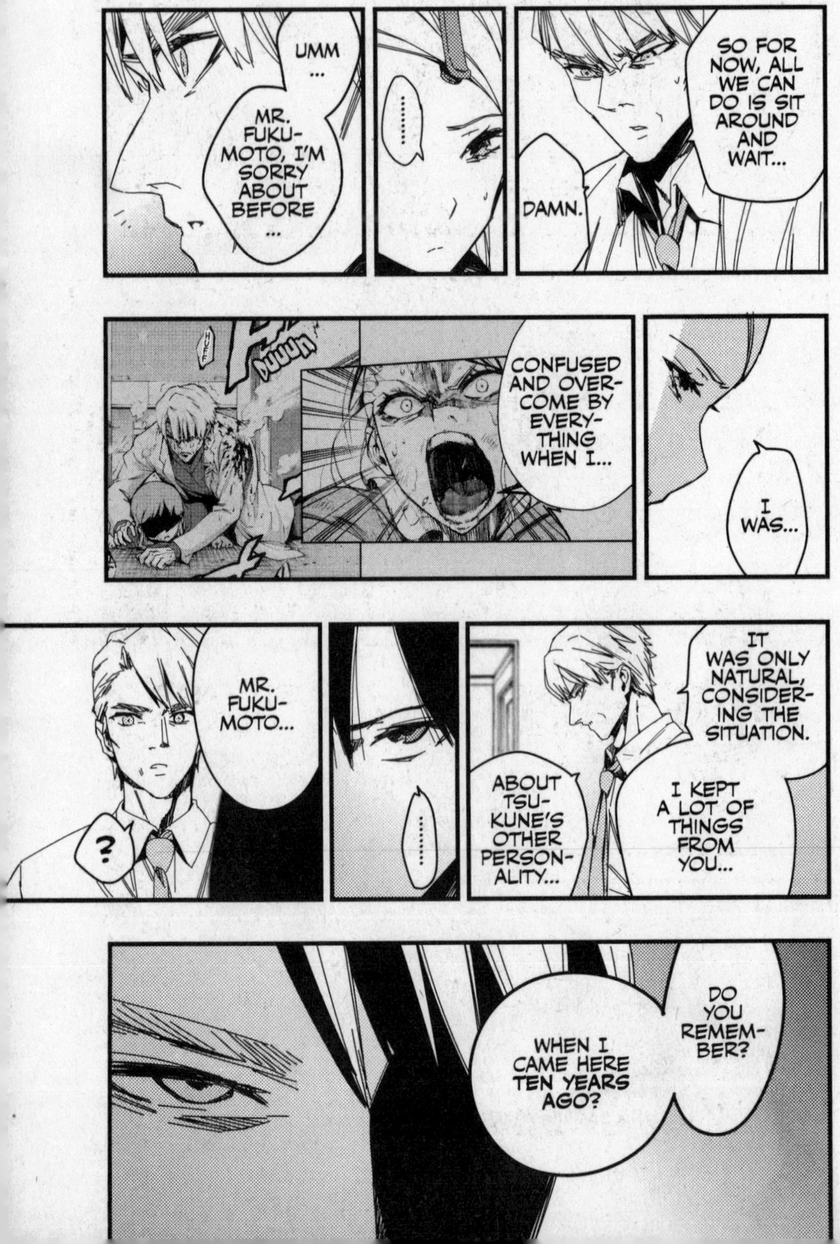
SO FOR NOW, ALL WE CAN DO IS SIT AROUND AND WAIT...
DAMN.
....
UMM ...
MR. FUKUMOTO, I'M SORRY ABOUT BEFORE ...
I WAS...
CONFUSED AND OVERCOME BY EVERYTHING WHEN I...
HUFF
IT WAS ONLY NATURAL, CONSIDERING THE SITUATION.
I KEPT A LOT OF THINGS FROM YOU...
ABOUT TSUKUNE'S OTHER PERSONALITY...
....
MR. FUKUMOTO...
?
DO YOU REMEMBER?
WHEN I CAME HERE TEN YEARS AGO?

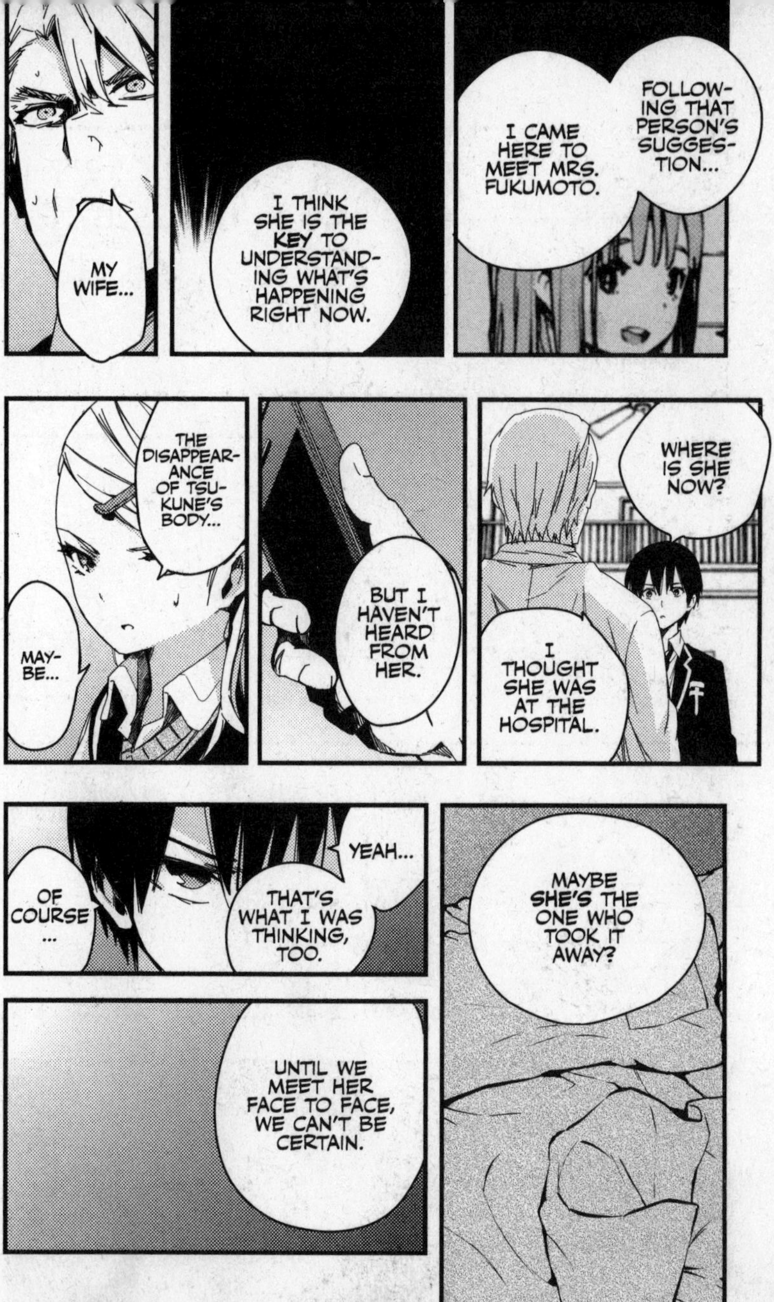
FOLLOWING THAT PERSON'S SUGGESTION...
I CAME HERE TO MEET MRS. FUKUMOTO.
I THINK SHE IS THE KEY TO UNDERSTANDING WHAT'S HAPPENING RIGHT NOW.
MY WIFE...
WHERE IS SHE NOW?
I THOUGHT SHE WAS AT THE HOSPITAL.
BUT I HAVEN'T HEARD FROM HER.
THE DISAPPEARANCE OF TSUKUNE'S BODY...
MAYBE...
MAYBE SHE'S THE ONE WHO TOOK IT AWAY?
YEAH...
THAT'S WHAT I WAS THINKING, TOO.
OF COURSE...
UNTIL WE MEET HER FACE TO FACE, WE CAN'T BE CERTAIN.

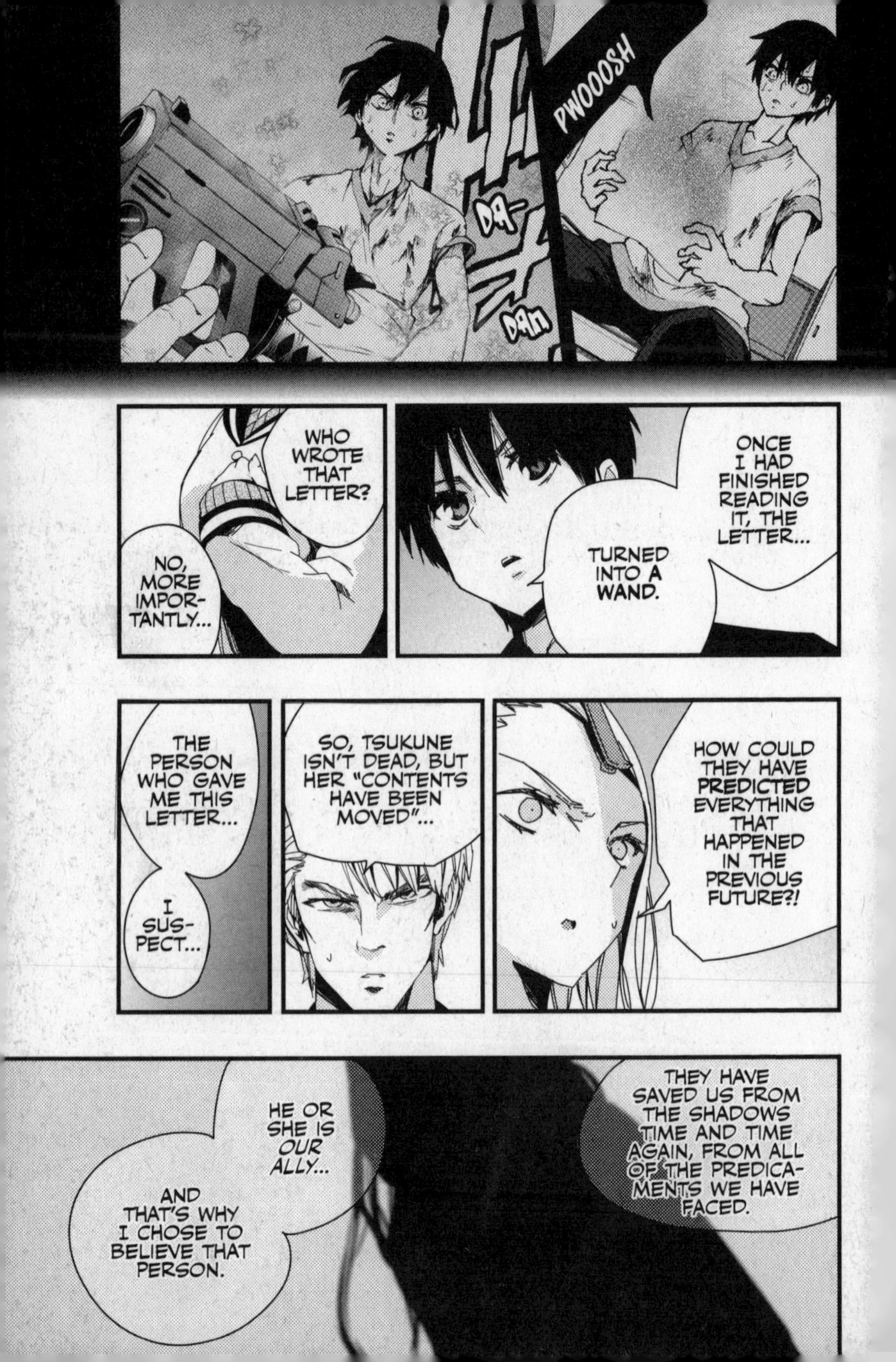
PWOOOSH
DA-
DAM
ONCE I HAD FINISHED READING IT, THE LETTER...
TURNED INTO A WAND.
WHO WROTE THAT LETTER?
NO, MORE IMPOR-TANTLY...
HOW COULD THEY HAVE PREDICTED EVERYTHING THAT HAPPENED IN THE PREVIOUS FUTURE?!
SO, TSUKUNE ISN'T DEAD, BUT HER "CONTENTS HAVE BEEN MOVED"...
THE PERSON WHO GAVE ME THIS LETTER...
I SUS-PECT...
THEY HAVE SAVED US FROM THE SHADOWS TIME AND TIME AGAIN, FROM ALL OF THE PREDICA-MENTS WE HAVE FACED.
HE OR SHE IS *OUR ALLY*...
AND THAT'S WHY I CHOSE TO BELIEVE THAT PERSON.

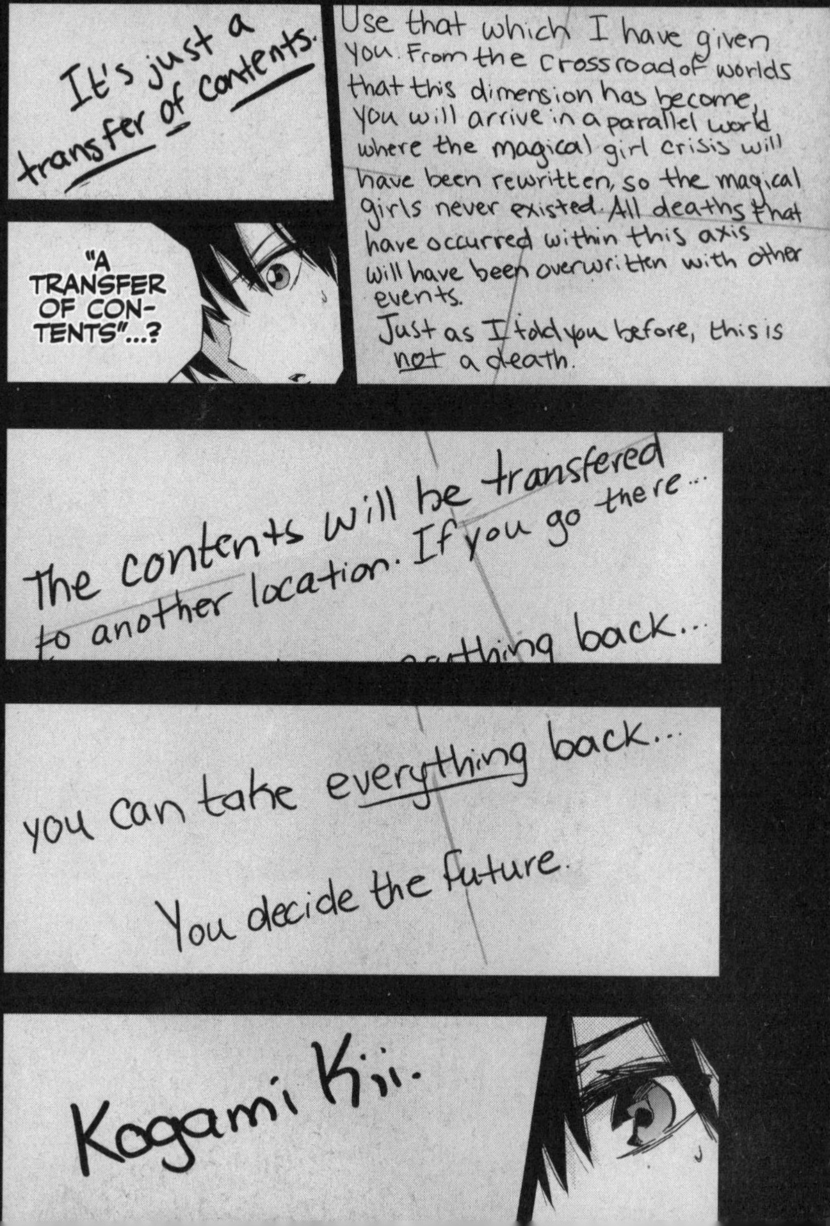
Use that which I have given you. From the crossroad of worlds that this dimension has become, you will arrive in a parallel world where the magical girl crisis will have been rewritten, so the magical girls never existed. All deaths that have occurred within this axis will have been overwritten with other events.
Just as I told you before, this is not a death.
It's just a transfer of contents.
"A TRANSFER OF CONTENTS"...?
The contents will be transfered to another location. If you go there...
you can take everything back...
You decide the future.
Kogami Kii.

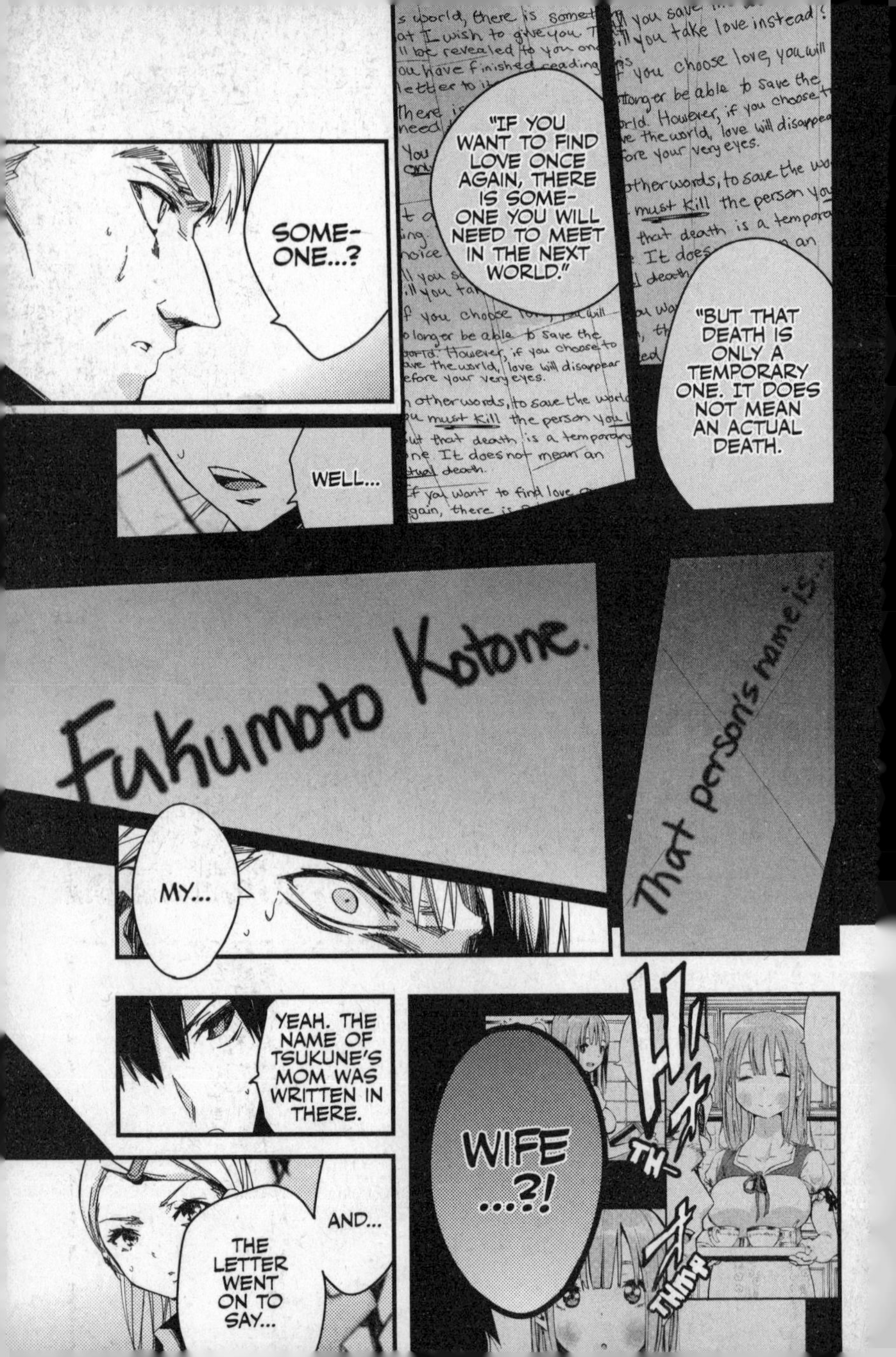
"BUT THAT DEATH IS ONLY A TEMPORARY ONE. IT DOES NOT MEAN AN ACTUAL DEATH.
"IF YOU WANT TO FIND LOVE ONCE AGAIN, THERE IS SOME-ONE YOU WILL NEED TO MEET IN THE NEXT WORLD."
SOME-ONE...?
WELL...
That person's name is...
Fukumoto Kotone.
MY...
WIFE ...?!
TH-
THMP
YEAH. THE NAME OF TSUKUNE'S MOM WAS WRITTEN IN THERE.
AND...
THE LETTER WENT ON TO SAY...

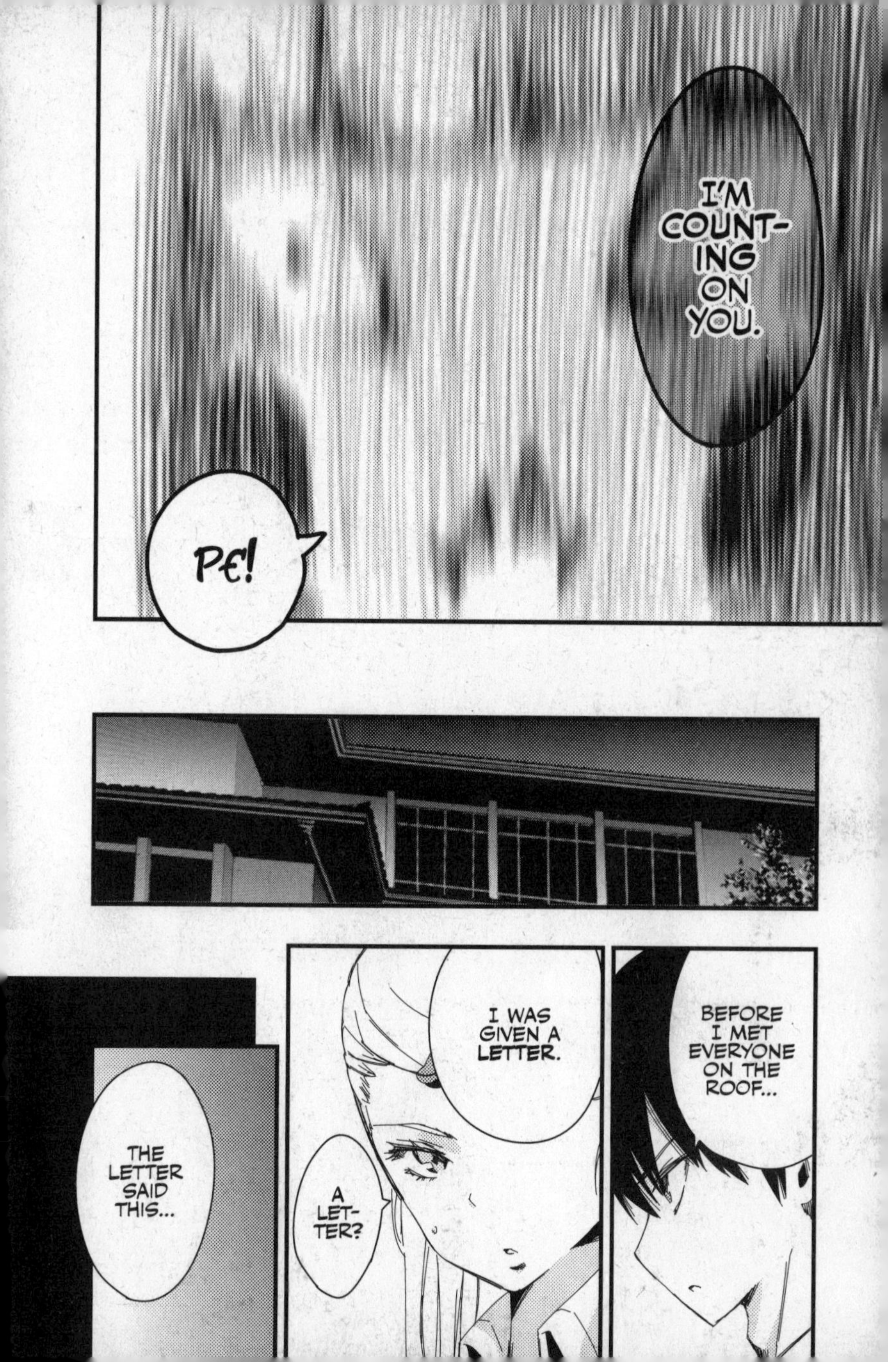
I'M COUNTING ON YOU.
PE!
BEFORE I MET EVERYONE ON THE ROOF...
I WAS GIVEN A LETTER.
A LETTER?
THE LETTER SAID THIS...

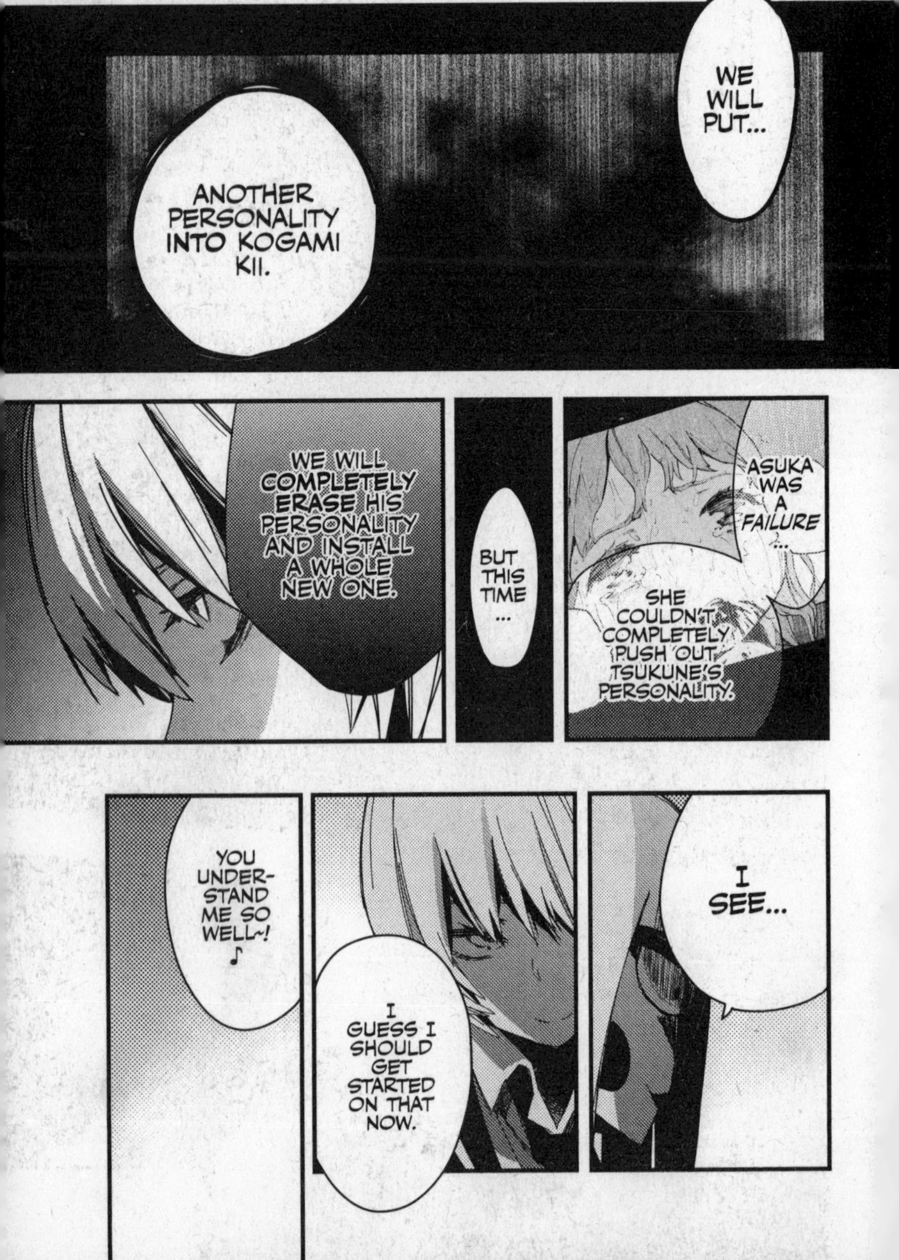
WE WILL PUT...
ANOTHER PERSONALITY INTO KOGAMI KII.
ASUKA WAS A FAILURE...
SHE COULDN'T COMPLETELY PUSH OUT TSUKUNE'S PERSONALITY.
BUT THIS TIME...
WE WILL COMPLETELY ERASE HIS PERSONALITY AND INSTALL A WHOLE NEW ONE.
I SEE...
I GUESS I SHOULD GET STARTED ON THAT NOW.
YOU UNDER-STAND ME SO WELL~! ♪

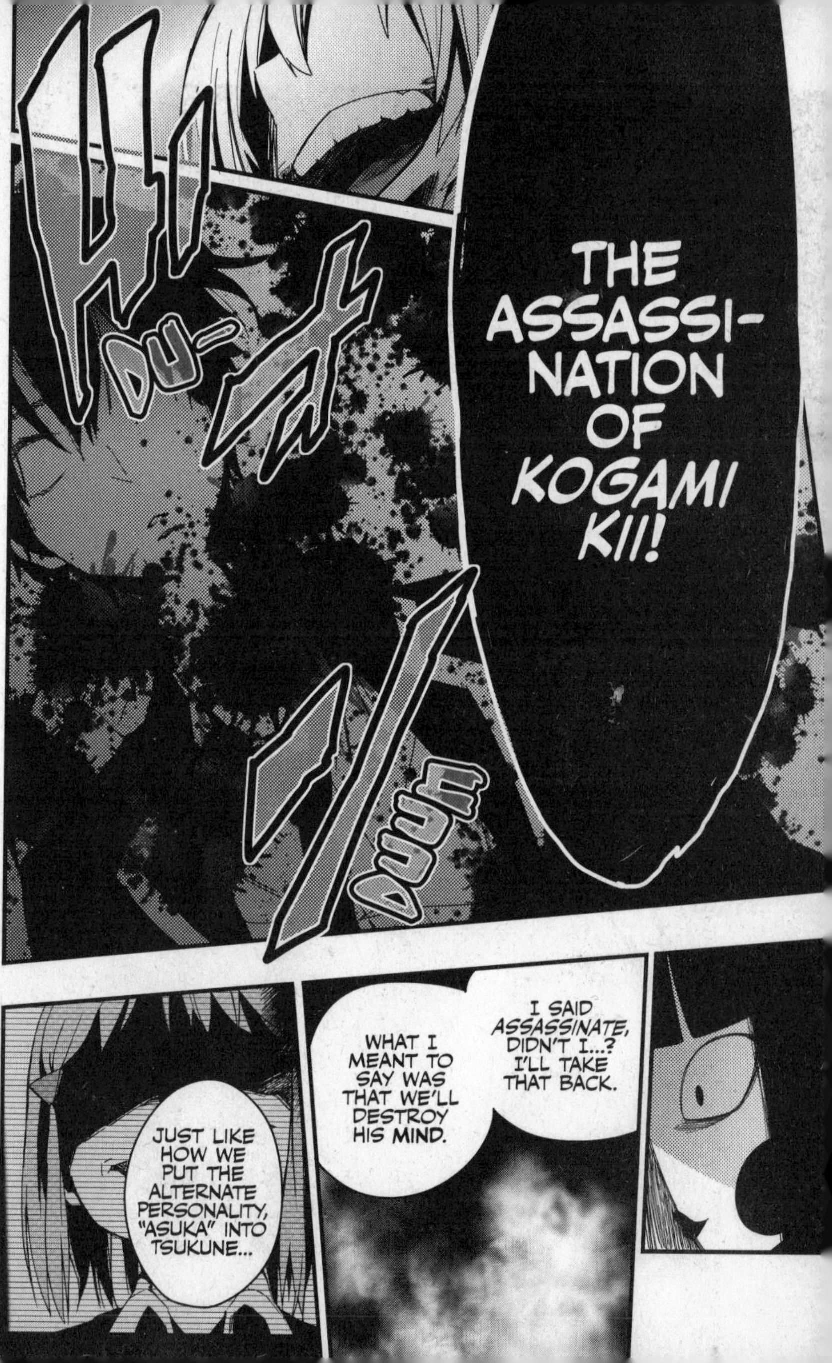
THE ASSASSI-NATION OF KOGAMI KII!
DU-
DUUUN
I SAID ASSASSINATE, DIDN'T I...? I'LL TAKE THAT BACK.
WHAT I MEANT TO SAY WAS THAT WE'LL DESTROY HIS MIND.
JUST LIKE HOW WE PUT THE ALTERNATE PERSONALITY, "ASUKA" INTO TSUKUNE...

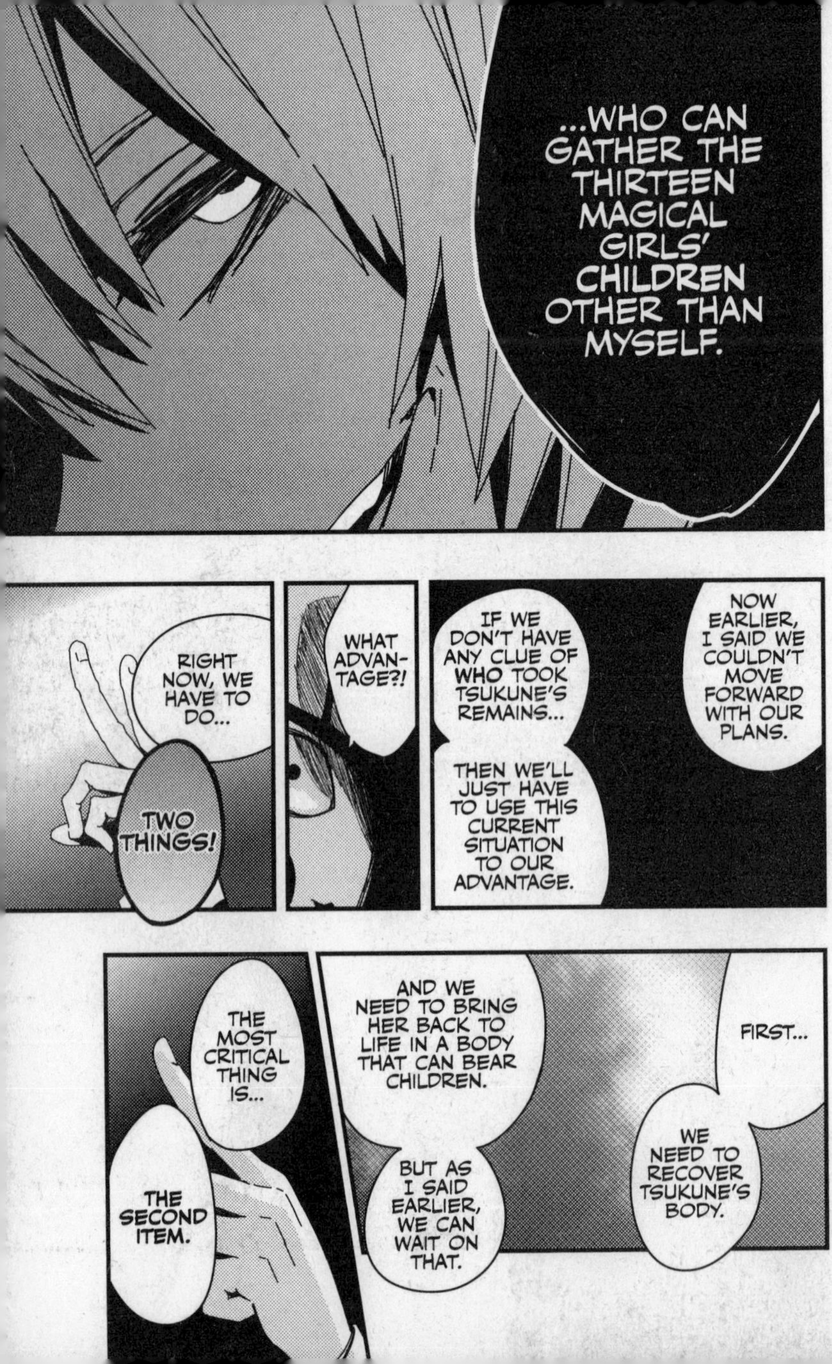
...WHO CAN GATHER THE THIRTEEN MAGICAL GIRLS' CHILDREN OTHER THAN MYSELF.
NOW EARLIER, I SAID WE COULDN'T MOVE FORWARD WITH OUR PLANS.
IF WE DON'T HAVE ANY CLUE OF WHO TOOK TSUKUNE'S REMAINS...
THEN WE'LL JUST HAVE TO USE THIS CURRENT SITUATION TO OUR ADVANTAGE.
WHAT ADVANTAGE?!
RIGHT NOW, WE HAVE TO DO...
TWO THINGS!
FIRST...
WE NEED TO RECOVER TSUKUNE'S BODY.
AND WE NEED TO BRING HER BACK TO LIFE IN A BODY THAT CAN BEAR CHILDREN.
BUT AS I SAID EARLIER, WE CAN WAIT ON THAT.
THE MOST CRITICAL THING IS...
THE SECOND ITEM.

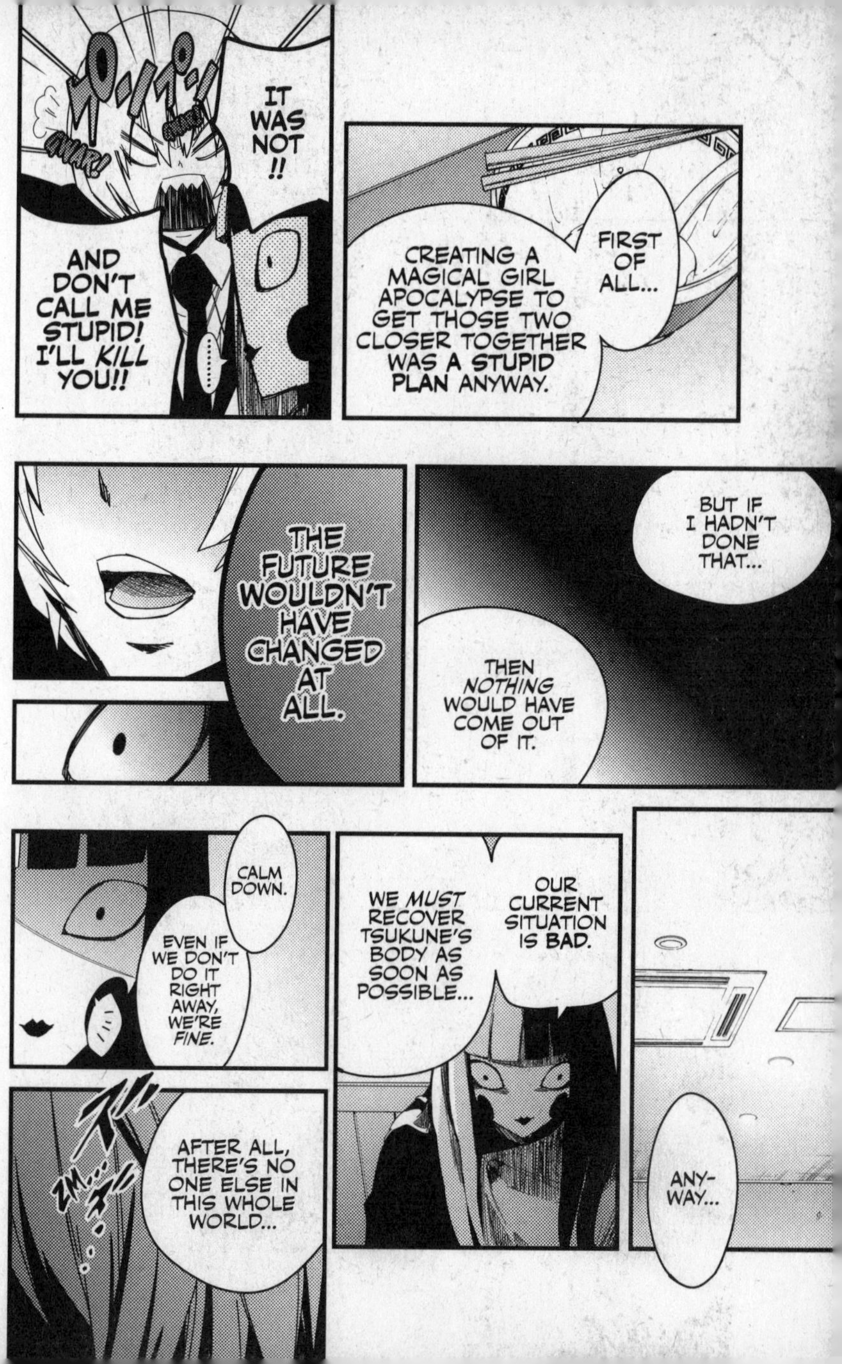
FIRST OF ALL...
CREATING A MAGICAL GIRL APOCALYPSE TO GET THOSE TWO CLOSER TOGETHER WAS A STUPID PLAN ANYWAY.
GWAR!
IT WAS NOT!!
AND DON'T CALL ME STUPID! I'LL *KILL* YOU!!
......
BUT IF I HADN'T DONE THAT...
THEN *NOTHING* WOULD HAVE COME OUT OF IT.
THE FUTURE WOULDN'T HAVE CHANGED AT ALL.
ANY-WAY...
OUR CURRENT SITUATION IS BAD.
WE *MUST* RECOVER TSUKUNE'S BODY AS SOON AS POSSIBLE...
CALM DOWN.
EVEN IF WE DON'T DO IT RIGHT AWAY, WE'RE *FINE*.
ZM...
AFTER ALL, THERE'S NO ONE ELSE IN THIS WHOLE WORLD...

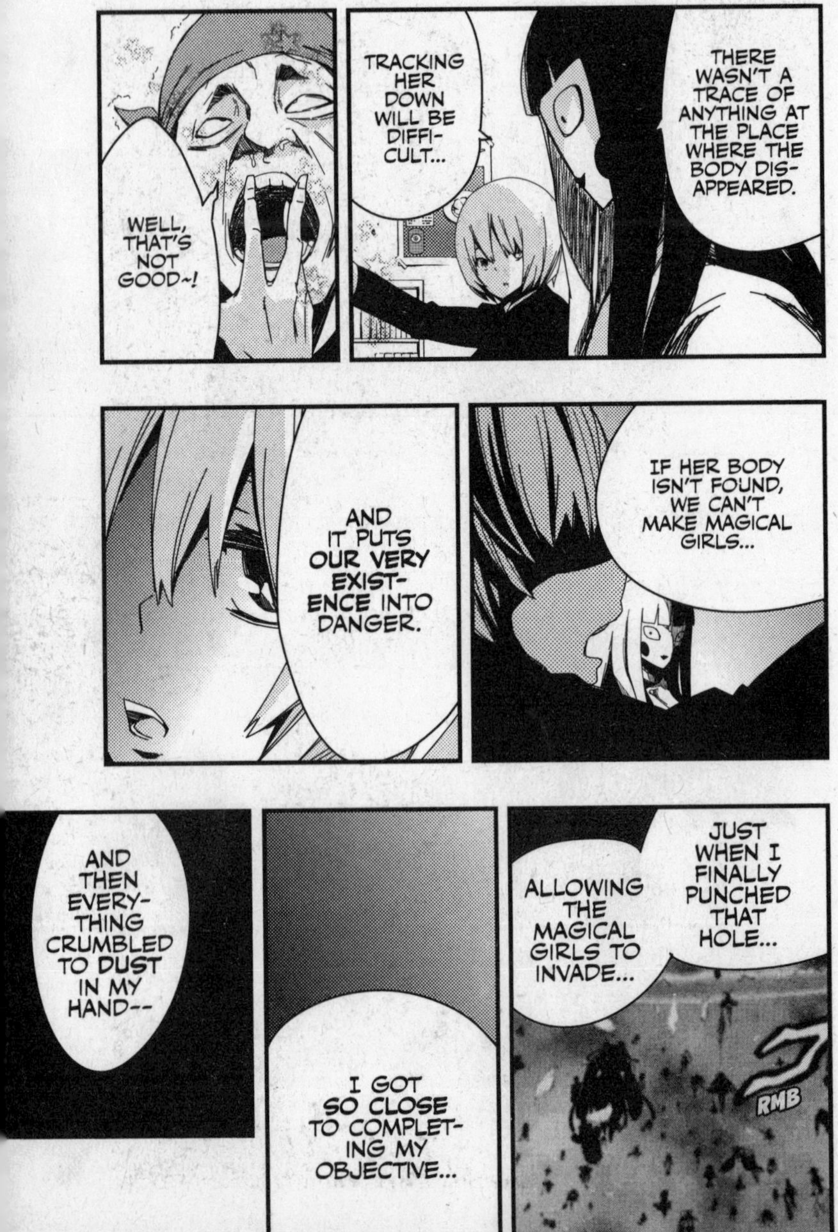
THERE WASN'T A TRACE OF ANYTHING AT THE PLACE WHERE THE BODY DISAPPEARED.
TRACKING HER DOWN WILL BE DIFFICULT...
WELL, THAT'S NOT GOOD~!
IF HER BODY ISN'T FOUND, WE CAN'T MAKE MAGICAL GIRLS...
AND IT PUTS OUR VERY EXISTENCE INTO DANGER.
JUST WHEN I FINALLY PUNCHED THAT HOLE...
ALLOWING THE MAGICAL GIRLS TO INVADE...
RMB
I GOT SO CLOSE TO COMPLETING MY OBJECTIVE...
AND THEN EVERYTHING CRUMBLED TO DUST IN MY HAND--

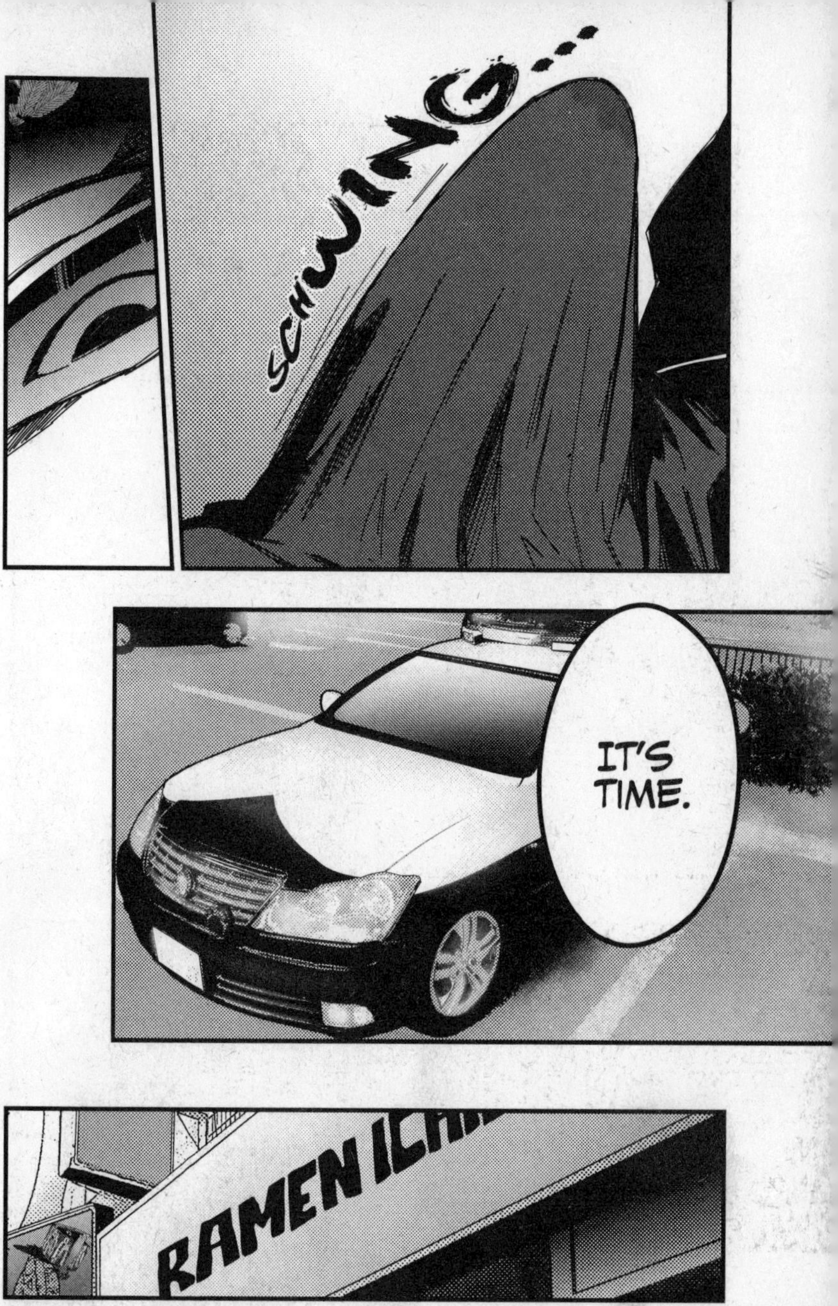
SCHWING...
IT'S TIME.
RAMEN ICH

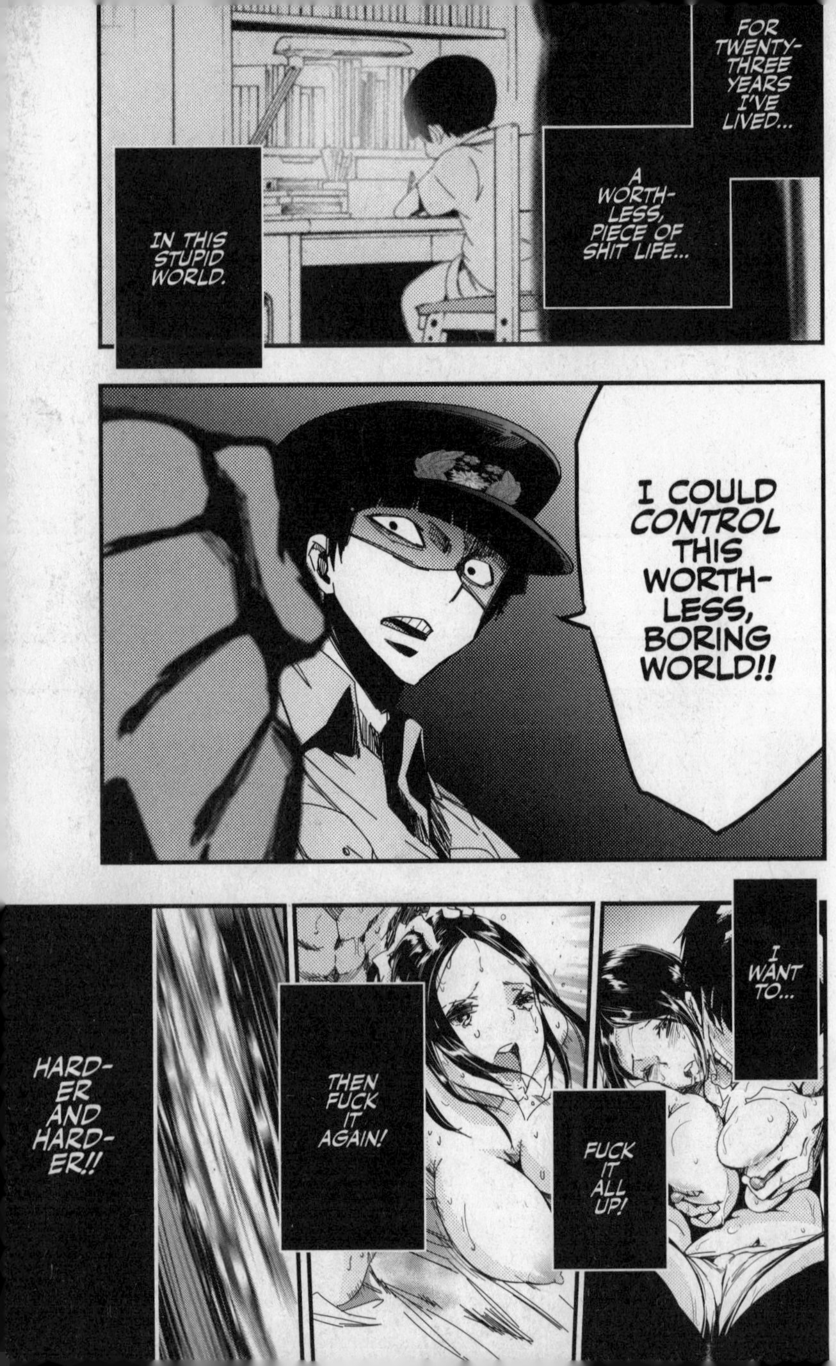
FOR TWENTY-THREE YEARS I'VE LIVED...
A WORTHLESS, PIECE OF SHIT LIFE...
IN THIS STUPID WORLD.
I COULD CONTROL THIS WORTHLESS, BORING WORLD!!
I WANT TO...
FUCK IT ALL UP!
THEN FUCK IT AGAIN!
HARDER AND HARDER!!

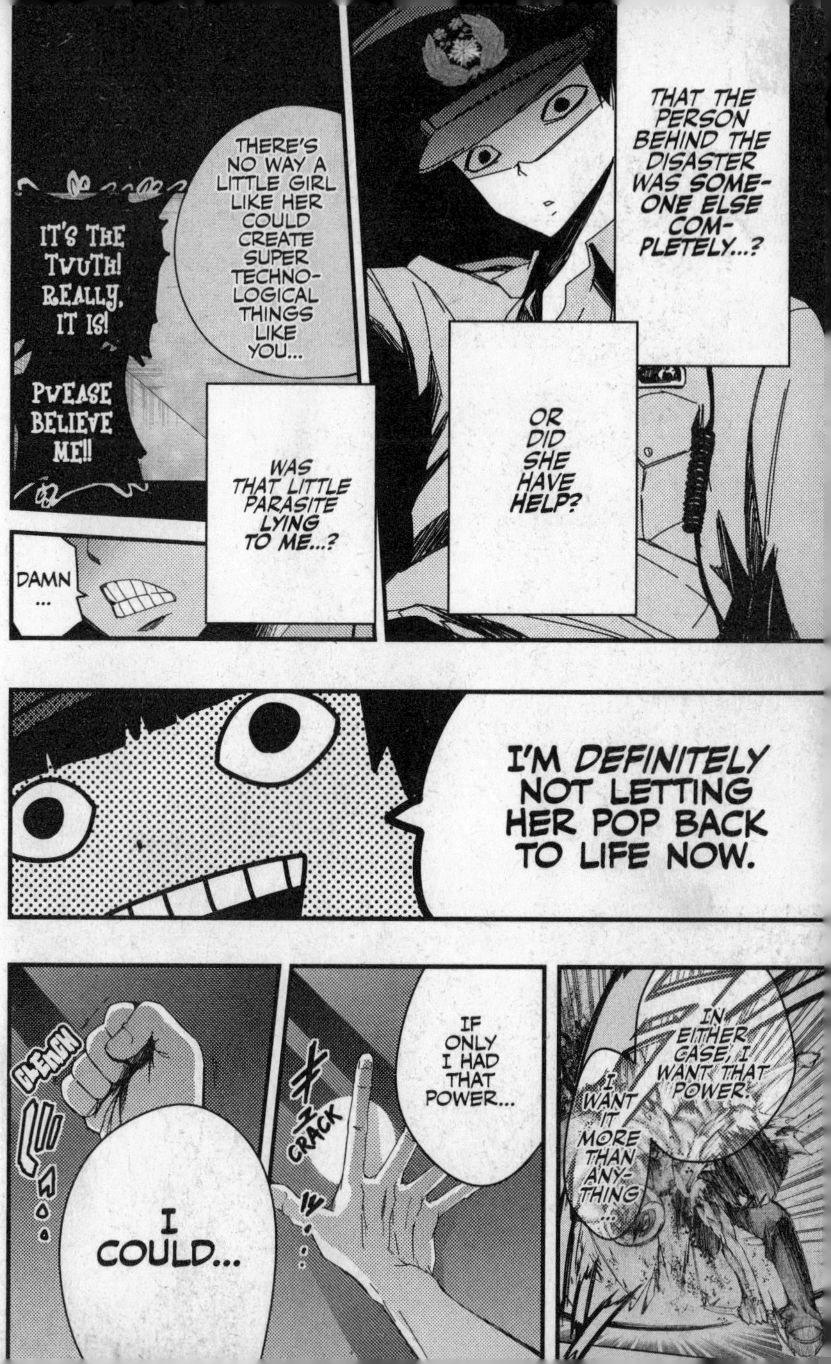
THAT THE PERSON BEHIND THE DISASTER WAS SOME-ONE ELSE COM-PLETELY...?
OR DID SHE HAVE HELP?
WAS THAT LITTLE PARASITE LYING TO ME...?
THERE'S NO WAY A LITTLE GIRL LIKE HER COULD CREATE SUPER TECHNO-LOGICAL THINGS LIKE YOU...
IT'S THE TWUTH! REALLY, IT IS!
PWEASE BELIEVE ME!!
DAMN...
I'M DEFINITELY NOT LETTING HER POP BACK TO LIFE NOW.
IN EITHER CASE, I WANT THAT POWER.
I WANT IT MORE THAN ANY-THING...
IF ONLY I HAD THAT POWER...
CRACK
I COULD...
CLENCH

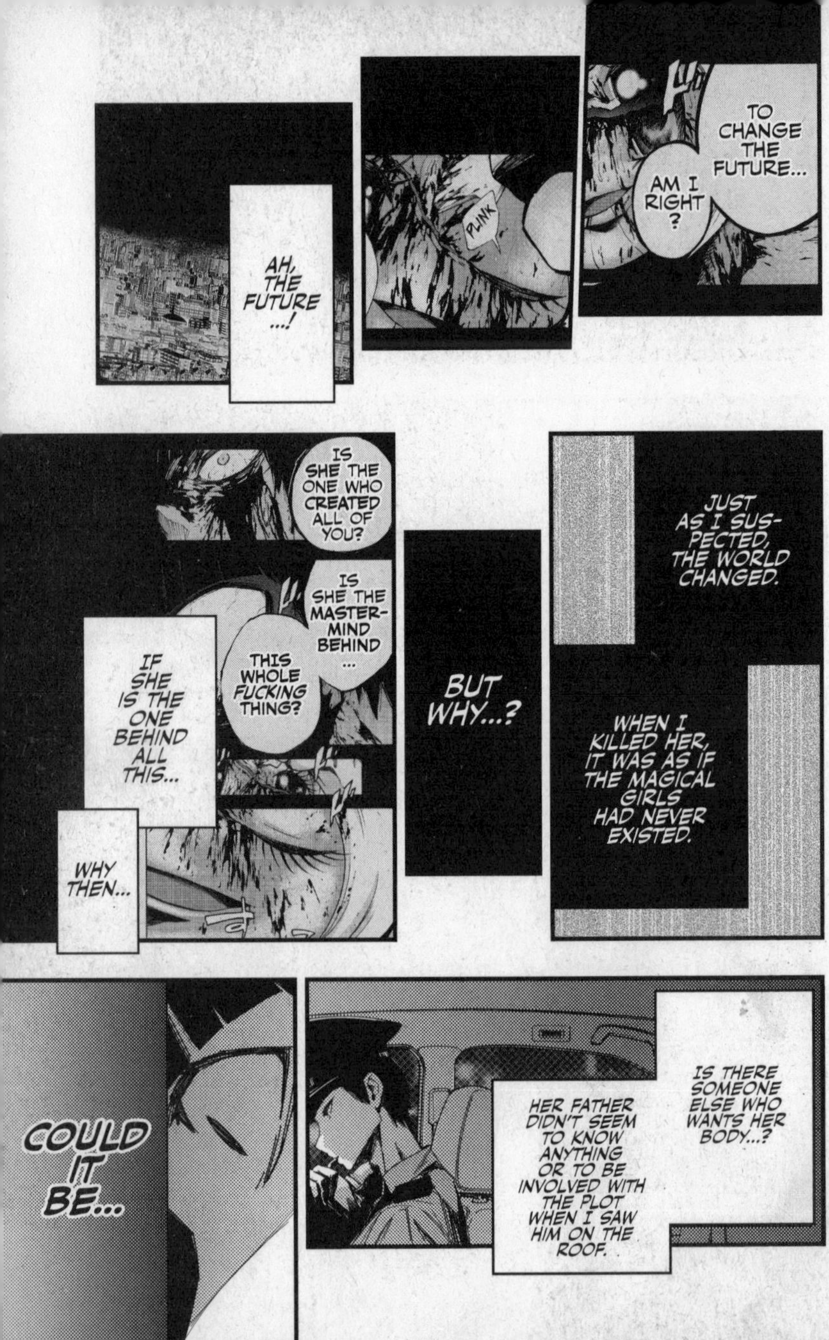
TO CHANGE THE FUTURE...
AM I RIGHT?
PLINK
AH, THE FUTURE ...!
JUST AS I SUSPECTED, THE WORLD CHANGED.
WHEN I KILLED HER, IT WAS AS IF THE MAGICAL GIRLS HAD NEVER EXISTED.
BUT WHY...?
IS SHE THE ONE WHO CREATED ALL OF YOU?
IS SHE THE MASTER-MIND BEHIND ...
THIS WHOLE FUCKING THING?
IF SHE IS THE ONE BEHIND ALL THIS...
WHY THEN...
IS THERE SOMEONE ELSE WHO WANTS HER BODY...?
HER FATHER DIDN'T SEEM TO KNOW ANYTHING OR TO BE INVOLVED WITH THE PLOT WHEN I SAW HIM ON THE ROOF.
COULD IT BE...

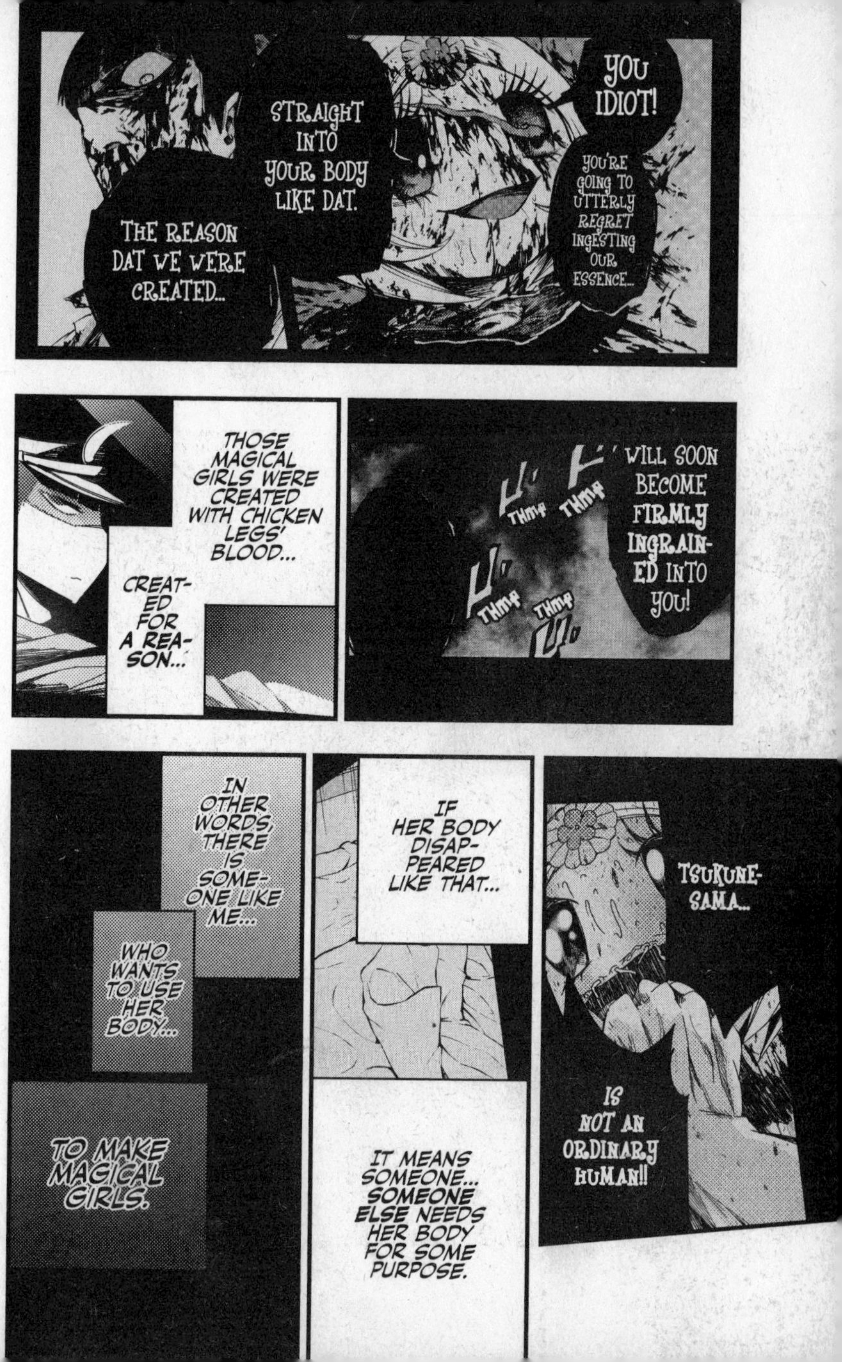
YOU IDIOT!
YOU'RE GOING TO UTTERLY REGRET INGESTING OUR ESSENCE...
STRAIGHT INTO YOUR BODY LIKE DAT.
THE REASON DAT WE WERE CREATED...
THMP THMP
THMP THMP
WILL SOON BECOME FIRMLY INGRAIN-ED INTO YOU!
THOSE MAGICAL GIRLS WERE CREATED WITH CHICKEN LEGS' BLOOD...
CREAT-ED FOR A REA-SON...
TSUKUNE-SAMA...
IS NOT AN ORDINARY HUMAN!!
IF HER BODY DISAP-PEARED LIKE THAT...
IT MEANS SOMEONE... SOMEONE ELSE NEEDS HER BODY FOR SOME PURPOSE.
IN OTHER WORDS, THERE IS SOME-ONE LIKE ME...
WHO WANTS TO USE HER BODY...
TO MAKE MAGICAL GIRLS.

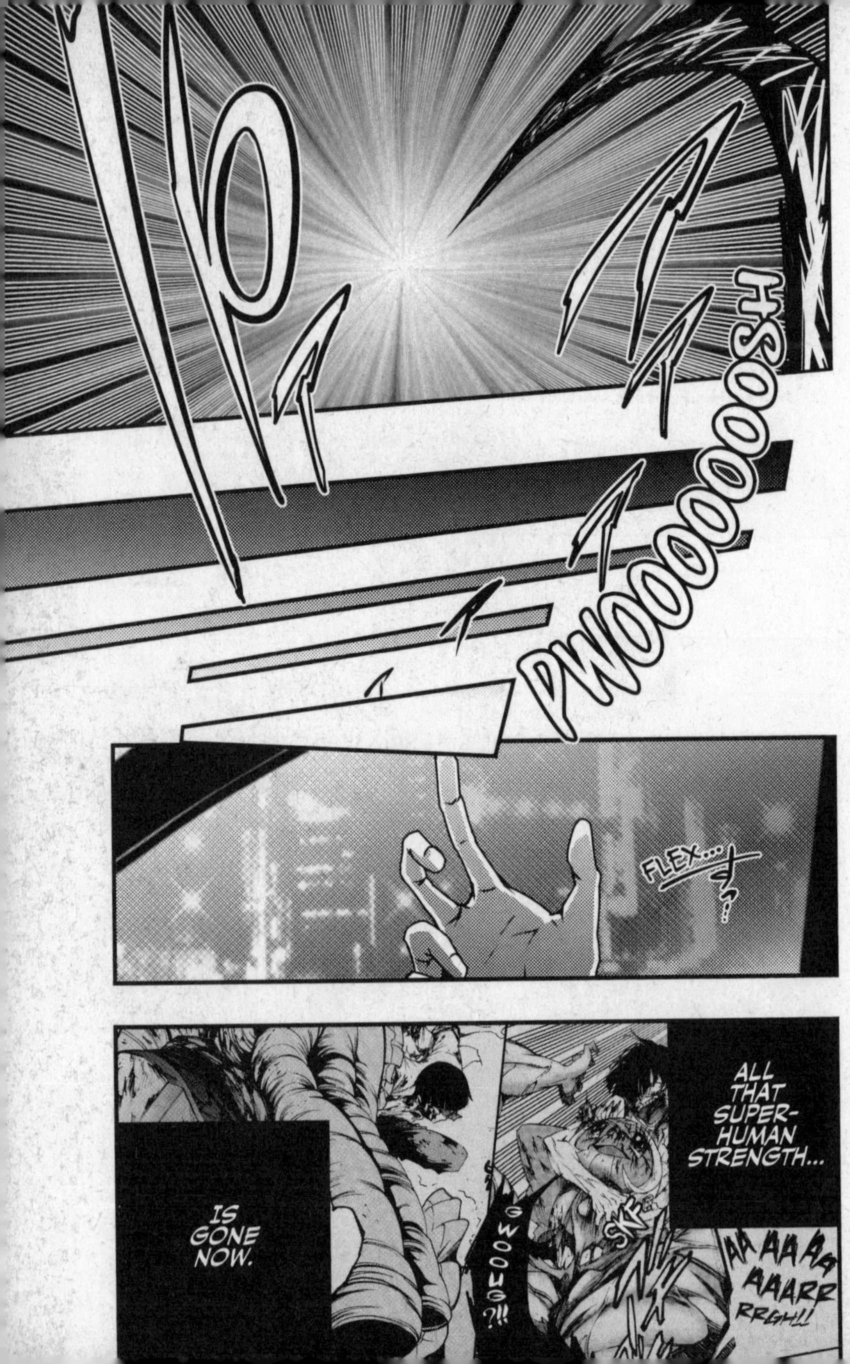
PWOOOOOOOSH
FLEX...
すっ...
ALL THAT SUPER-HUMAN STRENGTH...
AAAAAAAARRRGH!!
SKF
GWOOUG?!!
IS GONE NOW.

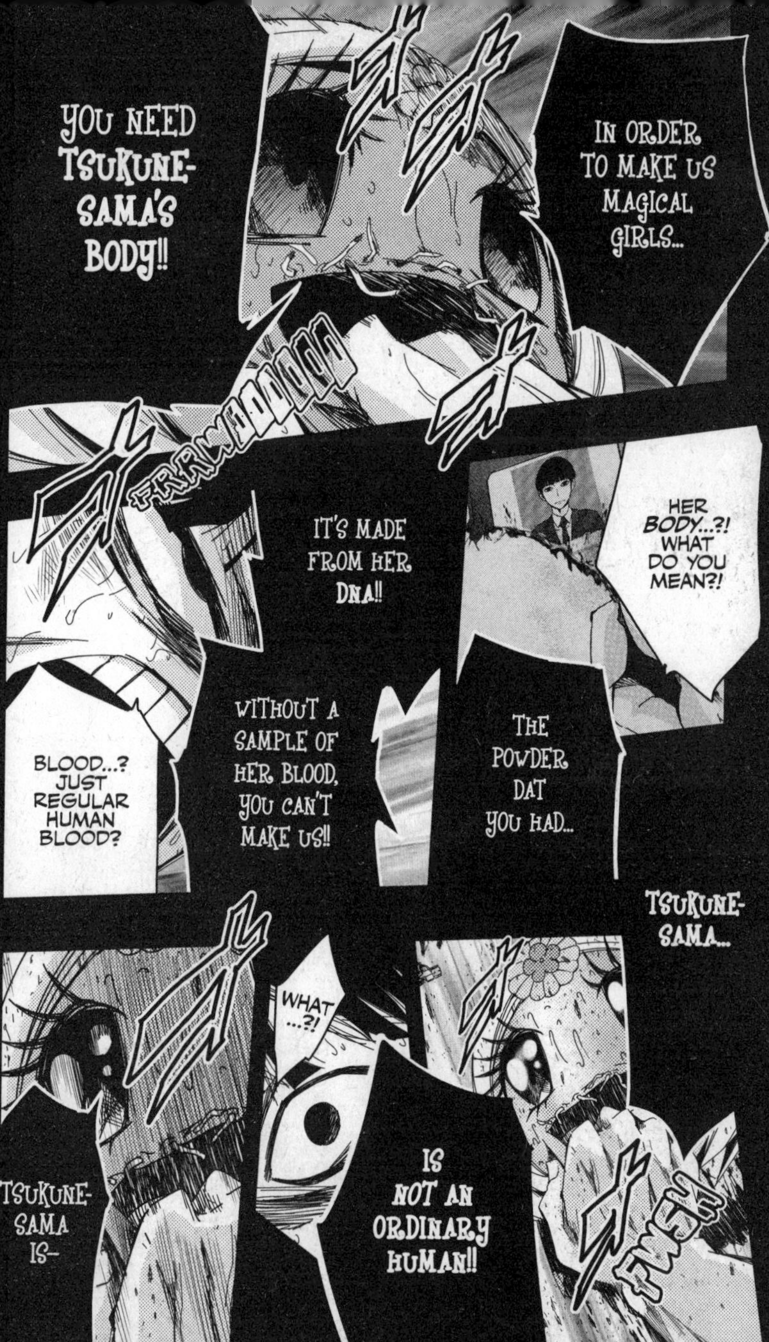
IN ORDER TO MAKE US MAGICAL GIRLS...
YOU NEED TSUKUNE-SAMA'S BODY!!
FRRWOOOOOSH
HER BODY...?! WHAT DO YOU MEAN?!
IT'S MADE FROM HER DNA!!
THE POWDER DAT YOU HAD...
WITHOUT A SAMPLE OF HER BLOOD, YOU CAN'T MAKE US!!
BLOOD...? JUST REGULAR HUMAN BLOOD?
TSUKUNE-SAMA...
IS NOT AN ORDINARY HUMAN!!
FWSH
WHAT...?!
TSUKUNE-SAMA IS-

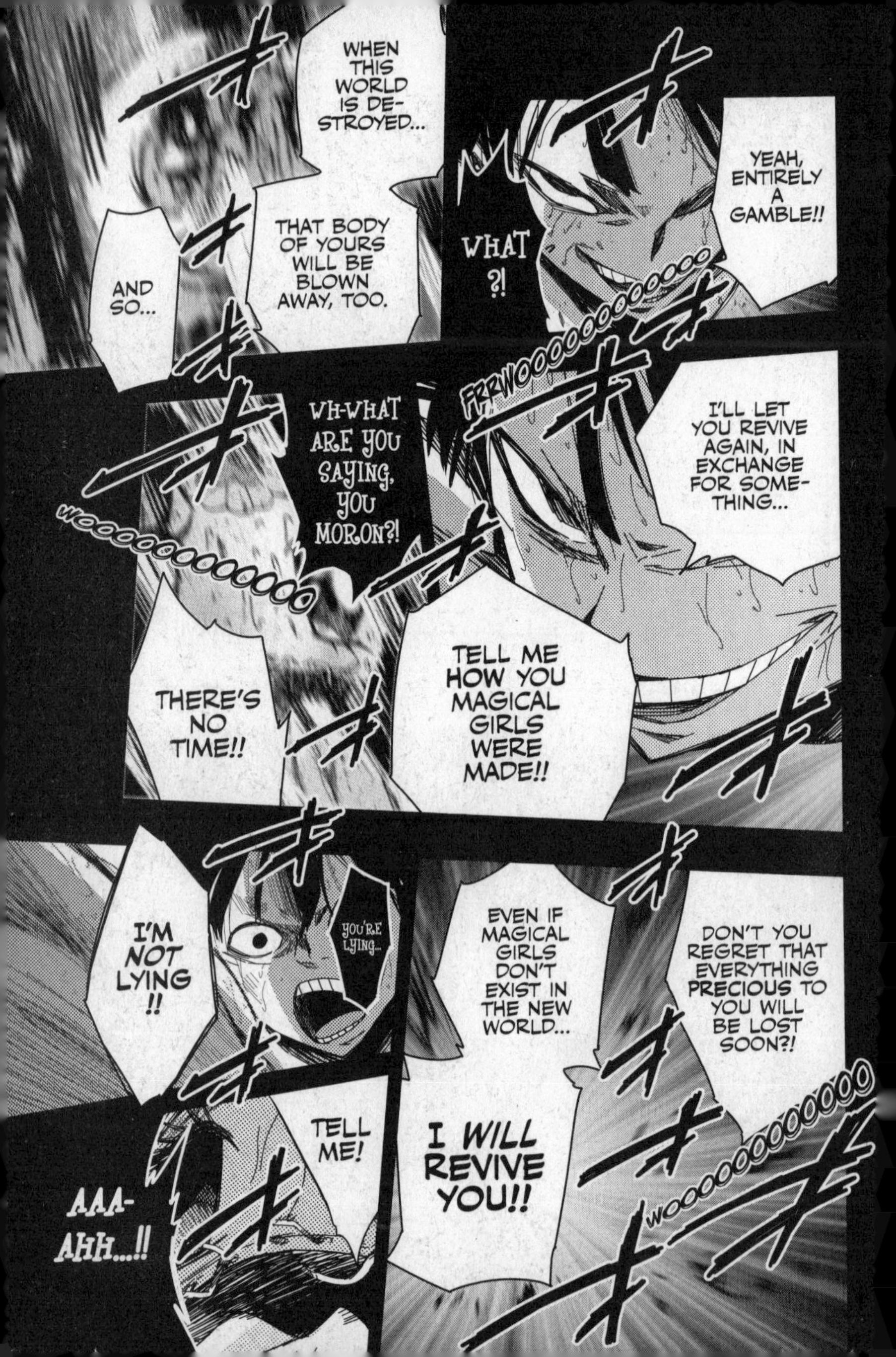
YEAH, ENTIRELY A GAMBLE!!
WHAT ?!
FRRWOOOOOOOOOOOOOO
WHEN THIS WORLD IS DE-STROYED...
THAT BODY OF YOURS WILL BE BLOWN AWAY, TOO.
AND SO...
I'LL LET YOU REVIVE AGAIN, IN EXCHANGE FOR SOME-THING...
WH-WHAT ARE YOU SAYING, YOU MORON?!
WOOOOOOOOOOOOOO
TELL ME HOW YOU MAGICAL GIRLS WERE MADE!!
THERE'S NO TIME!!
DON'T YOU REGRET THAT EVERYTHING PRECIOUS TO YOU WILL BE LOST SOON?!
EVEN IF MAGICAL GIRLS DON'T EXIST IN THE NEW WORLD...
YOU'RE LYING...
I'M NOT LYING!!
WOOOOOOOOOOOOOOO
I WILL REVIVE YOU!!
TELL ME!
AAA-AHH...!!

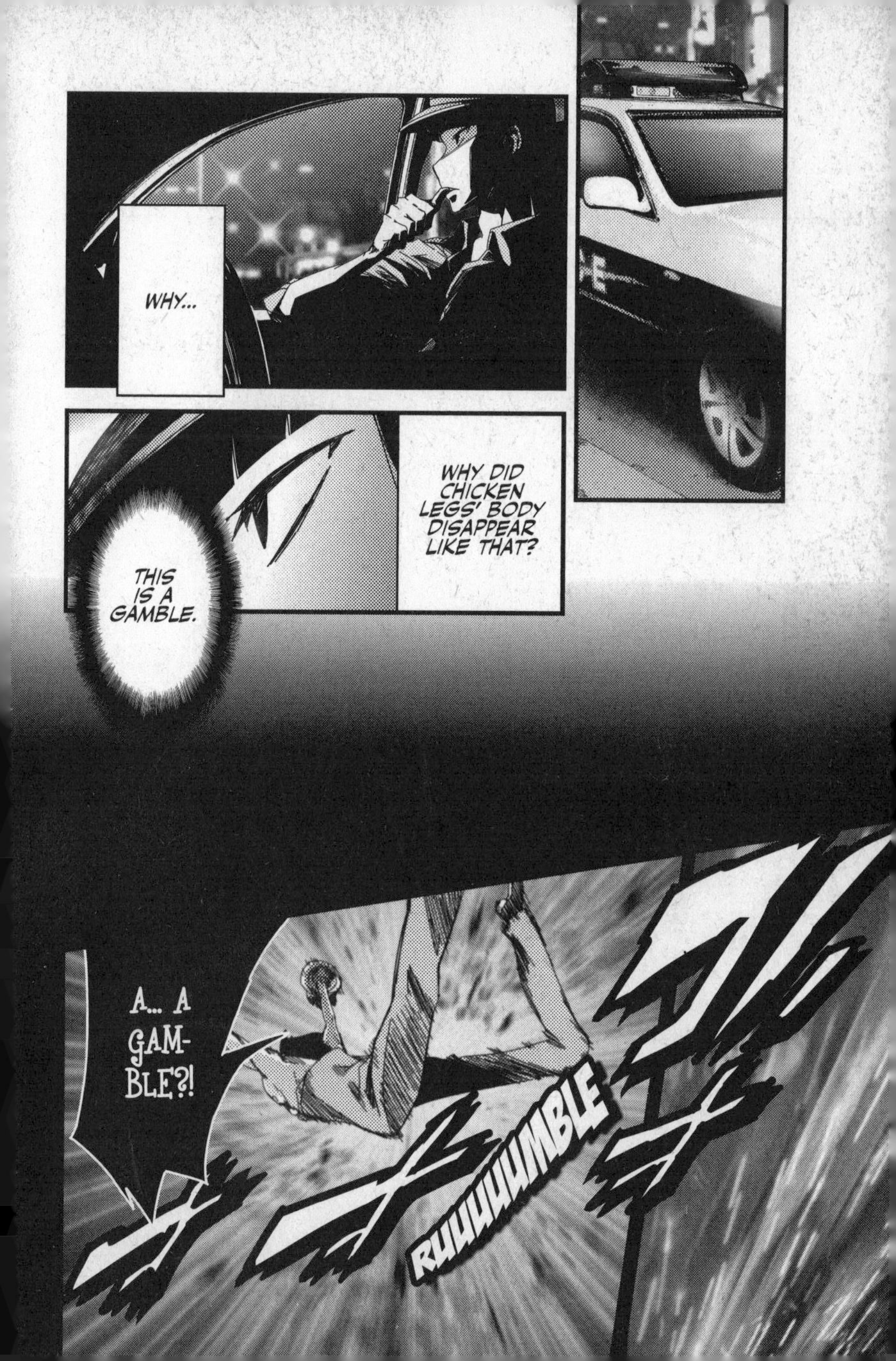
WHY...
WHY DID CHICKEN LEGS' BODY DISAPPEAR LIKE THAT?
THIS IS A GAMBLE.
A... A GAM-BLE?!
RUUUUUMBLE

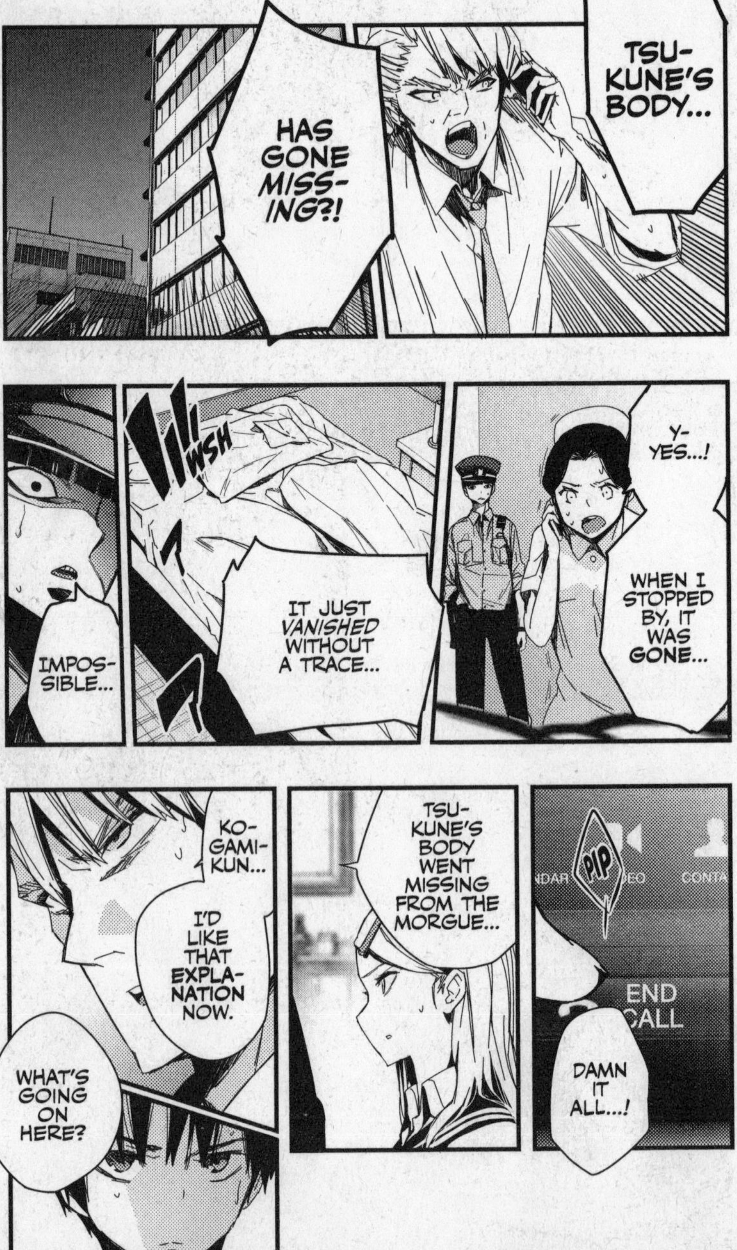
TSU-KUNE'S BODY...
HAS GONE MISS-ING?!
Y-YES...!
WHEN I STOPPED BY, IT WAS GONE...
WSH
IT JUST VANISHED WITHOUT A TRACE...
IMPOS-SIBLE...
PIP
END CALL
DAMN IT ALL...!
TSU-KUNE'S BODY WENT MISSING FROM THE MORGUE...
KO-GAMI-KUN...
I'D LIKE THAT EXPLA-NATION NOW.
WHAT'S GOING ON HERE?

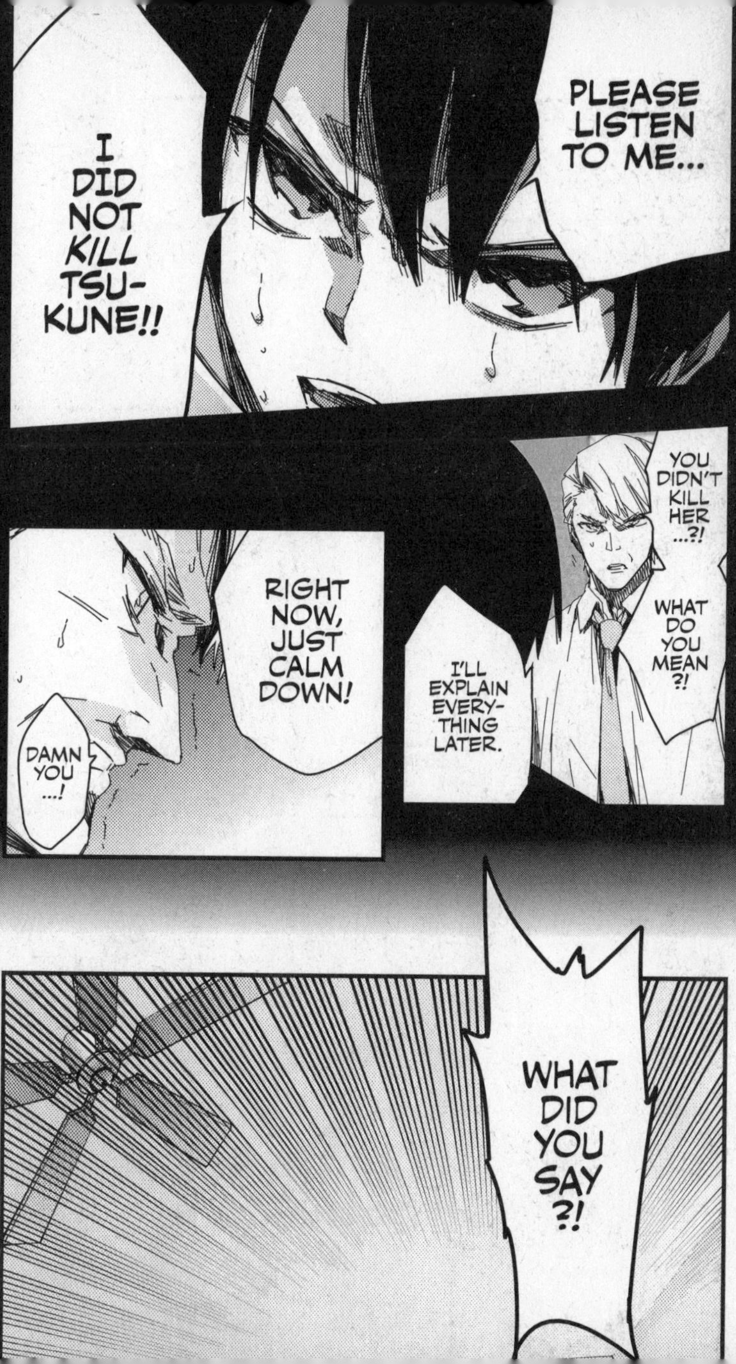
PLEASE LISTEN TO ME...
I DID NOT *KILL* TSU-KUNE!!
YOU DIDN'T KILL HER ...?!
WHAT DO YOU MEAN ?!
I'LL EXPLAIN EVERY-THING LATER.
RIGHT NOW, JUST CALM DOWN!
DAMN YOU ...!
WHAT DID YOU SAY ?!

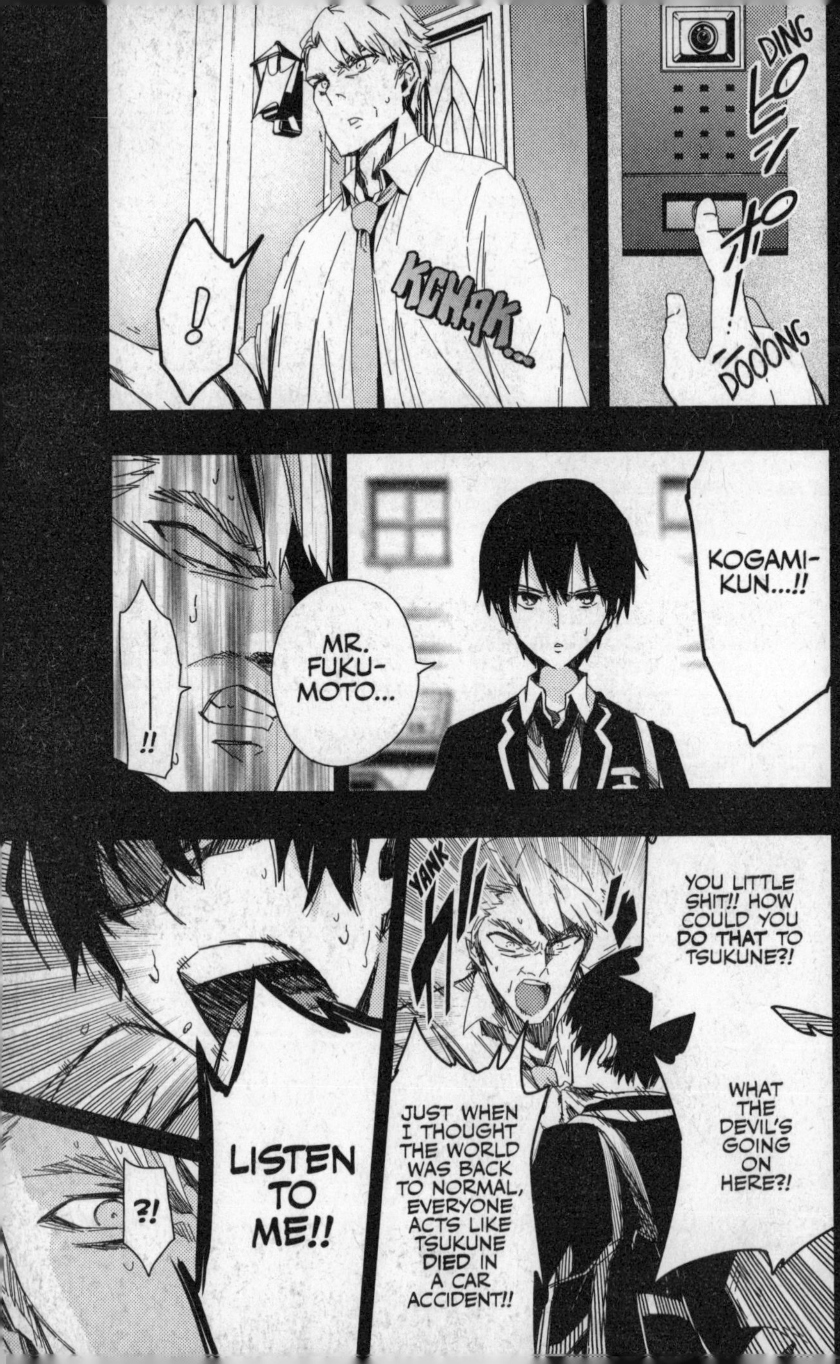
DING DOOONG
KCHAK...
!
KOGAMI-KUN...!!
MR. FUKU-MOTO...
......!!
YANK
YOU LITTLE SHIT!! HOW COULD YOU DO THAT TO TSUKUNE?!
WHAT THE DEVIL'S GOING ON HERE?!
JUST WHEN I THOUGHT THE WORLD WAS BACK TO NORMAL, EVERYONE ACTS LIKE TSUKUNE DIED IN A CAR ACCIDENT!!
LISTEN TO ME!!
?!

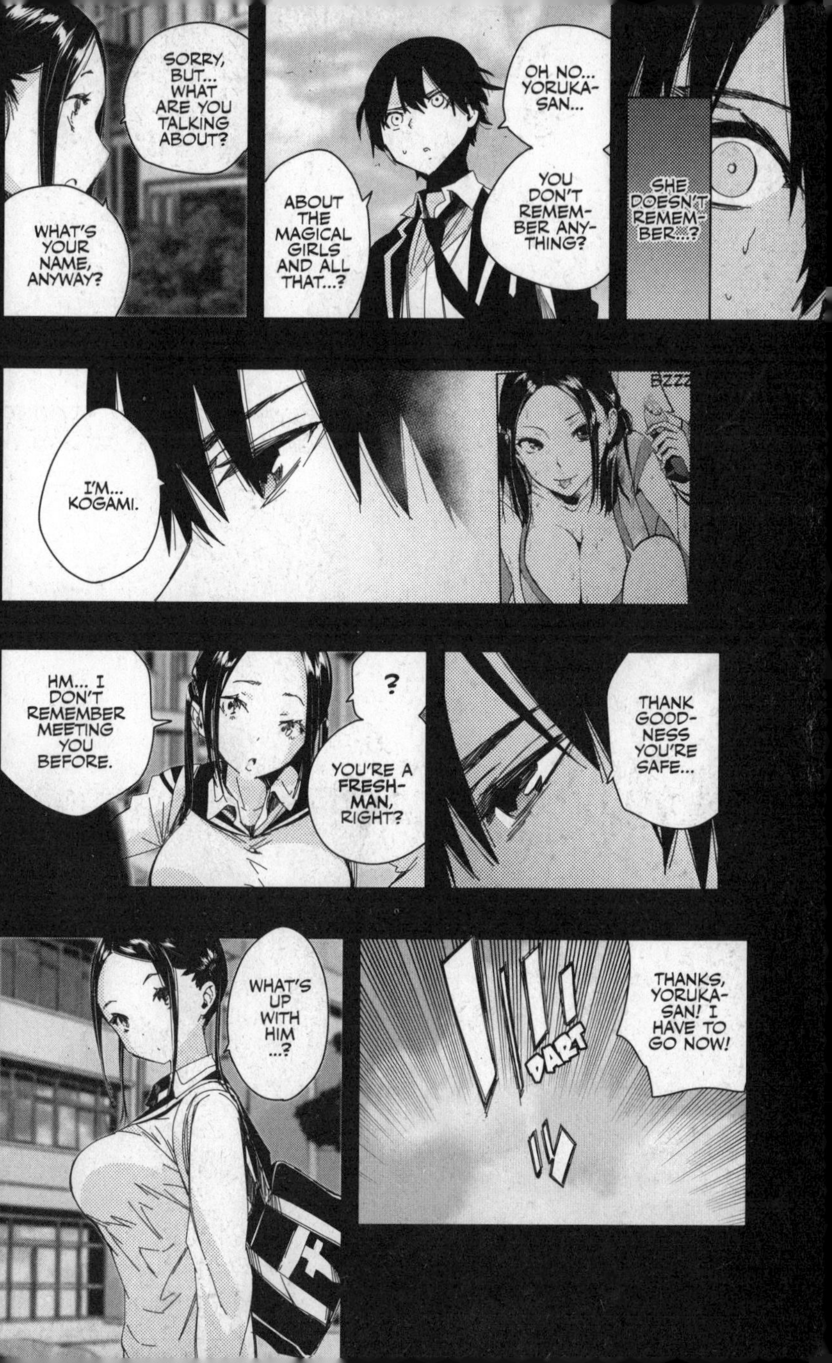
SHE DOESN'T REMEMBER...?
OH NO... YORUKA-SAN...
YOU DON'T REMEMBER ANYTHING?
ABOUT THE MAGICAL GIRLS AND ALL THAT...?
SORRY, BUT... WHAT ARE YOU TALKING ABOUT?
WHAT'S YOUR NAME, ANYWAY?
BZZZ
I'M... KOGAMI.
THANK GOODNESS YOU'RE SAFE...
?
HM... I DON'T REMEMBER MEETING YOU BEFORE.
YOU'RE A FRESHMAN, RIGHT?
THANKS, YORUKA-SAN! I HAVE TO GO NOW!
DART
WHAT'S UP WITH HIM ...?

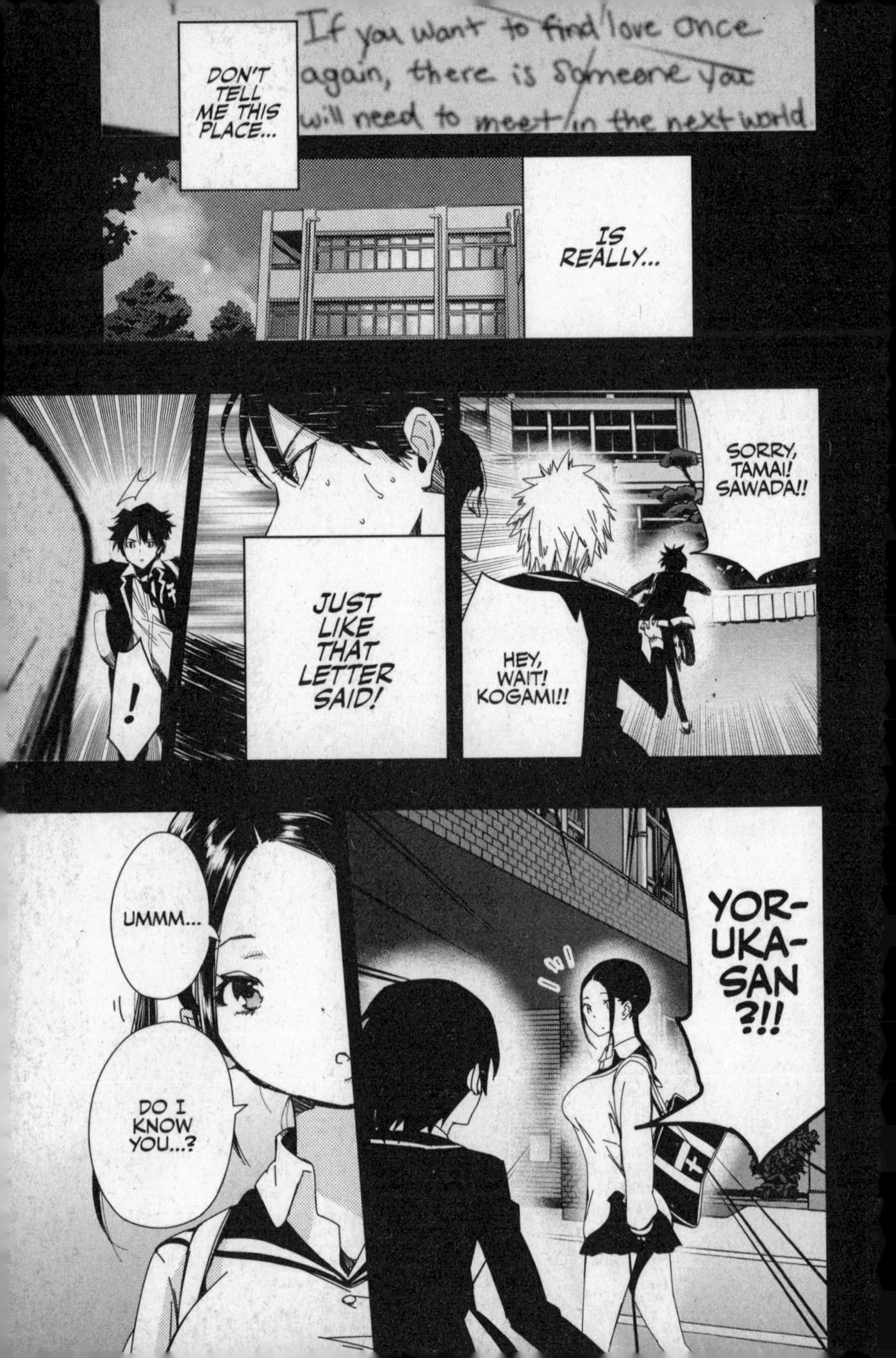
If you want to find love once again, there is someone you will need to meet in the next world
DON'T TELL ME THIS PLACE...
IS REALLY...
SORRY, TAMAI! SAWADA!!
HEY, WAIT! KOGAMI!!
JUST LIKE THAT LETTER SAID!
!
YOR-UKA-SAN?!!
UMMM...
DO I KNOW YOU...?

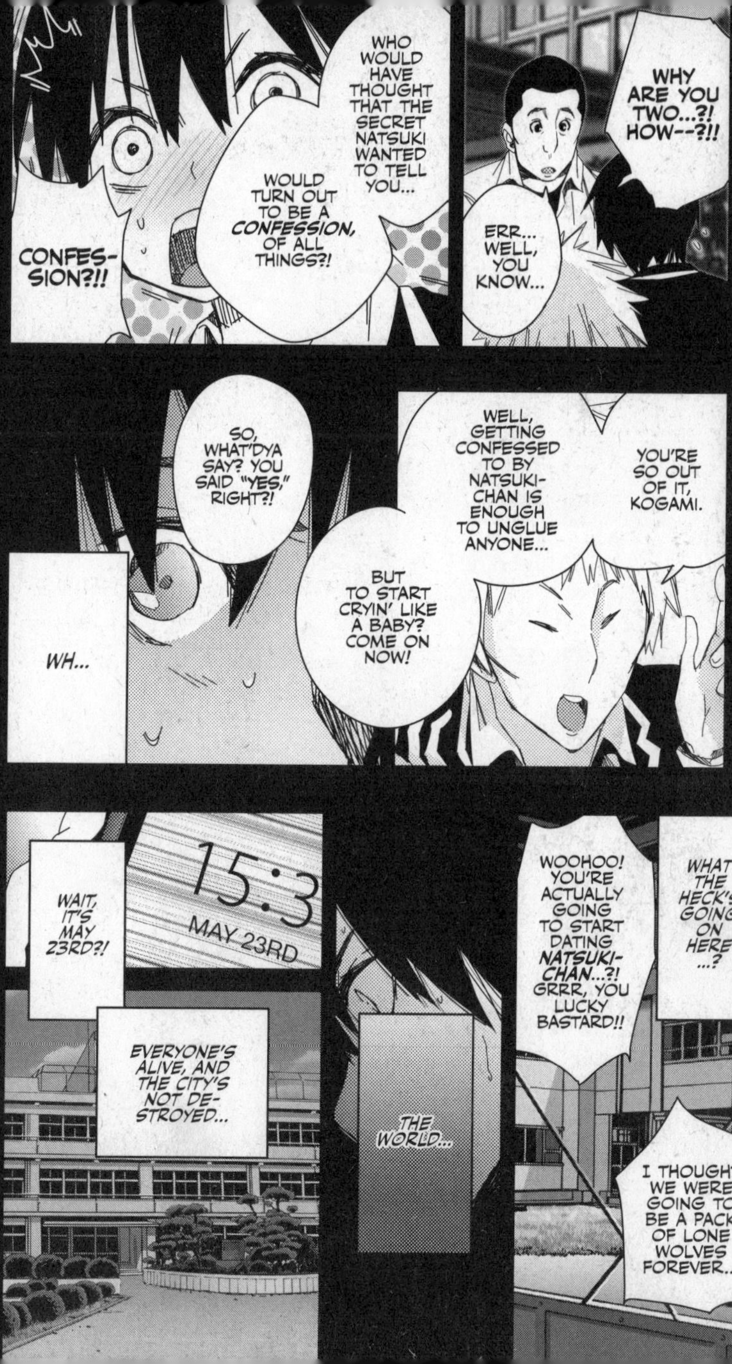
WHY ARE YOU TWO...?! HOW--?!!
ERR... WELL, YOU KNOW...
WHO WOULD HAVE THOUGHT THAT THE SECRET NATSUKI WANTED TO TELL YOU...
WOULD TURN OUT TO BE A *CONFESSION,* OF ALL THINGS?!
CONFES-SION?!!
YOU'RE SO OUT OF IT, KOGAMI.
WELL, GETTING CONFESSED TO BY NATSUKI-CHAN IS ENOUGH TO UNGLUE ANYONE...
BUT TO START CRYIN' LIKE A BABY? COME ON NOW!
SO, WHAT'DYA SAY? YOU SAID "YES," RIGHT?!
WH...
WHAT THE HECK'S GOING ON HERE...?
WOOHOO! YOU'RE ACTUALLY GOING TO START DATING *NATSUKI-CHAN*...?! GRRR, YOU LUCKY BASTARD!!
I THOUGHT WE WERE GOING TO BE A PACK OF LONE WOLVES FOREVER...
THE WORLD...
15:3
MAY 23RD
WAIT, IT'S MAY 23RD?!
EVERYONE'S ALIVE, AND THE CITY'S NOT DE-STROYED...

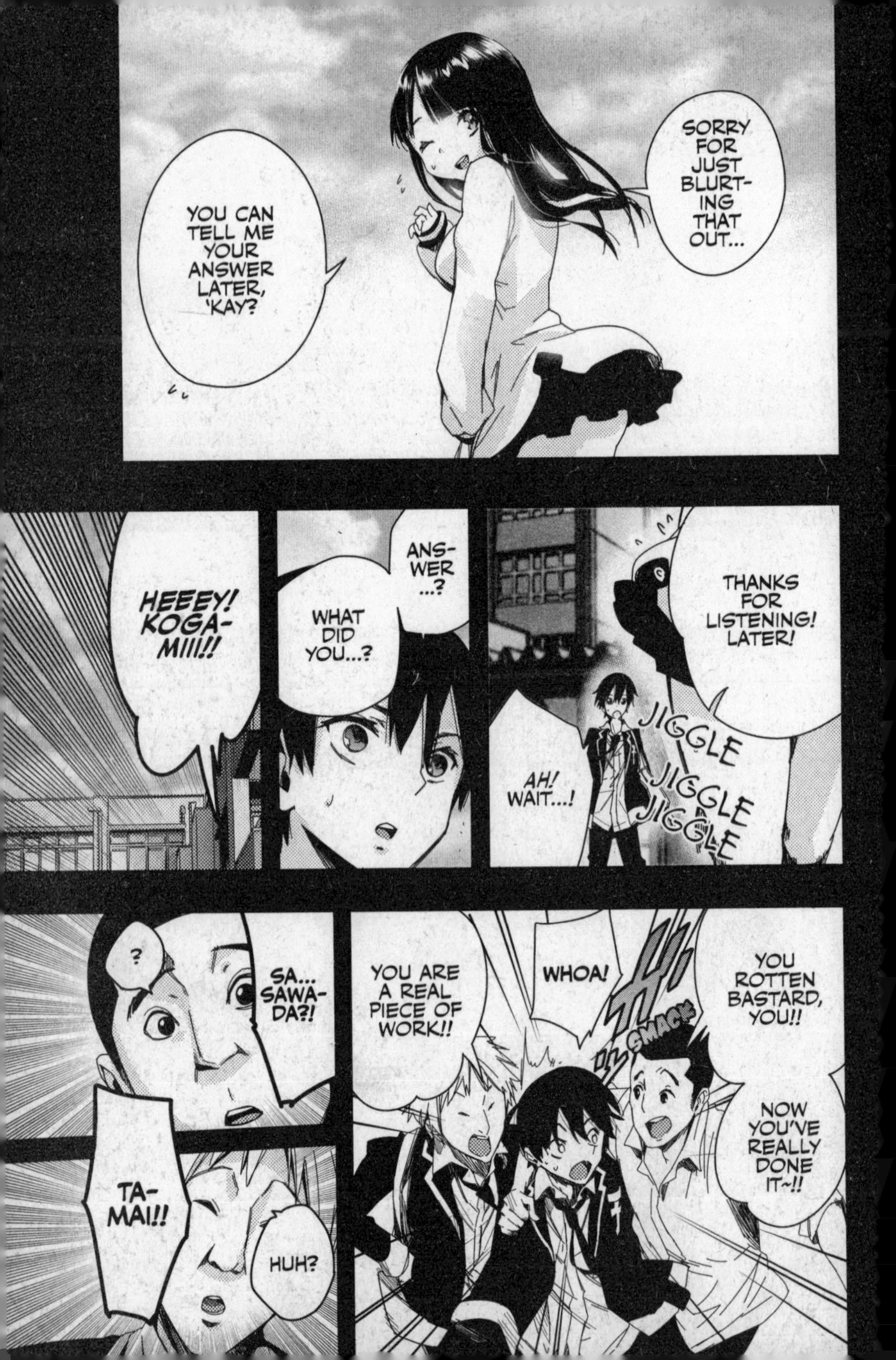
SORRY FOR JUST BLURT-ING THAT OUT...
YOU CAN TELL ME YOUR ANSWER LATER, 'KAY?
THANKS FOR LISTENING! LATER!
JIGGLE JIGGLE JIGGLE
AH! WAIT...!
ANS-WER ...?
WHAT DID YOU...?
HEEEY! KOGA-MIII!!
YOU ROTTEN BASTARD, YOU!!
WHOA!
SMACK
YOU ARE A REAL PIECE OF WORK!!
NOW YOU'VE REALLY DONE IT~!!
?
SA... SAWA-DA?!
TA-MAI!!
HUH?

KOGAMI-KUN... YOU JUST SUDDENLY STARTED CRYING...

IT STARTLED ME.

THIS IS...

MY SCHOOL ...?

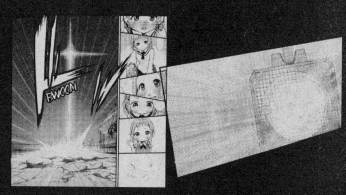

BWOOM

I SHOT...

BACK THEN, I...

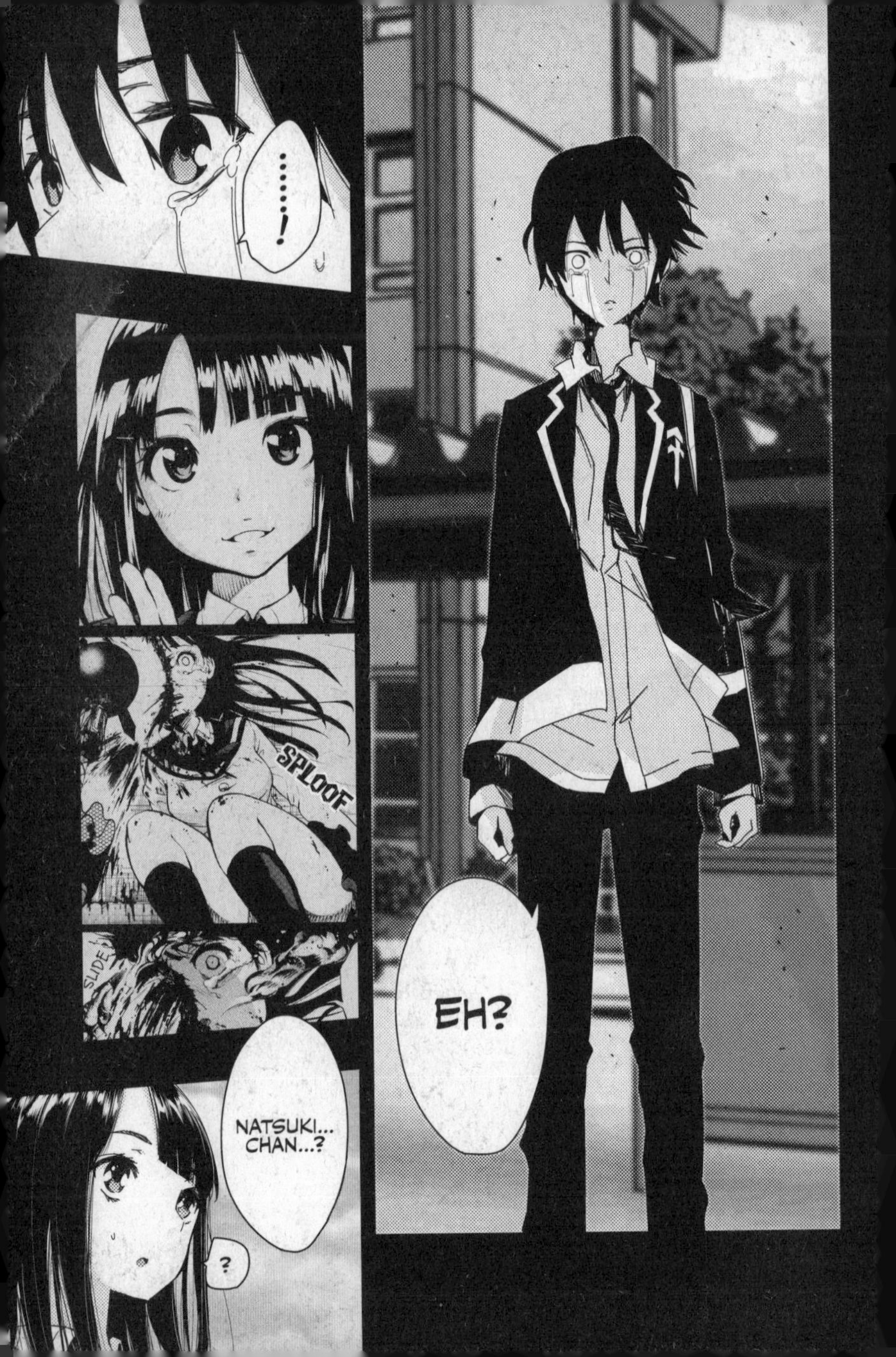
EH?
......!
SPLOOF
SLIDE
NATSUKI... CHAN...?
?

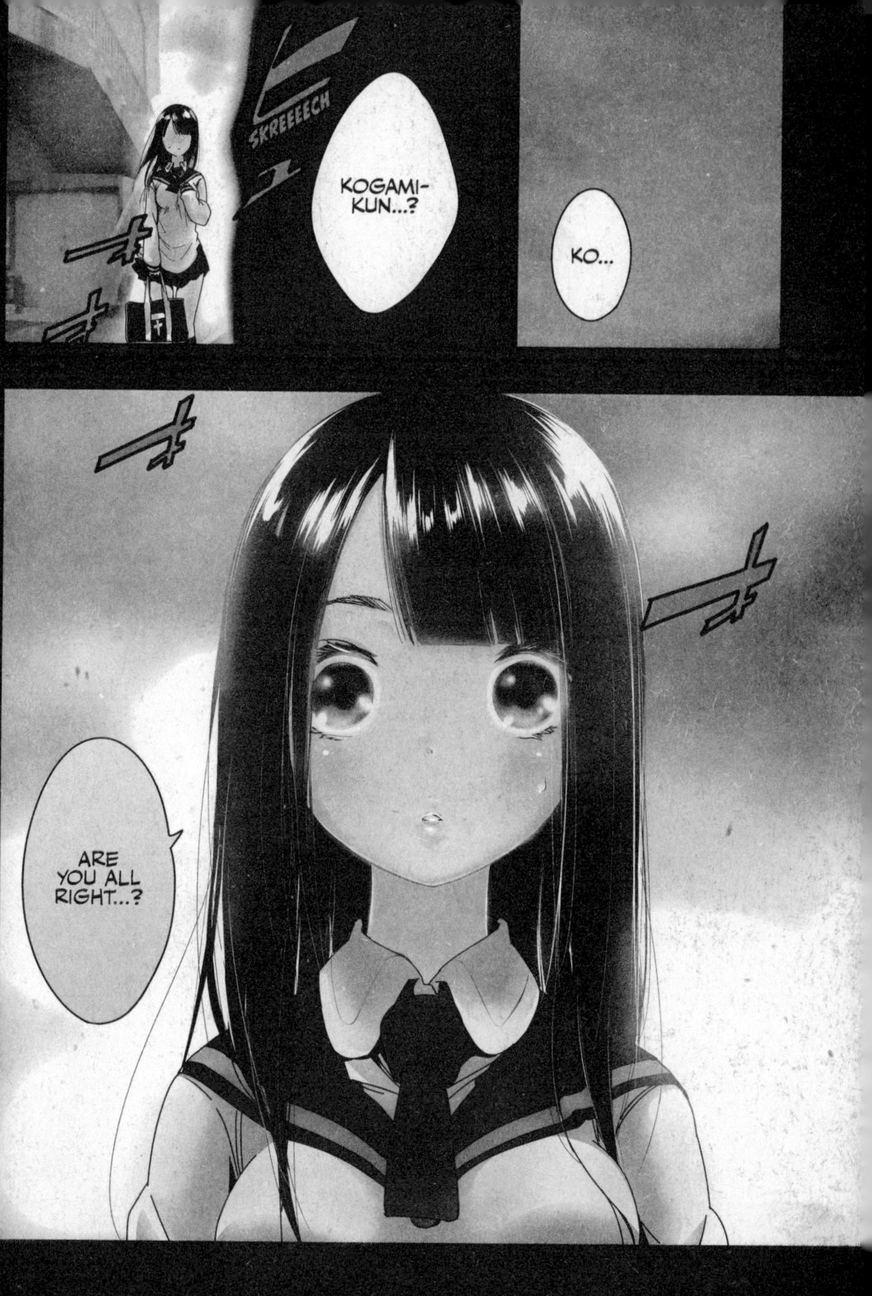
KO...
KOGAMI-KUN...?
SKREEEECH
ARE YOU ALL RIGHT...?

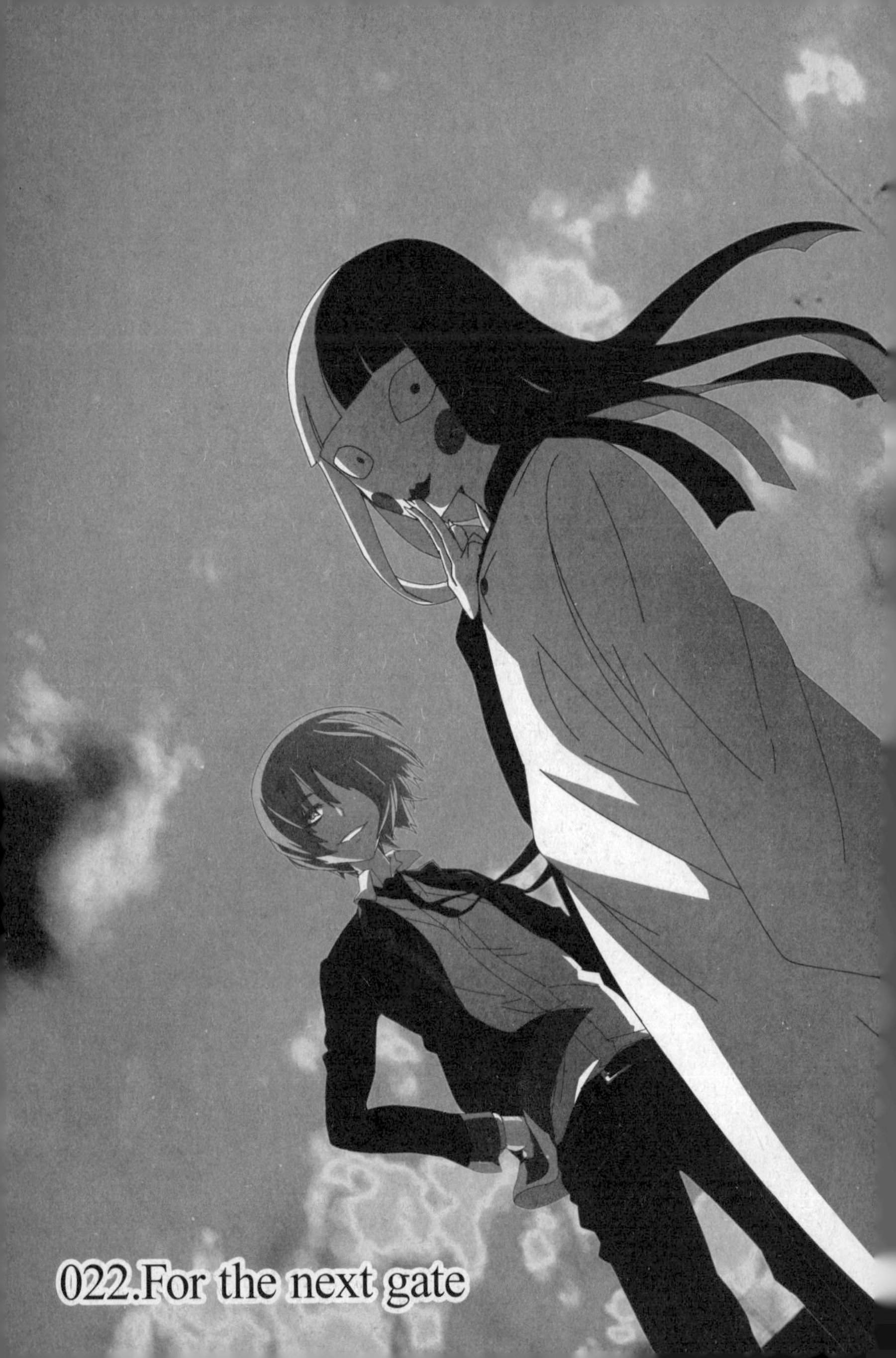

022.For the next gate

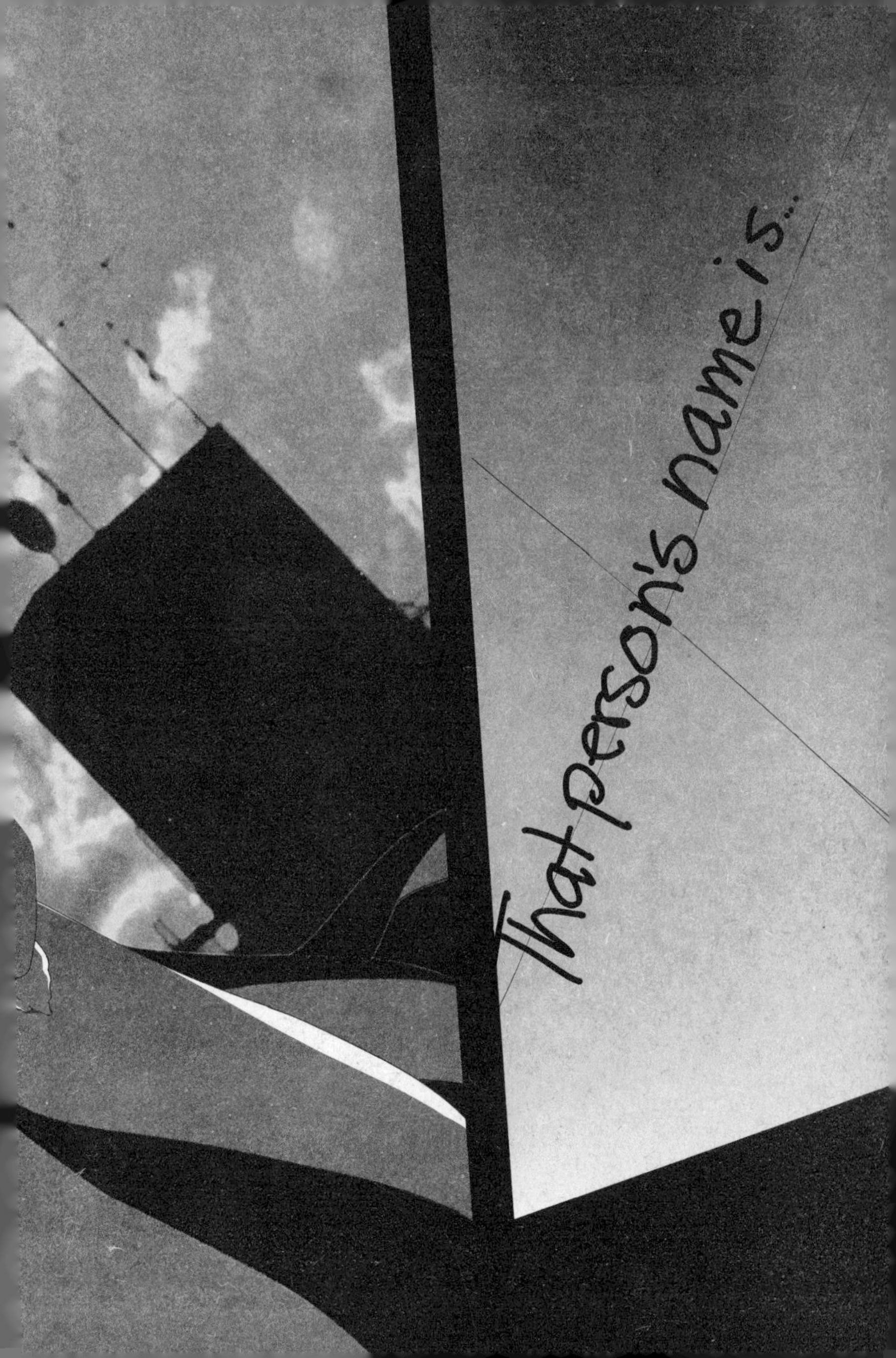
That person's name is...

022.For the next gate

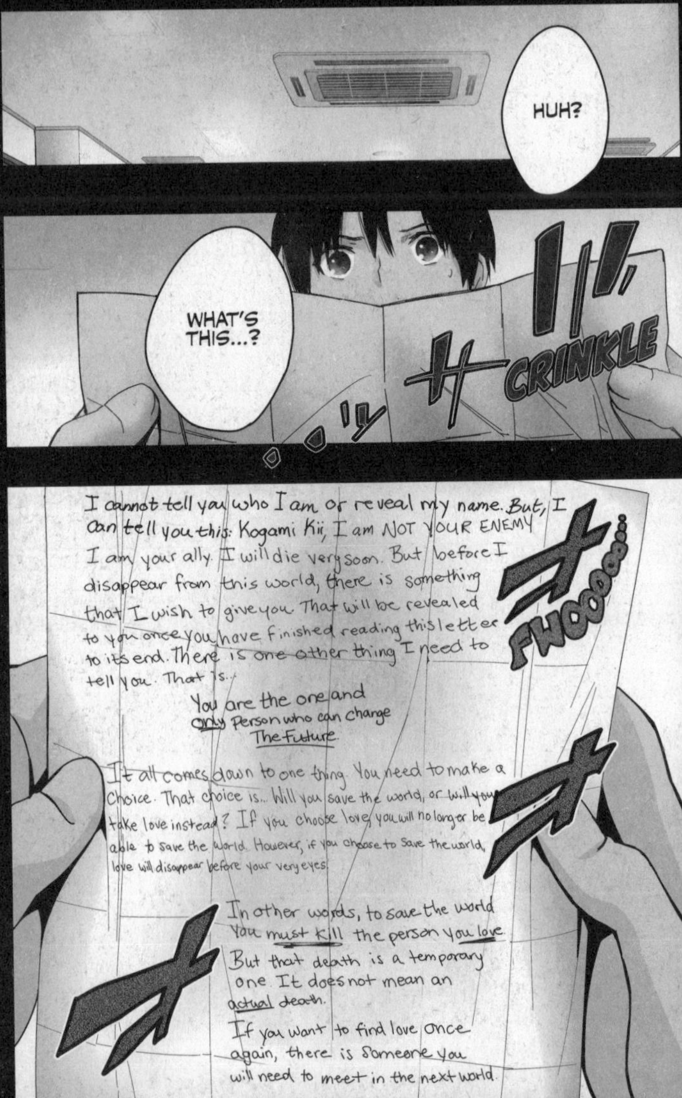
HUH?
WHAT'S THIS...?
CRINKLE
I cannot tell you who I am or reveal my name. But, I can tell you this: Kogami Kii, I am NOT YOUR ENEMY I am your ally. I will die very soon. But before I disappear from this world, there is something that I wish to give you. That will be revealed to you once you have finished reading this letter to its end. There is one other thing I need to tell you. That is...
You are the one and only person who can change The Future.
It all comes down to one thing. You need to make a choice. That choice is... Will you save the world, or will you take love instead? If you choose love, you will no longer be able to save the world. However, if you choose to save the world, love will disappear before your very eyes.
In other words, to save the world you must kill the person you love.
But that death is a temporary one. It does not mean an actual death.
If you want to find love once again, there is someone you will need to meet in the next world.
FWOOOO...

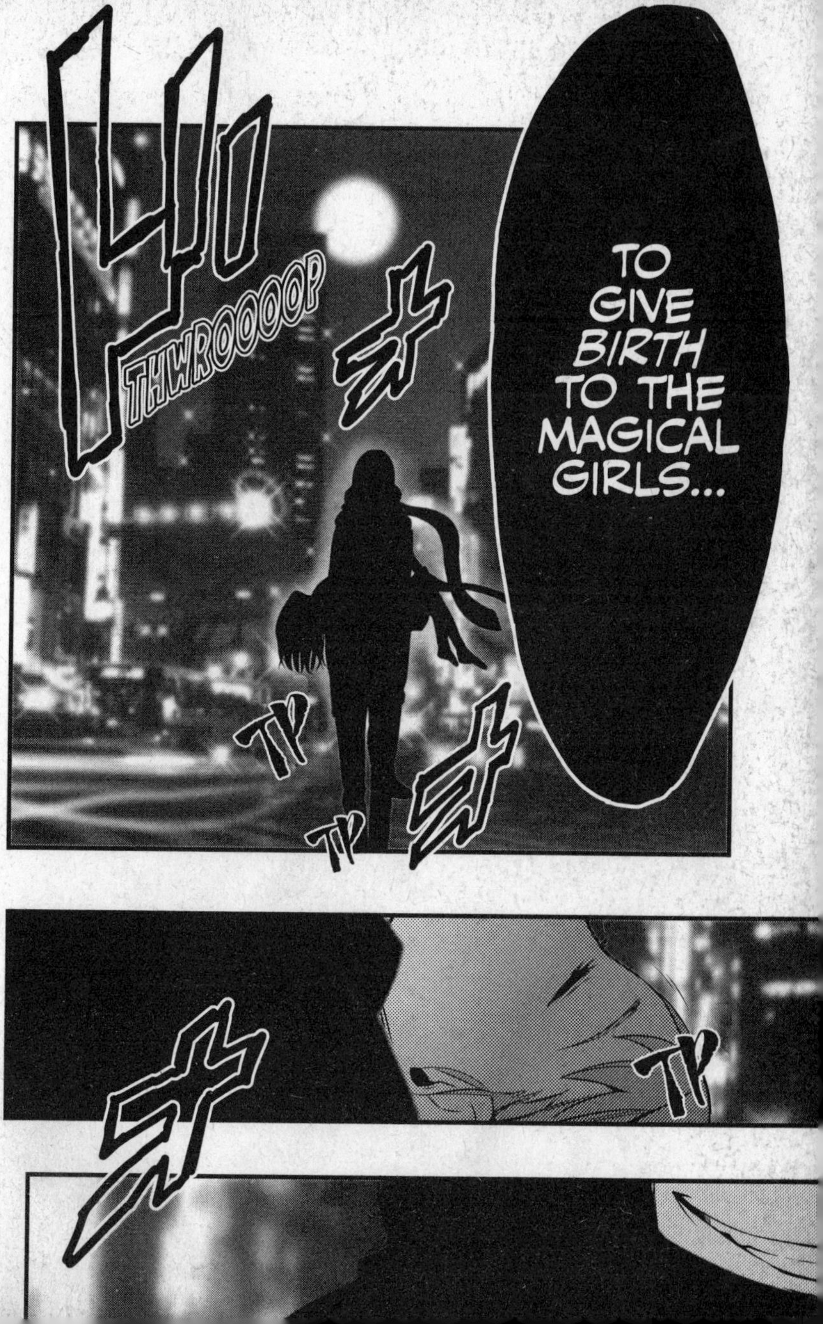
TO GIVE BIRTH TO THE MAGICAL GIRLS...
THWROOOOP
TP
TP
TP

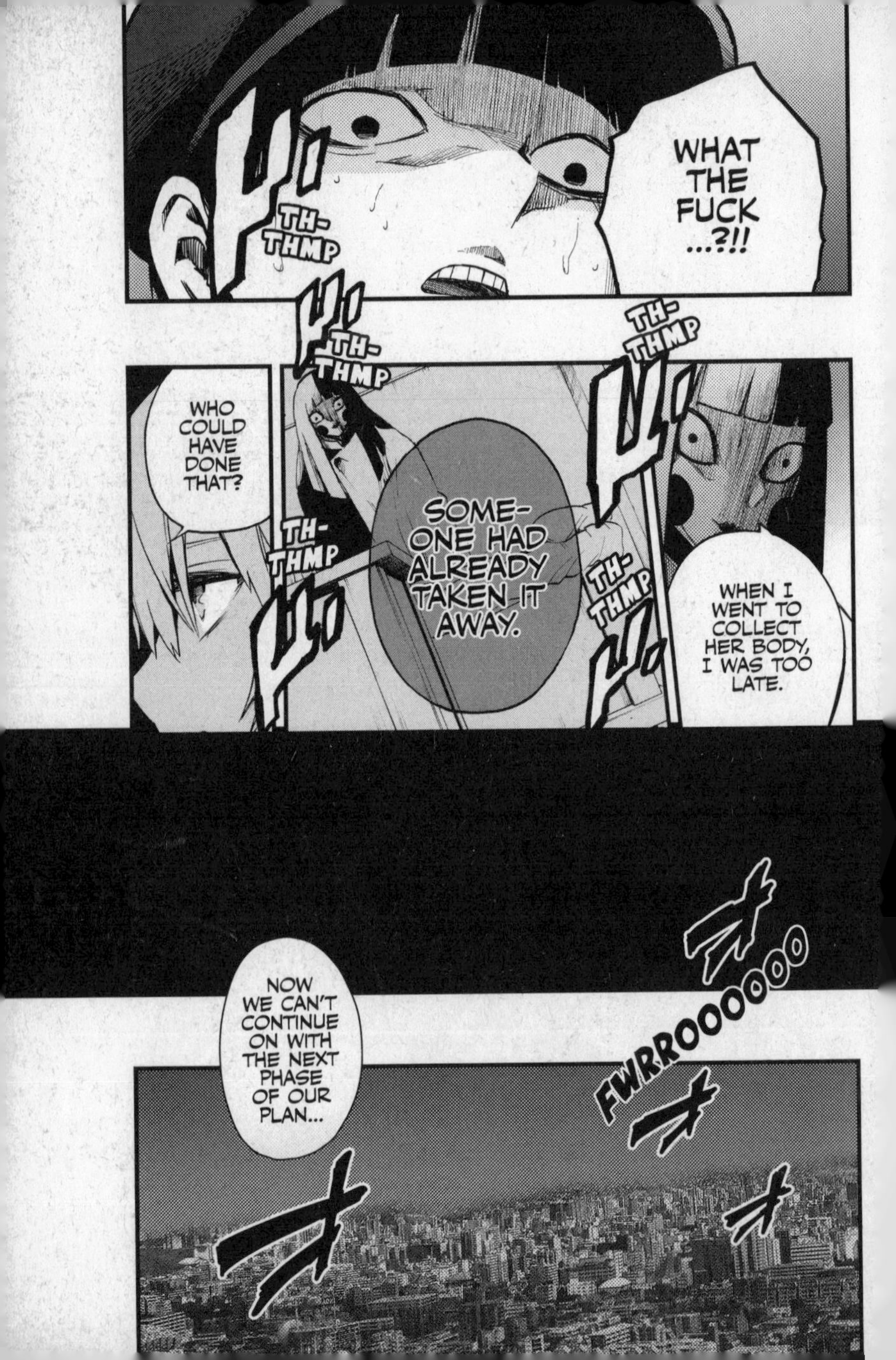
WHAT THE FUCK ...?!!
TH-THMP
TH-THMP
TH-THMP
WHEN I WENT TO COLLECT HER BODY, I WAS TOO LATE.
TH-THMP
SOME-ONE HAD ALREADY TAKEN IT AWAY.
TH-THMP
WHO COULD HAVE DONE THAT?
FWRROOOOOOO
NOW WE CAN'T CONTINUE ON WITH THE NEXT PHASE OF OUR PLAN...

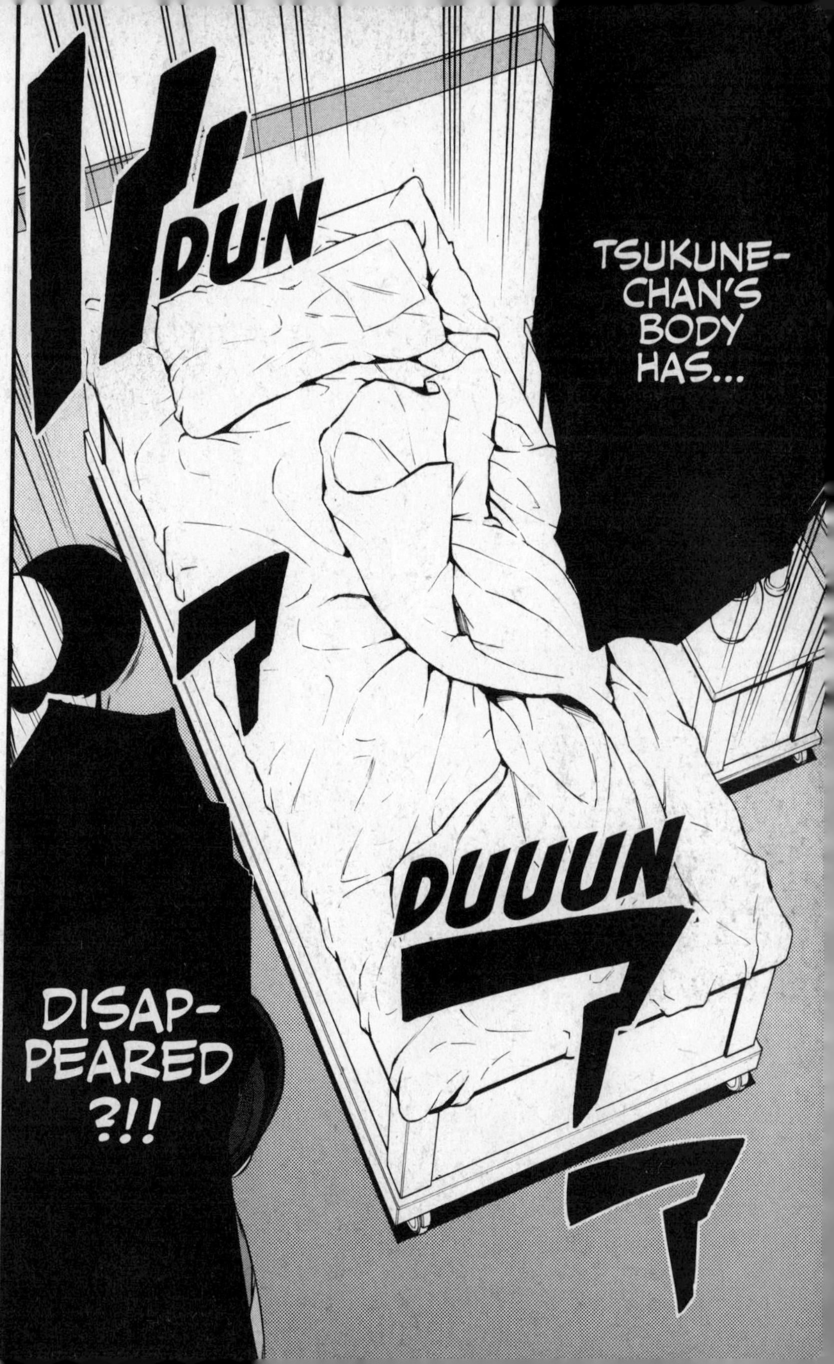
TSUKUNE-CHAN'S BODY HAS...
DUN
DUUUN
DISAP-PEARED ?!!

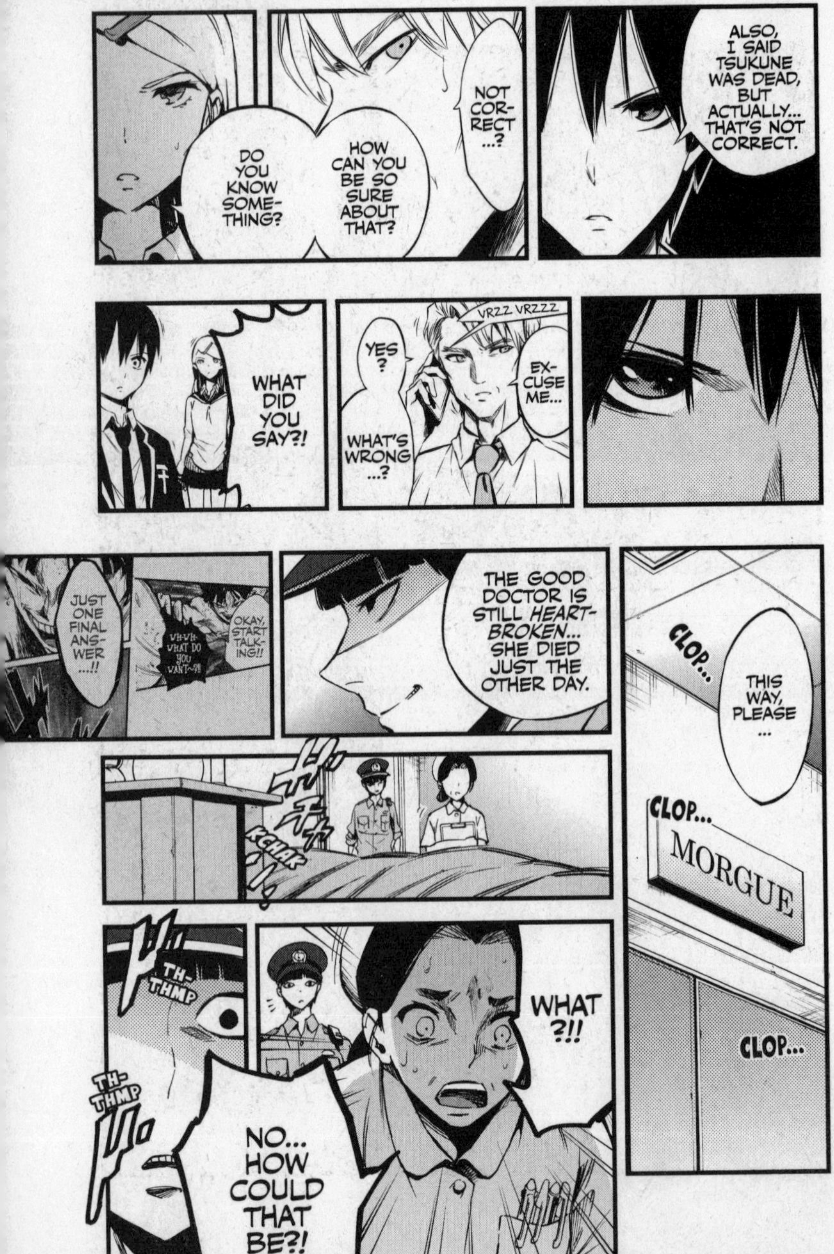
ALSO, I SAID TSUKUNE WAS DEAD, BUT ACTUALLY... THAT'S NOT CORRECT.
NOT CORRECT...?
HOW CAN YOU BE SO SURE ABOUT THAT?
DO YOU KNOW SOMETHING?
VRZZ VRZZZ
EXCUSE ME...
YES?
WHAT'S WRONG...?
WHAT DID YOU SAY?!
CLOP...
THIS WAY, PLEASE...
CLOP...
MORGUE
CLOP...
THE GOOD DOCTOR IS STILL *HEART-BROKEN*... SHE DIED JUST THE OTHER DAY.
OKAY, START TALKING!!
VH-VH-WHAT DO YOU WANT~?!!
JUST ONE FINAL ANSWER...!!
KCHAK
WHAT?!!
TH-THMP
NO... HOW COULD THAT BE?!
TH-THMP

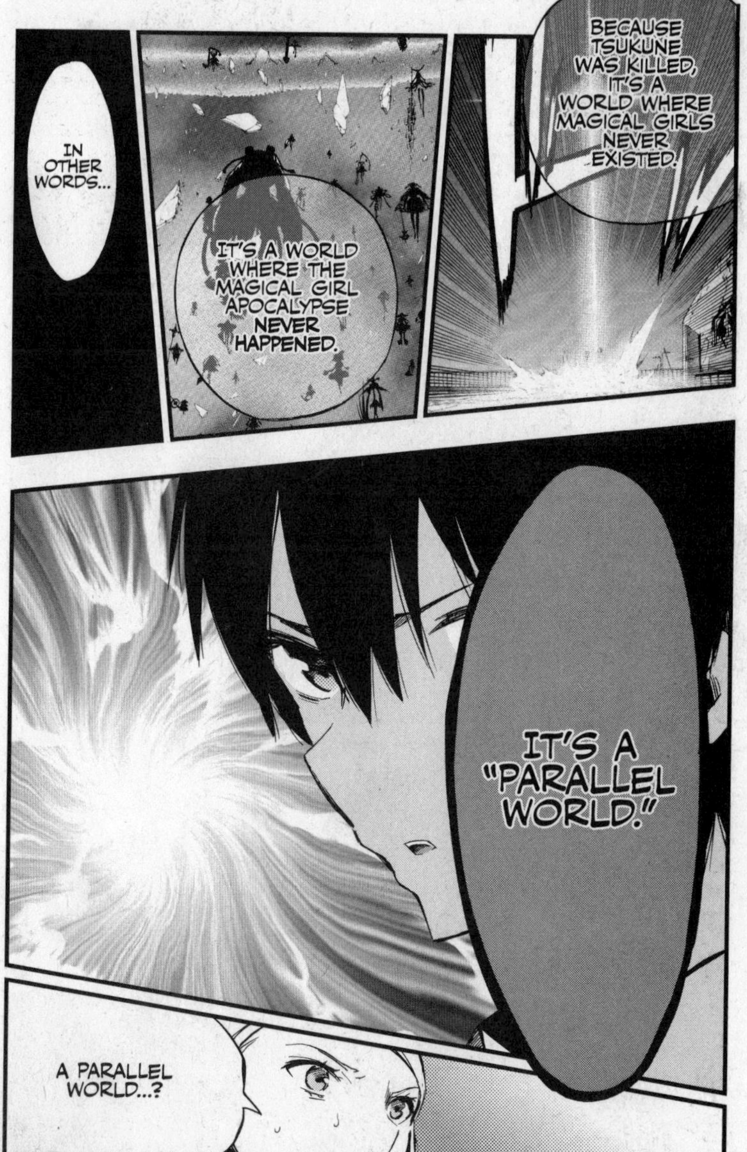
BECAUSE TSUKUNE WAS KILLED, IT'S A WORLD WHERE MAGICAL GIRLS NEVER EXISTED.
IT'S A WORLD WHERE THE MAGICAL GIRL APOCALYPSE NEVER HAPPENED.
IN OTHER WORDS...
IT'S A "PARALLEL WORLD."
A PARALLEL WORLD...?

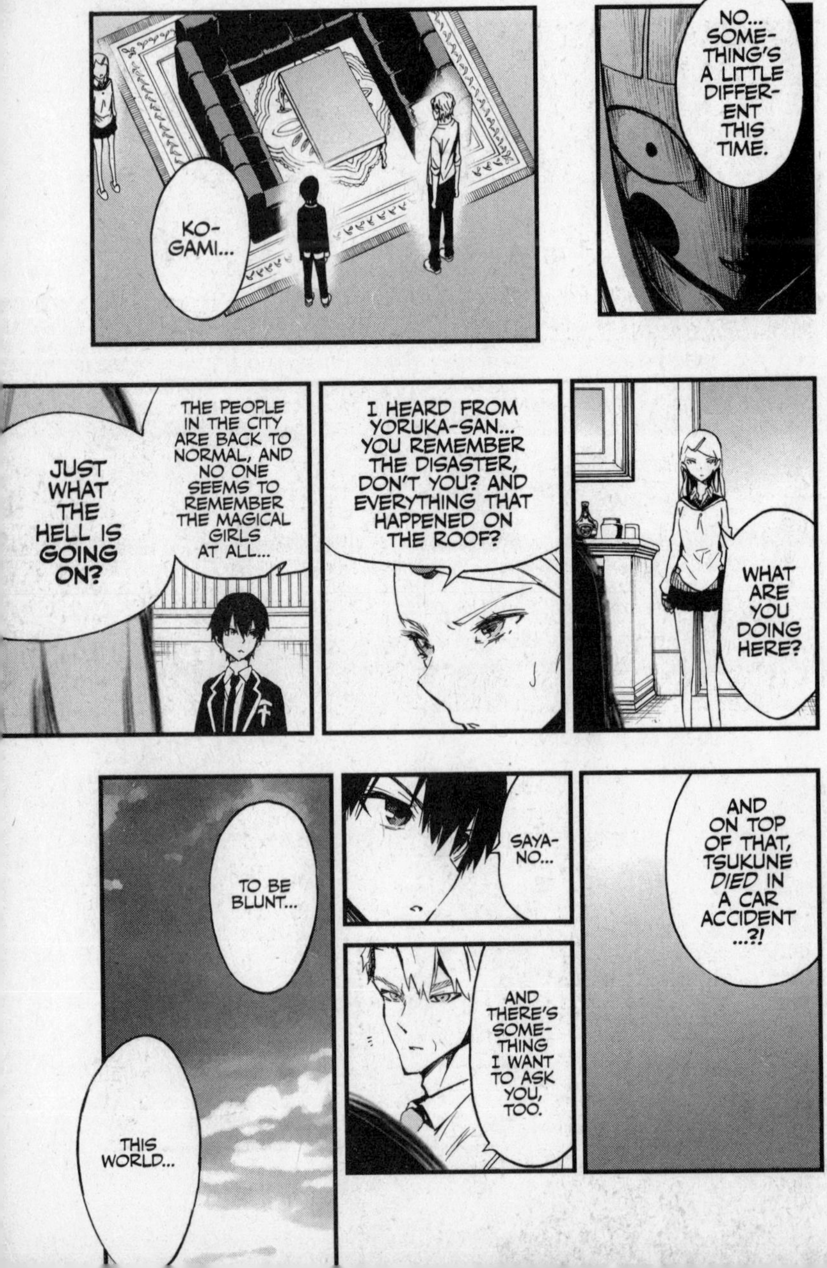
NO... SOMETHING'S A LITTLE DIFFERENT THIS TIME.
KO-GAMI...
WHAT ARE YOU DOING HERE?
I HEARD FROM YORUKA-SAN... YOU REMEMBER THE DISASTER, DON'T YOU? AND EVERYTHING THAT HAPPENED ON THE ROOF?
THE PEOPLE IN THE CITY ARE BACK TO NORMAL, AND NO ONE SEEMS TO REMEMBER THE MAGICAL GIRLS AT ALL...
JUST WHAT THE HELL IS GOING ON?
AND ON TOP OF THAT, TSUKUNE *DIED* IN A CAR ACCIDENT...?!
SAYA-NO...
AND THERE'S SOMETHING I WANT TO ASK YOU, TOO.
TO BE BLUNT...
THIS WORLD...

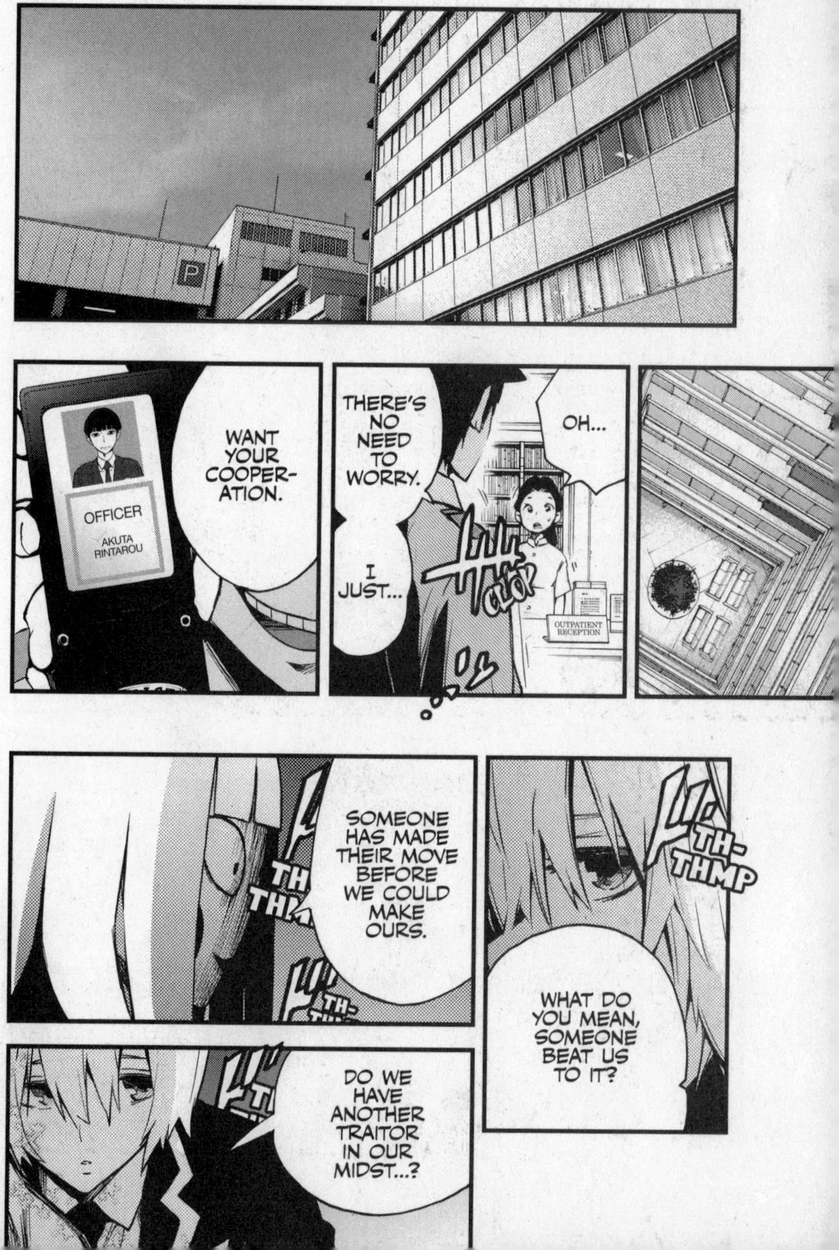
P
OH...
THERE'S NO NEED TO WORRY.
I JUST...
CLOP
OUTPATIENT RECEPTION
WANT YOUR COOPER-ATION.
OFFICER
AKUTA RINTAROU
TH-THMP
WHAT DO YOU MEAN, SOMEONE BEAT US TO IT?
TH-THMP
SOMEONE HAS MADE THEIR MOVE BEFORE WE COULD MAKE OURS.
DO WE HAVE ANOTHER TRAITOR IN OUR MIDST...?

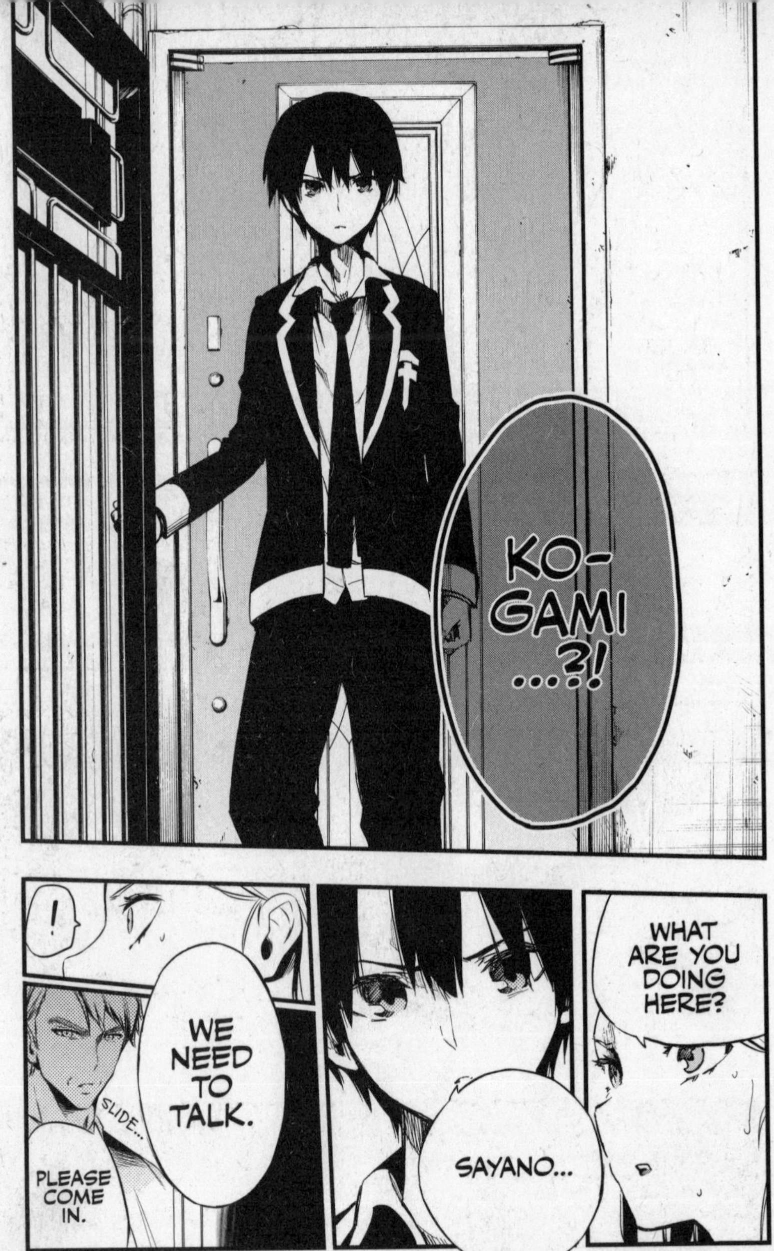
KO-GAMI ...?!
WHAT ARE YOU DOING HERE?
SAYANO...
!
WE NEED TO TALK.
SLIDE...
PLEASE COME IN.

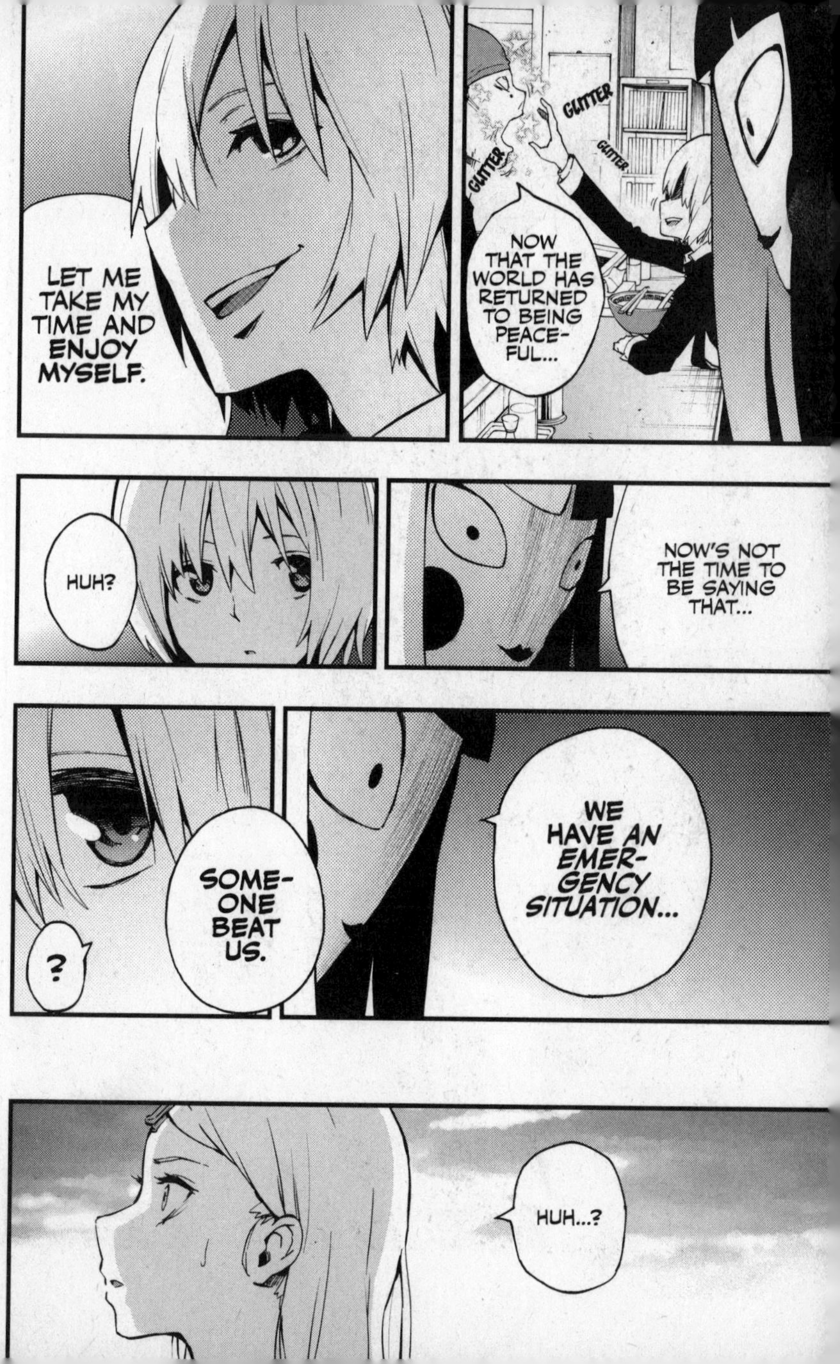
GLITTER
GLITTER
GLITTER
NOW THAT THE WORLD HAS RETURNED TO BEING PEACE-FUL...
LET ME TAKE MY TIME AND ENJOY MYSELF.
NOW'S NOT THE TIME TO BE SAYING THAT...
HUH?
WE HAVE AN EMER-GENCY SITUATION...
SOME-ONE BEAT US.
?
HUH...?

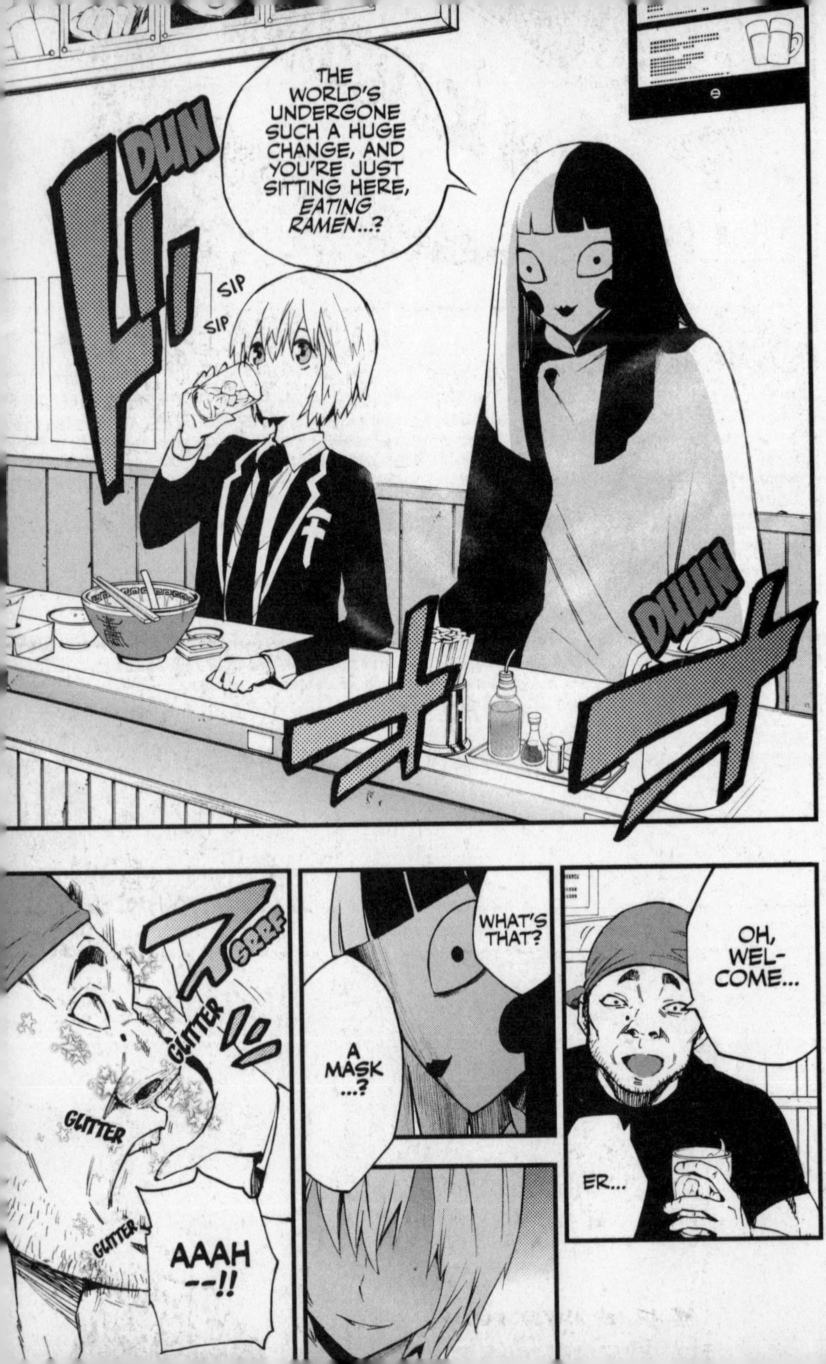
THE WORLD'S UNDERGONE SUCH A HUGE CHANGE, AND YOU'RE JUST SITTING HERE, *EATING RAMEN*...?
DUN
SIP
SIP
DUN
OH, WEL-COME...
ER...
WHAT'S THAT?
A MASK ...?
SRRF
GLITTER
GLITTER
GLITTER
AAAH --!!

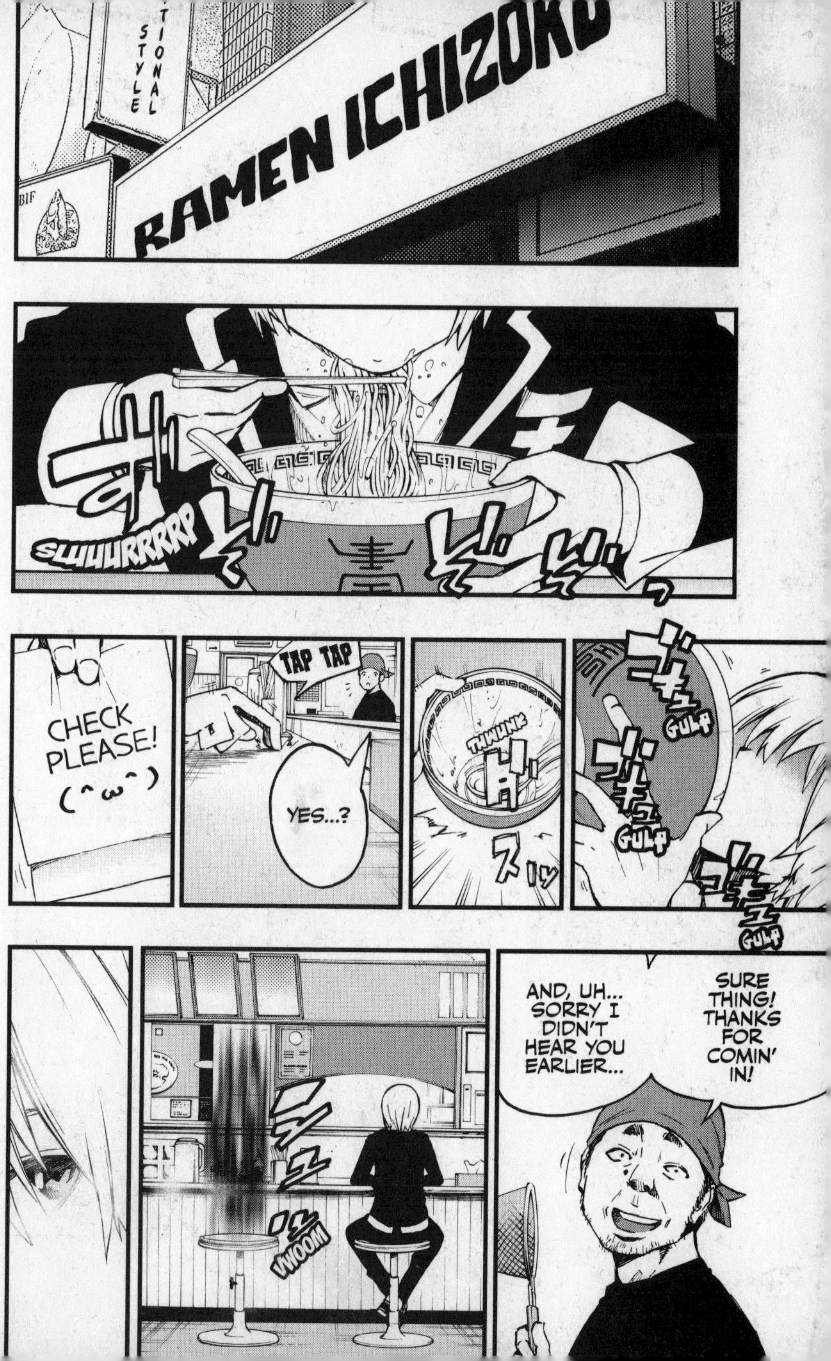
RAMEN ICHIZOKU
TIONAL
STYLE
BIF
SWUUURRRRP
GULP
GULP
GULP
THWUNK
TAP TAP
YES...?
CHECK PLEASE!
(^ω^)
SURE THING! THANKS FOR COMIN' IN!
AND, UH... SORRY I DIDN'T HEAR YOU EARLIER...
VWOOM

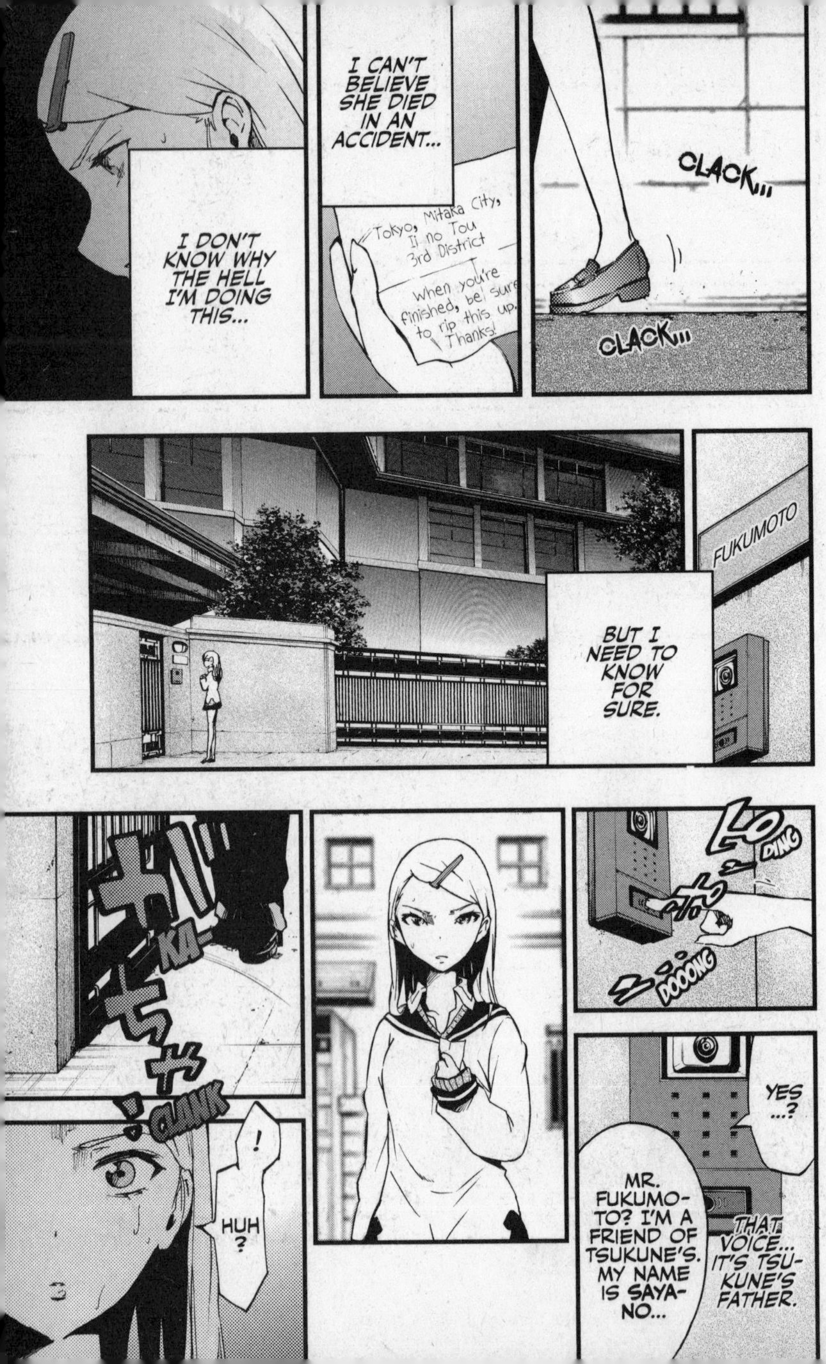
CLACK...
CLACK...
I CAN'T BELIEVE SHE DIED IN AN ACCIDENT...
Tokyo, Mitaka City, Ii no Tou 3rd District
When you're finished, be sure to rip this up. Thanks!
I DON'T KNOW WHY THE HELL I'M DOING THIS...
FUKUMOTO
BUT I NEED TO KNOW FOR SURE.
DING
DOOONG
YES ...?
MR. FUKUMOTO? I'M A FRIEND OF TSUKUNE'S. MY NAME IS SAYANO...
THAT VOICE... IT'S TSUKUNE'S FATHER.
KA-
CLANK
!
HUH ?

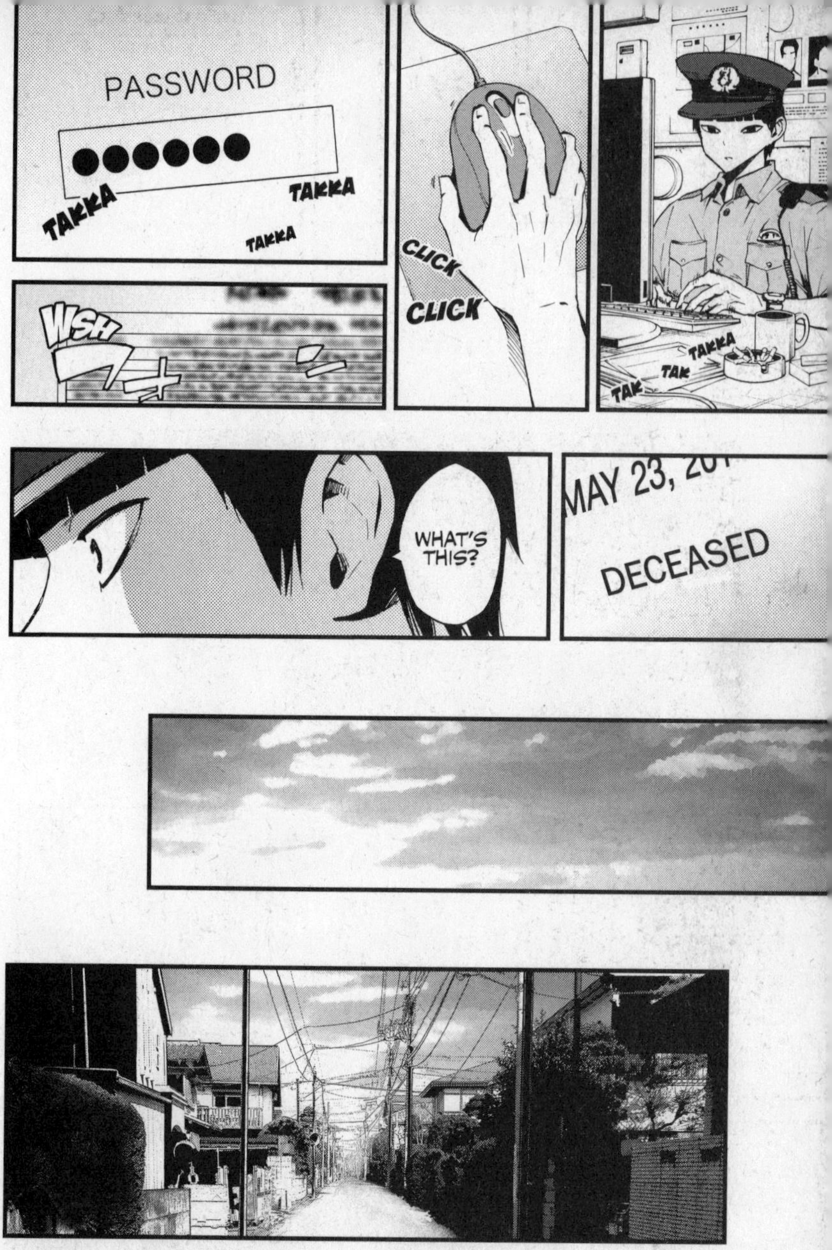
TAKKA
TAK
TAK
CLICK
CLICK
PASSWORD
TAKKA
TAKKA
TAKKA
WSH
MAY 23, 20
DECEASED
WHAT'S THIS?

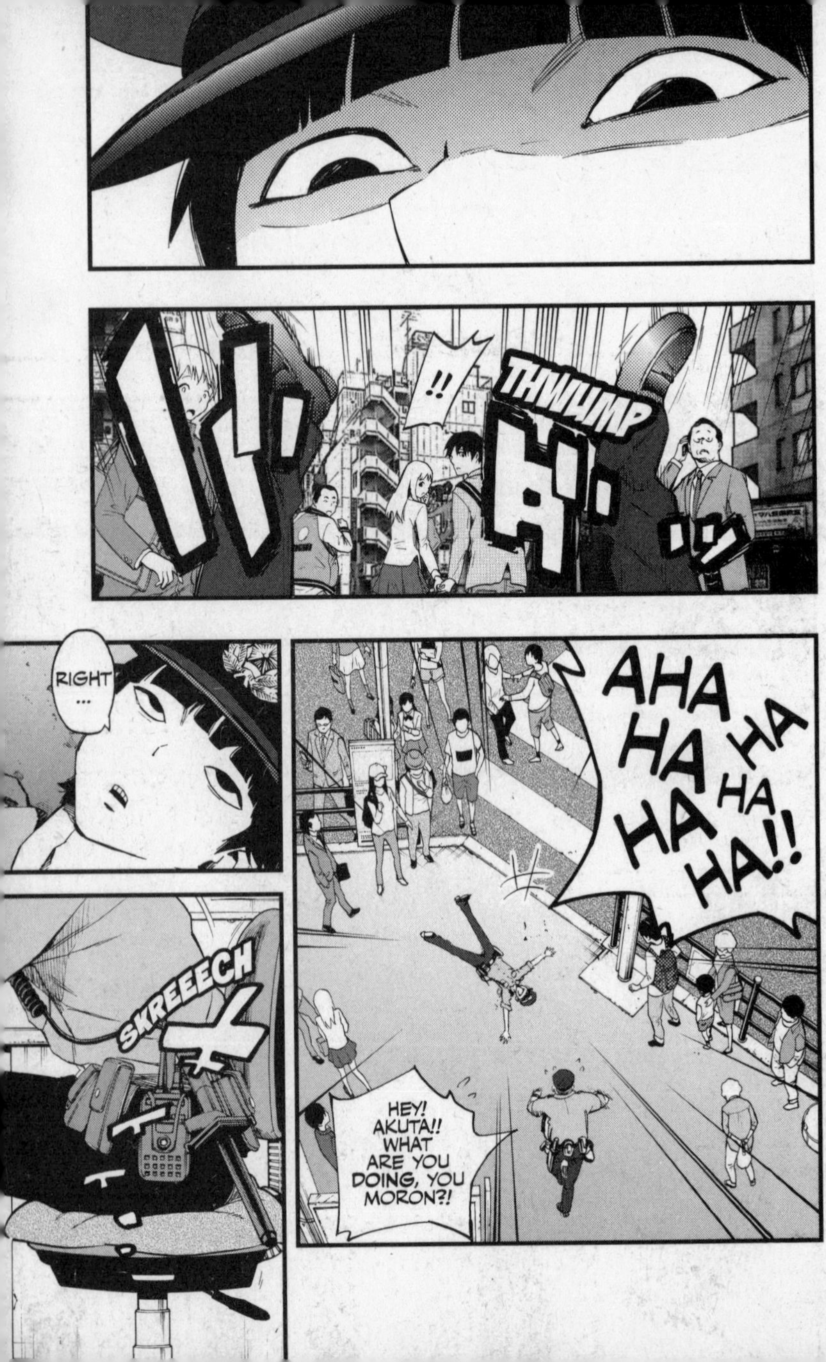

!!
THWUMP
AHA HA HA HA HA HA!!
HEY! AKUTA!! WHAT ARE YOU DOING, YOU MORON?!
RIGHT ...
SKREEECH

HUH?

OFFICER TSU-TSUMI...?

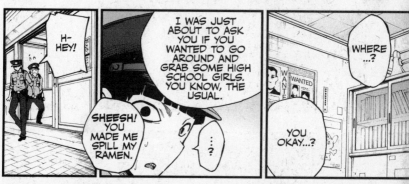

H-HEY!

I WAS JUST ABOUT TO ASK YOU IF YOU WANTED TO GO AROUND AND GRAB SOME HIGH SCHOOL GIRLS. YOU KNOW, THE USUAL.

SHEESH! YOU MADE ME SPILL MY RAMEN.

...?

WHERE ...?

YOU OKAY...?

BUSTLE

BUSTLE

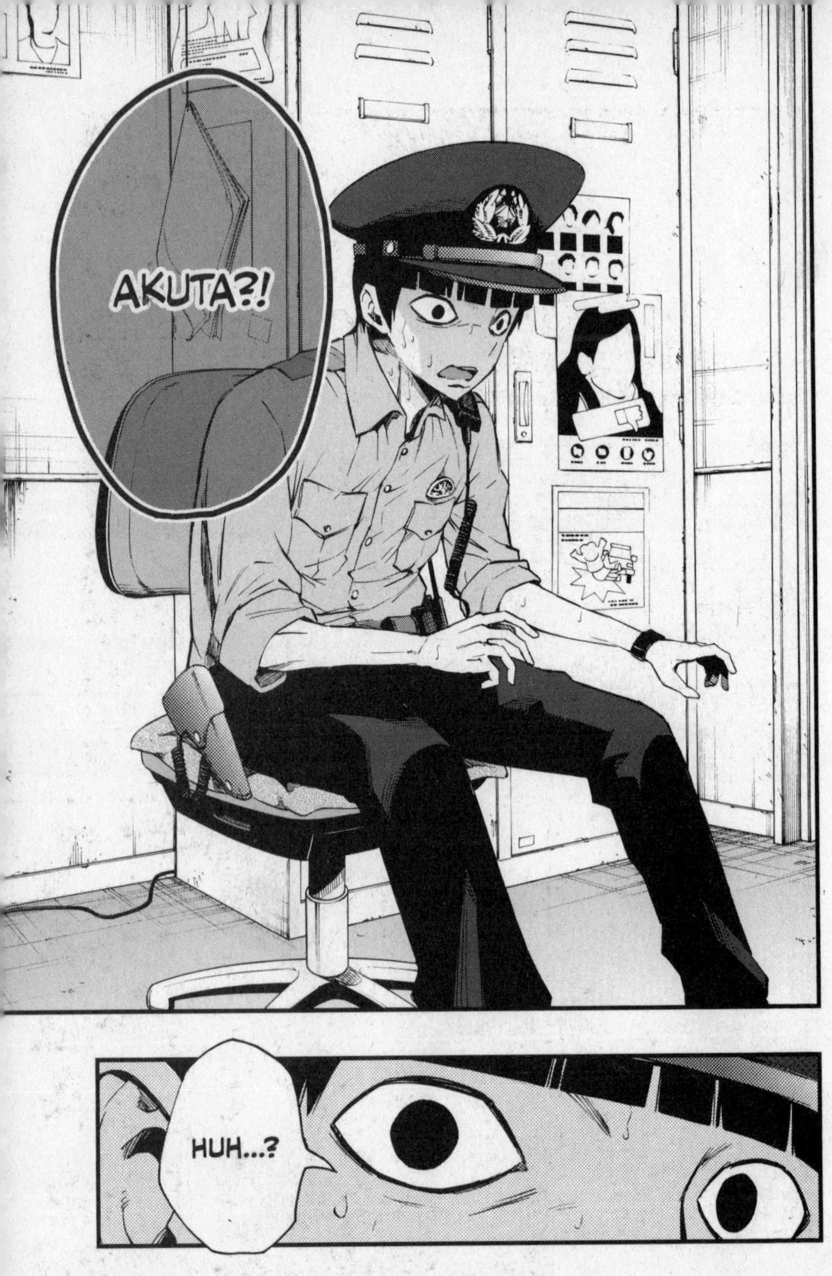
AKUTA?!
HUH...?

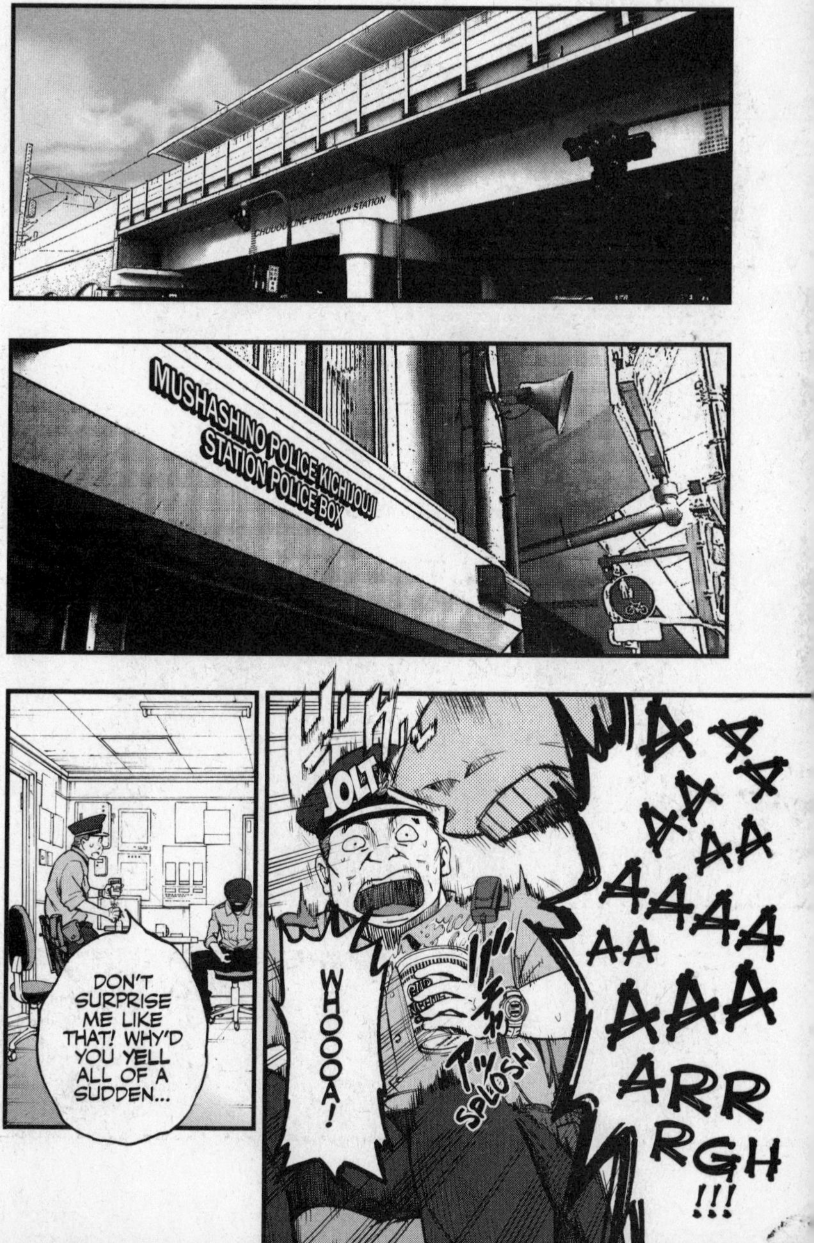
KICHIJOUJI STATION
MUSHASHINO POLICE KICHIJOUJI STATION POLICE BOX
WAAAAAAAAAAAAAAAAAAAARRRRGH!!!
WHOOOA!
SPLOSH
DON'T SURPRISE ME LIKE THAT! WHY'D YOU YELL ALL OF A SUDDEN...

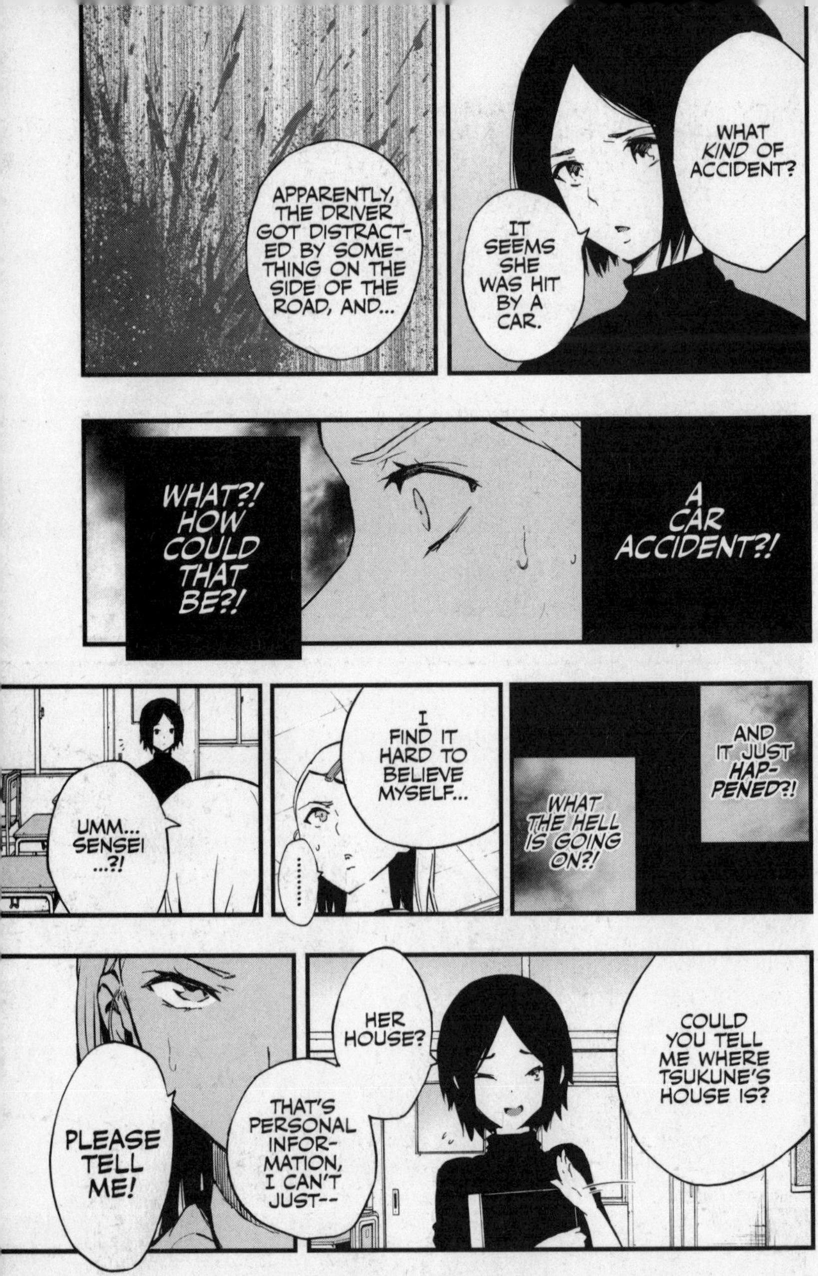
WHAT KIND OF ACCIDENT?
IT SEEMS SHE WAS HIT BY A CAR.
APPARENTLY, THE DRIVER GOT DISTRACTED BY SOMETHING ON THE SIDE OF THE ROAD, AND...
A CAR ACCIDENT?!
WHAT?! HOW COULD THAT BE?!
AND IT JUST HAPPENED?!
WHAT THE HELL IS GOING ON?!
I FIND IT HARD TO BELIEVE MYSELF...
......
UMM... SENSEI ...?!
COULD YOU TELL ME WHERE TSUKUNE'S HOUSE IS?
HER HOUSE?
THAT'S PERSONAL INFORMATION, I CAN'T JUST--
PLEASE TELL ME!

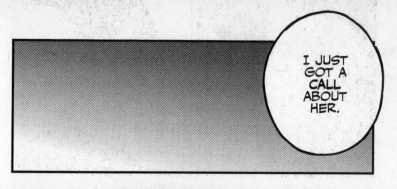

I JUST GOT A CALL ABOUT HER.

SHE WAS RUSHED TO THE HOSPITAL...

EVEN THOUGH...

SHE DIED IN THAT ACCIDENT.

AN ACCIDENT...?

HOLD ON...

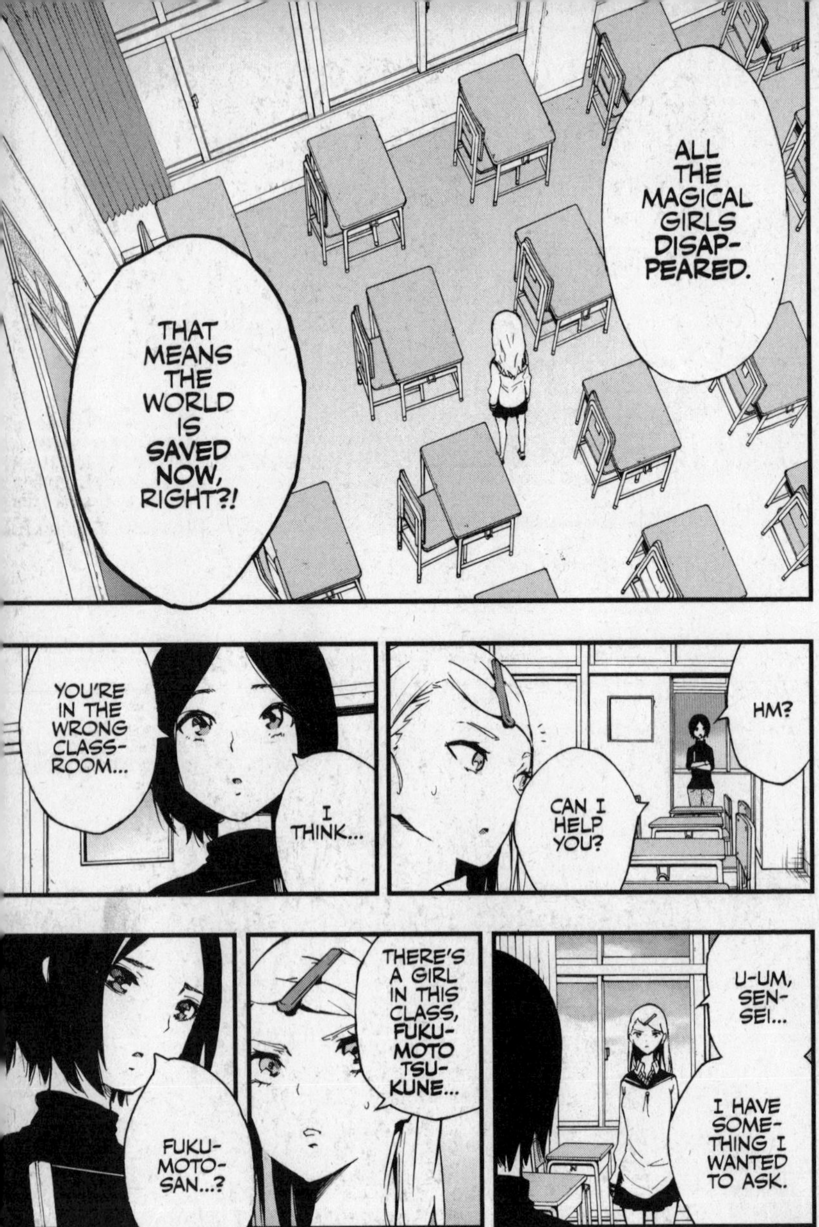
ALL THE MAGICAL GIRLS DISAPPEARED.
THAT MEANS THE WORLD IS SAVED NOW, RIGHT?!
HM?
CAN I HELP YOU?
YOU'RE IN THE WRONG CLASSROOM...
I THINK...
U-UM, SENSEI...
I HAVE SOMETHING I WANTED TO ASK.
THERE'S A GIRL IN THIS CLASS, FUKUMOTO TSUKUNE...
FUKUMOTO-SAN...?

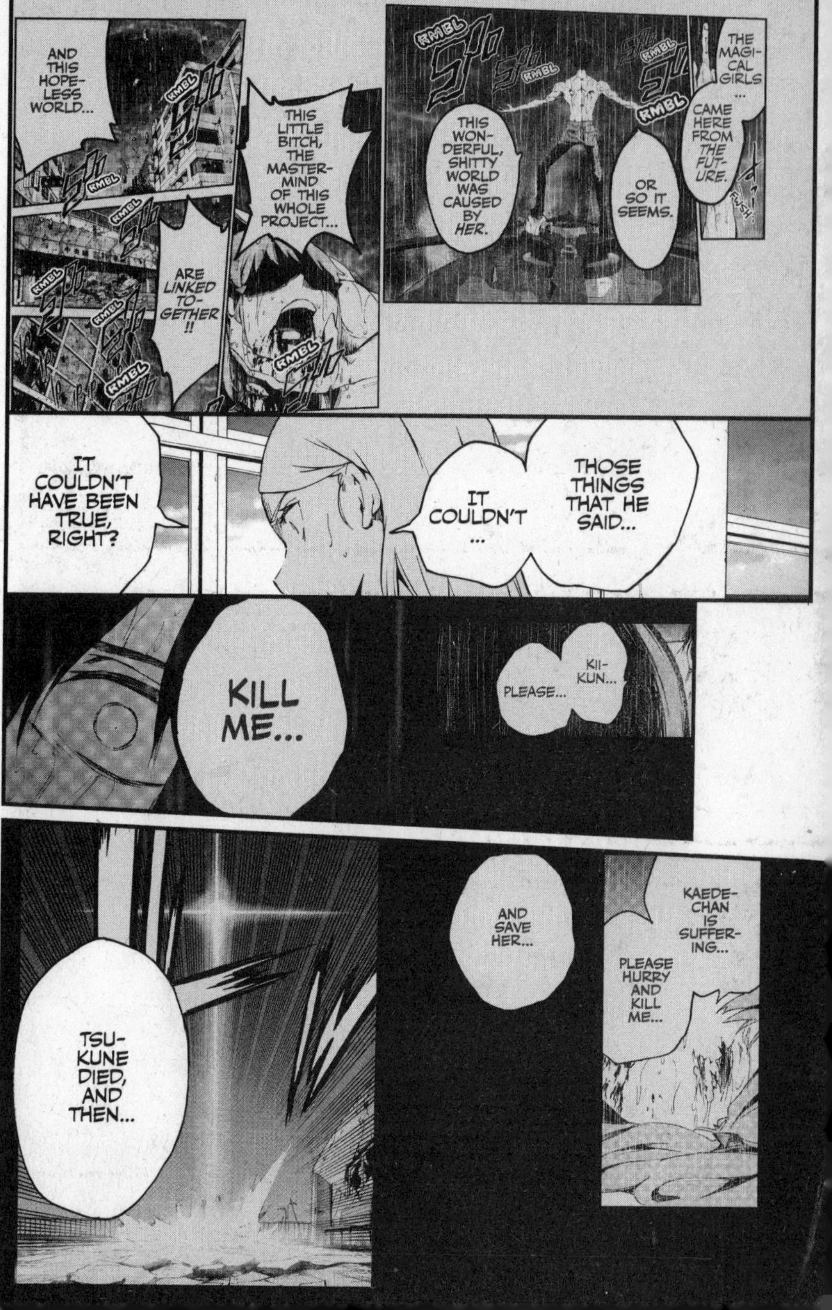
THE MAGICAL GIRLS... CAME HERE FROM THE FUTURE.
FWSH
OR SO IT SEEMS.
THIS WONDERFUL, SHITTY WORLD WAS CAUSED BY HER.
RMBL
THIS LITTLE BITCH, THE MASTERMIND OF THIS WHOLE PROJECT...
AND THIS HOPELESS WORLD...
ARE LINKED TOGETHER!!
RMBL
THOSE THINGS THAT HE SAID...
IT COULDN'T...
IT COULDN'T HAVE BEEN TRUE, RIGHT?
KII-KUN...
PLEASE...
KILL ME...
KAEDE-CHAN IS SUFFERING...
PLEASE HURRY AND KILL ME...
AND SAVE HER...
TSUKUNE DIED, AND THEN...

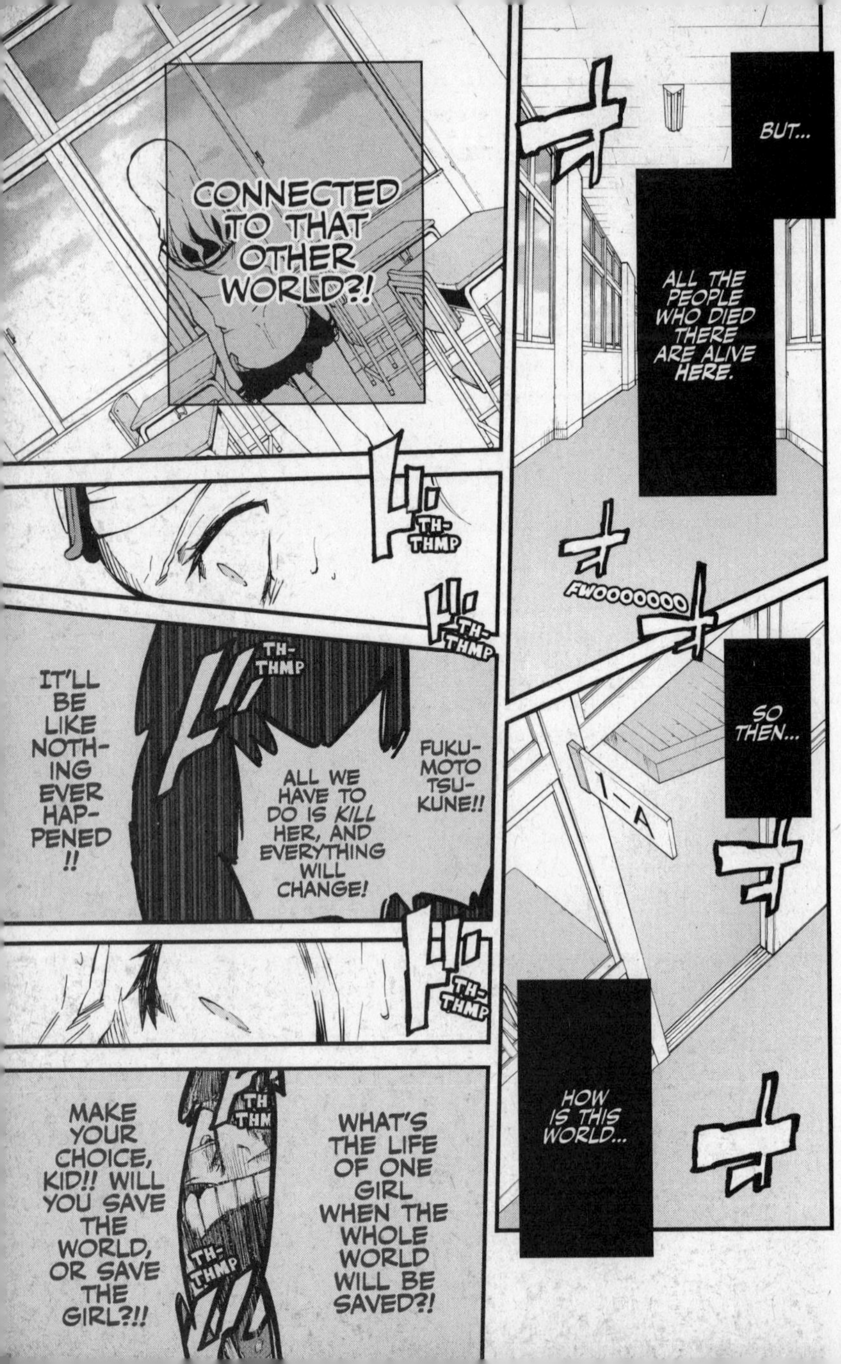
BUT...
ALL THE PEOPLE WHO DIED THERE ARE ALIVE HERE.
FWOOOOOOO
SO THEN...
1-A
HOW IS THIS WORLD...
CONNECTED TO THAT OTHER WORLD?!
TH-THMP
TH-THMP
TH-THMP
FUKUMOTO TSUKUNE!!
ALL WE HAVE TO DO IS *KILL* HER, AND EVERYTHING WILL CHANGE!
IT'LL BE LIKE NOTHING EVER HAPPENED!!
TH-THMP
TH THM
WHAT'S THE LIFE OF ONE GIRL WHEN THE WHOLE WORLD WILL BE SAVED?!
MAKE YOUR CHOICE, KID!! WILL YOU SAVE THE WORLD, OR SAVE THE GIRL?!!
TH-THMP

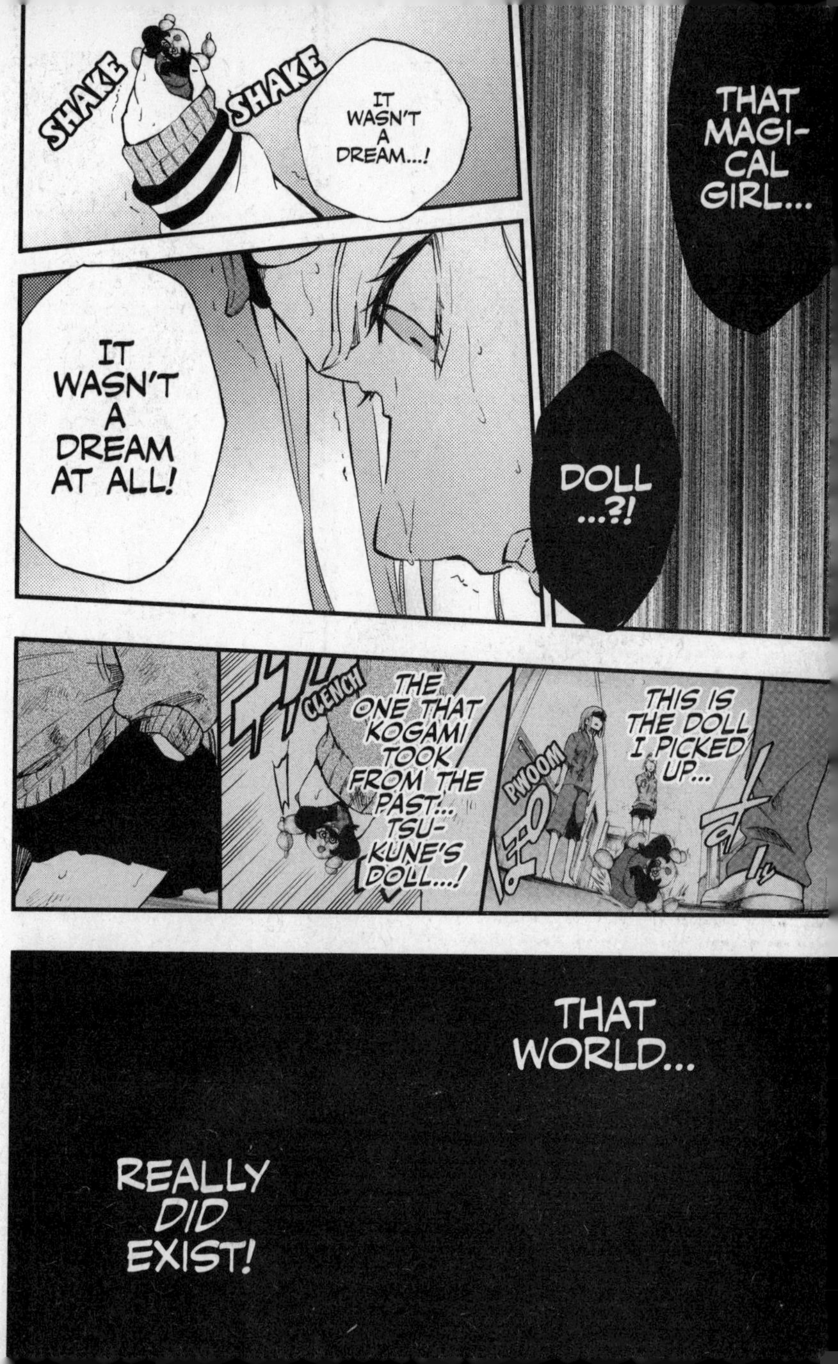
THAT MAGI-CAL GIRL...
DOLL ...?!
SHAKE
SHAKE
IT WASN'T A DREAM...!
IT WASN'T A DREAM AT ALL!
PWOOM
THIS IS THE DOLL I PICKED UP...
CLENCH
THE ONE THAT KOGAMI TOOK FROM THE PAST... TSU-KUNE'S DOLL...!
THAT WORLD...
REALLY *DID* EXIST!

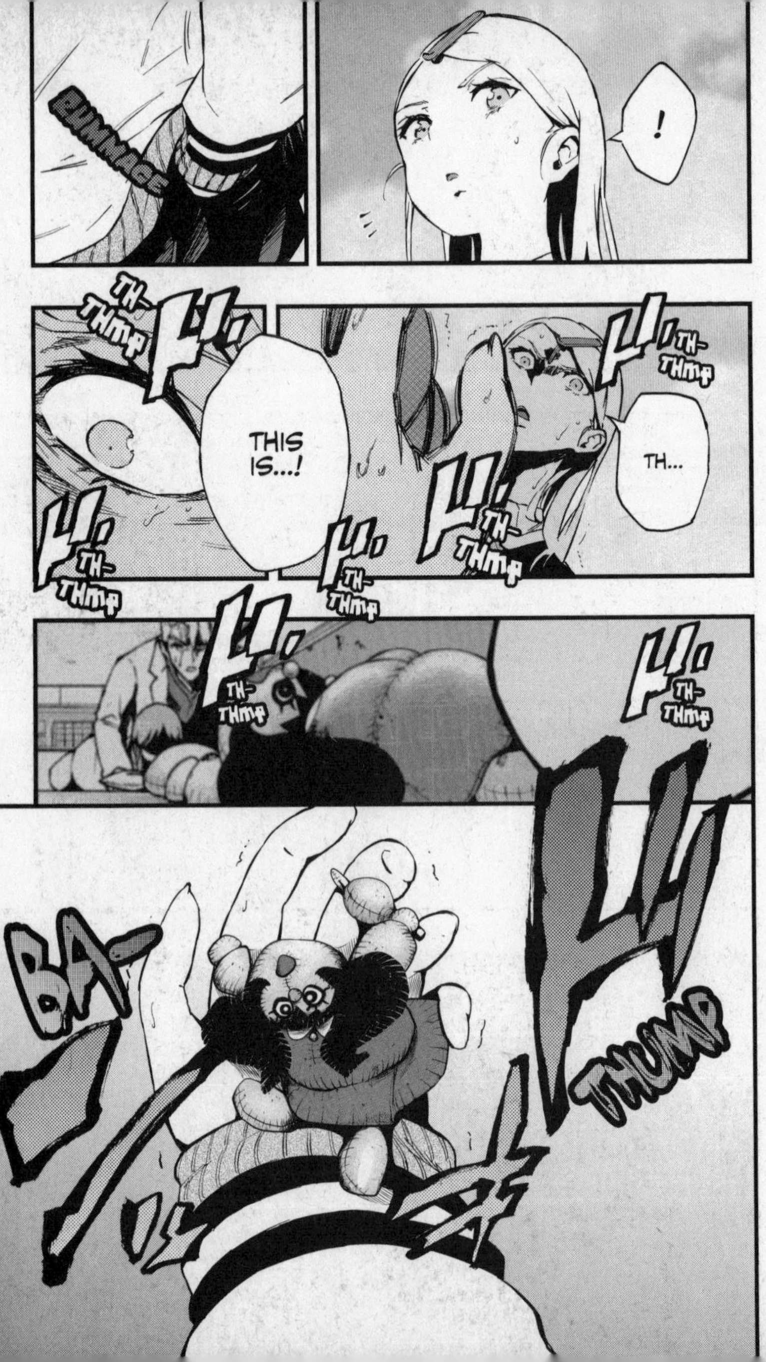
!
RUMMAGE
TH-THMP
TH...
TH-THMP
TH-THMP
THIS IS...!
TH-THMP
TH-THMP
TH-THMP
TH-THMP
THUMP
BA

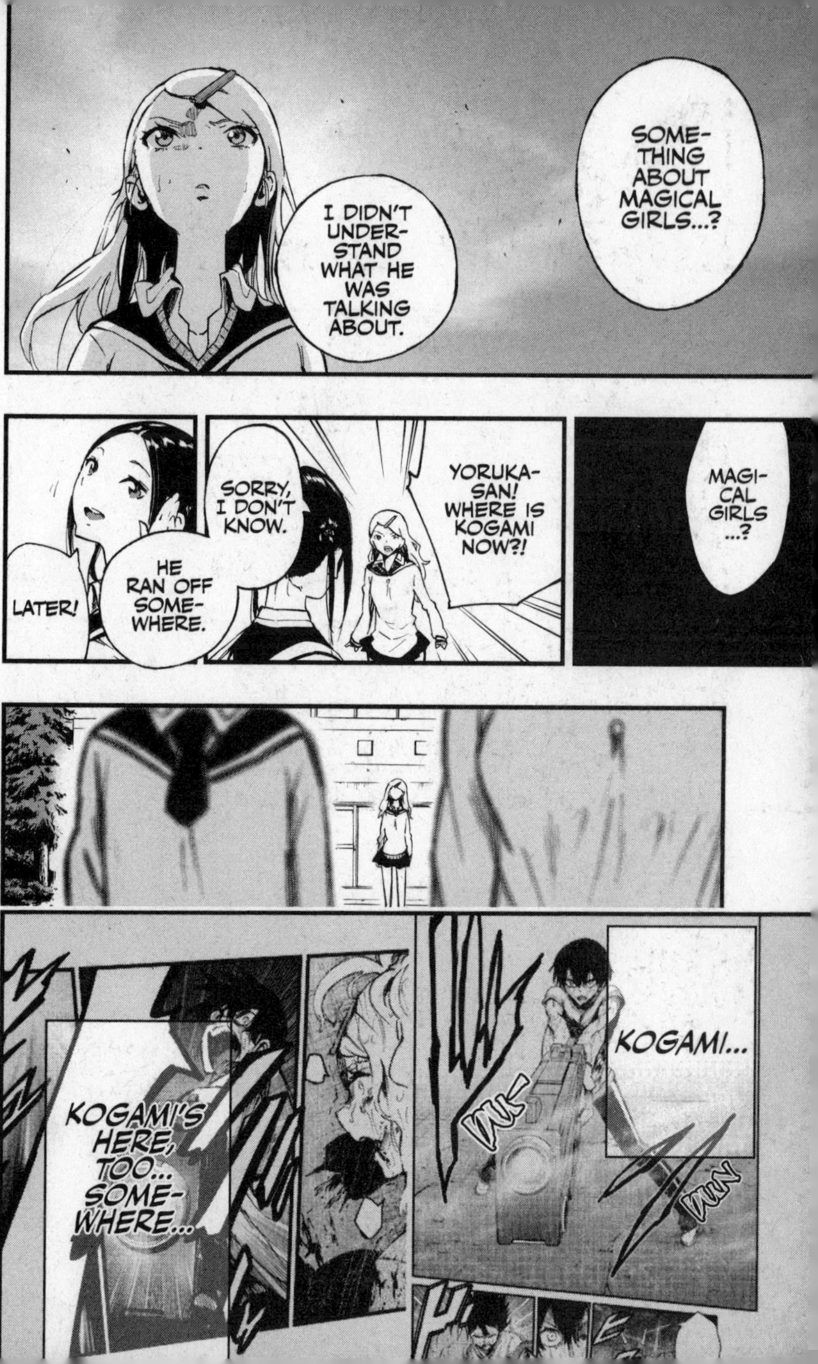
SOME-THING ABOUT MAGICAL GIRLS...?
I DIDN'T UNDER-STAND WHAT HE WAS TALKING ABOUT.
MAGI-CAL GIRLS ...?
YORUKA-SAN! WHERE IS KOGAMI NOW?!
SORRY, I DON'T KNOW.
HE RAN OFF SOME-WHERE.
LATER!
KOGAMI...
KOGAMI'S HERE, TOO... SOME-WHERE...

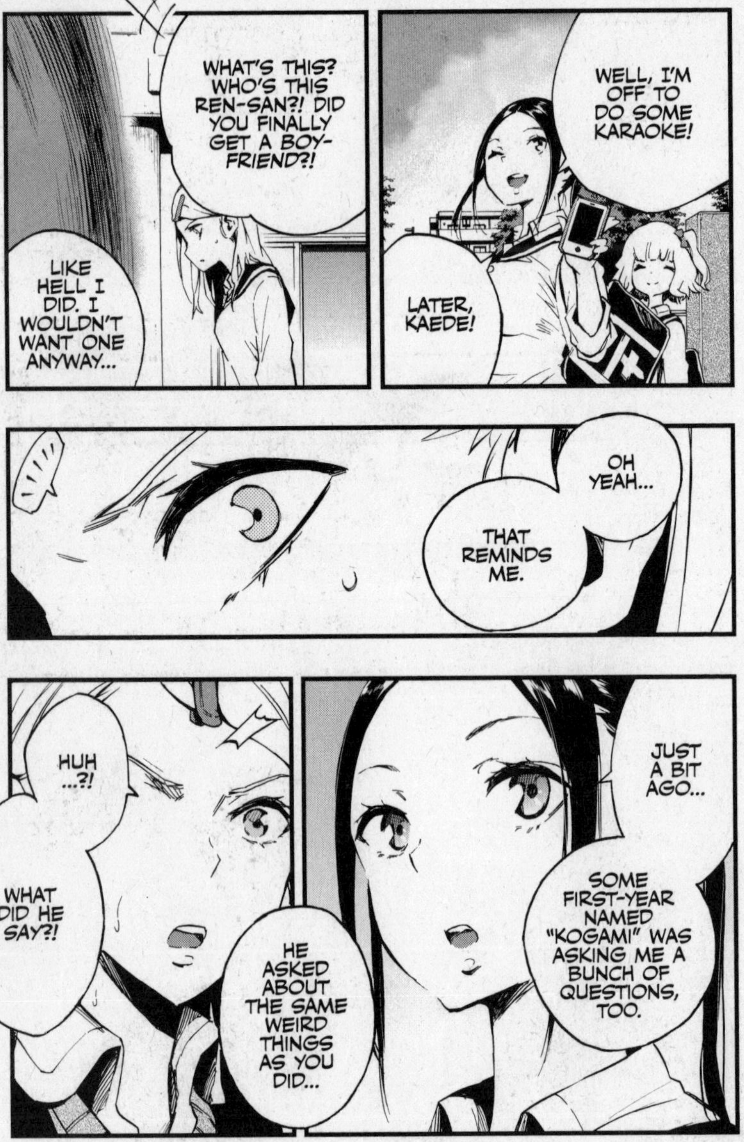
WELL, I'M OFF TO DO SOME KARAOKE!
LATER, KAEDE!
WHAT'S THIS? WHO'S THIS REN-SAN?! DID YOU FINALLY GET A BOY-FRIEND?!
LIKE HELL I DID. I WOULDN'T WANT ONE ANYWAY...
OH YEAH...
THAT REMINDS ME.
JUST A BIT AGO...
SOME FIRST-YEAR NAMED "KOGAMI" WAS ASKING ME A BUNCH OF QUESTIONS, TOO.
HUH ...?!
WHAT DID HE SAY?!
HE ASKED ABOUT THE SAME WEIRD THINGS AS YOU DID...

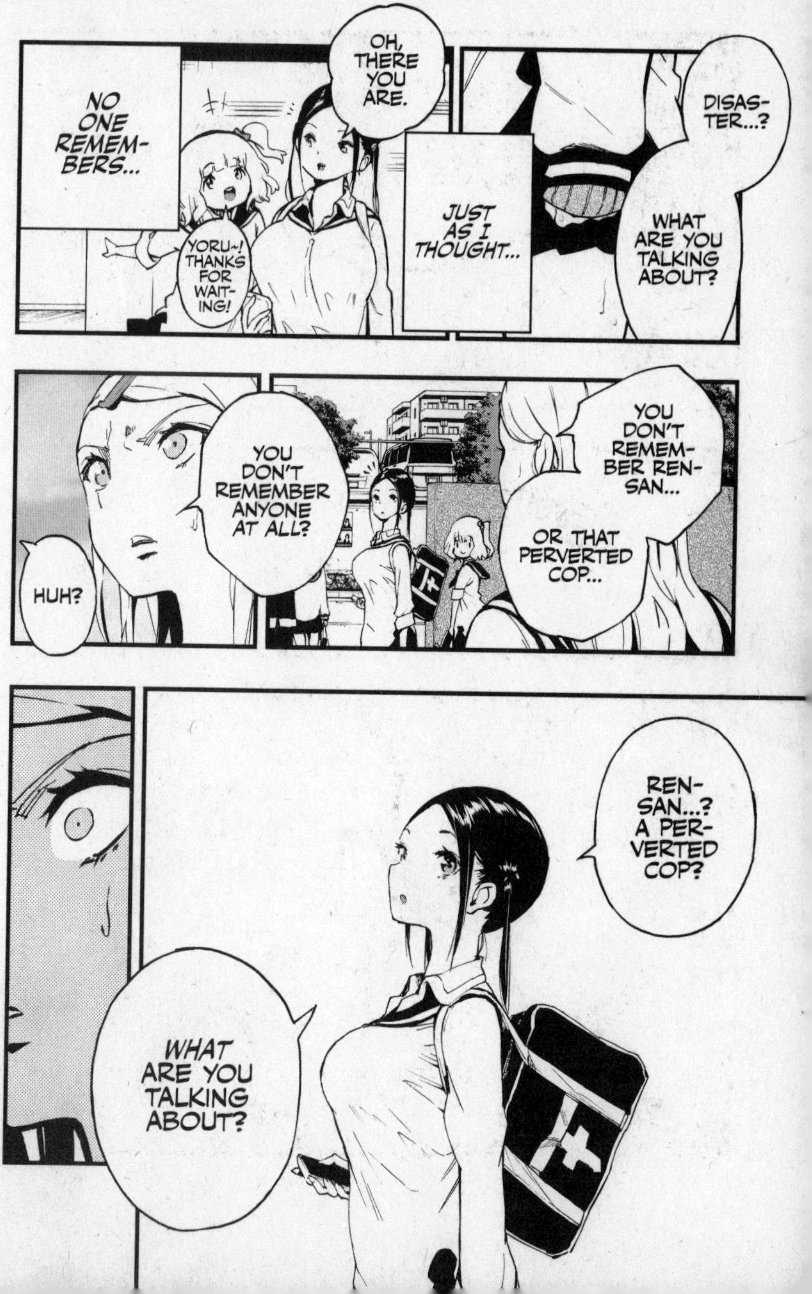
DISASTER...?
WHAT ARE YOU TALKING ABOUT?
JUST AS I THOUGHT...
OH, THERE YOU ARE.
NO ONE REMEMBERS...
YORU~! THANKS FOR WAITING!
YOU DON'T REMEMBER REN-SAN...
OR THAT PERVERTED COP...
YOU DON'T REMEMBER ANYONE AT ALL?
HUH?
REN-SAN...? A PERVERTED COP?
WHAT ARE YOU TALKING ABOUT?

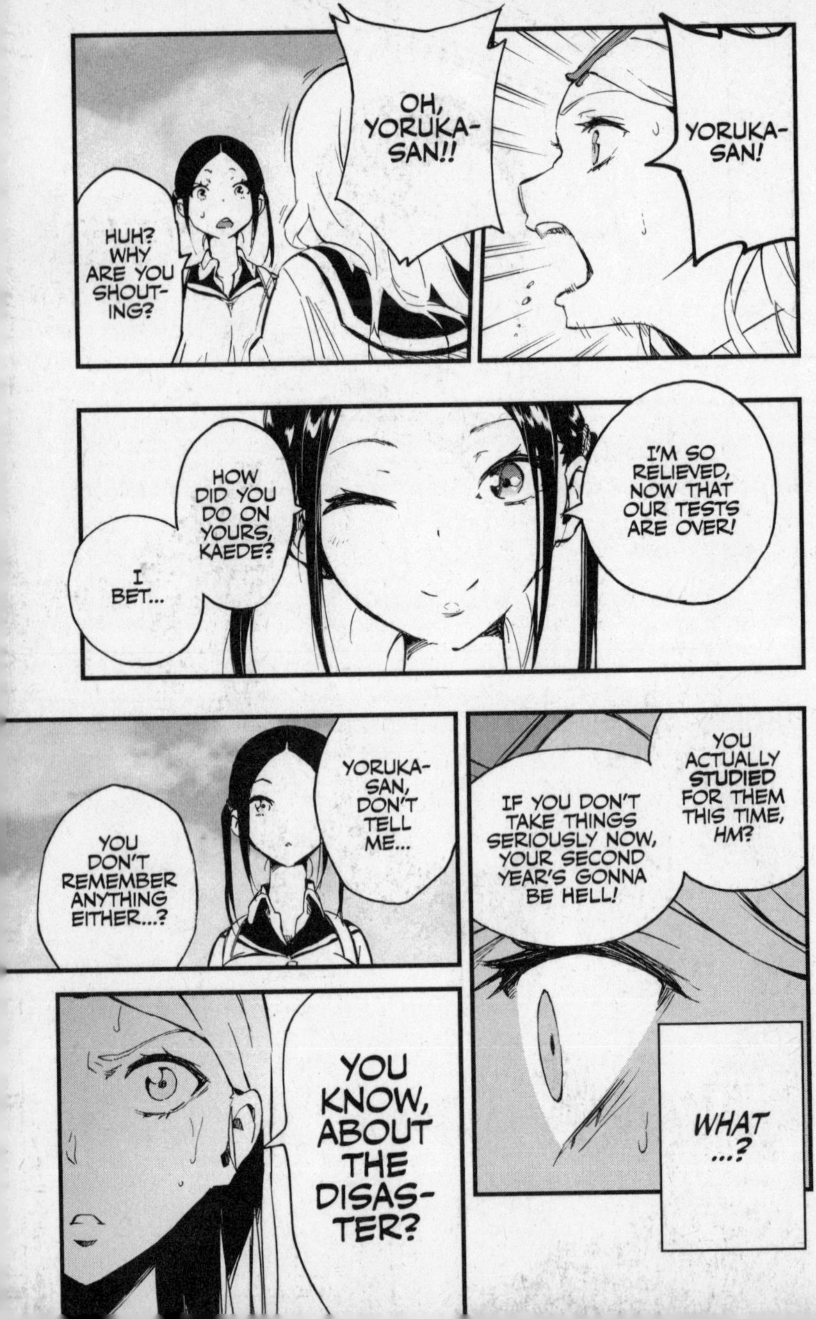
YORUKA-SAN!
OH, YORUKA-SAN!!
HUH? WHY ARE YOU SHOUTING?
I'M SO RELIEVED, NOW THAT OUR TESTS ARE OVER!
HOW DID YOU DO ON YOURS, KAEDE?
I BET...
YOU ACTUALLY STUDIED FOR THEM THIS TIME, HM?
IF YOU DON'T TAKE THINGS SERIOUSLY NOW, YOUR SECOND YEAR'S GONNA BE HELL!
WHAT ...?
YORUKA-SAN, DON'T TELL ME...
YOU DON'T REMEMBER ANYTHING EITHER...?
YOU KNOW, ABOUT THE DISASTER?

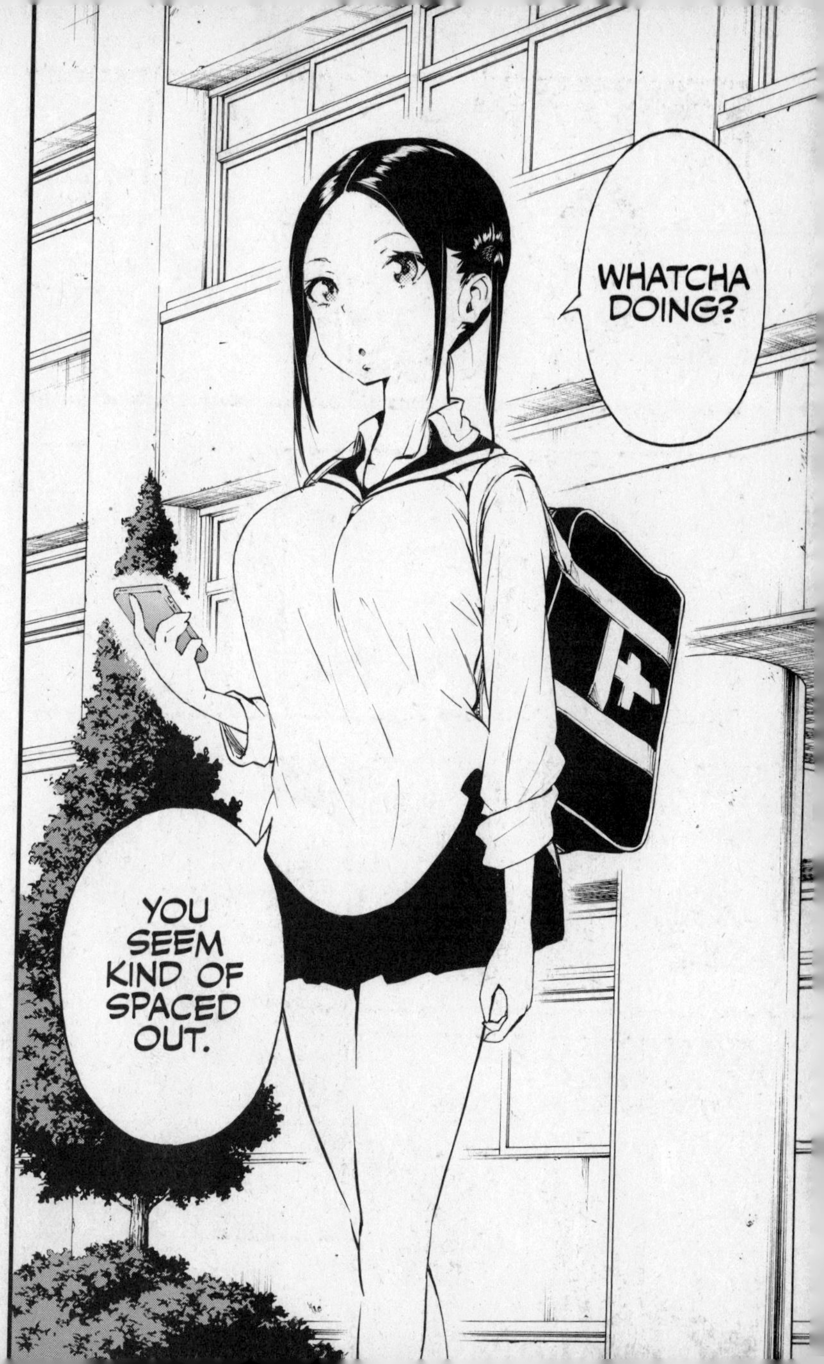
WHATCHA DOING?
YOU SEEM KIND OF SPACED OUT.

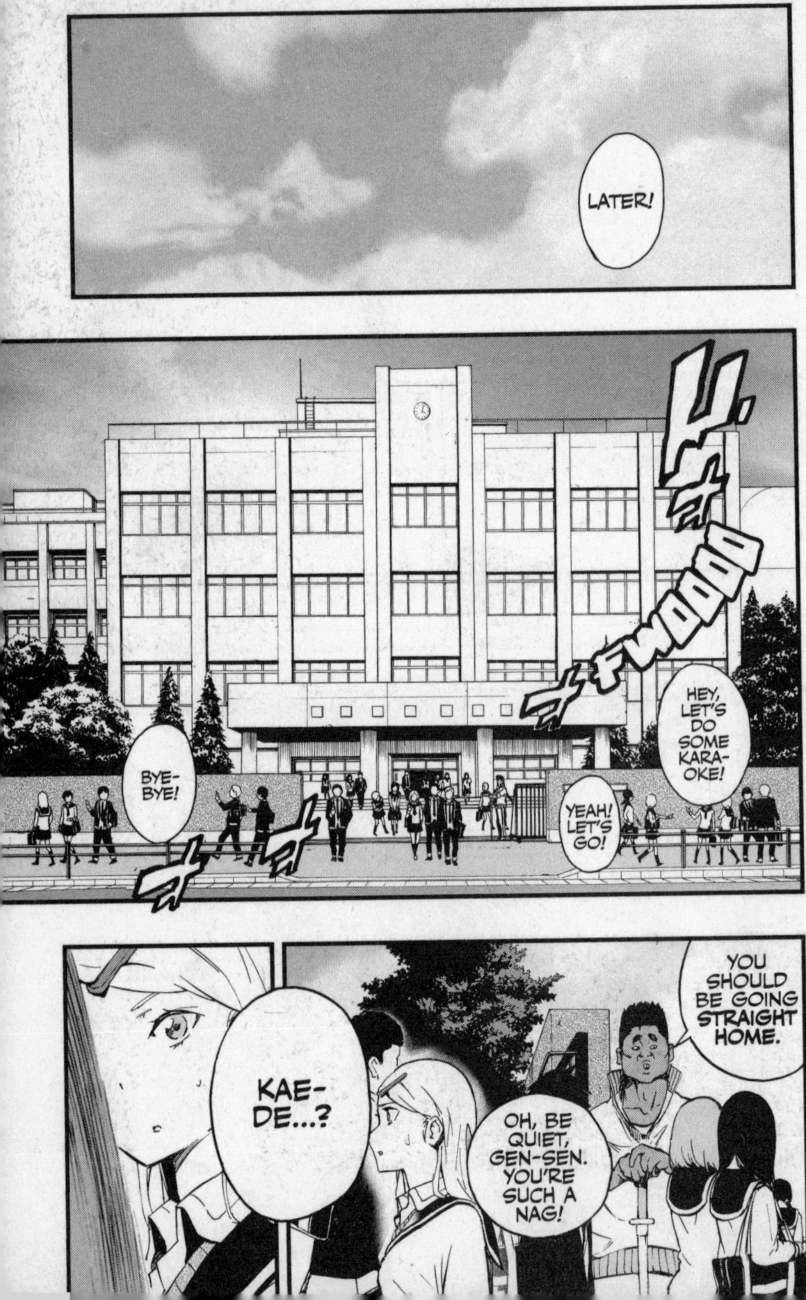
LATER!
FWOOOO
HEY, LET'S DO SOME KARA-OKE!
YEAH! LET'S GO!
BYE-BYE!
YOU SHOULD BE GOING STRAIGHT HOME.
OH, BE QUIET, GEN-SEN. YOU'RE SUCH A NAG!
KAE-DE...?

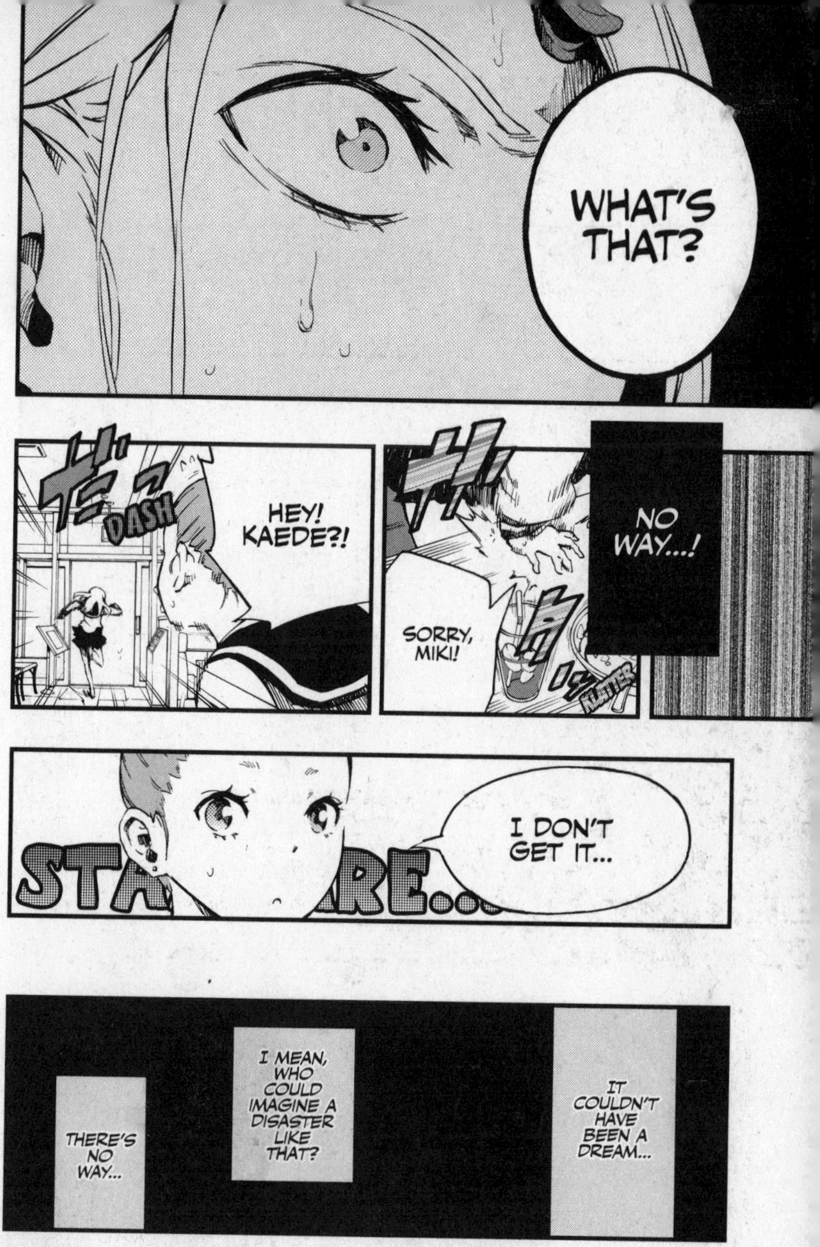
WHAT'S THAT?
NO WAY...!
SORRY, MIKI!
KLATTER
DASH
HEY! KAEDE?!
I DON'T GET IT...
IT COULDN'T HAVE BEEN A DREAM...
I MEAN, WHO COULD IMAGINE A DISASTER LIKE THAT?
THERE'S NO WAY...

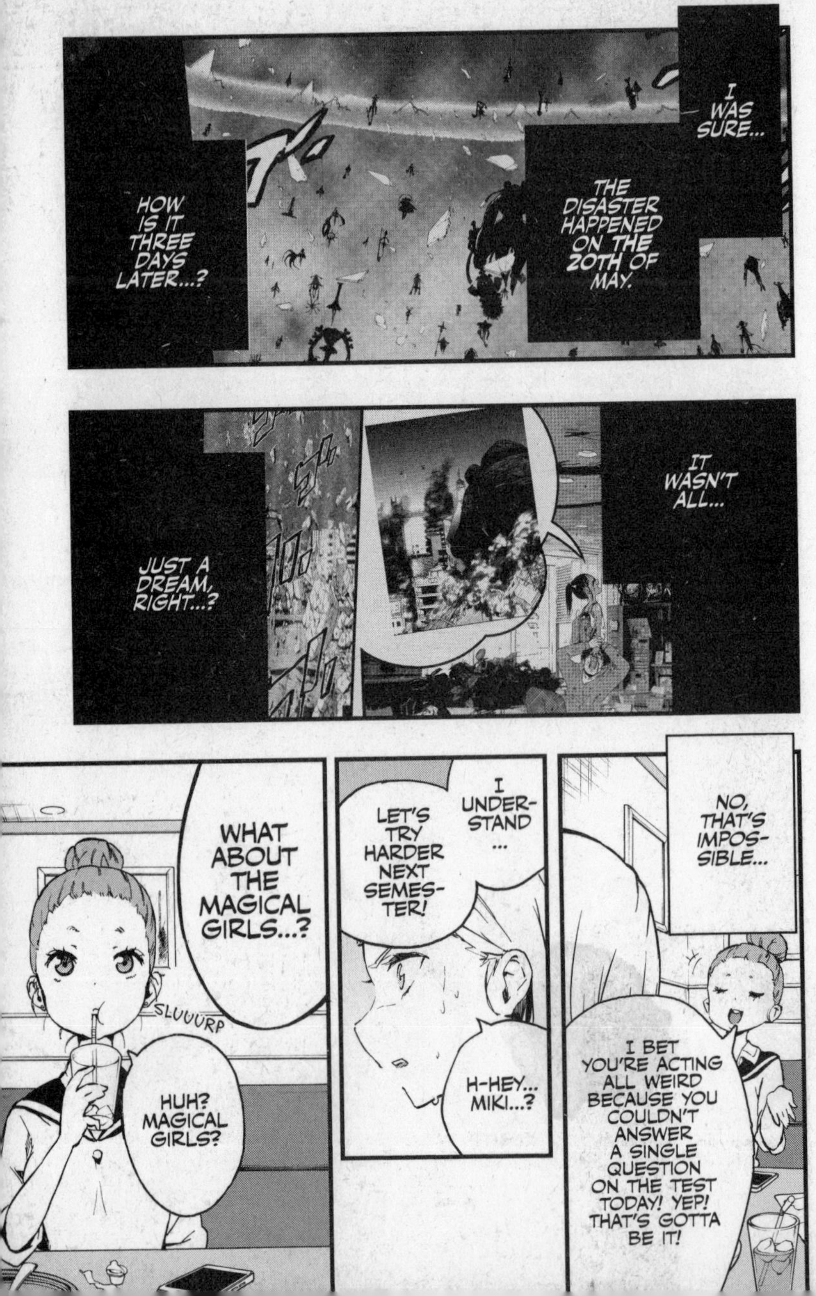
I WAS SURE...
THE DISASTER HAPPENED ON THE 20TH OF MAY.
HOW IS IT THREE DAYS LATER...?
IT WASN'T ALL...
JUST A DREAM, RIGHT...?
NO, THAT'S IMPOS-SIBLE...
I BET YOU'RE ACTING ALL WEIRD BECAUSE YOU COULDN'T ANSWER A SINGLE QUESTION ON THE TEST TODAY! YEP! THAT'S GOTTA BE IT!
I UNDER-STAND...
LET'S TRY HARDER NEXT SEMES-TER!
H-HEY... MIKI...?
WHAT ABOUT THE MAGICAL GIRLS...?
SLUUURP
HUH? MAGICAL GIRLS?

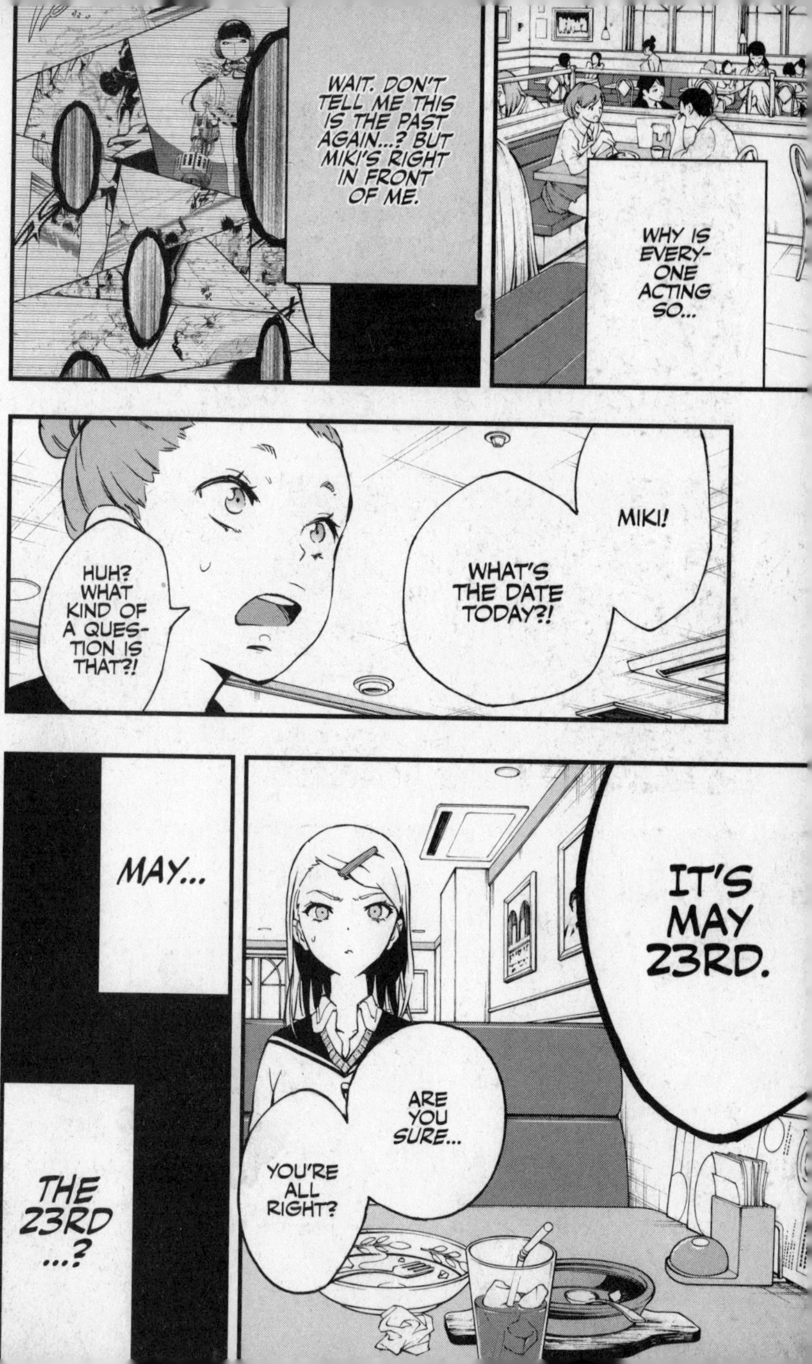
WHY IS EVERY-ONE ACTING SO...
WAIT. DON'T TELL ME THIS IS THE PAST AGAIN...? BUT MIKI'S RIGHT IN FRONT OF ME.
MIKI!
WHAT'S THE DATE TODAY?!
HUH? WHAT KIND OF A QUESTION IS THAT?!
IT'S MAY 23RD.
ARE YOU SURE...
YOU'RE ALL RIGHT?
MAY...
THE 23RD ...?

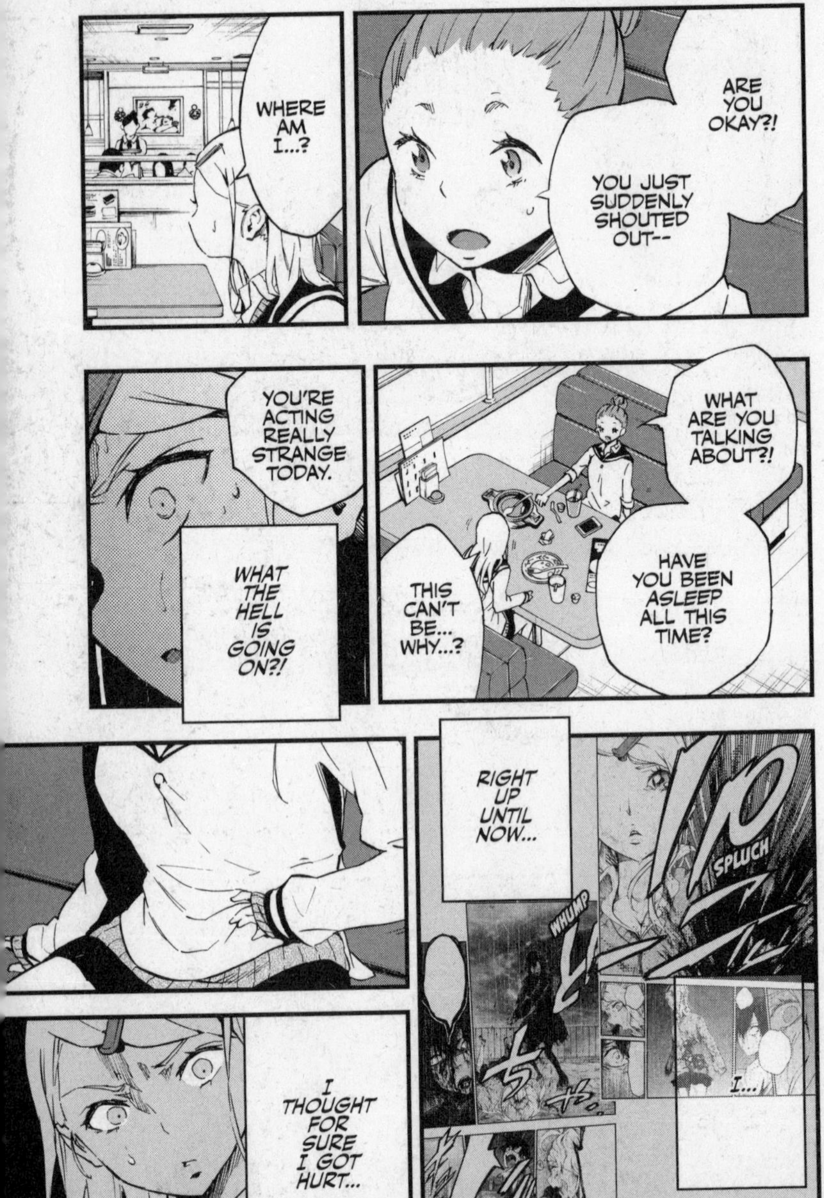
ARE YOU OKAY?!
YOU JUST SUDDENLY SHOUTED OUT--
WHERE AM I...?
WHAT ARE YOU TALKING ABOUT?!
HAVE YOU BEEN ASLEEP ALL THIS TIME?
THIS CAN'T BE... WHY...?
YOU'RE ACTING REALLY STRANGE TODAY.
WHAT THE HELL IS GOING ON?!
RIGHT UP UNTIL NOW...
SPLUCH
WHUMP
I...
BWAN
I THOUGHT FOR SURE I GOT HURT...

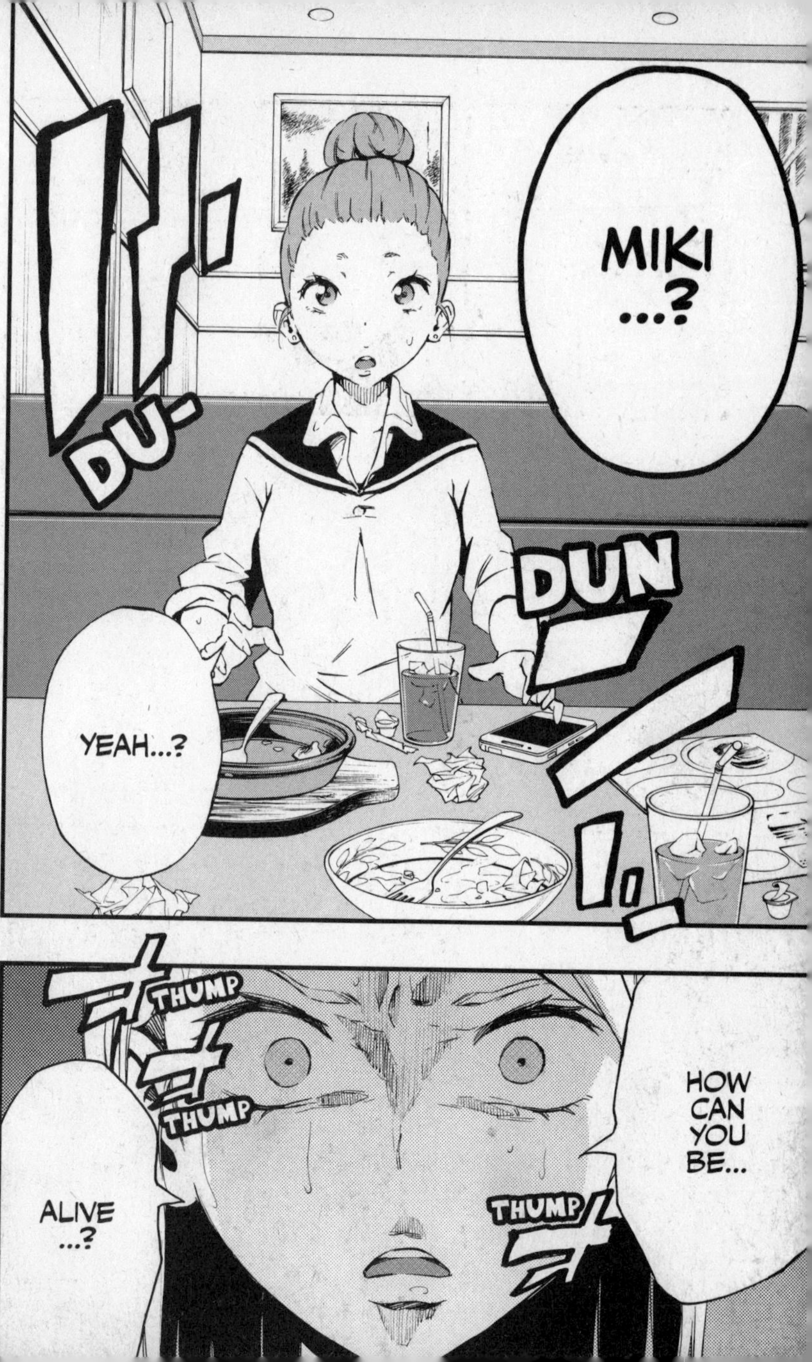
MIKI ...?
DU-
DUN
YEAH...?
HOW CAN YOU BE...
THUMP
THUMP
THUMP
ALIVE ...?

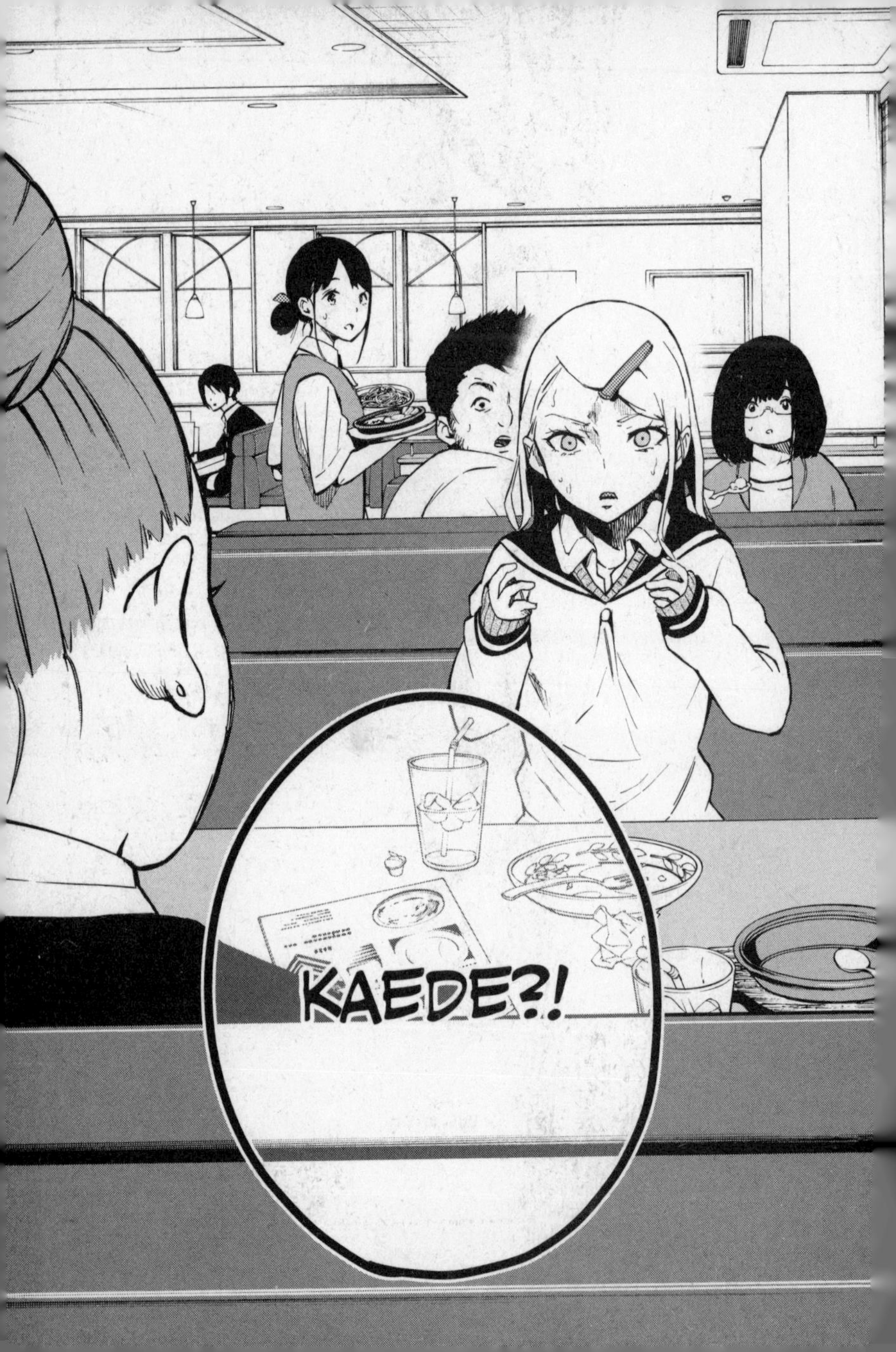
KAEDE?!

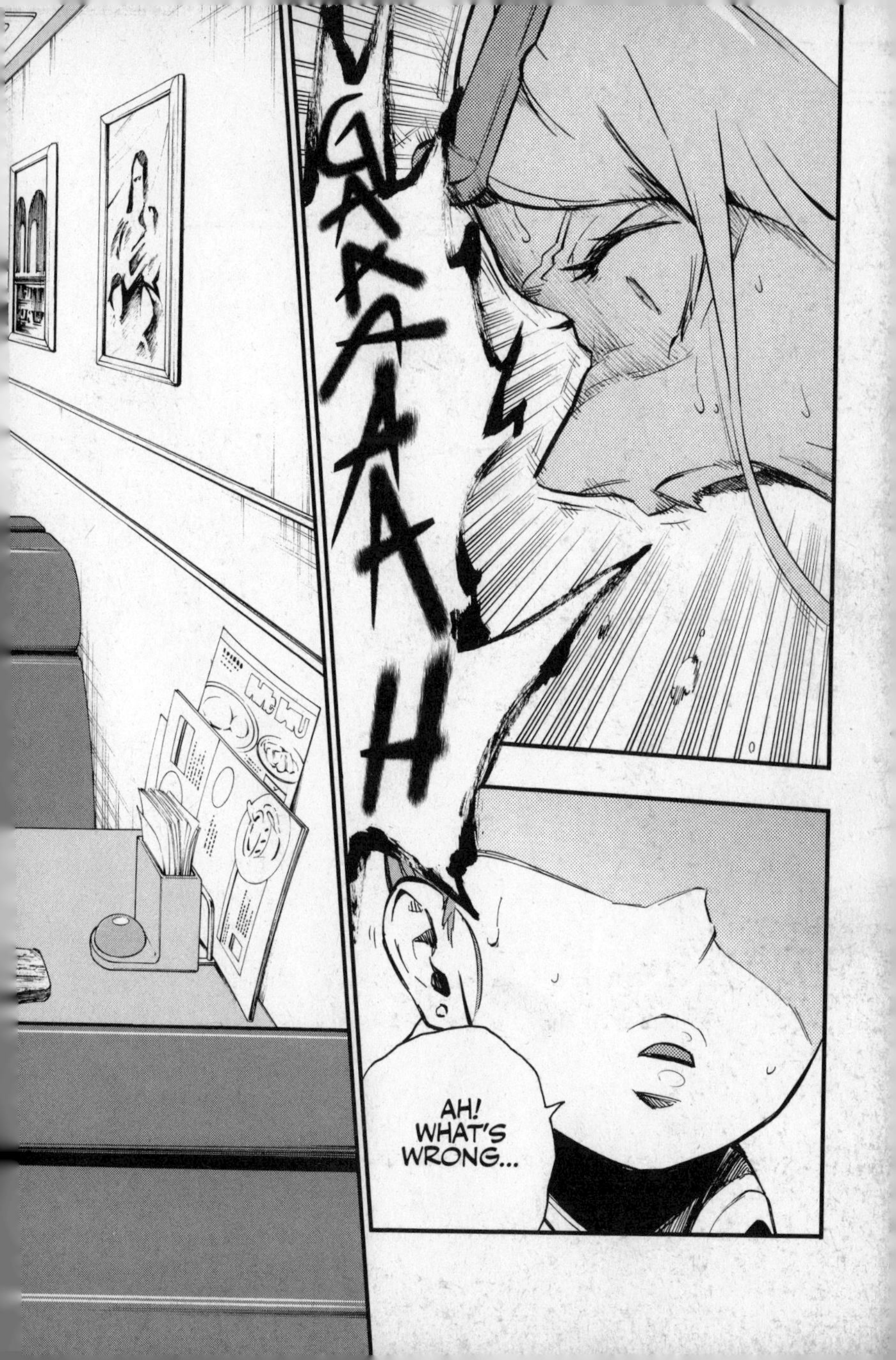

NGAAAAAH
AH! WHAT'S WRONG...

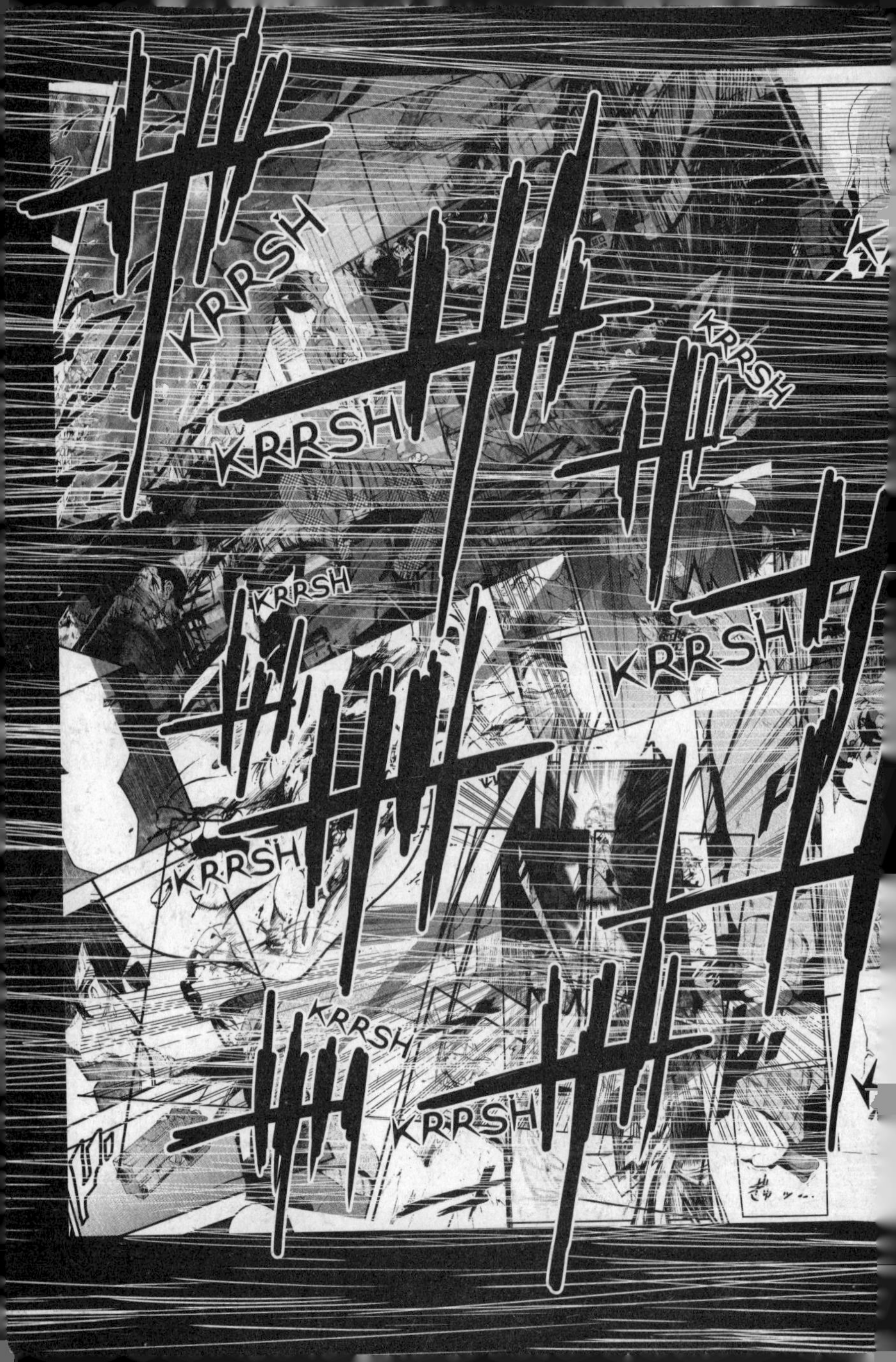
KRRSH
KRRSH
KRRSH
KRRSH
KRRSH
KRRSH
KRRSH
KRRSH

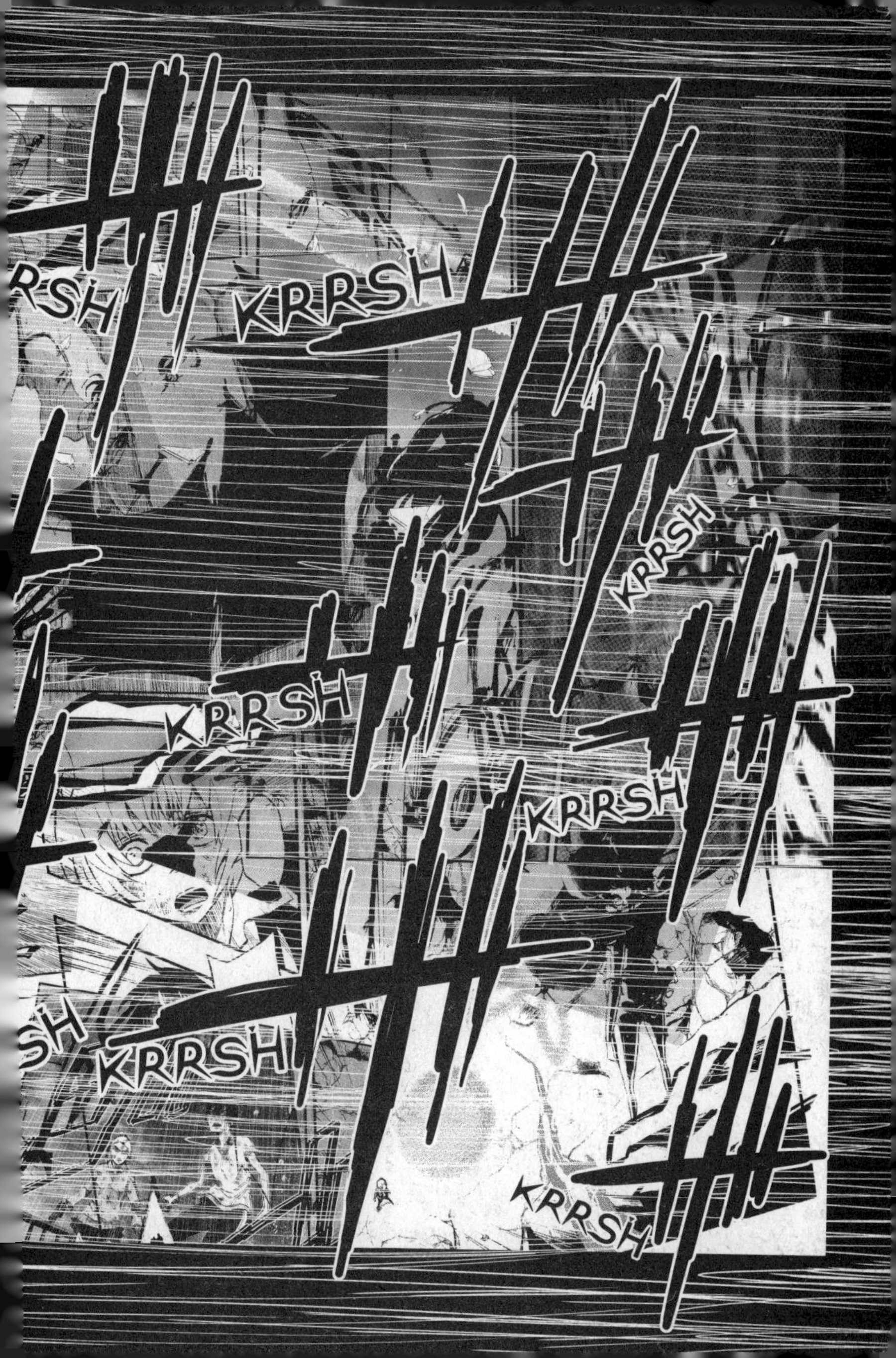
KRRSH
RSH
KRRSH
KRRSH
KRRSH
KRRSH
KRRSH
SH

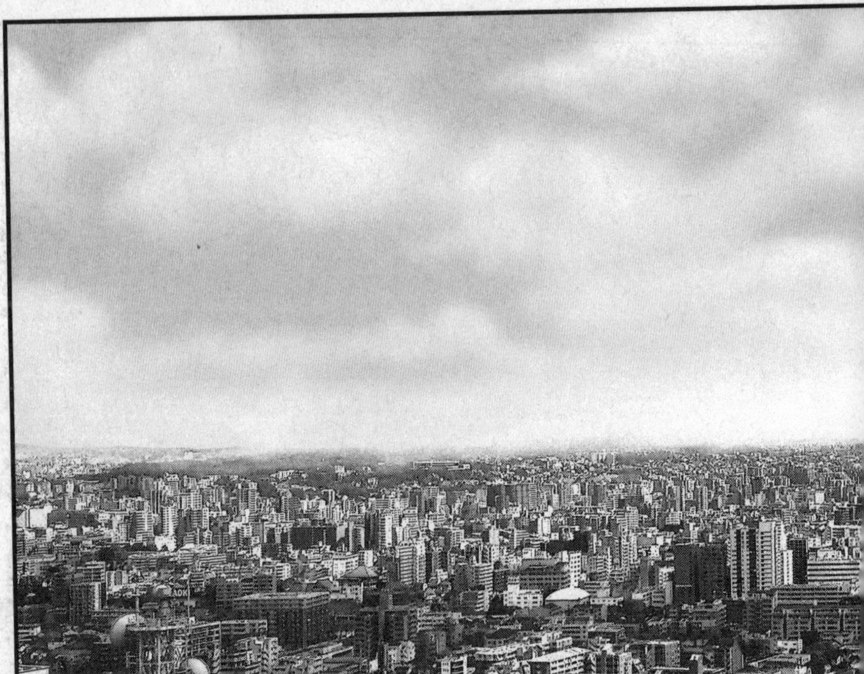

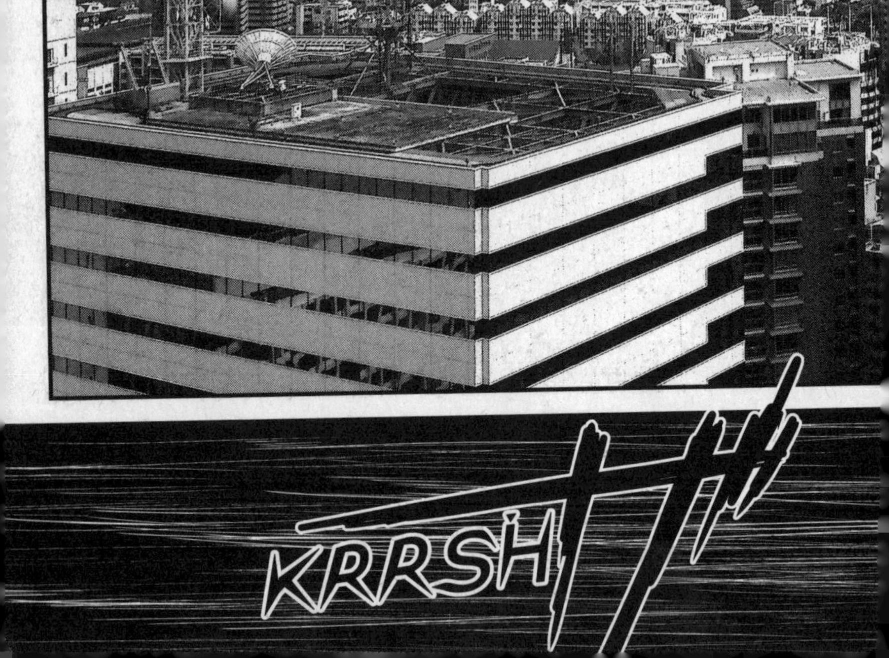
KRRSH

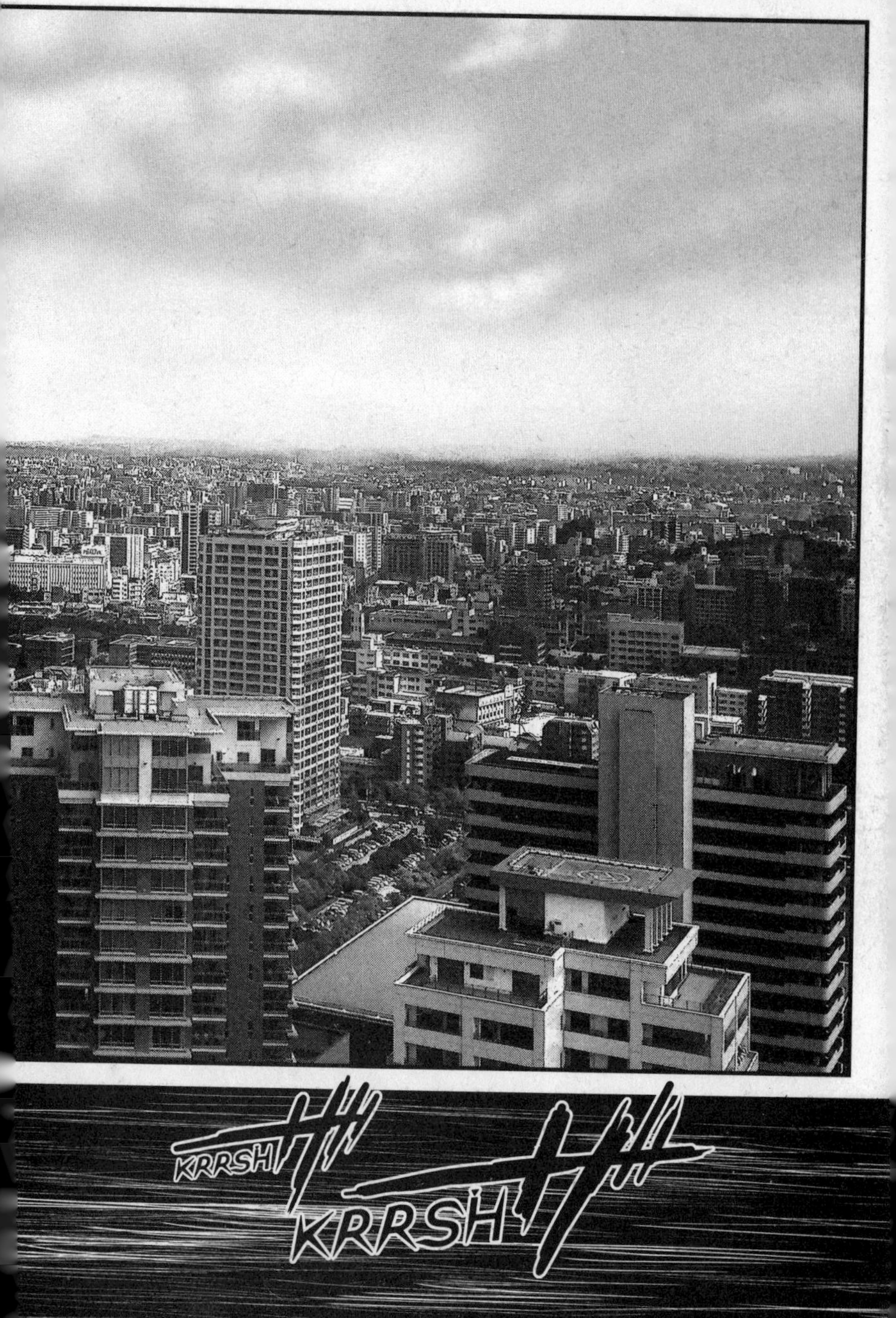
KRRSH
KRRSH

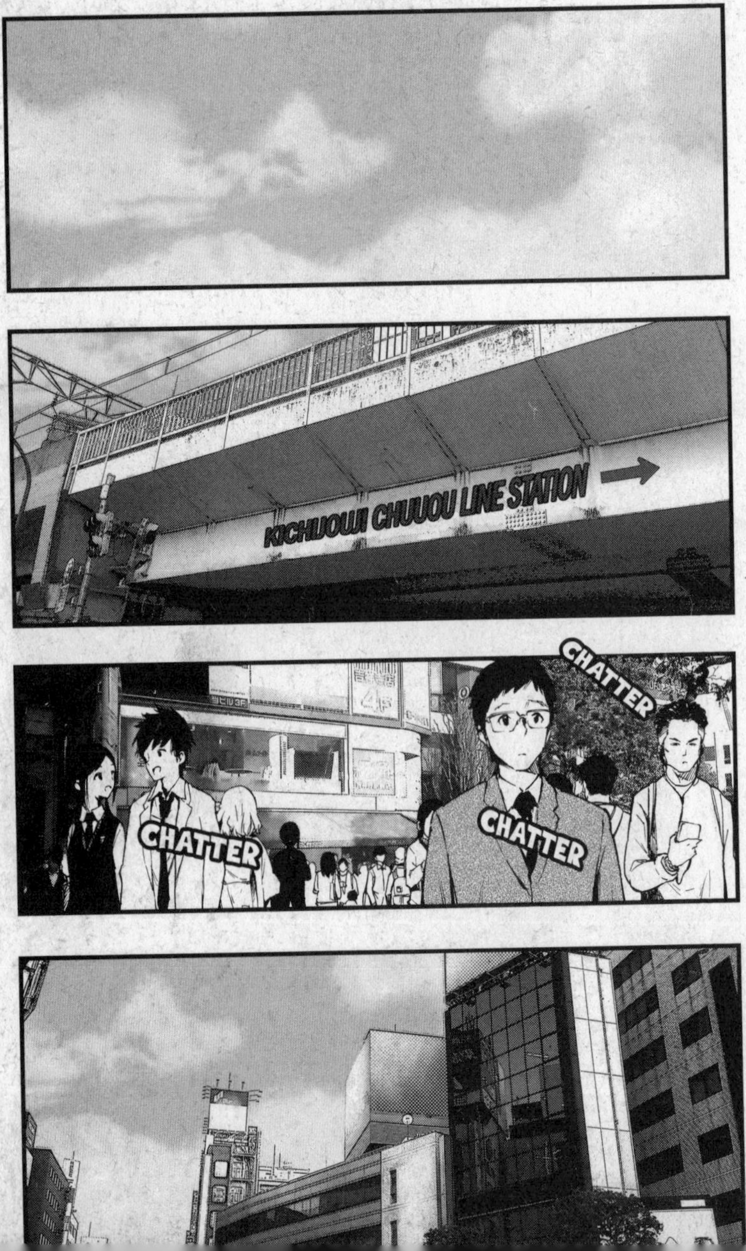
KICHIJOUJI CHUUOU LINE STATION
CHATTER
CHATTER
CHATTER

I NEVER EXPECTED THINGS TO TURN OUT THIS WAY...

I DID SOME CHECKING, REGARDING YOU...

OR RATHER, I SHOULD SAY, ALL OF YOU.

AND...

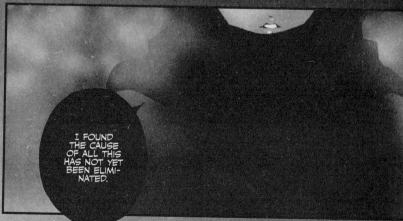

I FOUND THE CAUSE OF ALL THIS HAS NOT YET BEEN ELIMINATED.

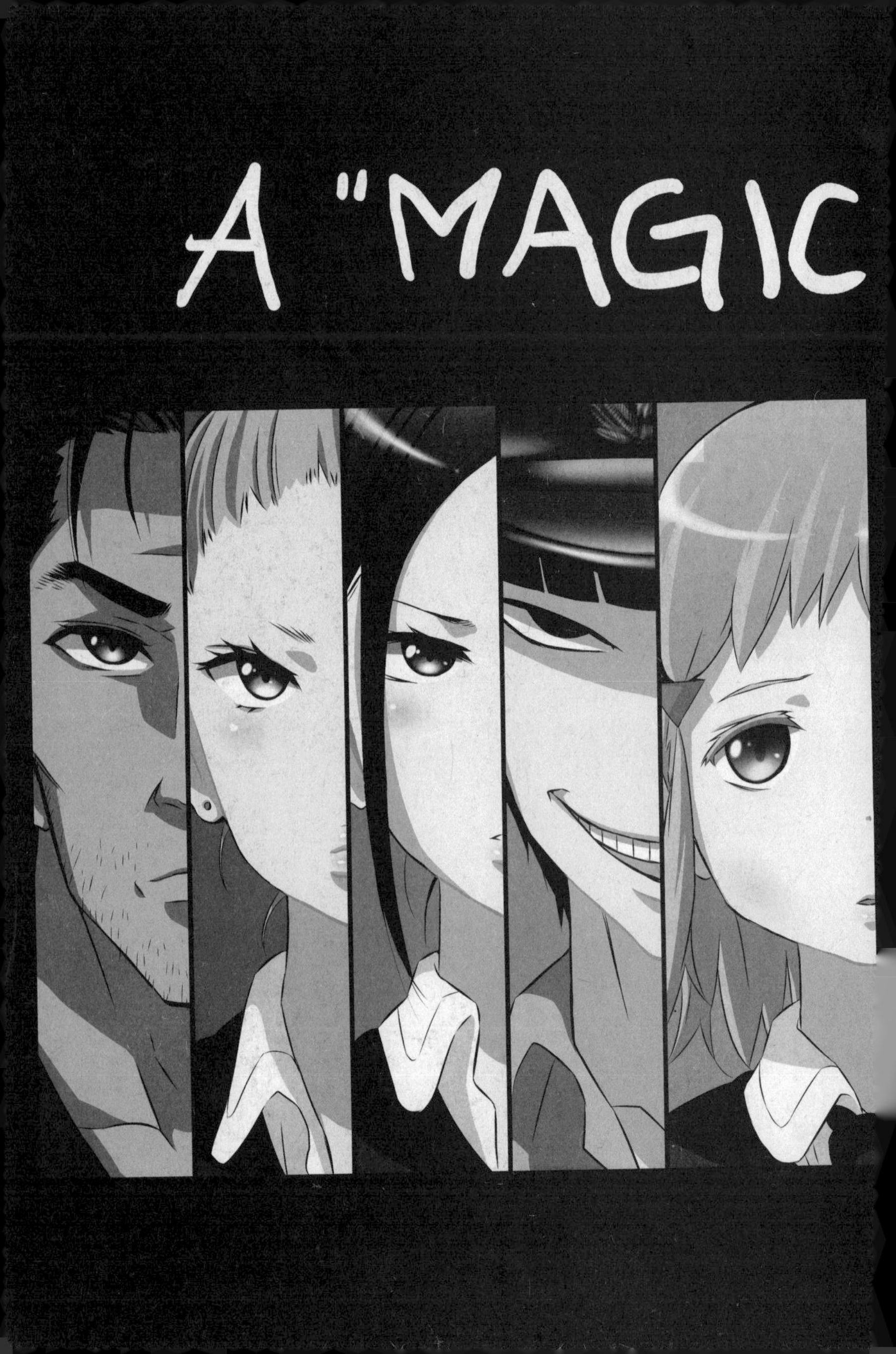
A "MAGIC

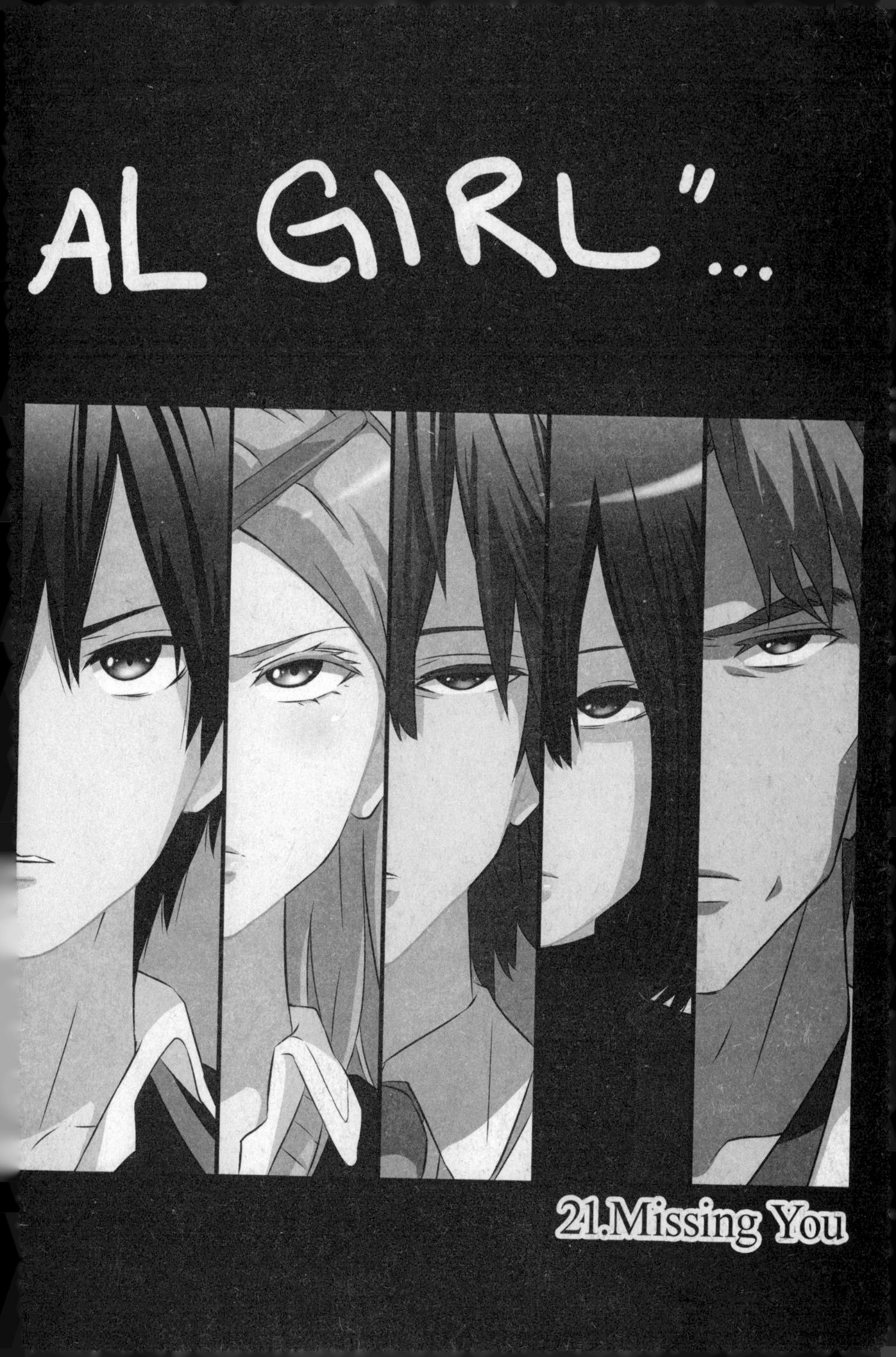
AL GIRL"...

21.Missing You

Witches—

That is to say, the children born when
a human makes a pact with a demon.

People loathed and despised such power.
They hated it more than anything else.

One day, some influential people of the time came
up with a solution: "Burn the Witches."

Knowing that their lives were now in danger,
the witches hid themselves.

From then on, people were persecuted for the slightest
suspicion of witchcraft, and they were executed,
one after the other. Later on, this time would be
recalled as the time of the witch hunts.

Meanwhile, the witches continued to live on alone,
isolating themselves from all...

And then one day, a human man appeared.

This man found a witch living in solitude, and he
extended his kindness towards her.

The witch loved the man, and the man loved the witch.

Even when the witch revealed herself to be a witch,
the man still loved her.

The two of them exchanged vows, and soon
thereafter, a child was born to them.

A child born to a witch will have some of
the witch's power within them.

And the two of them called their child...

SEVEN SEAS ENTERTAINMENT PRESENTS

MAGICAL GIRL APOCALYPSE

story and art by KENTARO SATO   VOLUME 6

TRANSLATION
Wesley Bridges

ADAPTATION
Janet Houck

LETTERING AND LAYOUT
Jaedison Yui

LOGO DESIGN
Phil Balsman

COVER DESIGN
Nicky Lim

PROOFREADER
Shanti Whitesides

PRODUCTION MANAGER
Lissa Pattillo

EDITOR-IN-CHIEF
Adam Arnold

PUBLISHER
Jason DeAngelis

MAHO SYOJYO OF THE END Volume 6
© Kentaro Sato 2014
Originally published in Japan in 2014 by Akita Publishing Co., Ltd..
English translation rights arranged with Akita Publishing Co., Ltd. through
TOHAN CORPORATION, Tokyo.

Seven Seas books may be purchased in bulk for educational, business, or
promotional use. For information on bulk purchases, please contact Macmillan
Corporate & Premium Sales Department at 1-800-221-7945 (ext 5442)
or write specialmarkets@macmillan.com.

Seven Seas and the Seven Seas logo are trademarks of
Seven Seas Entertainment, LLC. All rights reserved.

ISBN: 978-1-626922-34-1

Printed in Canada

First Printing: January 2016

10 9 8 7 6 5 4 3 2 1

FOLLOW US ONLINE: *www.gomanga.com*

READING DIRECTIONS

This book reads from *right to left*, Japanese style.
If this is your first time reading manga, you start
reading from the top right panel on each page and
take it from there. If you get lost, just follow the
numbered diagram here. It may seem backwards at
first, but you'll get the hang of it! Have fun!!

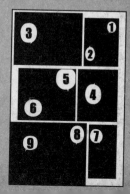

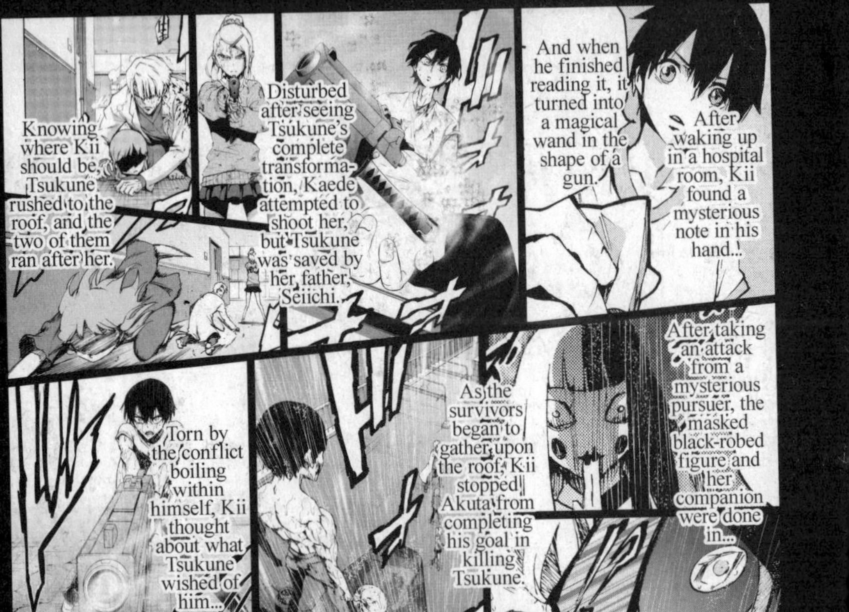
After waking up in a hospital room, Kii found a mysterious note in his hand...
And when he finished reading it, it turned into a magical wand in the shape of a gun.
Disturbed after seeing Tsukune's complete transformation, Kaede attempted to shoot her, but Tsukune was saved by her father, Seiichi.
Knowing where Kii should be, Tsukune rushed to the roof, and the two of them ran after her.
After taking an attack from a mysterious pursuer, the masked black-robed figure and her companion were done in...
As the survivors began to gather upon the roof, Kii stopped Akuta from completing his goal in killing Tsukune.
Torn by the conflict boiling within himself, Kii thought about what Tsukune wished of him...
And he turned his stick on her and fired.
Once he did, the sound of crumbling echoed throughout the world...
Recording the destruction was the one who had been pulling the strings behind the whole disaster: Himeji, who was thought to have been killed by the magical girls...?!
And then, the world finally...

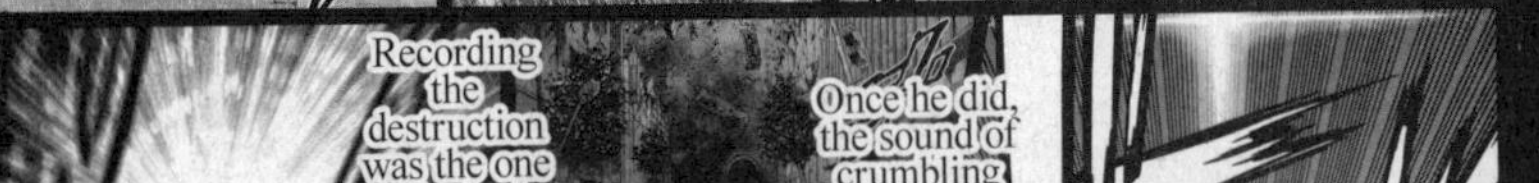

MAGICAL GIRLS

They kill people by shooting "magic" out of their wands. Those that die from their attacks end up rising from the dead to attack the living. Their wands are their only weakness.

MASKED BLACK·ROBE

A mysterious individual who has been observing Kii's movements. Whether she is friend or foe is yet unknown.

PUPPET MASTER

Someone who is able to transform into various Magical Girls and use their powers. Possibly Himeji's servant...?

WATARU HIMEJI

Kii's classmate. The one behind this entire disaster?!

AKUTA RINTAROU

A perverted policeman that does whoever and whatever he wants.

FUKUMOTO SEIICHI

Tsukune's father and a surgeon. He is sometimes called the "Hand of God."

Previously, in *Magical Girl Apocalypse...*

Finding themselves in a desperate situation, Yoruka, and Miu learned of Akuta's secret plan:
To locate the Magical Girl that sends people back in time and allow her to attack them.
Then they would go into the past and kill Tsukune there, which would undo everything that the Magical Girls have done.
Kii, who was facing troubles of his own, ran into a Magical Girl while searching for Tsukune in the hospital...
Only to be saved by the masked figure in black robes.
While searching for the Magical Girl he needed, Akuta ran across the parasitic Magical Girl. Yoruka was killed.
Flying into a rage, Akuta attacked the Magical Girl, but was instead run through.
However, the blow allowed the magical girl powder he had gathered earlier to mix with his blood and empower Akuta with inhuman strength and regeneration powers.
Making a miraculous comeback against his would-be killer, Akuta pressed the parasitic Magical Girl for information.
He then swore to kill Tsukune and headed toward the roof to find her.
Meanwhile, the now-alone Miu was attacked by the Magical Girl who had sent the group back in time previously.

CAST

ANAI MIU

An elementary student that the group met at the mall. She was looking for her mother at the time.

SAYANO KAEDE

A high school freshman. She bullied Tsukune at school with her friend, Miki.

HANZAWA YORUKA

A high school junior. She is strong, beautiful, and kind, but she always carries a stun gun to ward off perverts.

FUKUMOTO TSUKUNE

A high school freshman and childhood friend of Kii. She has been relentlessly bullied by her classmates.

KOGAMI KII

A high school freshman and childhood friend of Tsukune. He hates involving himself in relationships that add to his stress.

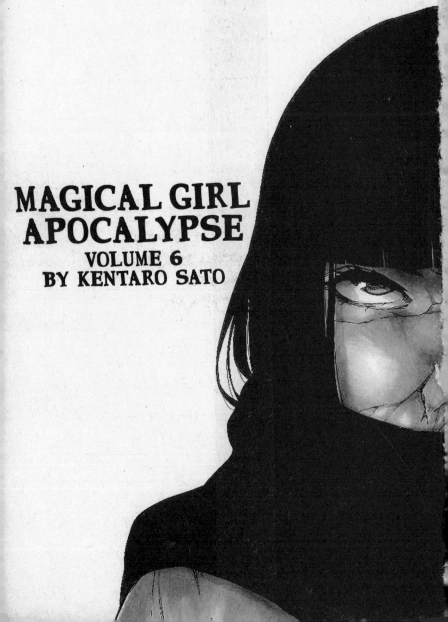

MAGICAL GIRL APOCALYPSE

VOLUME 6

BY KENTARO SATO

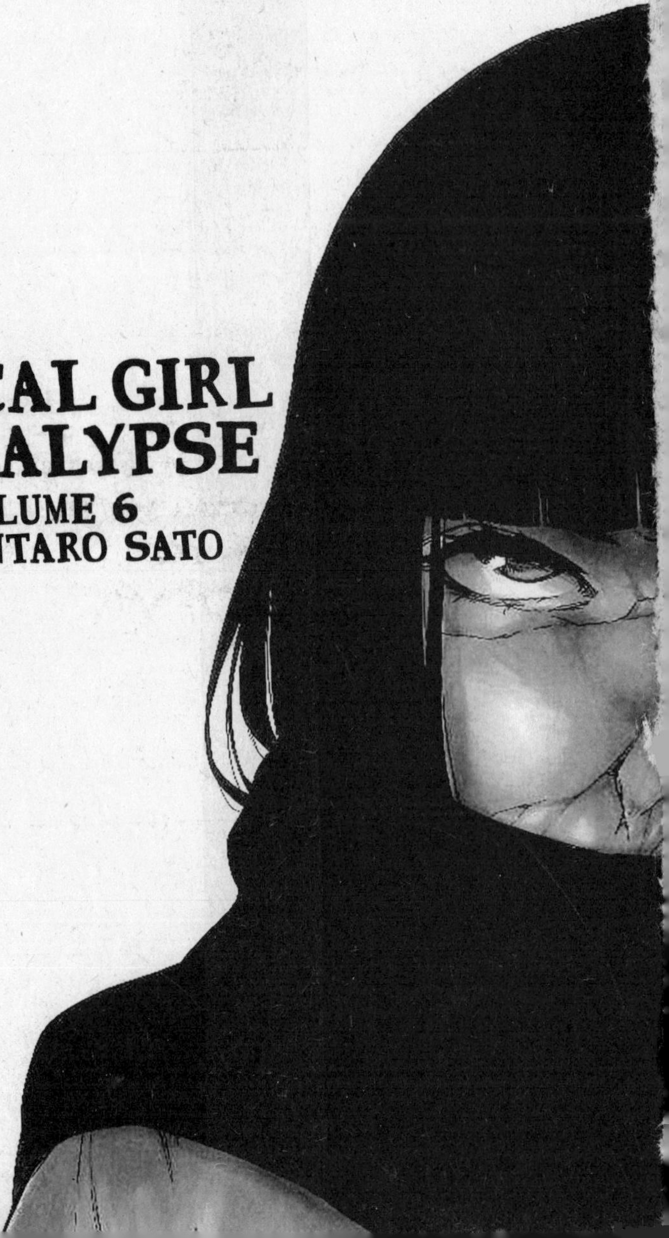